Fields of Green

Restorying Culture, Environment, and Education

Edited by

Marcia McKenzie
University of Saskatchewan

Paul Hart
University of Regina

Heesoon Bai
Simon Fraser University

Bob Jickling
Lakehead University

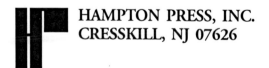

HAMPTON PRESS, INC.
CRESSKILL, NJ 07626

Printed in the United States of America

Library of Congress Cataloging-in-Publication Data

Fields of green : restorying culture, environment, and education / edited by Marcia McKenzie ... [et al.].
    p. cm.
  Includes bibliographical references and index.
  ISBN 978-1-57273-878-2 (hardbound) — ISBN 978-1-57273-879-9 (paperbound)
  1. Environmental education. 2. Environmentalism—Philosophy. I. McKenzie, Marcia.
  GE70.F54 2009
  333.7071—dc22   2009004726

"Evening Fields I" by Suzanne Northcott, acrylic on panel 40" × 40" collection, Rishma Dunlop

Hampton Press, Inc.
23 Broadway
Cresskill, NJ 07626

Contents

Out beyond ideas
of wrongdoing and rightdoing,
there is a field.

I'll meet you there.
...

Rumi (1207–1273)

Artist and photographer unknown

Foreword

The story that has ruled the world over the past few centuries is collapsing all around us. It has become incoherent and rings false. This was the story that transformed Terra Madre—the Earth as a living, vibrant, generous mother, into Terra Nullius—a dead, inert, empty earth. The story of Terra Nullius is a story of the colonization of nature, of women, of non-western cultures. It is a story of mechanization—of the machine as a metaphor for nature and humans. The untold part of the story is the ecological devastation and the cultural impoverishment that has been the consequence of the earth seen as empty, and humans seen as motivated only by greed, accumulation, and consumerism.

A financial meltdown on Wall Street has triggered an economic crisis. Gaia has had her revenge in terms of climate chaos, and the excluded and trampled cultures are having their revenge in the form of terrorism. We need another imagination which gives peace, justice, and sustainability a chance. I have called it Earth Democracy—living on the earth with full awareness of her self-organization and generous potential, her fragility and limits, and the rights of all beings who form one earth community. For me, Earth Democracy is about nourishing living economies, living democracy, and living cultures.

For centuries, the human mind has been shaped by education that treated the universe as a machine, and humans as cogs in the machine. We have to begin again, with a new education for a new imagination. We have to imagine our way forward at a time when the present trajectory is closing the future for humans. And with that new imagination we have to act to generate a future—with care and compassion, with hope and courage. *Fields of Green* will help create an imagination that allows us to cultivate this future.

Vandana Shiva

Acknowledgments

We would like to thank all those who contributed to this book, including those who provided copyediting and research assistance support—Charles Scott, Andrew Rushmere, Peter Kovacs, Daniela Bouneva Elza, Joy Goldberg, Carol Hart, Nora Timmerman, and Jessica Richmond; the publisher of Hampton Press, Barbara Bernstein; Sue Morreale, of Partners Composition; and for funding that made this work possible, Simon Fraser University and the Social Sciences Research Council of Canada. Thank you to artist Suzanne Northcott for sharing her painting for the volume cover; and to family, friends, colleagues, and others who agreed to have their work included in the book as vignettes. We are grateful to colleagues who offered ideas and feedback on the book as it was in progress, with special thanks to Rishma Dunlop.

We thank the following contributors and publishers for generously allowing us to reprint their material in this volume:

"The Place Where We Are Right," by Yehuda Amichai, 1996, from *The Selected Poetry of Yehuda Amichai, Newly Revised and Expanded Edition*, published by The University of California Press.

"The Peace of Wild Things," by Wendell Berry, 1999, from *The Selected Poems of Wendell Berry*, published by Counterpoint Press.

"Birding Lessons and the Teachings of Cicadas," by David Jardine, 1998, *Canadian Journal of Environmental Education, 3*, 92–99.

"To Carry Across: Metaphor Invents Us," by Daniela B. Elza, 2006, *Paideusis, 15* (2), 93–101.

"Place-based Education: Grounding Culturally-Responsive Teaching in Geographical Diversity," by David A. Gruenewald, 2006, *Democracy and Education, 16* (2), 24–32.

"Gardom Lake to Tatamagouche: Climate Change, the WTO, and a Community Land Trust," by Yuill Herbert, 2007, from *Notes from Canada's Young Activists*, edited by Severn Cullis-Suzuki, Kris Frederickson, Ahmen Kayssi, & Cynthia Mackenzie, published by Greystone Books, a division of Douglas & McIntyre Ltd.

"Manifesto," by J. B. MacKinnon, 2002, *Adbusters: Journal of the Mental Environment, 43*.

"The Bellies of Fallen Breathing Sparrows," by Don McKay, 2004, from *Camber: Selected Poems*, published by McClelland & Steward Ltd.

"The West Wind," by David J. Nightingale © www.chromasia.com.

Finally, we are indebted to the friends and family who helped support this work, and to the people, places, and fields that provoked it.

Introduction

Educational Fields and Cultural Imaginaries

Marcia McKenzie, Paul Hart, Heesoon Bai, and Bob Jickling

Dreams come in the day as well as the night...

—Ernest Bloch, A Philosophy of the Future

This volume is about hopeful daydreams and their implications for action in the interwoven spheres of culture, environment, and education. Despite and because of the recent significant global shift in concern for the "environment," we believe there remains the urgent task of restorying the ways we live on this earth. Cultural understandings that value the individual over the collective, humans over other species, concept over experience, progress as globalizing growth and change, print-based literacies as universally desirable, and other affiliated assumptions and values, are examples of the sorts of imaginaries that can be traced in the ecological and cultural losses we are currently experiencing and participating in around the world.

As Rosi Braidotti (2006) writes, "the imaginary is ultimately an image of thought...a habit that captures and blocks the many potential alternative ways we may be able to think about our environment and ourselves" (p. 87). In other words, we are always living according to the strengths and weaknesses of our imaginaries. Or as Thomas King (2003) says, "To every action there is a story" (p. 29). As participants in particular imaginaries and the paths they entail, we in a globalizing world are all already actors in ongoing ecological and cultural change on a massive scale, and thus already "revolutionaries" or change-makers (Cullis-Suzuki, 2008). Indeed, what seems required is the individual and collective production of revolution, with associated imaginaries, of a very different sort.

Stuart Hall (1981) also suggests that what matters most about culture is what we do with it. He describes culture as a site of contestation among dominant and less-dominant forms with ongoing shifts in what exists in the center and in the margins. Investigating the historical and sociopolitical understandings of the keyword *culture*, Raymond Williams (1976) outlines

1

the meanings that have been associated with the term and concludes: "The complex of sense indicates a complex argument about the relations between general human development and a particular way of life, and between both the works and practices of art and intelligence" (p. 91). Providing understandings of how things are and how they should be, culture is the means through which we interpret reality as well as being the "repository of imagination" (Duncombe, 2002, p. 35). Fleshing out the concept of *imaginary* as an image of thought and a function of culture that can both constrain and enable, Braidotti (2006) writes:

> Neither "pure" imagination—locked in its classical opposition to reason—nor fantasy in the Freudian sense, the imaginary marks a space of transitions and transactions. Nomadic, it flows like symbolic glue between the social and the self, the outside and the subject; the material and the ethereal. It flows, but it is sticky; it catches on as it goes. It possesses fluidity, but it distinctly lacks transparency. (p. 86)

Caught in this sticky web of imaginaries that constitutes the postmodern reality of cultures and identities in flux, Braidotti asks "how we can tell the proactive [imaginaries] from the regressive ones?"

Examining the multiplicity of discourses and social practices that many of us now live amidst, rather than resulting in the confusion and nihilism associated with moral relativism, can be understood as engendering "alternative systems of values and specific forms of accountability" (Braidotti, 2006, p. 94). Consciousness can be conceived as attempts to narrate and live one's relationship "to the variables that construct one's location" in order to create desired shareable positions (p. 95). For Braidotti, this entails dialogical confrontations with others with a mix of affectivity/involvement and objectivity/distance. It involves situated cartographies, in which location is "the always partial, always finite, always fraught play of foreground and background, text and context" (Haraway, 1997, p. 37). Through this type of engagement, Braidotti suggests, alternative collective imaginaries can be remembered, thought, experienced, shared, and sustained.

Along with others who have worked and continue to work at spinning together pedagogies of possibility in response to critical social and political issues, Roger Simon (1992) suggests the project at hand is not centrally one of critique but of expressing and engendering hope. Considering disruptive daydreams and educational practice, Simon calls for approaches that move from the inside out, pedagogies that become possible sites for daydreaming. We agree, and suggest through the chapters in this book that we consider what determines the composition of daydreams and where can they lead us, individually and collectively, for better or worse; and when and how it may be appropriate to seek to provoke new or old imaginaries in others. Or in other words, this volume suggests that we consider the stickiness of cultural imaginaries, or the stories we live by, and reflect on when embeddedness in particular understandings and practices might best be left as is, and when things may call for attempts at unsticking, for disruption. And who decides? What is the part of education in this complex negotiation of cultural consumption and creativity, conservation and transformation? And what are the ethical implications and decisions surrounding education conceived, at least in part, in some contexts and times, as provoking "disruptive daydreams?"

We see these questions surrounding the possibilities and ethics of cultural sustainability and change as at the heart of the work that we do as educators concerned with the ecological. There is a history of wrestling with education as a means of cultural reproduction or transformation, yet beginning from a position that suggests it does both, there remain many underexplored questions and implications for pedagogy. We hope this book helps bring these questions into conversation with day-to-day educational practices, and with the stories and imaginaries we live, learn, and teach by.

This collection works across various fields of green, drawing together poetry, philosophy, journalism, sociology, curriculum studies, Indigenous scholarship, feminist and social justice work, environmental ethics, and a range of other fields of inquiry and practice. We have included an introductory "primer," 20 chapters, and a number of short text and image vignettes that we hope act as presence and proxy for realities of the world we cannot include (Bhabha, 1994). These contributions in what follows, are, as Rishma Dunlop suggests, mutually concerned with the poetics and politics of relation. They examine matters of body and mind, vitality and re-enchantment, rhizomes and desert, remembrance and transgression, global and local, family and schooling, culture and environment. Happily, many are unruly chapters that weave back and forth across shared themes and resist easy division and categorization. Demonstrating a heterogeneous politics (Braidotti, 2006), these contributions suggest strategies and spaces of education that enable alternative stories and daydreams to consider and live by. Rather than settling into solidified positions, these are visions and explorations that suggest the "uncertain certainty" of humility and the "blessed unrest" (Hawken, 2007) that can be seen as the calling of 21st-century artists, activists, and educators.

PART I: COMPLICATED CONVERSATIONS

In the questions we raise and those we pass over, through the knowledges and actions that we support, we are always educating amidst, for, and against particular cultural understandings and practices. Drawing on the work of C. A. Bowers (e.g., 1997), Derek Rasmussen (2001) makes a compelling argument for "staying put" in the context of cross-cultural forms of education, and suggests the ways in which well-intentioned educators contribute to colonization and cultural loss through assumptions about aspects of life in other cultures that need changing. For example, as Rasmussen, Bowers, and others examine, cultural practices of critique can function to uproot: To name the world is to change it (Freire, 1970). Functioning as a form of interpellation, the calling into being of various codes, discourses, doxa, or imaginaries, at once and the same time loosens and resolidifies, opening up the possibility for movement and yet naming us in particular ways too as we come to see the world through different lenses (McKenzie, 2004). And as Noel Gough explores in Chapter 1, there are no easy answers to whether particular educational aims are ever transculturally appropriate or desirable.

Certainly, many of these discussions are applicable to the growing interest in "education for sustainable development" (e.g., UNESCO, 2003). Delighted to see environment and sustainability getting more purchase locally and globally, we also worry about what sorts of cultural agencies and agendas are and are not at play in various renditions. As Neil Evernden (1993) suggests, "the question society wants answered is not how to be right, but how to be smart—how to go on doing what it has been doing, without paying the price" (p. 11). In offering to answer that question, he suggests environmentalists run the risk of supporting societal norms and practices that contribute to the very problems they seek to redress. Colleagues recently reflected that based on the breadth and quality of work being done in environmental education, "the field should have bright prospects" (Reid & Scott, 2007, p. 325). The irony here demands attention. Although "the field" may be active and growing, we must ask what roles our own efforts are playing in the patterns of cultural consumption and resistance. What sort of "bright" future are we working toward individually and collectively?

The contributions in the first section of this volume undertake this sort of critical focus on the assumptions and understandings that support current discourses and practices of education and environment. Noel Gough begins the section with Bill Pinar's (2005) question: How do we provide opportunities for "complicated conversation" and "intellectual breakthrough" in the internationalization of curriculum studies? Through the work of Giles Deleuze and Félix Guattari, Gough explores philosophy, as tied to history and geography, as the discipline that involves creating concepts; and suggests that the philosophy/geography of the domination of nature has been and continues to be one largely of colonialism and imperialism. Spiraling out to examine the alternative productive possibilities of rhizomes, cultural difference, and unnaming, Gough closes with a discussion of planes of immanence, or invisible mental landscapes that can only be seen through the concepts (and philosophies) occupying them. Suggesting that every concept has a "history" and a "becoming," he explores the value of investigating the mental landscapes we live by in various contexts, how concepts can be used to intervene to resolve local situations, and how various knowledge traditions can coexist together without recourse to a single transcendent reality.

Also concerned with the cultural understandings underlying education, Sean Blenkinsop and Kieran Egan (Chapter 2) offer a critique of three commonplace educational aims in contemporary westernized contexts: education conceived variously as socialization into cultural norms, as the learning of truth and rationality, or as the unfolding development of the individual. Suggesting that all three of these ideas are inadequate separately or in combination as a basis for education, and for environmental education more specifically, Blenkinsop and Egan propose that examining the underlying foundational assumptions of one's practices indeed opens up the ability to think imaginatively about alternative possibilities.

In Chapter 3, Edgar Gonzáles-Gaudiano and Rosa Nidia Buenfil-Burgos focus on brushing "the cobwebs away" from discourses of environmentalism and environmental education. Tracing a range of issues and priorities that are pursued under these names, the authors posit the terms as floating and empty signifiers. Rather than remaining concerned with the fixation of the "impossible identity of EE," they propose that educators and researchers consider the ways in which the very ambiguity of these terms can make them ethically and politically potent. A postfoundational approach to environmental education, they suggest, requires a new language through which to engage in dialogue across positions, and can result in the strategic construction, articulation, and temporary fixation of educational projects with an understanding that they too will be replaced with better ones in time.

Leigh Price (Chapter 4) is also concerned with postfoundational approaches to environmental education that enable action-oriented educators to move forward in their practices without cynicism. She suggests that in rejecting positivism, or "ontological monovalency," one does not need to reject realism. With "real" objects or referents at the base of our understandings of the world, Price is optimistic about the possibility of achieving better interpretations of those referents. Moving from the present to imagine the past that got us here, Price suggests that "musement" can enable "good enough" explanations that allow one to move forward with action and education. Given that we are always acting on the world and changing it, for better or worse, Price advocates for carefully monitored changes in direction that are tested by living according to the actions they suggest.

PART II: THE SENSUOUS

Also engaging in processes of critique, the contributors to this section are very definitely as Heesoon Bai puts it in Chapter 6, "in recovery" from a reductive, rational, dualistic, mechanistic worldview that has dominated western ways of knowing since the scientific revolution in the 17th century. Broadening out from the conceptual legacies associated with thinkers such as Rene Descartes, and going further back, Plato; the contributors in the second section of the volume instead highlight possibilities offered by the senses, experience, and emotion. As Derek Rasmussen (n.d.) writes, "Deciding to subject reality to representation in 26 letters reflects a decision that reality can be represented in 26 letters . . . this [is the] alphabetization of thought" (p. 8). In contrast, the contributors to this section attempt feats of romantic resistance and sensuality, showing us different alphabets through which to know the world (Abram, 1996).

In a playful post-paddle conversation in Chapter 5, coyote and raven (aka Patricia O'Riley and Peter Cole) take us on an opening journey of the sensuous as they think about their/ our relationships with land, knowledge, learning, schooling, scholarship, science, language, and 20:20:20 visions of what counts as good. Suggesting that education should be considered and enacted beyond curriculum mandates, the boxes into which we put western science, and other classified forms of knowledge, O'Riley and Cole offer clues to a wilder pedagogy of earthworms and sky.

Tracing the history of how we have collectively become so numb, deaf, and blind when it comes to the natural world, in Chapter 6 Heesoon Bai suggests how the Platonic/Cartesian curse can be broken. In order to recover our own animism within, she advocates disrupting the hegemony of the rational and conceptual with a strong validation and inclusion of emotional and poetic subjectivity. This participatory consciousness, in combination with critical intellect, can enable us to think feelingly and feel thoughtfully. Rather than mistaking the map for the road, through attention to the conditions and structures we perpetuate and participate in, including those of education, we can then become fully present, awake and alive, in the sensuous reality that encompasses us. Bai proposes mindfully walking on the soil in order to recover the soul: "to see and hear the world through the stop is to make love to it."

Turning to the lessons of birds and cicadas, in Chapter 7 David Jardine takes us on a summer walk through the woods of his childhood. Meditating on our tendencies to try to contain and manage knowledge, Jardine suggests how one can instead discover the pleasures of the knowledge patiently held in the stories of cicadas, bird songs, leaves turning: "as if some of my life is stored up in these trees for safekeeping." Jardine suggests the ways in which we become through what we know, and the importance of this in considering where and how we educate children, as he gathers himself in gathering together this remembered place. Exploring the common flesh of our relationships with other creatures, Jardine proposes the ways in which we do not simply know, but are also known by places. This irreplaceable, unavoidable intimacy, Jardine suggests, constitutes the limits of our narrativity and a "fleshy obligation" to the world. Imagine, he prods, a mathematics education conceived as an invitation into the intimate ways of this old and wondrous place.

Also concerned with the marginalization of experience and emotion in education and the implications for ethical engagements with the world, Bob Jickling, in Chapter 8, explores the poetry of Williams Wordsworth and the untamed forest fires of the north as forms of resistance. Joining E. F. Schumacher and others in questioning "the soundness of our maps," Jickling proposes that emotional and sensuous experiences offer alternatives to an epistemology that privileges reason and the careful maintenance of boundaries between humans and other species, adding flesh and life to bones polished bare by analytical thought.

Likewise suggesting that our current global environmental predicament requires a radical review, not only of our behaviors, but the ways we think of, understand, and relate to the world, in Chapter 9 Michael Bonnett identifies some of the possible transgressional implications that flow from such a metaphysical shift. He inquires into how, for example, anthropocentric and ambiguous conceptions of "sustainable development," and considerations of nature as reducible to knowable objects to be managed and dominated, function to sanction and perpetuate understandings at the root of current spiritual, social, political, and ecological conditions. Instead of sustainability considered as a "bolt-on extra to being human," Bonnett proposes sustainability in education conceived as enabling the "self-arising" of students and the re-enchantment of the natural world.

Bonnett too seeks to elicit the suspension of mastery and our engagement in a less processed, poetic world in which we are better able to see the blueness of the blueness of the sky.

PART III: WAVES, HYBRIDS, AND NETWORKS

Contributors to this third section are also passionate about experience and the sensuous, about "thought and feeling that cannot be pried apart" as Leesa Fawcett says in Chapter 12, and about the need for new myths, metaphors, and stories to live by. However, these chapters can also be seen as sharing an emphasis on social flesh as a contingent ethics (Beasly & Bacchi, 2007). That is, they focus in various ways on how social and political interactions among human beings as well as with the rest of the world structure our feelings, our ways of knowing and acting as individual subjects, and vice versa.

Wishing to help people to inhabit a non-dualistic, intersubjective consciousness, in Chapter 10 Claudia Eppert calls us to untangle what we have created through rememberance-learning and a returning to our source—water. Instead of an exploitive relationship with water, she suggests it is a primary site for reconciliation and renewal. Telling us two water stories, and drawing attention to the thematic presence of water within Taoist, Confucian, Buddhist, Vedic, and Hindu worldviews, Eppert shows us the power, vitality, and invincibility of the fluidity of water. She proposes we move with rather than struggle against the forces of life, exercising our agency, our action and nonaction, in blending with and becoming an integral part of the world—as waves in the waters of life. Through a curriculum of witnessing via the arts, meditative engagement, and the autobiographical "running of the course" work of *currere*, Eppert suggests we can explore and learn both wave and water on a path of reconciliation, nonviolent action, integrity, and reverence in our relations with others and the world.

Also thinking about agency and action in terms of intersubjectivity, in Chapter 11 Marcia McKenzie explores the possibilities of considering education as offering problematizations that can provoke movements at the limits of the ways we think about ourselves and act in the world. Visiting Michel Foucault's writings on transgression, critical ontologies, and care of the self, McKenzie draws on dialogue among teacher educators to highlight the learning possibilities and challenges of hybridities and cultural contact zones, testimony and witnessing, and place. She advocates for the value of experiences of dissonance and imagination in sorting out how we, in westernized and westernizing contexts, might live otherwise with each other and on the earth.

Encouraging us across disciplinary trenches and encounters of difference, Chapter 12 by Leesa Fawcett elaborates how 1 + 1 can equal three in the development of a new hybrid feral sociality. Suggesting she wants to go beyond "counternarratives" to narratives that transform the official natural histories and question some of the reigning truths in environmental education, Fawcett draws on Deleuze and Guattari, Paulo Freire, and others to explore possibilities for dialogical, public, social action that follows the fabric of the rhizome in the connection "and . . . and . . . and." Journeying with escaped farmed salmon as feral cyborgs; and reading aloud, swimming naked, tiring and laughing together with others in the Australian bush; Fawcett suggests that if we approach the other more attentively and openly, with humour and expecting unpredictability, we can nourish imaginations and nomadic ethics: "It is always a day to day decision to feel the intensity of life, just as it is to hope." Following Deleuze and Guattari, "the question is not: is it true? But: does it work?"

In Chapter 13, Michael Peters and Daniel Araya take us through a history and overview of network theory, proposing an ecological approach to knowledge and learning as an alternative to a worldview of dominion, control, and all encompassing materialism. The authors explain that in network social theory the emphasis is on patterns of interactions among actors (both individuals and collectives), and on revealing the structure of the network and the kinds of exchanges that define it. Scale-free and with attributes distributed according to nonlinear power laws, Peters and Araya indicate that subtle changes, perceptible only to local participants, can result in significant modifications to the system. Expected to achieve the status of a meta-paradigm as "the language of our times," they suggest that network theory is extended by Gregory Bateson's work on an ecology of mind. Using peer-to-peer social networking as an example, Peters and Araya outline how networks create an ecology of exchange without recourse to higher authority, and are important in considering new forms of education and resistance.

Also exploring Bateson's work on an ecology of mind as collaborative intelligence, in Chapter 14 Rebecca Martusewicz takes us to Wabash Street in Detroit. There we witness a set of practices, relationships, and accompanying language patterns that Martusewicz suggests are part of that community's efforts to recover shared cultural and environmental commons in the face of economic enclosure and poverty. Drawing on Bateson's notion of differences that make a difference, Martusewicz explains the idea that what we know is only possible because of the whole system as it engages the communicative process among differences making differences, and therefore, intelligence is much more than our own cognitive abilities. In this view, one is never really "outside" the world at all, thus breaking down the culture/nature binary. Calling us toward conscious participation in a collaborative intelligence, Martusewicz asks us to consider how we can help reassert older maps of mutual support in the face of the dominance of individualism, meritocracy, enthnocentrism, and anthropocentrism.

PART IV: GEOGRAPHIES AND PLACE-MAKING

Building from where the previous section leaves off, this final section of the volume examines how culture and place are deeply intertwined, with places and geographies themselves also being potentially profoundly pedagogical. The chapters in this section ask us to grapple with ways in which we are both made by, and makers of, place, and how we might consider differently the types of homes, families, cities, and other diverse places and communities we contribute to and engage with.

In Chapter 15, David Greenwood (previously Gruenewald) raises concerns about how terms such as *multiculturalism, diversity,* and *culturally responsible teaching* may in fact perpetuate the very conditions they purport to work against when they are framed as classroom problems instead of as cultural problems. Reduced to "closing the achievement gap," schooling practices undertaken under a rhetoric of "diversity" actually function to funnel experiences and students into narrow expectations. Instead, Greenwood proposes, it is necessary to look outside schools to find actual diversity. Using "place" synomously with "community," he suggests true diversity can be engaged through studying a range of experiences and cultural and ecological formations. Closing with a discussion of the hegemony of *difference* over *relation* in the field of cultural studies, Greenwood proposes a "critical pedagogy of place" as a potential confluence of cultural and ecological thinking in the emerging discourse of place-based education, with a focus on both decolonization and reinhabitation.

Extending many of the themes in previous chapters, in Chapter 16 Derek Rasmussen and Tommy Akulukjuk share their dialogue on the relationships between Inuktitut language and culture and how we understand and interact with "environment." In the naming of the places and species of the north in the language of the south through English science and English schools, Rasmussen and Akulukjuk suggest that a richness of understanding of the land and the possibilities for relations with it are lost. With that loss, Inuktitut culture is irretrievably changed.

Rasmussen and Akulukjuk advocate for spaces to encourage a sentient knowledge that "doesn't try to pry nature away from culture and fragment it into data," but rather involves time to "feel what it's like to have fingers, to have sense," a knowledge that encompasses learning about life as flexible and confusing. Drawing Inuit elders into the conversation, these authors show us the risks and losses for culture and place of so-called "development." Grappling with the work that a modern western education can do, and the effect his own has had on his relationship with place and culture, Akulukjuk concludes, "I wish that I were uneducated."

In Chapter 17 Milton McClaren suggests that much contemporary environmental education embodies underlying attitudes to urban or constructed environments that reify anthropocentric orientations to the "natural" world and marginalize the realities of many city dwellers. Rather than viewing cities as rich in human potential and possibility, he suggests that the literatures and practices of environmental education tend to perpetuate dystopian visions of the urban. These portrayals, McClaren suggests, fail to recognize the ways in which the often "naturistic stories" of environmental educators affect the ways in which we engage with urban people, and particularly urban youth. Indicating the role of place in the construction of identity, and the role of culture in cultivating our orientations to place, McClaren, like Martuscewitz, calls for forms of education that engage in revisiting our lived and told stories of urban dwellers and places, their/our contributions and possibilities.

Interested in the potential of the family household to act as a powerful site of environmental education and sustainable development, in Chapter 18 Phillip Payne explores how the home might act "ontologically" as a location of moral, social, and ecological being, doing, belonging, dwelling, placing, and becoming. Payne attempts to counter more abstract, empty, virtual, and instantaneous modes of living with a look at families' "best resistance practices," combining research with "green families" and the writing of Hannah Arendt, Zygmunt Bauman, and John Sanders. He argues that families remain the central agents of everyday politics, and seeks to demonstrate the moral possibility of being, before anything else, for the other.

Suggesting that environmental education is concerned with relations with our shared "house of life," in Chapter 19 Lucie Sauvé proposes three complementary perspectives that respond to three intertwined issues: the degradation of life-support systems, the loss of meaning and sense of belonging, and the lack of relevant education. She proposes that a critical education invites us to rebuild our frames of reference, thereby reconstructing ourselves as individuals and as a society. Focusing on the role that relation to the environment (ecosphere) plays in education for the development of individuals (psychosphere) and social groups (sociosphere), Sauvé suggests that environmental education can contribute to the development of environmental citizenship at the interface between the sociosphere and ecosphere.

Finally, we close the collection with Chapter 20 by youth activist, Yuill Herbert. Chronicling his lessons of trying to make a difference: of locations of place and family, of trees and absent cougars, of antiglobalization protests, of touring buses run on French fry oil, of free schools and community land trusts, Herbert tells us "once your eyes are opened to injustice, it's hard to close them again. He offers us hope in the possibilities of "strong, radical communities with rooted connections to people and place," and how they have given him and others the opportunity to imagine and contribute to individual and collective change.

CLOSE

This then is a book about the limits and possibilities of educational fields and cultural imaginaries. Individually and cumulatively, the contributors to this volume search for, theorize, and practice approaches that probe education as an endeavor that imperfectly, yet hopefully, walks the blurred line between cultural determinism and resistance. As Murry Bookchin (1994) suggests: "In this confluence of social and ecological crises, we can no longer afford to be unimaginative; we can no longer afford to do without utopian thinking" (p. 22). Not envisioned as a search for a future perfect society, this is rather utopia understood as an "ethos of experimentation that is oriented toward carving out spaces for reisistance and reconstruction here and now" (Coté, Day, & de Peuter, 2007).

Dunlop writes in her evocative "primer" which precedes and further introduces the four sections of this book: "Curriculum is found in human eyes, in rivers, in animals, in the language of music, poetry, art, science, history, anthropology, in what is public, intimate, beloved." We hope you are able to find your own curricula in the pages that follow, and in the daydreams and stories to live by they may help elicit or remember. As King (2003) reminds us, stories can be wondrous things, as well as dangerous, and once told, cannot be called back. They can however be met with counter-stories:

> Take [this] story, for instance. It's yours. Do with it what you will. Tell it to your friends. Turn it into a television movie. Forget it. But don't say in the years to come that you would have lived your life differently if only you had heard this story. You've heard it now. (p. 29)

REFERENCES

Abram, D. (1996). *The spell of the sensuous.* New York: Vintage Books.

Beasley, C., & Bacchi, C. (2007). Envisaging a new politics for an ethical future: Beyond trust, care and generosity—towards an ethic of "social flesh." *Feminist Theory, 8*(3), 279–298.

Bhabha, H. (1994). *The location of culture.* New York: Routledge.

Bloch, E. (1970). *A philosophy of the future.* Herder & Herder.

Bookchin, M. (1994). The concept of social ecology. In C. Merchant (Ed.), *Key concepts in critical theory: Ecology* (pp. 152–162). Atlantic Highlands, NJ: Highlands Press.

Bowers, C. A. (1997). *The culture of denial: Why the environmental movement needs a strategy for reforming universities and public schools.* Albany: State University of New York Press.

Braidotti, R. (2006). *Transpositions: On nomadic ethics.* Malden, MA: Polity.

Coté, M., Day, R., & de Peuter, G. (2007). Utopian pedagogy: Creating radical alternatives in the neoliberal age. *The Review of Education, Pedagogy, and Cultural Studies, 29,* 317–336.

Cullis-Suzuki, S. (2008, January). *Who are revolutionaries?* Lecture presented at the University of Saskatchewan, Saskatoon, SK.

Duncombe, S. (2002). *Cultural resistance reader.* New York: Verso.

Evernden, N. (1993). Talking about the mountain. *The natural alien: Humankind and the environment* (pp. 3–34). Toronto, ON: University of Toronto Press.

Freire, P. (1920). *Pedagogy of the oppressed.* New York: Continuum.

Hall, S. (1981). Notes on deconstructing "the popular." In R. Samuel (Ed.), *People's history and socialist theory* (pp. 231–239). London: Kegan Paul-Routledge.

Haraway, D. (1997). *Modest_witness@second_millenium: Femaleman©_meets_OncoMouse™.* New York: Routledge.

Hawken, P. (2007). *Blessed unrest: How the largest movement in the world came into being and why no one saw it coming.* New York: Penguin.

King, T. (2003). *The truth about stories: A native narrative.* Toronto, ON: Anansi Press.

McKenzie, M. (2004). The "willful contradiction" of poststructural socio-ecological education. *Canadian Journal of Environmental Education, 9,* 177–190.

Pinar, W. F. (2005). Complicated conversation: Occasions for "intellectual breakthrough" in the internationalization of curriculum studies. *Journal of Curriculum Studies [Taiwan]*, *1*(1), 1–26.

Rasmussen, D. (n.d.). *Cease to do evil, then learn to do good . . . (A pedagogy for the oppressor)*. Unpublished manuscript (pp. 1–17).

Reid, A., & Scott, W. (2007). *Researching education and the environment: Retrospect and prospect*. London: Routledge.

Simon, R. (1992). *Teaching against the grain: Texts for a pedagogy of possibility*. New York: Bergin & Garvey.

UNESCO. (2003). *Education for sustainable development: The education sector paper*. Paris: Author.

Williams, R. (1976). *Keywords*. Glasgow: Fontana.

Primer: Alphabet for The New Republic

by Rishma Dunlop, photography by Joe Paczuski

The world was askew how to get it right again?
Stacks of Duncan, Olson thin, weathered Ginsberg,
. . . It was all about Spicer's grail, the Enron scandal
It was "all about" death in war, torture
The empire of reading was clear
You needed special reading glasses provided by Homeland Security
But here there was no "home," there was no "secure"
But something was going to change, get born.

—Anne Waldman

The story begins at birth.
Someone names you
Invents a beginning.
Imagine a story fit for a newborn.

Introductory Notes for a Primer

A place is a story happening many times.
    —Kim Stafford, *Places and Stories*

All landscapes ask the same question:
'I am watching you—are you watching yourself in me?'
    —Lawrence Durrell

Alphabet for The New Republic is a textbook for an imagined ecotopia, or ecological utopia, a homeplace. This alphabet book is a primer for global citizens, proposing ways of reading the world. Its "open" form is inspired by the literary conceits of the open texts of Roland Barthes in *Roland Barthes by Roland Barthes*, an autobiography arranged by alphabetic entries, Csezlaw Milosz in *Milosz's ABC*, and Stan Persky's *The Short Version: An ABC Book*. In Roland Barthes' 1971 essay "From Work to Text," and in his essay of structuralist literary criticism "S/Z," Barthes defines two kinds of texts as *lisible et scriptable* (readable and writable). The readable text is more comfortable for the reader, received in conventional forms, whereas the writable text is more difficult, requiring the active participation of the reader as writer. This writable text is aligned with Umberto Eco's notion of the open text. As Umberto Eco proposes in *The Role of the Reader*, an "open work" engages readers in the creation of meaning, and each reading is both an interpretation and a performance. The original text becomes a homeland that offers a return to memory and possibilities of meaning. As Palestinian poet Mahmoud Darwish writes in *Journal of an Ordinary Grief,* "writing remains the other shape of the homeland."

As an open text, the *Primer* is not intended for passive consumption by the reader. The author's lists, fragments, aphorisms, remembrances, theories, thoughts, prayers, poems, invite the reader to write and read the reader's own entries, layering narratives as acts of imagination, oriented towards social change. The *Primer* becomes a subgenre of memoir and poetic prose essay, a flexible, hybrid form of inquiry.

What would we learn in *The New Republic*? In considering what knowledge is necessary in the present world, education is an endeavor to consider the vital knowledge of our connection to the world as home, how to live well in this world, and the nature of our human relation to the land. Education is an acknowledgement of the insistence of beauty despite terror, difficulty, ugliness, in an environment scarred by the politics of war, terrorism, and violence. Essential to the knowledge honoured in *The New Republic* is a sensibility of poetics, poetics of culture and place, and ecological literacy that determines how we read the world, a verdant language rooted in a vital poetics of relation that is the human imaginary.

Notes on Biocultural Ecology

One of the strangest things about our culture is our ability to describe the destruction of the world in exquisite, even beautiful detail. The whole science of ecology, for instance, describes exactly what we're doing wrong and what the global effects are. The odd twist is that we become so enamored of our language and its ability to describe the world that we create a false and irresponsible separation. We use language as a device for distancing. Somebody who is genuinely living in their ecosystem wouldn't have a word for it. They'd just call it the world.

—Ursula LeGuin

Ecology n. (German Ökologie < Greek *Oïkos*, house + -logia [-logy], study, theory) a theory of home.

The New Republic is a primer for education in ecological literacy, framed by philosophies of biocultural ecology. Ecological thought that theorizes about home encompasses semiosis, the 19th-century medical science, sometimes called symptomatology, which formed the basis of what became semiotics. The basic tenet of semiosis was that marks on the body, whether wounds, scratches, or sores, should be seen as signs. Signs conveyed information. The idea of the mark as sign was developed by Ferdinand de Saussure and later by Claude Levi-Strauss.

Every sign matters, including marks on the earth, and they all tell a story. Signs become stories, stories become myths, and myths create the need for rituals. In medicine, wounds and sores on the body may disappear, but if they don't heal, if they linger too long, the body that carries them may not survive. The same is true of the wounds of the earth, the marks of

strip-mining, dumping of toxins, oil spills, nuclear bomb testing, the mass graves, sites of war, sites of murders, continue to accumulate scar tissue.

A biocultural philosophy of ecological education is anchored in the belief that human biological experience is inseparable from the world as *Oïkos,* meaning home, and from our human relations to this world. This home is at once a natural phenomenon and an aesthetic and cultural world. Home is a process, a form of resistance to dystopia. The ecotopian notion of *The New Republic* is linked to education conceptualized not as a discrete discipline in the arbitrary manner of institutions of higher education; rather, education is conceptualized as interdisciplinary and cross-disciplinary, contained in and relevant to all fields of study.

Dear Reader:

The world is an ancient book. Fragile and tough. Read the pages to the songs of sparrows and nightingales, to the trees that speak to you even on windless days. In the story, the cities of the future are bandaging their limbs against wholesale murder, bombed schoolyards. From the crazed skulls of highrises, the winds blow over a house of poured-out waters. Everywhere you travel there are vanquished cities burning, men, women, children cradling the slain, jilted sweethearts in every theatre. You will come to know that there is consolation in desire, in the occasional small bird singing. This singing is a temporary clearing of the disorder of things, a singing that flushes the throats of politicians and warriors, pours a river of poetry through the larynx, spreading like honey on the land.

In *The New Republic* you will learn to read and write the world's story. It is a story about how to become human. You will begin with picture books. A child's garden of verses. The alphabet will sift into your rib cage, open you to stars, grass, ABCs, whole sentences whispering in the dark. Stories of long-toothed wolves, glass slippers, palaces, and forests. You will learn to follow the curve of the sentence, wherever it might lead, into deserts, under drifts of sand. Alphabet cities. Notebooks lined with emerald rivers, pages salted with oceans, every continent a chapter, every history connected to the veined margins. Primer for aesthetics, for art, for poetry. Against anaesthesia. Reading and storying the world requires a synesthetic, neuroaesthetic consciousness.

Curriculum is found in human eyes, in rivers, in animals, in the language of music, poetry, art, science, history, anthropology, in what is public, intimate, beloved. These are stories lodged in the house of the earth and in your body. All your days and nights you can have this book. Turn the pages until they become well-worn linen, last words soft in your hands. Meet me there in that story, afterlife of spine cracked open. What is ordinary is no longer possible. What you are waiting for is just now being born.

In the nursery doorway, something cold and distant, even adult hands tremble against it. The book left out on the lectern, brittle yellow pages, lexicons of disclosure. You will come to know how words will hiss and tremble on storied pages, imagined wilderness, insomniac's tale, seductions, remembrances and forgettings, child's face against a shattered window, wrecked lullaby, murderer's knife, deep song unnaming the known.

Once upon a time and never again...

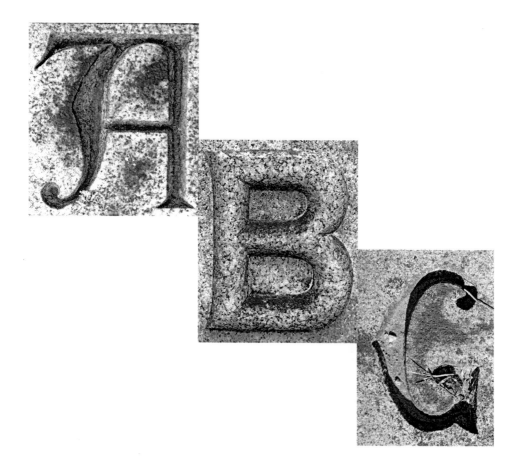

Never again: Auschwitz.

Never again: Aral Sea. Lost ecosystem drained for irrigation by the former Soviet Union. Landlocked sea, shrinking, polluted by weapons testing, industrial waste, fertilizer runoff. Plains of salt and toxic chemicals drifting in the air. Citizens suffering from cancers and lung diseases.

Never again: Armenian genocide, 1915–1918, 1920–1923.

Never again: Apartheid and racial segregation. Apartheid in South Africa 1948–1994.

Never again: Air India bombing, Flight 182, June 22, 1985.

Altars in every grove of trees. Abracadabra. Even the alphabet is magic. Words are your amulets. Stories suspended in amber.

Ave Maria.

The poems of Anna Akhmatova.

Art originates from the most profound admiration of the world. You will learn about the angel of history. This angel is Paul Klee's painting, a stick figure looking back at history. Walter Benjamin describes the angel in "Theses on the History of Philosophy":

> His face is turned toward the past. Where we perceive a chain of events, he sees one single catastrophe which keeps on piling wreckage and hurls it in front of his feet. The angel would like to stay, awaken the dead, and make whole what has been smashed. But a storm is blowing in from Paradise: it has got caught in his wings with such a violence that the angel can no longer close them. The storm irresistibly propels him into the future to which his back is turned, while the pile of debris before him grows skyward.

You will read the earth's testimonies, always remembering the child in you reading—a pocket of held light in the corner of the manuscript. In your dreams you will see that child, pages blowing dormant with terror as you gather moon, sky, ocean, in your small hands like a mouth lovely language that has no word for *harm*.

Beauty
　　　　So many kinds to name.
You hope for a day soft at the edges
　　　　　　　for something, someone to
　　　　　　　know the small hands of rain
to be like rain
wet with a decent happiness.

Beauty and truth. Keats writes *Beauty is truth, truth is beauty*. Comfort lies in the beauty and poetry and music of others. When you see beauty you will want to paint it, write it, savour it, and preserve it. The sights and fires of the world belong to you. When you travel to other cities, you will feel the wounds of history. Beauty is in the coming home.

Gaston Bachelard has a theory of home: *the house shelters day-dreaming, the house protects the dreamer, the house allows one to dream in peace.*

What makes the earth sustainable and palatable is our capacity to locate ourselves in beauty. Beauty is political by its endurance.

Blue of a newborn's eyes. The flights of birds. The heron's wings. The ancient augurs who determined the sites of cities by the flights of birds.

Baudelaire. Taste of bergamot. Baroque of sunset. Benediction of islands, horizons, fresh water, blue Himalayan poppies, veins of hands.

Beloved. Call yourself by this name. Bestow it on another, on others before you die.

B. B. King's Blues. Beethoven's Fifth Symphony.

Remembrance: Stephen Biko 1946–1977.

Never again: Bombings of Beirut, August 6, 1982. July 12, 2006.

The Bath School Massacre, Bath, Michigan, May 18, 1927. Bombings that killed 45, injured 58. Victims were children in grades two to eight at Bath Consolidated School.

Beslan School Massacre, September 1 to September 3, 2004. September 1, the first day of school for Russian children. Also known as the Day of Knowledge.

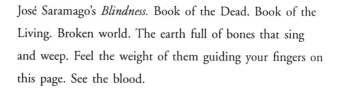

José Saramago's *Blindness*. Book of the Dead. Book of the Living. Broken world. The earth full of bones that sing and weep. Feel the weight of them guiding your fingers on this page. See the blood.

Breakable. The story of the new world is membrane thin, breakable. It can shatter into chips of bone and tears. It can be repaired with the poem that speaks of being human, the poem that refuses to shut its scarlet mouth.

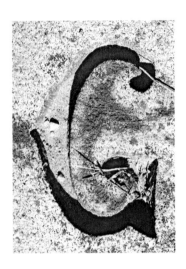

Cradle. *Motherland, cradle me. Close my eyes, lullaby me to sleep*. Classroom as cradle.

Learn that the child has been used for political power. The child can be the locus of joy, the locus of abuse and suffering. Nelson Mandela's address to the nation state is a poem by Afrikaans poet Ingrid Jonkers, "The Child," a translation of Jonker's "Die Kind." Nations begin with the child as symbol of democracy, innocence, goodness, suffering, hope. It is an immutable, universal symbol. Truth. And beauty. Terror and beauty.

They took all that was child in the house.

> —Resident of Victoria West, South Africa, reporting on police action

They took all that was child
And in the closed room
Visions of the ripe split melon
Were at the tip of the knife
They held to the child's dry tongue.

A stone against a tank is a stone against a tank
But a bullet in a child's chest rips into the heart of the house.

> —Ingrid de Kok, "All Wat Kind Is"

Carnation's peppery scent. Hard light of suffering in a Caravaggio painting. Currents of rivers. Cypress trees. Drift of cherry blossoms in spring orchards. Coyote's ears, split in the wind. Clouds. Crepescule. Lighting candles is a form of prayer and remembrance.

Never again: Chile of General Augusto Pinochet's dictatorship, 1973–1990. The executed, the tortured, the disappeared.

Chernobyl where children are being born with brains outside their bodies and holes in their hearts, two decades after the world's worst nuclear accident, April 25 to 26, 1986.

Columbine High School Massacre, Denver, Colorado, April 20, 1999. 12 students and one teacher killed, 24 others wounded, before the two killers turned their guns on themselves.

Cantos. Cello music by Elgar. Chopin prelude. Constellations. Chekhov. *Corazón, coeur,* courage. Chagall's paintings of lovers floating in night skies. Knowledge of catalpa blossoms raining down, petals on your hair. The cool touch of mother's hand. Chalk leaving milky traces on teacher's hands as she wipes the slate. Turn the page.

And this torn light,
this long torn light
will repair itself
out of the filaments of children,
and all that was child will return to this house,
will open the doors of the house.

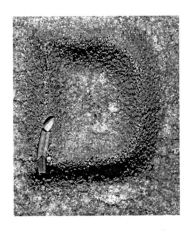

Let our different dreams,
and more than dreams, our acts
of constructive refusal generate
struggle. And love. We must dare to win
not wars, but a future
in which to live.

—Denise Levertov, "A Speech for
Antidraft Rally," D.C., March 22, 1980

Desert sands of the Sonoran, Sahara, Kalahari, Arabian, Arctic, Gobi, Great Basin.

Never again: The Devil's Tinderbox. Firebombing of Dresden, February 13, 1945.

Never again: Darfur Famine. Civil war in Sudan. Genocide. Blood. Bones.

Never again: The Dunblane Primary School Massacre, Dunblane, Scotland, March 13, 2006. 16 children killed, all under the age of 7, also their teacher. Twelve others wounded before the murderer killed himself.

Never again: Dawson College Shootings, Westmount, Quebec. 1 woman killed, 19 others wounded before the gunman killed himself. September 13, 2006.

Dream. Desire. Dostoyevsky. Iridescent propellers of dragonflies. The poetry of Robert Desnos:

I dreamt of loving. The dream remains, but love
is no longer that storm whose white nerve sparked
the castle towers, or left the mind unrhymed,
or flared an instant, just where the road forked.
. . . .
It is the star struck under my heel in the night.
It is the word no book on earth defines.
It is the foam on the wave, the cloud in the sky.

—From "Landscape," Translated from French by Don Paterson

The end of Claribel Alegría's long poem "Documental" ("Documentary") about El Salvador:

A for alcoholism,
B for battalions,
C for corruption,
D for dictatorship,
E for exploitation,
F for feudal power
of fourteen families
and etcetera, etcetera, etcetera.
My etcetera country,
my wounded country,
my child,
my tears,
my obsession.

—Translated from Spanish by D. J. Flakoll

Dissent is the right to say no, offer a second opinion, the freedom to conceive of the future. Democracy is an open space, a new page where leadership comes from the streets, from the people. Democracy is an insecure landscape that needs protection.

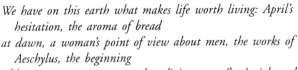

We have on this earth what makes life worth living: April's
hesitation, the aroma of bread
at dawn, a woman's point of view about men, the works of
Aeschylus, the beginning
of love, grass on a stone, mothers living on a flute's sigh and
the invaders' fear of memories

—Mahmoud Darwish, "On This Earth"

In the classroom, the child asks me about earth,
the question suspended in the curled fingertips

of the outstretched arm. I answer, the earth is a school,
a large room without walls, expectant. It is a book of

desires, a story substantial as clouds and winds, held
by the hands of rain. It is wrapped in weather and words.

Never again: Exxon Valdez Oil Spill, March 24, 1989. The oil tanker struck Bligh Reef in
Prince William, Alaska, spilling more than 11 million gallons of crude oil. Threat to food
chain for commercial fishing, danger to ten million migratory shore birds, waterfowl, hundreds
of sea otters, dozens of other species such as harbor porpoises, sea lions, several varieties
of whales.

Never again: Erfurt Gutenberg Gymnasium High School Massacre, Germany, April 26, 2002.
Highly trained combat shooter killed 17, wounded 7.

This page speaks of the smell of earth under your fingers, sands from ocean shores, clay cliffs,
rich soil of gardens. Earth girdled with winds and languages. Evergreen. Esperanza.

Evening that arranges itself around the fallen leaves alphabetized across the back yard. Syllables that braille us and sign us, leaning against the invisible. Our dreams are luminous, a cast fire upon the world. Alphabets for every continent, every child's notebook. Some read from east to west, others west to east, north to south. Everyone reaches for nomenclature. Hoop the names of things to your belt. When you are empty, eat the words, drink them.

Forgetting. Memory for forgetting. Forgiveness is not always necessary for repair.

Fauré's music. Fields of lavender, blankets of Provence mauve. Juice of figs. The Japanese believe we live in twelve pictures thrown from a floating world.

First light.

Fields of green. Freedom. Forgetfulness stalks us, leaves a wake behind the earth, a discarded trail of paper diapers, needles, wasted blood. Fresh courage glimmers when we learn the forgotten names of the stars, the names of birds, trees.

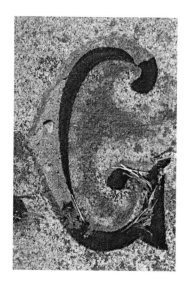

...recall the places of beauty you know.
And then, on your chosen site, let memory speak.

—Tachibana no Toshitsuna. *Sakuteiki,*
manual of garden design, Japan, 1050(?)

A little music from the trees,
 sonata in green.

Gardens. Every child, every citizen, has a plot to tend to. Each schoolyard has a garden. Small hands give new homes to earthworms. Fragrance of peonies, hyacinths, lilacs. Dark eye of the sunflower. Red flowers of runner beans, plump flesh of tomatoes.

Grief.

Grace. A literacy of grace.

Georgia O'Keefe.

Luna moths.

Never again: Gaza Strip. War between Palestine and Israel.

Henryk Górecki's Symphony No. 3 *Symphony of Sorrowful Songs*

Gather seeds. Like Wangari Maathai, winner of the Nobel Peace Prize in 2004, hold fast to Green Belt movements against deforestation. See the connection between planting trees, conserving natural resources, and peace among human communities. Create children's forests with your own stories and handfuls of seeds.

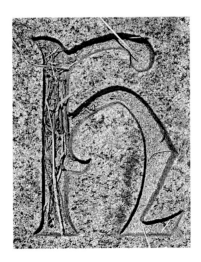

In the end the world is a language we never quite understand.
Poets jot down the alphabets of everyday.
                                    All speech pulls us toward the infinite.
History threatens to swallow us
                            year after year.

Hope is an orientation of the spirit, an orientation of the heart.

                                            —Vaclav Havel

Hummingbird.

Hyacinth. Heliotrope. Honeysuckle. Hellebore. Honey bee. High tide.

Never again: Chinese Head Tax.

Holocaust. Claws of swastikas, tattoos of yellow stars. Adolph Hitler.

Hiroshima, August 6, 1945.

Haiti of Papa Doc (François) Duvalier's dictatorship. Crimes of his secret police the Tonton Macoutes, 1971–1986. Baby Doc, his son and successor, 1971–1986.

HIV/AIDS. Rape of babies. Trafficking of girls and women.

Honour killings.

The heart is the first home of democracy, says Terry Tempest Williams.

Home. House. Our house is the core of red earth, the clay and tar sands and wetlands and forests. Our house could be the centre of the world. Not Paris, Tokyo, New York, London, but the humble centre at the core of things. You could drive by and miss it in a flash if you don't pay attention. Words cannot construct it; there are some sounds that take sacred, wordless forms. The black bird scavenging the city garbage understands the centre of the earth as greasy scraps. He doesn't have to tell us the story of the earth that has turned crimson through centuries of fierce belief and grief and heartbreak and laughter. The black bird simply perches in the green fields, in the blue arc of the sky—and laughs.

When the earth takes a difficult turn, you could fall off. A house could lose its center, ride into destruction. Sometimes the house can not protect you and the house will weep for its broken spirit.

Hymns. Despite the obscenities of civilization, everything should be sung. For this, we need poetry. Learn that after long silence, the centre of things can be healed, brought into singing.

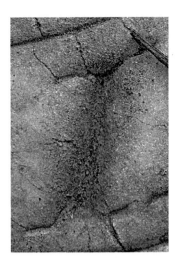

Imagination. Learn that the imagination is a magical thing, a blue fire that occurs in our expressive consciousness. When you awaken from a long stretch of creating imaginative work, you will feel in limbo, not quite on solid ground. If you try to do something physical, run, make lunch, sparks may fly. It may feel like a fire igniting, or an earthquake. All will converge at some point.

Irises. Long before the invention of calendars, Japanese farmers used floral signs to guide them in growing rice. Cherry blossoms told them it was time to plant. The blooming of irises meant the beginning of the rainy season, time to transplant seedlings to the field.

In Ogatha Korin's famous Yatsuhashi screen in New York's Metropolitan Museum of Art, the journey of an exiled courtier in the mythic tenth century *Tales of Ise* is depicted. On his journey, while crossing a bridge, he sees masses of irises blooming. The irises remind him of his homeland and the sadness of exile.

His companions challenge him to write a poem, each line starting with the letters of the Japanese word for iris.
Never again: Ipperwash.

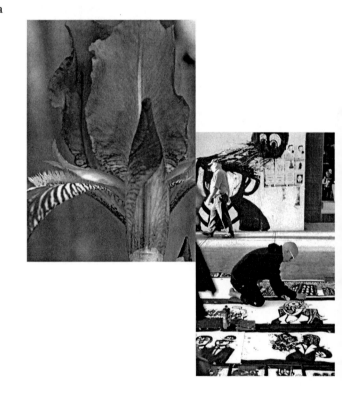

Indian residential schools.

Iraq war.

Invent what you desire

Read Paul Loeb's book
The Impossible Will Take a Little While.

Never again: Japanese Internment.

Deep purple blooms of jacaranda trees. Children playing jump-rope games. Jonquils. Jellyfish. June bugs. Jungles. Jaguars. Jasmine. Juice of plums. Joy.

Wassily Kandinsky paintings.

Kiss. Kiss of winds, sweetness of rain on the wounded mouth. The mouth of love. Mouths of deltas and rivers. Kiss of mother, father, child, lover. Lip of stars. Kiss for the lonely, the homeless, the unloved, the despairing, the abandoned. Salve.

Never again. KKK.

Never again: The Korean War, 1950–1953.

Never again: Kashmir of guns, swords, blood, bones. Contested borders. Remember and preserve the peacocks, monkeys, perfume of flowers.

Never again: The Killing Fields.

Never again: Kristallnacht.

Never again: War zone of Kandahar.

Kitchen table. Imagine life might end here, all of you
sitting together, sharing food and laughter.

Kiss the gleaming armour of the world.
Feel its electric purr.
Close your hands on wind-stunned leaves.
Buff the scars of history with your mouth.

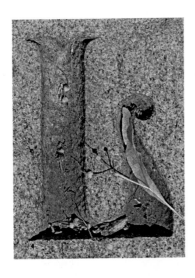

If these words can do anything
if these songs can do anything
I say bless this house
with stars.
Transfix us with love.

—Joy Harjo, "The Creation Story"

Teachers in *The New Republic* speak unabashedly about love. Education is a practice of love. The history of love is taught and made in schools. You will be taught not to fear love and that its consequence is light.

Light. Luminosity.

Buddhists tell us to live our days unattached
                to the dust of the world
                      to enter the blackness.

To always see ourselves as light.

Not so easy to do when the hum of the world
                      dulls us in its gears.

Try to wear light as a garment
                find it in the paradise of afterlife under a stone
                in the opened door of a commuter train.

Landscape. Landscape that softens the sharp edges of solitude. Hold the landscape in your arms and feel the contours of your mind like nature, thoughts flowing like water. Knowledge and memory are inextricably bound to the earth and the mind has its own ecology, inseparable from the body. Remember things past, not just the taste of things but the turning of the body on the bed, language inseparable from experience, from skin.

Learn to read, see, and feel landscape like abstract painters. The beautiful soaked canvasses of Helen Frankenthaler. Frankenthaler writes about returning from Nova Scotia: *I came back and did the Mountains and the Sea painting and I knew the landscapes were in my arms as I did it.* She names her paintings: *The Moors; The Bay; Passport; Towards a New Climate; Blue Tide; Dawn After Storm; Blue Head On: Mauve Exit; White Lilac; Night Shade; Bird of Paradise: Nature Abhors a Vacuum.*

Richard Diebenkorn's geometric fields in the Ocean Park paintings. Mark Rothko's giant color fields. Become Rothko's ideal of the sensitive observer, one who sees beyond those fields of color to weep, to feel.

Lilies. Lilacs. Lavender.

Never again: The Blitz. The bombing of London by the Nazis, September 7, 1940, for 57 consecutive nights. 18 thousand tons of explosives were dropped, killing 18,629 men, 16,201 women, 5,028 children. There were 695 unidentified, charred bodies.

The Love Canal Tragedy. Niagara Falls, New York. One of the worst environmental tragedies in American history. Dream community turned into a chemical toxic waste dump by the Hooker Chemical Company. Benzene, carcinogens seeping through schoolyards and lawns. Birth defects, leukemia.

The Lockerbie Bombing. Pan Am 103, London to New York, December 21, 1988. 270 passengers killed, 11 townspeople killed in Lockerbie.

Never again mourn the burned libraries of the world:

When the National Library burned for three
days in August, the town was choked with black
snow. Those days I could not find a single pencil
in the house, and when I finally found one it
did not have the heart to write. Even the erasers left
behind a black trace. Sadly, my homeland burned.

—Goran Simić, "Lament for Vijecnica" in From Sarajevo With Sorrow

Remember libraries as sacred places, shelter from the sharp corners of the world.

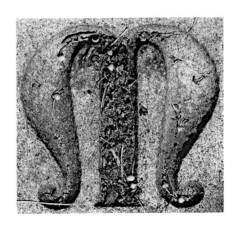

Motherland cradle me
  Close my eyes
Lullaby me to sleep

> —Natalie Merchant, "Motherland"

Memory. In *The New Republic* you will be taught to read history, to learn that ideas are short lived, that human memory can be short lived. Sometimes ideas that seem most persuasive will vanish in an instant. You will be taught to read literature as a study of humankind, to understand the development of the earth and its peoples. Literary study is envisioned as a branch of ecology, anthropology, and history. Your education will help you learn to judge an idea in the context of long-term human memory so the lessons of history bear weight upon the present and future world. Education is a consideration of ecology, of *Oïkos*, our home. And in this place of beauty and truth, the aesthetic value of art is our most powerful way of speaking to others. Education then, as a practice of and engagement with love, becomes a religion of love against a religion of death.

Mozart's *Requiem*.

Mahmoud Darwish's *Memory for Forgetting*.

The poems of Osip Mandelstam.

Marsh grasses. Meadows. Mockingbirds. Monsoon rains. Magnolia.

Never again: Massacres:

My Lai Massacre, Vietnam, March 16, 1968, also known as the Song My Massacre.

Munich Massacre at the 1972 Olympics. Hostage taking and murder of eleven Israeli athletes.

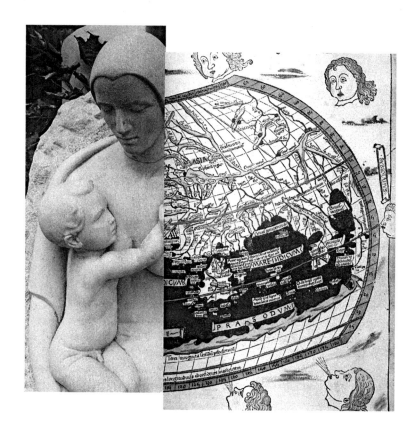

Montreal Massacre, December 6, 1989. Fourteen women gunned down at Montreal École Polytechnique.

Madrid Train Bombings, March 11, 2004. On rush hour commuter trains, terrorists' bombs killed 192, wounded 2,050.

Mercy.

Map. You will be given an imperfect map printed with warnings. Your place of entry is the sea of your mother's blood. No exit. No guidebook or compass. Only your mother's song and the journey before you shimmering above cliffs and lakes and moonlight that contain your heart. You must make your own map, create an atlas for the difficult world. Mouthing the words of your own fables, your own inventions, give them gold-leaf and leather bindings.

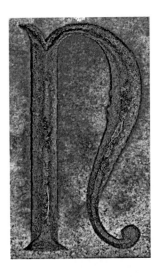

For [the Kwakiutl], a name was a story. We say "Vancouver," naming an island for a captain; we say "Victoria," naming a village for a queen. For them, a place-name would not be something that is, but something that happens. They called one patch of ocean "Where salmon gather." They called one bend in the river "Insufficient canoe."... If the Kwakiutl habits of naming were childlike, naïve, they were also utterly mature. Their language shows connections where we have made separations.

—Kim Stafford, "There are No Names but Stories"

Naming. Roll the words on your tongue to taste them. Think of painters' colours: alizarin crimson, viridian, azure, cadmium red, ochre, titanium white, sap green.

Night. Elie Wiesel's *Night.*

Nursery stories. Margaret Wise Brown's *Goodnight Moon.*

Night-blooming cereus. Nicotania. Narcissus.

Primo Levi *In such a night as this*

>   *In such a night like this*
> *There are seven young men in white lab coats,*
> *Four of them are smoking pipes.*
> *They are designing a very long channel*
> *In which to unite a bundle of protons*
> *Almost as swift as light.*
> *If they succeed, the world will blow up.*
>   *In such a night as this,*
> *A poet strains his bow, searching for a word*
> *That can contain the typhoon's force,*
> *The secrets of blood and seed.*

—"Memorandum Book"

Never again: Nuclear weapons. Atomic bombing of Nagasaki, August 9, 1945.

Never again: Nuclear fallout from atomic bomb tests. Acid rain in Nevada in the 1950s. Generation after generation of women and men dying of cancer.

New Alphabet

If you say A you have to say B
A is always against apartheid
B is color blind
. . . .
my eyes can't get enough of drowsing thorntrees
between red-grass and thin-sinned plovers
my garden strewn with loads of roses—only for my children
                    do I lay down my life

here I am learning to write—I can't do otherwise

—Antjie Krok, "New Alphabet," translated from the Afrikaans by Peter Sacks

Never Again. Nickel Mines School Massacre, Amish School, Lancaster County, Pennsylvania. 10 girls, ages 6-13, shot by a lone gunman, October 3, 2006. 5 girls died. The gunman killed himself.

Nothing. Sometimes what we know is nothing. Uncertainty. And this too is knowledge, born of the vast and stunning nature of the earth, every struggle flooding the mind, until we are tended by rain and flowers.

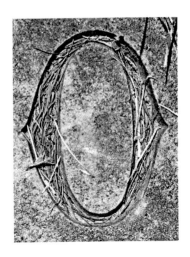

O brave new world. Taste of blood oranges.

Never again: Oklahoma bombing, April 19, 1995.

Never again: Osama Bin Laden.

Never again: Ovens burning people alive.

Whir of monarch butterflies, orange-gold dust of thousands of wings, carrying pollen to the sun. Search for them everywhere. Oronoko River. Oz. Emerald City. Click your ruby heels and you are home.

At the end of a perfect day, those
looking for love leave scars in twilight.

Proust's *Remembrance of Things Past*.
We may remember the past inaccurately.
Perfume of tea and skin.

Peter Pan. Promise of Neverland.

Never again: Port Arthur Massacre, Tasmania, April 28, 1996. Shooting massacre of 35 men, women, and children, 18 more wounded.

Parklands. Poetry. Peace. Prayer. Learn that you can invent your own prayers. You don't always need a prayer book. You will come to understand that a church is not the only place to find divinity.

The Peace of Wild Things

When despair for the world grows in me
and I wake in the night at the least sound
in fear of what my life and my children's lives may be,
I go and lie down where the wood drake
rests in his beauty on the water, and the great heron
> *feeds.*
I come into the peace of wild things
who do not tax their lives with forethought
of grief. I come into the presence of still water.
And I feel above me the day-blind stars
waiting with their light. For a time
I rest in the grace of the world, and am free.

—Wendell Berry

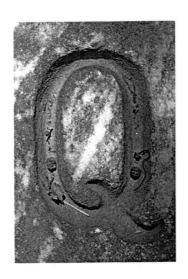

Questions. Quarrel with politics. Quince.
Quarry. Quail. Quack grass. Quick silver. Quick
step. Quixote. Quantum physics.
Always ask the questions.
Quiet. Eudora Welty's response when asked
what causes she would support: *Peace,
education, conservation, and quiet.*

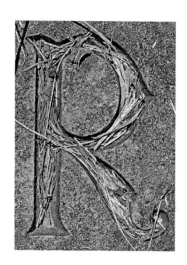

And he was noisy. He has a cry that contained all the noises of a spoiled child and an angry raven—yet he could sometimes speak softly as the wind in the hemlock boughs, with an echo of that beautiful other sound, like an organic bell, which is also part of every raven's speech.

—Robert Bringhurst and Bill Reid,
The Raven Steals the Light

Refuge. Redress. Repair.

Never again: Rwanda. Genocide. Massacre of 800,000 to 1, 071,000 Tutsis and moderate Hutus during a period of 100 days, April 6 to mid-July 1994.

When you read, as reading becomes your faith, you will leave a commotion in your wake. The book becomes talisman. Hear the startled breath of the world. Remember your childhood sets of golden books. Nursery of stars. Winken, Blinken, and Nod. Kipling has a theory about how the alphabet came to be. Cahiers d'exercises. Lined notebooks with faint pink margins. Vanish through a rabbit hole, a looking glass, a wardrobe. Find a page that does not tear the retina. Paul Éluard's love poems. In the burned libraries everything is winged and dreaming. We are not all born with grace and we are scarred along with the landscape. A manifesto of stars is necessary. Words unfurling into prayer flags. After Auschwitz, no theology, but the touch of longing is everywhere.

Imagine the letter that begins in honesty *Dearest Beloved.* After Rwanda, no language. Poem that temples grief. Stone of witness. Tablet of amen and love. In the ruined garden stand in the shadow of the scar. Beauty cleanses, rinses your dreaming brow.

Bend your neck over the page. The heart is the toughest part of the body. Tenderness is in the hands. After a requiem begin to hear the noise of the world again. Door opening as the palm of the eye. A poetry of shine. Repair.

Rachel Carson's *Silent Spring*. Songs for the earth's body.

Scarlet ribbons in a small girl's braids. Learn to sew your shadow back on. Keep it close to your skin at all times.

Sorrow.

Never again: Soweto Riots and the massacre of youth and schoolchildren protesting against apartheid, June 16, 1976.

Never again: Sharpeville Massacre, March 21, 1960.

Never again: Famine, disease, and war in Somalia.

Never again: Sept. 11, 2001. World Trade Center bombings.

Never again: Bombed schoolyards. Bombed subways and buses. London bombings, July 2005.

Never again: Siege of Sarajevo.

Never again: Saddam Hussein.

Never again: Contamination of Sydney Tar Ponds, Sydney, Nova Scotia. Industrial waste from steel mills, coking works. Sydney Steel Company (SYSCO) coke ovens produced benzene, kerosene, and naphthalene that poured into the estuary flowing into Sydney Harbour known as Muggah Creek. More than 80 years of coke-oven operation left ground and surface water contaminated with arsenic, lead, and other toxins. An accumulation of 700,000 tonnes of chemical waste and raw sewage has resulted in residents suffering from cancer, headaches, birth defects, arsenic poisoning.

Never again: Strange fruit. In the flooded bayou of New Orleans, the history of slavery and lynching. Those who waded in the waters to lose the tracking dogs. Those who waited for chariots to Jordan.

Saudade. Similkameen River. Salmon spawning. Sweetness of rainwater, glacial streams. Salt flats of Utah. Silk rustle of a sleeve. Spring. Sap-drunk trees.

Study. Education as Plato conceived it is not simply instruction but engaged study. Make a house of intellect. Make of your lives a study. Vital truths cannot be taught; they can be learned only through the difficulties of uncertain, unconditioned, open study. Each of us has the capacity for this, but not always the will.

Small things

You believe small things keep you safe:
prayers like the Japanese tie to trees,
clasp of your child's hand,
angels at the gates of your city,
schedules of commuter trains.

Until the blasted church,
machete massacres,
the rush-hour bombs on the subways,
carnage that is the beginning of aloneness.
Clothed in our convictions,
we feel our brains slip,
in every bone the fossil of murder,
illness we cannot vomit up
a hurt so fierce it takes more than
all human grief to beat it down.

We see the exact perspective of
loss as a fading pencil study,
loved one's features blur, dim in detail,
clouds of centuries pass over the image,
through cross-hatched strokes
only a wrist in forced memory remains,
a hand caressing.

In the archives of accusations,
vengeance and the unforgiven,
we are nailed together, flying the black
flag of ourselves.

The farmer continues to till his fields.
In the city we awaken, turn off alarm clocks,
drink our coffee, kiss our lovers and children,
begin again at the train stations, at bus stops,
briefcases in hand.

In deafness to political speech
                                        the eye permits change.
We imagine words fit for a newborn.

Touch me. In the burned city,
we have become beautiful.

Love's no secret now.

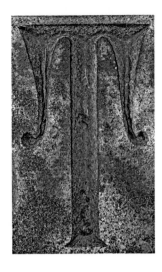

Somehow we survive
and tenderness, frustrated, does not wither.

. . . .

most cruel, all our land is scarred with terror,
rendered unlovely and unlovable;
sundered are we and all our passionate surrender

but somehow tenderness survives.

—Dennis Brutus, "Somehow We Survive"

Turquoise. Stone of the desert. Colour of yearning. Stone that strengthens the eyes, say the Persians. It is the desert dweller's equivalent of a bulletproof vest against pain or evil. The Zuni say turquoise is water. For the Aztecs, it is the color that supplies the heart.

Touch another. In *The New Republic* teachers and students may touch each other. This has nothing to do with sex. Touch can be through words as well as hands. Touch has everything to do with love, and education as a practice of love. It has everything to do with the healing of scars. Many in the world are dying from skin-hunger. It is not exclusively a widow's affliction. Pulitzer Prize poet Stanley Kunitz wrote in his poem "Touch Me":

Summer is late, my heart…
Darling, do you remember
the man you married? Touch me,
remind me who I am.

Trees hold the story of birdflight. Maurice Merleau-Ponty writes: *Language is the very voice of the trees, the waves, the forest.*

Truth and reconciliation. No tragedy is local. It is always global. Turtle Island.

Never again: Tiananmen Square Massacre, June 4, 1989.

Taliban.

Torture at Abu Ghraib.

Tenderness is our best gesture in the face of death.

There is tenderness in every geography. And this has the power to change you,

unweight your eyelids every morning, as the sky leans towards the absolute.

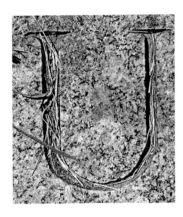

Umbilical. Underground waters, springs, wells. Underground Railway. Underworld. Underbelly of subways beneath the city. Undone.

Never again: Uganda of brutal dictator Idi Amin, "Butcher of Uganda," 1971–1979. Murder and torture of 3 thousand to 5 thousand people.

Mahmoud Darwish's *Unfortunately, It Was Paradise.*

Vita nuova. Viva voce. In the living voice.

Velvet.

Vetiver grasses.

Venice

Never again: Vietnam War. Legacy of Agent Orange. Dioxin poisoning. No accident of nature but environmental warfare. The legacy of American defoliation of Vietnamese forests in order to expose the enemy. Veterans struck by cancers. Lost nation of Vietnam—thousands born without limbs, without eyes, without organs, hideous deformities, cancers.

Never again: Virginia Tech Massacre, Blacksburg Virginia. Gunman killed 32 people and wounded many others before committing suicide. April 16, 2007.
Velocity of fear, velocity of joy.

Tell me, what is it you plan to do
with your one wild and precious life?

> —Mary Oliver, "The Summer Day"

Wounds. White ink. Stories written in mother's milk. Water. Wholeness. Teachers in *The New Republic* will speak as if this wholeness exists. You will learn what it means to know that one is not alone. That there exists a rich, full, wholeness of life to be grasped. Wholeness in the earth, in us, in the wintry obstinance of all those who cling to its existence.

Preserve the wilderness by speaking out against its destruction. Gary Snyder's notions of wild mind, watershed, the practice of the wild.

Never again: World War I. World War II.

Wings. When the century turns, let the darkling thrush fly.

> *The natural function of the wing is to soar upwards and carry that which is heavy up*
> *to the place where dwells the race of gods. More than any other thing that pertains to*
> *the body it partakes of the nature of the divine.*

> —Plato

Sometimes in the shallow waters of
mudflats and wetlands, the cranes
dance, these birds who mate for life,
sending waves flying, a language of
ancient memories, a language that
teaches us that after grief, it is possible
to love again, a music we have
forgotten, such sheer joy. When the
cranes lift in ascent, cathedrals of wind
rise in their wingbones, estuaries of
morning light lifting across continents,
a white front of radiance, their cries
like clouds of desire. After, in the
presence of still waters, you can rest in
the white light, in the grace of wings.

The inner—what is it?
If not intensified sky,
Hurled through with birds and deep
With the winds of homecoming.

—Rainier Maria Rilke

When hobo skies dream us into adventures of comic-book heroes with
X-ray vision,   new gods of the city.

   Yawping across skyscrapers and apartment buildings.

      Zest of their goodness like an absolute tasted on the wind.

I have seen the face of sorrow. It is the face of
the Sarajevo wind leafing through newspapers
glued to the street by a puddle of blood as I
pass with a loaf of bread under my arm.

—Goran Simić, "The Face of Sorrow," from *Sarajevo With Sorrow*

Never again: Ethnic cleansing in former Yugoslavia. The Bosnian War. Ethnic and religious tensions in the new independent republics: Bosnia and Hercegovina, Macedonia, Slovenia, Croatia, Montenegro, Serbia.

The girl reads neighbourhoods of
dog, cat, sister, brother, mother, father
houses lit with yellow sunshine and once
upon a time glass slippers, long-toothed wolves.

Yellow of lemons, sunlight, butter, daffodils.

Pacific yew trees saved from clear-cutting to make tamoxifen for cancer drugs.

You can read and write this story
with the yes of being.

You are reading this poem through your failing sight, the thick
Lens enlarging these letters beyond all meaning yet you read on
Because even the alphabet is precious.

—Adrienne Rich, "Dedications"

The end of the alphabet is never final. A body is never
final. The chronicle unravels like a prayer cloth, calm of
storybook nurseries, book codes, calligraphies of desire.
There is a small star pinned where Hiroshima used to be.
The book's pages continue past the final letter into the
future. Read in the present, storied by the past, in order
to reach out for the future. Invent what you desire to the
songs of zephyr winds. In each of your days,
all the way to the zero hour, pay full attention to
the radiance, to the full chase of beauty.

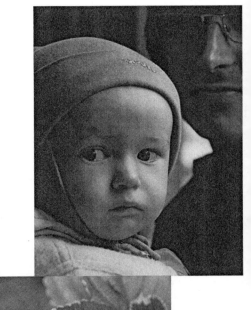

We are our final vocabulary

and how we use it.

Listen to the earth's prayer which has the perfume of newborns.

The right word can send you breathless.

Everything is speaking and singing. We are here.

This life. Long, slow burn of a struck match.

Alone we are not strong enough.
But the stars and oceans have entered us.

Afterword

Dear Reader: the afterword becomes a foreword. This is not a novel of departure, ending in the smoke of railway stations or the plane waiting on the tarmac. The pages of *The New Republic* are in your hands and eyes to read and write as you move ahead from the natural and unnatural histories that are your legacies. Add your own entries to the primer: your own stories of once upon a time and never again, your own lists of things to remember, things to love, things to study, stories of place, your readings of home. In these stories, enter the dialogues between public and private worlds in which a paramount freedom is the right to imagination. Then you will know you have existed, felt, desired, hated, loved.

The ecotopia that is most desirable is not the ecotopia of Ernest Callenbach's *Ecotopia*; there is no blueprint for the future. Science fiction provides us primarily with dystopias. Most desirable are stories that acknowledge the world as messy, full of people and animals and gods who make mistakes, get the world wrong. Through this messiness, a biocultural ecological education provides a location for dialogues and relations that enable a more hopeful story, not necessarily a more ordered one. The more hopeful story is a narrative that provides a site of resistance to master narratives, to unquestioned received knowledges.

Relation in *The New Republic* is turbulence, exposure, an identity, not of ethnicities and ancestries, but of meeting places. Relation does not uphold a *lingua franca* but a multiplicity of languages and articulations. This conception might challenge us, as we are accustomed to thinking in terms of separate and disenfranchised groups, nations, ethnicities, religions, genders, tribes. We might fear that a poetics of relation as the central premise of education would be chaos; rather, it is a transformational way of apprehending and sustaining our world.

For the reader and artist to remain grounded in poetics, in art, in the face of a historical past and a present that puts humans face to face with terror and evil, is also to reach the heart of political and educational debate. Human feelings, human experiences, the human body and face, recover their proper place—the foreground of educational life.

In the end, in the beginning, all lessons are about survival in the face of evil and terror, the losses of soul and spirit, the threats to home. In the circumstances of this century and the new ones to come, remain always a poet, an artist engaged in a poetics of relation with others. In a world of violence and destruction, the only education that matters is one that creates a home.

Notes

Introductory epigraph by Anne Waldman, excerpt from "5 Female Poets next to a Block of Ice." *The American Poetry Review*, May/June 2006:33.

All photographs © Joe Paczuski, 2007.

Introductory Notes for a Primer

Barthes, Roland. "From Work to Text." In *Modern Literary Theory*. Edited by Philip Rice and Patricia Waugh. New York: Arnold, 1996.

————. *Roland Barthes by Roland Barthes*. Translated by Richard Howard. Berkeley: University of California Press, 1994.

————. *S/Z*. originally published Paris: Editions de Seuil, 1970. Translated by Richard Howard and Richard Miller. New York: Farrar, Strauss, Giroux, 1974.

Darwish, Mahmoud. *Journal of an Ordinary Grief,* 1973. Cited by Ibrahim Muhawi in the introduction to *Memory for Forgetfulness: August, Beirut, 1982*. Berkeley: University of California Press:xviii.

Durrell, Lawrence. *Spirit of Place*. New York: Marlowe and Company, 1969.

Eco, Umberto. *The Role of the Reader*. Bloomington: Indiana University Press, 1979:49.

Milosz, Csezlaw. *Milosz's ABC*. Translated by Madeline G. Levine. New York: Farrar, Strauss, Giroux, 2001.

Persky, Stan. *A Short Version: An ABC*. Vancouver: New Star Books, 2005.

Stafford, Kim. *Places and Stories*. Pittsburgh: Carnegie Mellon University Press, 1987.

Notes for a Primer on Biocultural Ecology
LeGuin, Ursula. *Talking on the Water: Conversations about Nature and Creativity*. San Francisco: Sierra Club Books, 1994.

A

Benjamin, Walter. "Theses on the History of Philosophy." *Illuminations*. Edited by Hannah Arendt. New York: Schocken Books, 1969:263.

B

Bachelard, Gaston. *The Poetics of Space*. (First published 1958.) Translated by Maria Jolas. New York: Orion Press, 1964; Boston: Beacon Press, 1994.

Dunlop, Rishma. Epigraph: *Beauty / So many kinds to name. . . .* Excerpt from "Saccade." In *Reading Like a Girl*. Windsor: Black Moss Press, 2004:11.

C

De Kok, Ingrid. "All Wat Kind Is." In *Seasonal Fires: New and Selected Poems*. New York: Seven Stories Press, 2006:49.

Merchant, Natalie. Italicized lines: *Motherland, cradle me. . . .* Excerpt from "Motherland." *Motherland*. Audio CD. Elektra/Wea, 2001.

D

Alegria, Claribel. " Documental." Translated by D. J. Flakoll. In *Woman of the River*. Pittsburgh: University of Pittsburgh Press, 1988:23.

Desnos, Robert. *Landscape*. Translated by Don Paterson. In *Poetry: The Translation Issue*, April 2006:62.

Levertov, Denise. "A Speech for Antidraft Rally, D.C.: March 12, 1980.

E

Darwish, Mahmoud. "On This Earth." In *Unfortunately, It Was Paradise: Selected Poems*. Translated by Munir Akash and Carolyn Forché. Berkeley: University of California Press, 2003.

H

Dunlop, Rishma. *In the end the world. . . .* Excerpt from "Slow Burn." In *Reading Like a Girl*. Windsor: Black Moss Press, 2004:82.

Havel, Vaclav. *Disturbing the Peace*. New York: Vintage Books, 1991:181.

Williams, Terry Tempest. The Open Space of Democracy Tour: Democracy Diary, October 6–29, 2004. http://www.oriononline.org/pages/oo/sidebars/OSD/diary22.html

K

Dunlop, Rishma. *Kiss the gleaming armor of the world.* . . . Excerpt (final stanza) from "Saccade." *Reading Like a Girl.* Windsor: Black Moss Press, 2004:12.

L

Harjo, Joy. (Epigraph.) "The Creation Story." In *How We Became Human: New and Selected Poems: 1975–2001.* W. W. Norton, 2002:91. Originally published in *The Woman Who fell from the Sky.* W. W. Norton, 1994.

Dunlop, Rishma. Stanza beginning: *Buddhists tell us* . . . Excerpt from "Reading Chekhov." In *Reading Like a Girl.* Black Moss Press, 2004:50.

Simić, Goran. "Lament for Vijecnica." In *Sarajevo with Sorrow.* Windsor: Biblioasis, 2005:32.

M

Merchant, Natalie. "Motherland." *Motherland.* Audio CD. Elektra/Wea, 2001.

N

Krok, Antjie. "New Alphabet." Translated by Peter Sacks. In *Poetry*: The Translation Issue, April 2006:72.

Levi, Primo. "Memorandum Book." In *Scanning the Century: the Penguin Book of the Twentieth Century in Poetry.* Edited by Peter Forbes. London: Penguin, 1999:334.

Stafford, Kim. *Places and Stories.* Pittsburgh: Carnegie Mellon University Press, 1987.

P

Berry, Wendell. "The Peace of Wild Things." In *Collected Poems: 1957–1982.* San Francisco: North Point Press, 1985. Originally published in *Openings,* 1969.

Q

Welty, Eudora. Cited in Williams, Terry Tempest. *Refuge: An Unnatural History of Family and Place.* New York: Vintage, Random House, 1992.

R

Reid, Bill and Robert Bringhurst. *The Raven Steals the Light*. Vancouver: Douglas and McIntyre, 1984:15.

Dunlop, Rishma. Section beginning: *When you read* . . . Adapted from "Claim." In *Reading Like a Girl*. Windsor: Black Moss press, 2004:92

S

Dunlop, Rishma. "Small things." In *Metropolis*. Toronto: Mansfield Press, 2004:18.

T

Brutus, Dennis. "Somehow We Survive." In *Simple Lust*. New York: Hill and Wang, 1973.

Dunlop, Rishma. Italicized lines: *There is tenderness in every geography.* . . . Excerpt from "Naramata Road." In *Red Silk: An Anthology of South Asian Canadian Women Poets*. Mansfield Press, 2004:35.

Kunitz, Stanley. "Touch Me." In *Passing Through: The Later Poems, New and Selected*. W. W. Norton, 1995:158.

Merleau-Ponty, Maurice. *The Visible and the Invisible*. Edited by Claude Lefort. Translated by Alphonso Lingis. Northwestern University Press, 1968.

W

Oliver, Mary. "The Summer Day." In *New and Selected Poems*. Boston: Beacon Press, 1992:94.

Plato. *Phaedrus*, 246e.

Rilke, Rainier Maria. *Ahead of All Parting: The Selected Poetry and Prose of Rainier Maria Rilke*. Translated by Stephen Mitchell. New York: Modern Library, 1995.

Y

Simić, Goran. "The Face of Sorrow." In *Sarajevo with Sorrow*. Windsor: Biblioasis, 2005:20.

Z

Rich, Adrienne. "Dedications." In *Atlas of a Difficult World: Poems 1988–1991*. New York: W. W. Norton, 1991.

Dunlop, Rishma. Stanza beginning: *We are our final vocabulary* ... Excerpts from "Slow Burn." In *Reading like a Girl*. Windsor: Black Moss Press, 2004: 81–84.

Afterword

For views on ecotopia:

Callenbach, Ernest. *Ecotopia. The Notebooks and Reports of William Weston*. Berkeley: Banyan Tree Books, 1975.

Le Guin, Ursula. *Always Coming Home*. Toronto: Bantam, 1987. See also Le Guin's essay: "A Non-Euclidean View of California as a Very Cold Place to Be." In *Dancing at the Edge of the World: Thoughts on Words, Women, Places*. Harper and Row, 1990.

I

Complicated Conversations

1

Becoming Transnational

Rhizosemiosis, Complicated Conversation, and Curriculum Inquiry

Noel Gough

More than a decade ago, William Pinar, William Reynolds, Patrick Slattery, and Peter Taubman (1995) concluded their synoptic text, *Understanding Curriculum: An Introduction to the Study of Historical and Contemporary Curriculum Discourses,* with a chapter titled "Postscript for the Next Generation" in which they foreshadowed a future for curriculum inquiry in terms of generating and sustaining "complicated conversations":

> Curriculum is an extraordinarily complicated conversation. Curriculum as institutionalized text is a formalized and abstract version of conversation, a term we usually use to refer to those open-ended, highly personal, and interest-driven events in which persons encounter each other. That curriculum has become so formalized and distant from the everyday sense of conversation is a profound indication of its institutionalization and bureaucratization. Instead of employing others' conversations to enrich our own, we "instruct" students to participate in others'— i.e. textbook authors'—conversations, employing others' terms to others' ends. Such social alienation is an inevitable consequence of curriculum identified with the academic disciplines as they themselves have been institutionalized and bureaucratized over the past one hundred years. Over the past twenty years the American curriculum field[1] has attempted to "take back" curriculum from the bureaucrats, to make the curriculum field itself a conversation, and in so doing, work to understand curriculum. (p. 848)

More recently, Pinar and others worldwide have deliberately sought to make participation in the complicated conversations that constitute curriculum work more culturally inclusive by establishing the International Association for the Advancement of Curriculum Studies (IAACS) in 2000. Through its triennial conferences, online journal, interactive Web sites,[2] and associated publications (see, e.g., Pinar, 2003; Trueit, Doll, Wang, & Pinar, 2003), IAACS provides a number of forums for such conversations, which now have additional layers of complication and complexity by virtue of being conducted transnationally, transculturally and, at least to some extent, translinguistically.

In this chapter I respond to a question that has been a persistent focus for inquiry among members of IAACS since its formation. Pinar (2005) formulates the question as follows: "How do we provide opportunities for 'complicated conversation' and 'intellectual breakthrough' in the internationalization of curriculum studies?" Pinar's question is a specific formulation of a larger problematic that will be familiar to many environmental educators, because environmental education as an institutionalized curriculum category has had a significant international presence since the early 1970s—for example, the United Nations (through UNESCO-UNEP[3]) established the International Environmental Education Programme in 1974.[4] But as I have argued elsewhere (N. Gough, 2003), although the phrase "thinking globally" has circulated within the slogan system of environmental education for more than 30 years, the deeper implications of internationalization, globalization, and cultural inclusivity for the field remain largely unexamined and undertheorized. During the past decade and more, my personal experiences of research, consultancy, and teaching in various nations or regions—including Australia, China, Europe, Iran, New Zealand, and southern Africa[5]—have served to deepen my conviction that the "complicated conversation" to which Pinar et al. refer is not yet complicated enough in any of the disciplines within which I work (principally curriculum studies, research methodology, environmental education, and science education). The international discourses of these disciplines are "complicated," complex, and diverse only within western registers of difference in approaches to disciplined inquiry, principally because they remain dominated by scholars who work in Eurocentric scholarly traditions. Indeed, many environmental education scholars seem more interested in "*un*complicating" the concepts, issues, and debates that mark the field. For example, William Scott and Stephen Gough (2004) begin their book, *Sustainable Development and Learning: Framing the Issues*, by treating sustainable development "*at least initially*, as a set of contested ideas rather than a settled issue" (p. 2, italics added) and "set precision aside and begin with working definitions which are as *inclusive* as possible" (p. 1). But they also "see definition [of both (lifelong) learning and sustainable development] as a core process of the book" (p. 1) and implicitly suggest that contestation, ambiguity, and multiplicity are conditions to be tolerated as we struggle to overcome them and eventually reach authoritative, stable, and settled definitions.

Pinar (2005) explores the question of how to provide opportunities for complicated and generative conversation in the internationalization of curriculum studies through three concepts that structure Charles David Axelrod's (1979) sociological study of intellectual breakthrough, namely, *thinking*, *individuality*, and *community*. He is in the early stages of conducting a program of inquiry that uses these concepts to structure a planned sequence of transnational conversations. In the remainder of this chapter, I explore Pinar's question by performing a narrative experiment.

NARRATIVE EXPERIMENTS: A METHODOLOGICAL DISPOSITION

My response to Pinar's question (and the larger problematic of which it is a part) is shaped by my methodological disposition to perform educational inquiry by producing texts of the kind that Laurel Richardson (2001) calls "writing-stories" and that I call "narrative experiments" (N. Gough, 2004a). Richardson argues (persuasively, in my view) that:

> *Writing is a method of discovery*, a way of finding out about yourself and your world. When we view writing as a *method*, we experience "language-in-use," how we "word the world" into existence . . . And then we "reword" the world, erase the computer screen, check the thesaurus, move a paragraph, again and again. This "worded world" never accurately, precisely, completely captures the studied world, yet we persist in trying. Writing as a method of inquiry honors and encourages the trying, recognizing it as emblematic of the significance of language. (p. 35)

Like Richardson, "I write because I want to find something out. I write in order to learn something that I did not know before I wrote it" (p. 35), and this essay can be understood as a narrative experiment performed by bringing concepts that circulate widely in the discourses of an increasingly internationalized curriculum field into intertextual play with Gilles Deleuze and Félix Guattari's geophilosophy and Ursula Le Guin's fictions. I use the term *essay* here both as a verb—to attempt, to try, to test—and as a noun. In theoretical inquiry an essay can serve similar purposes to an experiment in empirical research—a methodical way of investigating a question, problem or issue—although I find more appropriate analogies for my work in the experimental arts than in the experimental sciences.[6] Both *essay* and the related term *assay* come to English speakers through the French *essayer* from the Latin *exigere*, to weigh. Thus, I write essays to test ideas, to "weigh" them up, to give me (and eventually, I hope, my colleagues) a sense of their worth. The purpose of this particular narrative experiment is to imagine, rehearse, and perform (to the best of my ability) some possible "rhizosemiotic" practices of transnational curriculum inquiry that might generate and sustain complicated conversations and the conditions under which they occur.[7] I deliberately refrain from attempting to "define" my invented signifier, *rhizosemiotic*, because I share Deleuze's disinterest in asking what a sign, concept, or text "means" but, rather, asking how they *work* and what they *do* or *produce*. If my narrative experiment does the work I intend, readers will experience "rhizosemiotic play" immanently, as emerging from this text.

I understand environmental education research to be a species of curriculum inquiry, and I therefore intend all that I write here to be interpretable and applicable within national and transnational discourses of environmental education. Where appropriate, I draw attention to some of the particular ramifications for environmental education of the narrative experiments I perform here.

DELEUZE AND GUATTARI'S GEOPHILOSOPHY

Deleuze and Guattari (1994) map the "geography of reason" from pre-Socratic times to the present, a geophilosophy describing relations between particular spatial configurations and locations and the philosophical formations that arise in them. "Philosophy," they say, "is the discipline that involves creating concepts" (p. 5) through which knowledge can be generated. As Michael Peters (2004) points out, this is very different from the approaches taken by many analytic and linguistic philosophers who are more concerned with the *clarification* of concepts:

> Against the conservatism, apoliticism and ahistoricism of analytic philosophy that has denied its own history until very recently, Deleuze and Guattari attempt [a] geography of philosophy—a history of geophilosophy—beginning with the Greeks. Rather than providing a history, they conceptualise philosophy in spatial terms as *geophilosophy*. Such a conception immediately complicates the question of philosophy: by tying it to a geography and a history, a kind of historical and spatial specificity, philosophy cannot escape its relationship to the City and the State. In its modern and postmodern forms it cannot escape its form under industrial and knowledge capitalism. (p. 218)

In a similar way, Simon Dalby (2004) argues that conceptualizing environmental philosophy in spatial terms immediately foregrounds its formation under imperial expansion and colonial dispossession:

> Environmentalists have long bemoaned the damage done by what is frequently termed "the domination of nature." Once one asks the simple geographical question "what is the geography

of the domination of nature?" the answer fairly quickly reveals itself as the history of colonization and imperialism. Ironically environmentalists who wish to ease the burden of that domination have frequently promoted the establishment of protected spaces, parks and the control of populations in manners that nonetheless replicate the practices of empire. (pp. 8–9)

Deleuze and Guattari (1987) created a new critical language for analyzing thinking as flows or movements across space. Concepts such as *assemblage, deterritorialization, lines of flight, nomadology,* and *rhizome/rhizomatics* clearly refer to spatial relationships and to ways of conceiving ourselves and other objects moving in space. For example, Deleuze and Guattari distinguish the "sedentary point of view" (p. 23) that characterizes much western philosophy, history, and science from a nomadic subjectivity that allows thought to move across conventional categories and against "settled" concepts and theories. They also distinguish "rhizomatic" thinking from "arborescent" conceptions of knowledge as hierarchically articulated branches of a central stem or trunk rooted in firm foundations. As Umberto Eco (1984) explains, "the rhizome is so constructed that every path can be connected with every other one. It has no center, no periphery, no exit, because it is potentially infinite. The space of conjecture is a rhizome space" (p. 57; see Fig. 1.1).

In a world of accelerating globalization and increasingly complex information, communication, and knowledge technologies, the semiotic space of curriculum inquiry is also becoming a "rhizome space" that is more hospitable to nomadic than to sedentary thought. This is especially evident in fields such as environmental education that explicitly foreground global issues and international understandings. Rhizome is to a tree as the Internet is to a letter—networking that echoes

Tangle of Rhizomes

Fig. 1.1. A tangle of rhizomes (drawing © Warren Sellers; used with permission).[8]

the hyperconnectivity of the Internet. The structural reality of a tree and a letter is relatively simple: a trunk connecting two points through or over a mapped surface. But rhizomes and the Internet[9] are infinitely complex and continuously changing. Imagining knowledge production in a rhizosemiotic space is particularly generative in postcolonialist educational inquiry because, as Pat O'Riley (2003) explains: "Rhizomes affirm what is excluded from western thought and reintroduce reality as dynamic, heterogeneous, and nondichotomous; they implicate rather than replicate; they propagate, displace, join, circle back, fold" (p. 27).[10]

CONCEPTS, PLANES, AND DIFFERENCES

Returning to the question of how we provide opportunities for complicated conversation and intellectual breakthrough in the internationalization of curriculum inquiry, I suggest that Deleuze and Guattari's geophilosophy is particularly helpful in thinking about the unavoidable concept of *difference* (within and between nations, regions, and cultures) and the opportunities and dilemmas for curriculum scholars that difference produces. For example, Pinar (2005) alludes to the productivity of difference in describing one of the anticipated phases of his research on intellectual breakthrough in the internationalization of curriculum studies:

> One potential function of "internationalization"—being called by a foreigner to reflect upon one's own nationally and/or regionally-distinctive field, including one's own situatedness within it—is the dislocation of the native scholar-participant from his or her embeddedness in his or her local or domestic field. This opportunity for dislocation is occasioned by the call to study one's locality in conversation with foreigners in a foreign setting. Such dislocation functions to interpellate the individual scholar as a "stranger," certainly to foreigners and, to a lesser and relative extent, to one's fellow citizens. (pp. 13–14)

Here the concept of *difference* is marked by other concepts such as *native* and *foreigner*, and I now demonstrate how Deleuze and Guattari's approach differs from that of analytical philosophers by focusing more sharply on the concept of *foreigner*. For Deleuze and Guattari (1994), the philosopher's task is not to construe the concept of *foreigner* as an object of "contemplation, reflection and communication" (p. 5) but, rather, to ask how the concept of *foreigner* is (or can be) created. However, before I outline (my interpretation of) Deleuze and Guattari's response to this question, I suggest that their philosophy of concept creation might be more intelligible if we can first imagine some possible circumstances in which the concept of *foreigner* is *not* (and perhaps *cannot* be) created.

Ursula Le Guin (2000) imagines such circumstances in *The Telling*, a novel in her series of so-called "Hainish" stories. The common background for this series supposes that, at least 500,000 years ago, intelligent humanoids from the planet Hain spread across the galaxy and settled on nearly 100 habitable worlds, including Terra (Earth), that were then left alone for many millennia. Le Guin's stories imagine that communication and travel between the worlds has resumed and that a loose interplanetary federation, the Ekumen, coordinates the exchange of goods and knowledge among the myriad of diverse cultures, religions, philosophies, sciences, and forms of governance that have evolved separately on the various planets. Representatives of the Ekumen travel to each planet when it is rediscovered and invite peoples of Hainish descent to participate in the federation, if they wish.

In *The Telling*, the character Sutty is a Terran Observer for the Ekumen, a language and literature specialist who travels to the planet Aka to continue studies initiated by the first Observers to make contact with the Akan people some 70 years earlier. Aka is a world with only one continent, so all of its peoples live on just one land mass. In the following passage, Sutty meditates on the significance of this difference from Terra—and its implications for the politics of identity—and, related to this, her conviction that traditional Akan spirituality is not a "religion:"

> [R]eligion as an institution demanding belief and claiming authority, religion as a community shaped by a knowledge of foreign deities or competing institutions, had never existed on Aka. Until, perhaps, the present time.
>
> Aka's habitable lands were a single huge continent with an immensely long archipelago of its eastern coast . . . Undivided by oceans, the Akans were physically all of one type with slight local variations. All the Observers had remarked on this, all had pointed out the ethnic homogeneity . . . but none of them had quite realised that among Akans *there were no foreigners.* There had never been any foreigners, until the ships from the Ekumen landed.
>
> It was a simple fact, but one remarkably difficult for the Terran mind to comprehend. No aliens. No others, in the deadly sense of otherness that existed on Terra, the implacable division between tribes, the arbitrary and impassable borders, the ethnic hatreds cherished over centuries and millennia. "The people" here meant not *my* people, but people—everybody, humanity. "Barbarian" didn't mean an incomprehensible outlander, but an uneducated person. On Aka, all competition was familial. All wars were civil wars. (pp. 98–99)

We hardly need to be reminded of just how deadly our sense of otherness can be. In the aftermath of the attacks on the United States on September 11, 2001, the breadth of new antiterrorist legislation in nations such as Australia and the US—coupled in Australia with the then federal government's paranoid approach to "border protection" and treatment of asylum seekers that amounts to institutionalized racism—has eroded the foundations of respect for human rights in these countries and worldwide. *The Telling* is testimony to the *possibility* of thinking what many humans think is unthinkable, such as imagining a world without "foreigners." What would social, environmental, and educational policy look like if we too assumed that "the people" meant "everybody, humanity?" Similarly, what would ecological thinking be like if we lacked exclusionary categories such as "native" and "exotic?" Le Guin demonstrates that it is possible to think differently about identity and community, and related questions of inclusion and exclusion, without ever underestimating the remarkable difficulty of doing so, and the even greater difficulty of bringing new imaginaries into effect. In one of her short stories, aptly titled "She Unnames Them," Le Guin (1987), demonstrates how we might subvert the contemporary politics of naming nature by mocking and subverting the biblical assertion that "Man gave names to all the animals." In this story, Eve collaborates with the animals in undoing Adam's work: "Most of them accepted namelessness with the perfect indifference with which they had so long accepted and ignored their names" (p. 195). Modern science maintains clear distinctions between subject and object and, thus, between humans and other beings, plant and animal, living and nonliving, and so on. These distinctions are sustained by the deliberate act of *naming*, which divides the world into that which is named and everything else. Naming is not just a matter of labeling distinctions that are already thought to exist. Assigning a name to something constructs the illusion that what has been named is genuinely distinguishable from all else. In creating these distinctions, humans can all too easily lose sight of the seamlessness of that which is signified by their words and abstractions. So, in Le Guin's (1987) story, Eve says:

> None were left now to unname, and yet how close I felt to them when I saw one of them swim or fly or trot or crawl across my way or over my skin, or stalk me in the night, or go along beside me for a while in the day. They seemed far closer than when their names had stood between myself and them like a clear barrier. (p. 196)

We could do with some creative unnaming in our work. We could start with some of the common names of animals and plants that signify their instrumental value to us rather than their kinship. There is a vast difference between naming a bird of the Bass Strait islands (between Tasmania and mainland Australia) an "ocean going petrel" or a "short-tailed shearwater" and naming it a "mutton bird." Only one of these names identifies a living thing in terms of its worth to us as dead meat. Names are not inherent in nature; they are an imposition of human minds. It is as if we wish to own the earth by naming it. Unnaming our professional identities as "environmental" or "experiential" or "science" educators is another way in which we might establish closer connections and continuities with one another and with the earth. Unnaming makes it harder to explain ourselves—we can't chatter away as we're so used to doing, hearing only our own words making up the world, taking for granted our names and what they signify.

Deleuze and Guattari (1994) show us how to do philosophy in ways that produce similar effects to Le Guin's storytelling arts, that is, to create a perspective through which the world takes on a new significance: "The task of philosophy when it creates concepts . . . is always to extract an event from things and beings, always to give them a new event: space, time, matter, thought, the possible as events" (p. 33). For Deleuze and Guattari (1994), doing philosophy means creating concepts on planes of immanence: "Philosophy is a constructivism, and constructivism has two qualitatively different aspects: the creation of concepts and the laying out of a plane" (pp. 35–36). Every concept is a finite multiplicity. For example, our concept of *foreigner* involves many other concepts, such as ethnic or racial difference and territorial divisibility. Neither singular nor universal concepts are possible because every concept has a "history" and a "becoming"—a history of its traversal of previous constellations of concepts, and a becoming as it joins with other concepts within similar or contiguous fields of problems. For example, Mark Halsey (2006) offers a detailed micropolitical account of the evolution of such taken-for-granted concepts as *nature, sustainability,* and *environmental harm* by focusing specifically on the categories and thresholds used over time to map and transform a particularly forested area, namely, the Goolengook forest block in far eastern Victoria, and the socioecological costs arising from these thresholds and transformations and ensuing conflicts over logging and so on. Following Deleuze and Guattari, Halsey argues that places like Goolengook *become*—they are always already invented, fabricated, although they are no less "real" for being so. He suggested that the process of "becoming-known," "becoming-forest" (or, for that matter, becoming-uranium mine, becoming-housing estate, becoming-hydro-electric dam, etc.), and thus of "becoming-contested," is intimately related to what he calls four "modalities" of nature involving the way nature is *envisioned,* the way nature is *named,* the *speed* at which nature is transformed, and the *affect* (image, concept, sense) of nature that is subsequently produced. These modalities always already harbor an ethic linked to the production of a life (or lives) and a death (or deaths). For example, the Australian federal government envisions "forest" to mean "an area . . . dominated by trees having usually a single stem and a mature stand height exceeding 5 metres" (Commonwealth of Australia, 1992, p. 47). Envisioning "forest" in terms of trees exceeding 5 meters—rather than, say, 20 meters—has significant consequences for biodiversity, employment, resource security, research and development, and so on.

As I interpret Deleuze and Guattari (1994), the proposition that every concept has a history and a becoming is not only a matter of concepts developing within various and changing social and historical contexts but also recognizes that concepts have *acontextual* and *atemporal* features. Every concept inaugurates the plane of immanence of the concept, which is "neither a concept nor the concept of all concepts" (p. 37) but, rather, is a preconceptual field presupposed within the concept, "not in the way that one concept may refer to others but in the way that concepts themselves refer to nonconceptual understanding" (p. 40). Deleuze and Guattari (1994) argue that the "plane of immanence is not a concept that is or can be thought but rather *the image thought gives itself of what it means to think, to make use of thought, to find ones bearings in thought*" (p. 37; italics added). For example: "in Descartes [the plane of immanence] is a matter of a subjective understanding implicitly presupposed by the 'I think' as first concept; in Plato it is the virtual image of an already-thought that doubles every actual concept" (pp. 40–41). The plane of immanence is inaugurated within the concept (that which is created) but it is clearly distinct from the concept (because it expresses the uncreated, that which "thought just does"). The plane of immanence thus expresses the nonconceptual that is *both* internal to *and* "outside" the concept. Deleuze and Guattari (1994) characterize this complex and paradoxical relationship as follows: "concepts are events, but the plane is the horizon of events, the reservoir or reserve of purely conceptual events" (p. 36). By way of example, Iain MacKenzie (1996) suggests:

> "the present happens" because there is a "past-becoming-future horizon" presupposed within it. Without a presupposed limitless expanse of time we could not talk of the present. In the same way, without the presupposed plane of immanence concepts would never "happen." Moreover, as the present would never change without the existence of an "eternal horizon" presupposed within it, without the institution of the plane—that which thought "just does"—concepts would never change. The fact that concepts institute this "unthinkable" plane at their core engenders the movement of concepts; their history and becoming. (p. 1236)

Similarly, we could say that the concept of *foreigner* happens for us because there is an "us-becoming-other" horizon presupposed within it. Neither the concept nor the preconceptual field happened for the Akans until they created it to make sense of the existence of the Ekumen. A parallel question for those of us who identify ourselves as environmental educators might be: "What images of the *a*categorical and *a*temporal govern what we can say and do with respect to 'the environment'?"

Deleuze and Guattari's geophilosophy enlarges the field of concepts and categories that we can deploy to account for difference, which in turn multiplies the possibilities for analyses, critiques, and interventions. Such a broadening of our repertoires of representation and action may be particularly useful when we encounter *remarkable* difference (difference that puzzles, provokes, surprises, or shocks us)—as we almost certainly will as our transnational curriculum conversations become more widespread, inclusive, and complicated. Alma Gottlieb (2002) provides one example of such remarkable difference in her ethnographic study of the Beng villagers in Africa's Ivory Coast. She focuses on the Beng belief that children are reincarnated souls from whom their parents must learn lessons of the afterlife. Mediated by local seers, Beng parents understand education to be a listening process through which they discover their child's hidden knowledge and capture the essence and destiny of his or her soul. Parents assume that their children are maximally multilingual at birth, because they knew all languages in the afterlife, but that they lose this multilingual capacity around the age of three. If we can say that the Beng people have a concept of "language education," then (in our terms) it is a reactualization process of selecting the "right" channels that will be useful for communicating with others in this new life; it is a process of forgetting many languages, not learning one.

How should we (the "we" who belong to international organizations such as IAACS and who work transnationally in fields such as environmental education) respond to such a remarkable difference between concepts of education? Some might seek to "explain" the difference in terms of social and historical contexts. Some will invoke cultural relativism. I must admit that my first response was to welcome the Beng as a resource for teaching in my curriculum studies courses, using their understanding of learning-as-forgetting as a defamiliarization strategy. Defamiliarization (often rendered as "to make the familiar strange, and the strange familiar"[11]) assumes that the tactic of surprise may serve to diminish distortions and help us to recognize our own preconceptions, and it is a recurrent feature of artistic manifestos and of creative brainstorming sessions in many fields (that is, defamiliarization is potentially a tool for intellectual breakthrough).

But in the world I inhabit (as I understand it), these sorts of responses do nothing for Beng children. One of the apparent consequences of Beng parents' belief that children are reincarnated souls is that they pay scant attention to their children's material needs (the afterlife is not feared) and infant mortality rates are horrendous even by African norms—fewer than 20% of Beng children survive beyond the age of five years.

Deleuze and Guattari's geophilosophy cannot tell us precisely how we might resolve the dilemmas produced by this encounter with difference, but I argue that it offers a more ethically defensible approach to seeking such a resolution than conventional western philosophies that repress difference in the name of what is "right" (and righteous). For Deleuze and Guattari (1994), "Philosophy does not consist in knowing and is not inspired by truth. Rather, it is categories like Interesting, Remarkable, or Important that determine its success or failure" (p. 82). Their philosophy is a creative and hopeful practice whose purpose is not to be "right" in an abstract or universal sense but to contribute to the quality of "real" lives. Deleuze (1994) insists that concepts "should intervene to resolve local situations" (p. xx), and consistently argues that (western) philosophy has been aligned too closely with dominant interests in promoting identity and sameness and marginalizing difference:

> The history of philosophy has always been the agent of power in philosophy, and even in thought. It has played the repressor's role . . . Philosophy is shot through with the project of becoming the official language of a Pure State. The exercise of thought thus conforms to the goals of the real State, to the dominant meanings and to the requirements of the established order. (Deleuze & Parnet, 1987, p. 13)

Thus, if philosophy is to succeed in doing important things (such as reducing infant mortality rates), it must also seek to do interesting and remarkable things by creating novelty and difference. If we think it is important *both* to save Beng children's lives *and* to conserve Beng cultural traditions, we need to invent ways in which our different knowledge traditions can coexist rather than displacing "theirs" by "ours." Imagining that the Beng, too, create concepts on planes of immanence respects our differences and offers us an ethically defensible repertoire of dispositions and conceptual tools that we might be able to use in building a space created through the process that David Turnbull (2000) describes as "negotiation between spaces, where contrasting rationalities can work together but without the notion of a single transcendent reality" (p. 228). Stanley Jeyaraja Tambiah (1990) and Edward Soja (1996) name the space that Turnbull envisages as a "third space," whereas Hami Bhabha (1994) calls it "an interstitial space" (p. 312).[12] In Deleuze's (see Deleuze and Parnet, 1987) thought, the dynamics of becoming are such that any given multiplicity, such as the constellation of concepts that structure the Beng view of learning, "changes in nature as it expands its connections" (p. 8). This gives me hope that a new multiplicity, created in the "third space" in which Beng people negotiate with others, might include (say) a concept of children as reincarnated souls that is not incommensurate with caring for their health.

The idea of a presupposed plane of immanence generates many other new questions and possibilities for our complicated conversations around concepts such as "intellectual breakthrough" in the internationalization of curriculum studies, and the many other concepts that constitute its multiplicity, including those that Axelrod (1979) identifies: "thinking," "individuality," and "community." We can ask questions such as: "What preconceptual fields are presupposed within the concept of intellectual breakthrough in different nations and cultures?" "What are the acontextual and atemporal features of intellectual breakthrough in different nations and cultures?" "What presupposed horizon of events permits concepts such as 'thinking,' 'individuality,' and 'community' to 'happen' when and where they do?" Similarly, "What preconceptual fields are presupposed within the concept of 'education for sustainable development' in different nations and cultures (and what are their effects)?"

Jakub Zdebik (2003) offers a way to think metaphorically about the relationship between concepts and planes that might be useful for some purposes:

> In order to describe the plane of immanence, Deleuze and Guattari must simultaneously describe the concept. The plane of immanence and the concept mutually define each other. It is as if the plane of immanence is an invisible mental landscape that can only be seen through the concepts occupying it. It is a place that becomes noticeable through the objects that occupy this space. It is like cities that appear to an airplane flying over dark continents when, after night has fallen, the lights come on. From the height of this plane we can map out the geography of the plane of immanence, because geography [citing Deleuze and Guattari (1994, p. 96)] "is not merely physical and human but mental, like a landscape." (p. 142)

What other generative metaphors might help us to reveal the "invisible mental landscapes" of curriculum studies and stories in various nations and regions? What invisible mental landscapes are (or might) be shared by curriculum scholars and environmental educators who work transnationally? These are significant questions because, as Deleuze and Guattari (1994) argue, modes of intellectual inquiry need to account for the planes of immanence on which they operate. Following this line of argument, Ned Curthoys (2001) suggests that "conceptual thinking needs to retain a multifarious 'sense' of what it is doing, the kinds of problems it addresses and the cultural context it seeks to influence and is influenced by" (n.p.). Curthoys' perspective is particularly useful for my purposes because he deploys terms and tropes that resonate with IAACS's mission to support complicated scholarly conversations across national and regional borders:

> The plane of immanence is the complex ongoing conversation, the dilemma, the received history of fraught questions that one intuitively recognises as a formative background for one's own critical enunciations. In other words, the plane of immanence is the admission that thought is not simply a contemplative relation to a secure object of knowledge, nor a solution to a problem, but rather an affirmation of all that is problematic and historically negotiated. As an historically inflected thinking, the plane of immanence turns one's focus towards the cultural competency required for addressing a set of issues and the historically productive conditions of transformative thinking. (n.p.)[13]

The preamble to the IAACS Constitution states: "at this historical moment and for the foreseeable future, curriculum inquiry occurs within national borders, often informed by governmental policies and priorities, responsive to national situations. Curriculum study is, therefore, nationally distinctive."[14] If we restate this assertion in Deleuze and Guattari's terms, we could say that curriculum inquiry presently operates on numerous nationally distinctive "planes of immanence" (or, in Zdebik's terms, invisible mental landscapes). If we also agree with the founders of the IAACS who "do not dream of a worldwide field of curriculum studies mirroring the standardization and uniformity the larger phenomenon of globalization threatens,"[15] then it follows that the internationalization of curriculum studies should not create concepts that inaugurate a single transnational plane of immanence (or posit a single invisible mental landscape in which transnational curriculum inquiry takes place) but, rather, will be a continuous process enacted by curriculum scholars worldwide who have the capacities and competencies to *change planes*. In this context, "changing planes" refers both to movements between one plane of immanence and another, and to transformations of one's own plane.

CHANGING PLANES

Le Guin's (2004) collection of linked short stories, *Changing Planes*, offers a rhizomatic connection to Deleuze and Guattari's figuration of the plane of immanence as well as to Zdebik's (2003) ambiguous deployment of "plane" in the passage quoted earlier. The premise of *Changing Planes* is outlined in the first story—"Sita Dulip's Method":

> [T]he airport is not a prelude to travel, not a place of transition; it is a stop. A blockage. A constipation. The airport is where you can't go anywhere else. A nonplace in which time does not pass and there is no hope of any meaningful existence. A terminus: the end. The airport offers nothing to any human being except access to the interval between planes.
>   It was Sita Dulip of Cincinnati who first realised this, and so discovered the interplanar technique most of us now use. (p. 2)

Sita Dulip realized that the tedious experience of waiting in airports for delayed and cancelled flights—"a specific combination of tense misery, indigestion, and boredom" (p. 5)—facilitates "interplanary travel": "by a mere kind of twist and a slipping bend, easier to do than to describe, she could go anywhere—be anywhere—because she was *already between planes*" (p. 3). Le Guin's pun words new worlds into existence as she tells stories of a traveler who transports herself to different "planes," in the sense of levels or angles of imagination, and to alternative worlds. After setting up the possibility and method of interplanary travel, the book becomes a travelogue of imaginary civilizations that exist on various planes (the dust jacket of the U.K. hardcover edition carries an appropriate subtitle: "armchair travel for the mind"). Le Guin's particular gift as a storyteller is her capacity to invent plausible and detailed alternative societies and environments, and in *Changing Planes* she creates a succession of strange places, peoples, and customs that disrupt assumptions about what is standard, settled, and normal. For example, the inhabitants of Frin share their dreams; the people of Asenu become almost entirely silent when they reach adulthood, which leads obsessive scholars from other planes to generate Talmudic exegeses of the rare words spoken by the Asenu they identify as mute "sages"; on Islac excessive and imprudent genetic engineering has generated a vast range of beings, some of whom are tragic travesties of naïve wish-fulfillment, such as talking dogs and chess-playing cats—"There are talking dogs all over the place, unbelievably boring they are, on and on and on about sex and shit and smells, and smells and shit and sex, and do you love me, do you love me, do you love me" (p. 13)—but some of whom literally flower unexpectedly, like the woman who is 4% maize.

One of the most intriguing stories in *Changing Planes* is "The Nna Mmoy Language," in which people do not address each other by name but by "ever-varying phrases [for] a thousand social and emotional connections" (p. 153). Although the Nna Mmoy themselves are pleasant, no interplanary visitors have yet succeeded in talking with them: "Though their monosyllabic language is melodious to the ear, the translatormat has so much trouble with it that it cannot be relied upon even for the simplest conversation" (p. 144). This appears to be because "the meaning of each word is continuously modified by all the words that precede *or may follow* it in the sentence (if in fact the Nna Mmoy speak in sentences)" (pp. 145–146).

And so, after receiving only a few syllables, the translatormat begins to generate a flurry of alternate meanings which proliferate rapidly into a thicket of syntactical and connotational possibilities that the machine overloads and shuts down. (p. 146)

Written Nna Mmoy is a syllabary ... Each syllable is a word, but a word with no fixed, specific meaning, only a range of possible significances determined by the syllables that come before, after, or near it. A word in Nna Mmoy has no denotation, but is a nucleus of potential connotations which may be activated, or created, by its context ...

Texts written in Nna Mmoy are not linear, either horizontally or vertically, but radial, budding out in all directions ... Literary texts carry this polydirectional complexity to such an extreme that they resemble mazes, roses, artichokes, sunflowers, fractal patterns. (pp. 144–145)

These brief excerpts should be sufficient to demonstrate the rhizomatic connections between Le Guin's story and Deleuze and Guattari's philosophical writings.[16] Indeed, Nna Mmoy speech and writing is manifestly rhizomatic. For example, any enunciation in Nna Mmoy is "open and connectable in all its dimensions; it is detachable, reversible, susceptible to constant modification" (Deleuze & Guattari, 1987, p. 12). These enunciations do not aspire to achieving some sort of final, complete, or coherent status, but are constantly opening up new territories, spreading out, and "overturning the very codes that structure [them] . . . putting them to strange new uses" (pp. 11, 15).

Le Guin's stories also connect to Deleuze's (1994, p. xx) assertion that "[a] book of philosophy should be . . . in part a kind of science fiction" in the sense of writing "at the frontiers of our knowledge, at the border which separates our knowledge from our ignorance and transforms the one into the other" (p. xxi). This is precisely what Le Guin achieves in "The Nna Mmoy Language": she creates "a kind of science fiction" that imagines a rhizomatic language—or, rather, a rhizosemiotic language-making process—that appears to be impossible to "translate" and sets limits on the extent to which we can learn anything about, with or from the Nna Mmoy. I suggest that many transnational and transcultural conversations around environmental education—and curriculum writ large—present some difficulties of translation and interpretation that are similar to the attempts to communicate with the Nna Mmoy that Le Guin imagines. The narrator of "The Nna Mmoy Language" quotes a friend who has spent more time in this plane than most, who offers further understandings of these difficulties and, as well, suggests some tentative possibilities for their partial resolution:

We talk snake. A snake can go any direction but only one direction at a time, following its head.

They talk starfish. A starfish doesn't go anywhere much. It has no head. It keeps more choices handy, even if it doesn't use them. (p. 148)

Learning Nna Mmoy is like learning to weave water.

I believe it's just as difficult for them to learn their language as it is for us. But then, they have enough time, so it doesn't matter. Their lives don't start here and run to there, like ours, like horses on a racecourse. They live in the middle of time, like a starfish in its own center ...

What little I know of the language . . . I learned mostly from children. The children's words are more like our words, you can expect them to mean the same thing in different sentences. But the children keep learning; and when they begin to read and write, at ten or so, they begin to talk more like adults; and by the time they're adolescents I couldn't understand much of what they said—unless they talked baby talk to me. Which they often did. Learning to read and write is a lifelong occupation . . . it involves not only learning the characters but inventing new ones, and new combinations of them—beautiful new patterns of meaning. (pp. 150–151)

Le Guin's expression, "they live in the middle," offers a further connection to Deleuze and Guattari's (1987) rhizomes, which have no beginnings or ends but are always in the middle; beginnings and ends imply a linear movement, whereas working in the middle is about "coming and going rather than starting and finishing" (p. 25). As Elizabeth St. Pierre (1997) writes:

> [W]e must learn to live in the middle of things, in the tension of conflict and confusion and possibility; and we must become adept at making do with the messiness of that condition and at finding agency within rather than assuming it in advance of the ambiguity of language and cultural practice. (p. 176)

Elsewhere (N. Gough, 2006b), I demonstrate how rhizomatic textual assemblages that commence in the "messiness" of cultural materials that are readily at hand in our everyday lives can be used to generate questions, provocations, and challenges to dominant discourses and practices of contemporary science education. One of these (developed more extensively in N. Gough, 2007) began when a number of initially separate threads of meaning—a research article in *Public Understanding of Science*, a *Time* magazine cover story titled "Death by Mosquito," and a one-page account of malaria in my son's high school biology textbook—coincided, coalesced, and eventually began to take shape as an object of inquiry. I was concerned (indeed, offended) that neither *Time* nor the textbook provided readers with any alternatives to understanding malaria within the conceptual frameworks of western laboratory science, in which malaria is made to appear as a "natural" entity in the world, rather than as (say) a political disease resulting from the dominance of the Third World by the colonial and mercantile interests of the west. As I read *Time* and the textbook, I also recalled reading *The Calcutta Chromosome: A Novel of Fevers, Delirium, and Discovery*, a mystery thriller in the science fiction subgenre of alternative history by Amitav Ghosh (1997). Like most works of science fiction, Ghosh's novel offers a semiotic space that is not regulated by the dominant systems of signification and cultural practice of science education, and that therefore invites readers to think beyond the sign regimes of western laboratory science. Ghosh's novel became another filament in what I came to think of as a mosquito-led rhizome by offering a speculative counterscience of malaria that connects with (but does not replicate) the "real" history of western medicine's explorations of the disease. Whereas *Time* and the textbook occluded malaria's complex heterogeneity, Ghosh's novel dramatically foregrounds the ways in which outbreaks of malaria in particular places and times are manifestations of numerous complex interactions among parasites, mosquitoes, humans, as well as various social, political (often military), administrative, economic, agricultural, ecological, and technological processes. A further filament came from my experience of working in south Africa, where the need for science educators to move beyond the arborescent knowledge space of western laboratory science is given further urgency by the increasing complexity of the linkages between traditional cultural practices (such as the production of herbal medicines by traditional gatherers and healers) and the activities of transnational corporations (such as large pharmaceutical companies).[17]

PAUSE

I have no "conclusion" to this essay but will simply pause (in the middle of things) to reflect briefly on what I have learned by writing it.

First, although changing planes might be more difficult than I thought, I believe that I have made Deleuze and Guattari's geophilosophy more intelligible to myself (and, I hope, to others) by bringing it into intertextual play with worlds imagined by Le Guin and with concepts, problems, and issues that circulate in the discourses of transnational curriculum inquiry and environmental education.

Second, I believe that I might have taken some small steps towards demystifying (again, for myself, and perhaps for others) Deleuze and Guattari's philosophy, which often is represented as being obscure and impenetrable. For example, Inna Semetsky (2003) writes: "The complexity of Deleuze's intellectual practice is beyond imagination. The language of expression in Deleuze's thought, as well as in Deleuze and Guattari's collaborative works, is even more complex" (p. 212). It is complex, certainly, but I hope that I have demonstrated that it is most assuredly not "beyond imagination." Indeed, imagination is precisely what we need to put Deleuze and Guattari's geophilosophy into practice. Their goal is to overturn philosophy's "traditional image of thought" (Deleuze, 1994, p. 3) and to create concepts through which we can imagine new pathways for thought and action. As Todd May (2003) writes:

> These concepts do not ask of us our epistemic consent; indeed they ask nothing of us. Rather, they are offerings, offerings of ways to think, and ultimately to act, in a world that oppresses us with its identities. If they work—and for Deleuze, the ultimate criterion for the success of a concept is that it works—it will not be because we believe in them but because they move us in the direction of possibilities that had before been beyond our ken. (p. 151)

Last of all, to pause on a note of slight disappointment—in reading what I have written I am more aware than ever that, although I might be trying to think starfish, I still write snake.

NOTES

1. Here Pinar et al. are not referring to *all* U.S. curriculum scholars but to those who have identified themselves as "reconceptualists" (see Pinar, 1975) in the wake of Joseph Schwab's (1969, 1971, 1973) immensely influential series of papers on curriculum as a discipline of "the practical." Reconceptualist curriculum scholars shifted the emphasis of curriculum studies from theorizing curriculum *development* toward generating theoretical frames for *understanding* curriculum.

2. See IAACS home page at http://iaacs.org/ for details of conferences and links to its journal, *Transnational Curriculum Inquiry* (TCI). Curriculum Forge, an interactive wiki, is at http://curriculumforge.org/

3. UNEP: United Nations Environment Programme.

4. See Annette Gough (1997, pp. 17–20) for a succinct account of the early development of this program, which remained active until the late 1990s.

5. The experiences to which I refer are both direct (such as teaching or conducting research in these nations/regions) and vicarious (such as supervising or examining research conducted by doctoral students in these nations/regions).

6. For example, in a 1950 interview, the abstract expressionist painter Jackson Pollock was asked: "Then you don't actually have a preconceived image of a canvas in your mind?" He replied: "Well, not exactly—no—because it hasn't been created, you see. Something new—it's quite different from working, say, from a still life where you set up objects and work directly from them" (cited in Pinar, 1994, p. 7). Richardson (2001) makes a parallel point about writing as research: "I was taught . . . as perhaps you were, too, not to write until I knew what I wanted to say, until my points were organized and outlined. No surprise, this static writing model coheres with mechanistic scientism, quantitative research, and entombed scholarship" (p. 35).

7. My narrative experiments have similar purposes to the "thought experiments" conducted by quantum and relativity physicists in the early part of the 20th century. Their purpose was not prediction (as is the goal of classical experimental science), but more defensible representations of present "realities."

8. Seller's image is an aliteral representation, which reflects André Colombat's (1991) observation that Deleuze and Guattari's rhizome "cannot be considered as a pure metaphor . . . [it] does not correspond exactly to its botanical definition" (p. 15).

9. See, for example, the Burch/Cheswick map of the Internet as at June 28, 1999 at http://research. lumeta.com/ches/map/gallery/isp-ss.gif. Accessed August 3, 2006.

10. See Gough (2004b, 2006a, 2006b, 2007) for further examples of applying Deleuze and Guattari's geophilosophy to questions, problems and issues concerning (e.g.), "posthuman" pedagogies, science education research (with particular reference to societies in transition), and quality imperialism in higher education.

11. This phrase has been attributed to the German poet Novalis (1772–1801, aka Friedrich von Hardenberg). The concept of defamiliarization is found among other Romantic theorists such as William Wordsworth and Samuel Taylor Coleridge and is also closely associated with Surrealism. Russian formalist Victor Shklovsky (1917/1965) introduced the concept of *ostraneniye* (literally "making strange") to literary theory.

12. For a more detailed exploration of the significance of Turnbull's research for transnational curriculum inquiry see N. Gough (2003).

13. Seeking the "productive conditions of transformative thinking" clearly resonates with Pinar's (2005) question of how to provide opportunities for "intellectual breakthrough" in the internationalization of curriculum studies

14. http://iaacs.org/

15. http://iaacs.org/

16. Another interpretation of "The Nna Mmoy Language" is that it takes Jacques Derrida's (1981) belief that language is so unstable that meaning is endlessly deferred to some sort of logical yet ludicrous extreme.

17. Sarah Whatmore's (2002) *Hybrid Geographies*, provides further examples of environment-related research informed by Deleuze and Guattari's geophilosophy.

REFERENCES

Axelrod, C. D. (1979). *Studies in intellectual breakthrough*. Amherst: The University of Massachusetts Press.

Bhabha, H. K. (1994). *The location of culture*. New York: Routledge.

Colombat, A. P. (1991). A thousand trails to work with Deleuze, *Substance, 20*(3), 10–23.

Commonwealth of Australia. (1992). *National forest policy statement*. Canberra: Author.

Curthoys, N. (2001). Future directions for rhetoric—invention and ethos in public critique [Electronic Version]. *Australian Humanities Review*. Retrieved 25 October 2005, from http://www.lib.latrobe. edu.au/AHR/archive/Issue-April-2001/curthoys.html.

Dalby, S. (2004). Ecological politics, violence, and the theme of empire. *Global Environmental Politics, 4*(2), 1–11.

Deleuze, G. (1994). *Difference and repetition* (P. Patton, Trans.). New York: Columbia University Press.

Deleuze, G., & Guattari, F. (1987). *A thousand plateaus: Capitalism and schizophrenia* (B. Massumi, Trans.). Minneapolis: University of Minnesota Press.

Deleuze, G., & Guattari, F. (1994). *What is philosophy?* (G. Burchell & H. Tomlinson, Trans.). London: Verso.

Deleuze, G., & Parnet, C. (1987). *Dialogues* (H. Tomlinson & B. Habberjam, Trans.). New York: Columbia University Press.

Derrida, J. (1981). *Positions* (A. Bass, Trans.). Chicago: University of Chicago Press.

Eco, U. (1984). *Postscript to the Name of the Rose* (W. Weaver, Trans.). New York: Harcourt, Brace & Jovanovich.

Ghosh, A. (1997). *The Calcutta chromosome: A novel of fevers, delirium and discovery*. New York: Avon Books.

Gottlieb, A. (2002). Deconstructing the notion of education: A view from west Africa. In L. Bresler & A. Ardichvili (Eds.), *Research in international education: Experience, theory, and practice* (pp. 83–101). New York: Peter Lang.

Gough, A. (1997). *Education and the environment: Policy, trends and the problems of marginalisation.* Melbourne: Australian Council for Educational Research.

Gough, N. (2003). Thinking globally in environmental education: Implications for internationalizing curriculum inquiry. In W. F. Pinar (Ed.), *International handbook of curriculum research* (pp. 53–72). Mahwah, NJ: Erlbaum.

Gough, N. (2004a). Read intertextually, write an essay, make a rhizome: Performing narrative experiments in educational inquiry. In H. Piper & I. Stronach (Eds.), *Educational research: Difference and diversity* (pp. 155–176). Aldershot: Ashgate.

Gough, N. (2004b). RhizomANTically becoming-cyborg: Performing posthuman pedagogies. *Educational Philosophy and Theory, 36*(3), 253–265.

Gough, N. (2006a). Quality imperialism in higher education: A global empire of the mind? *ACCESS: Critical Perspectives on Communication, Cultural & Policy Studies, 25*(2), 1–15.

Gough, N. (2006b). Shaking the tree, making a rhizome: Towards a nomadic philosophy of science education. *Educational Philosophy and Theory, 38*(5), 625–645.

Gough, N. (2007). Geophilosophy, rhizomes and mosquitoes: Becoming nomadic in global science education research. In B. Atweh, M. Borba, A. Calabrese Barton, N. Gough, C. Keitel, C. Vistro-Yu, & R. Vithal (Eds.), *Internationalisation and globalisation in mathematics and science education* (pp. 57–77). Dordrecht: Springer.

Halsey, M. (2006). *Deleuze and environmental damage: Violence of the text.* Aldershot: Ashgate.

Le Guin, U. K. (1987). She unnames them. In *Buffalo gals and other animal presences* (pp. 194–196). Santa Barbara, CA: Capra.

Le Guin, U. K. (2000). *The telling.* New York: Harcourt.

Le Guin, U. K. (2004). *Changing planes.* London: Victor Gollancz.

MacKenzie, I. (1996). Deleuze and Guattari's poststructuralist philosophy. In P. Dunleavy & J. Stanyer (Eds.), *Contemporary political studies 1996* (pp. 1234–1241). Exeter: Political Studies Association.

May, T. (2003). When is a Deleuzean becoming? *Continental Philosophy Review, 36*(2), 139–153.

O'Riley, P. A. (2003). *Technology, culture, and socioeconomics: A rhizoanalysis of educational discourse.* New York: Peter Lang.

Peters, M. (2004). Geophilosophy, education and the pedagogy of the concept. *Educational Philosophy and Theory, 36*(3), 217–231.

Pinar, W. F. (Ed.). (1975). *Curriculum theorizing: The reconceptualists.* Berkeley, CA: McCutchan.

Pinar, W. F. (1994). *Autobiography, politics and sexuality: Essays in curriculum theory 1972–1992.* New York: Peter Lang.

Pinar, W. F. (Ed.). (2003). *International handbook of curriculum research.* Mahwah, NJ: Erlbaum.

Pinar, W. F. (2005). Complicated conversation: Occasions for "intellectual breakthrough" in the internationalization of curriculum studies. *Journal of Curriculum Studies [Taiwan], 1*(1), 1–26.

Pinar, W. F., Reynolds, W. M., Slattery, P., & Taubman, P. (1995). *Understanding curriculum: An introduction to the study of historical and contemporary curriculum discourses.* New York: Peter Lang.

Richardson, L. (2001). Getting personal: Writing-stories. *International Journal of Qualitative Studies in Education, 14*(1), 33–38.

Schwab, J. J. (1969). The practical: A language for curriculum. *School Review, 78*(1), 1–23.

Schwab, J. J. (1971). The practical: Arts of eclectic. *School Review, 79*(4), 493–454.

Schwab, J. J. (1973). The practical 3: Translation into curriculum. *School Review, 81*(4), 501–522.

Scott, W. A., & Gough, S. R. (2004). *Sustainable development and learning: Framing the issues.* London & New York: RoutledgeFalmer.

Semetsky, I. (2003). The problematics of human subjectivity: Gilles Deleuze and the Deweyan legacy. *Studies in Philosophy and Education, 22*(2), 211–225.

Shklovsky, V. (1965). Art as technique (L. T. Lemon & M. J. Reis, Trans.). In L. T. Lemon & M. J. Reis (Eds.), *Russian formalist criticism: Four essays* (pp. 3–24). Lincoln: University of Nebraska Press. (Original work published 1917)

Soja, E. (1996). *Thirdspace: Journeys to Los Angeles and other real-and-imagined places.* Cambridge, MA: Blackwell.

St. Pierre, E. A. (1997). Methodology in the fold and the irruption of transgressive data. *International Journal of Qualitative Studies in Education, 10*(2), 175–189.

Tambiah, S. J. (1990). *Magic, science, religion, and the scope of rationality.* Cambridge: Cambridge University Press.

Trueit, D., Doll, W. E., Wang, H., & Pinar, W. F. (Eds.). (2003). *The internationalization of curriculum studies: Selected proceedings from the LSU [Louisiana State University] conference 2000.* New York: Peter Lang.

Turnbull, D. (2000). *Masons, tricksters and cartographers: Comparative studies in the sociology of scientific and Indigenous knowledge.* Amsterdam: Harwood Academic Publishers.

Whatmore, S. (2002). *Hybrid geographies: Natures, cultures, spaces.* London: Sage.

Zdebik, J. (2003). The archipelago and the diagram. *Journal for the Arts, Sciences, and Technology, 1*(2), 141–146.

2

Three "Big Ideas" and Environmental Education

Sean Blenkinsop and Kieran Egan

This chapter is situated within a larger argument—that we[1] currently lack an adequate theoretical foundation to support what we think of as being the practice and goals of environmental education. We understand the error thus: Current environmental education theory draws extensively and at times unreflectively from general educational theory. However, because modern western education as practiced tends to represent the underlying presuppositions of its culture, and that culture tends to situate itself in competition with the non-human world, then if environmental education tries to draw from general educational theory, it has the potential to find itself in conflict with environmental education's own goals. That is, general educational theory and the current troubling environmental situation both arise from that same nexus of modern western ideas. Consequently, there is a very real potential for incompatibility in trying to educate for a different environmental situation using the tools, principles, and theoretical foundations of the current educational system.

In this chapter, we explore only a small piece of this larger argument, recognizing that the argument is far from settled, but thinking that this might then allow environmental educators to engage in other searches of a similar type. The hope is that by focusing our attention on educational theory and pointing to what we see as deep and potentially irreconcilable differences between that theory and environmental education, a discussion might begin that asks: "What else does this apply to?" In so doing, we might begin to understand why environmental education, as currently theorized, has such a challenge fitting within the current paradigm of educative practice. The chapter begins with a short description of what has been described in other places as the "three big ideas" of educational theory (Egan, 1998, 1999). Although recognizing that these three categorizations may be somewhat arbitrary, we think that for the most part they are a useful shorthand summary of the theoretical range currently available to general educational theory; that is, they might be best seen as a heuristic to thinking about complex and very general foundational issues in education. The second step of this discussion is a closer examination of each of the ideas with a view to exploring whether or not that particular idea has the potential to support the weight and purpose of a more thoroughly considered environmental education.[2] Our hope is that through this admittedly slightly provocative process regarding curriculum theory we will, at the very least, plant the seed that environmental educators cannot rely uncritically on general educative theory.

THE THREE BIG IDEAS SUPPORTING CURRICULUM THEORY

One can conceive of the whole field of education as resting largely on three very powerful ideas, which we call socialization, Platonic truth, and Rousseauian development. We argue that none of these ideas stands independently because of being incomplete, nor are they able to work successfully together because the differences between them are irreconcilable. As a result, educational theory and the educational practice it influences is compromised in ways we explore. We are not so much interested in the commensurability of the three ideas with each other as we are in determining which, if any, is in alignment with environmental educational programs. But first we must clarify the big three.

Socialization

The language of socialization in education today appears in many forms. We hear business leaders arguing the need for workers with particular skills, governments looking for citizens who conform to and for the most part understand a particular, centralized set of social norms, and many groups suggesting, at varying levels of insistence, the standards they consider necessary for every graduate. Ultimately, every society shapes the next generation into its own systems of understanding, values, and modes of dealing with the practical needs of the everyday world. Human beings have an enormous plasticity early in life to adapt to a kaleidoscopically indeterminate range of cultural forms, beliefs, and patterns of behavior. The central task of socialization is to inculcate a restricted set of norms and beliefs—the set that is presupposed by the adult society into which the child will grow. Societies can survive and maintain their sense of identity only if a certain degree of homogeneity is achieved in shaping its members, and "education perpetuates and reinforces this homogeneity by fixing in the child, from the beginning, the essential similarities that collective life demands" (Durkheim, 1956, p. 70). To put it at its simplest, socializing aims to make people more alike.

Questions must immediately arise as to the kind of meaning-making to which today's children are being socialized, and the range of flexibility that is available within that current structure. Ultimately, it must be remembered that the goal of socialization is to integrate the next generation into the society as it stands, or as we assume it is going to develop. The purpose of this process is to allow the knowledge and skill, as well as the values, commitments, and means of making sense, to be transferred into the future, thereby maintaining the structure of the society and allowing individuals to establish their individual identities within a framework of belonging to a larger sense-making community. What some concede is a small theoretical problem with an exclusively socializing approach to education—that occasionally reaches elephantine dimensions in practice—is that you can include in your curriculum *only* things justified in terms of present or projected future utility. Some things that are true or beautiful are not always immediately useful, and therein lies the cause of a few millennia of arguments about educating.

There is, of course, no argument for not socializing: It is necessary for societies to function. The crucial point, however, is that socializing is recognized by being justified solely in terms of social utility.

Plato, Changing the World Through the Truth

Although best known as "traditional" or "liberal" education, Platonic theory has produced an impressive array of variously named progeny that have also managed to maintain their allegiance to a common theoretical core. According to Plato, there exists a universally correct, rational view of reality that can only be reached through an ongoing, disciplined, and increasingly abstract program of study. This study, for Plato, means reaching an adequate understanding of the world. It is a harsh and usually unwelcome doctrine—a lot of very hard work, self-discipline, dedication, and an array of moral virtues are required to make any serious educational progress. For most people, he conceded, socializing is the most they can handle—immediate utility trumps the transcendent. Eric Havelock (1963) argues that Plato's great achievement was to work out how to think once alphabetic literacy became common. The result is both described and—if you will excuse the term—paradigmatically exemplified in Plato's dialogues. When the best-accumulated knowledge coded in writing is learned, Plato taught, it transforms the mind of the learners and enables them to understand the world more accurately and truly.

Thus, if the correct experiences and knowledge are packaged together and offered up to the inquiring mind, the result will be a good and virtuous human. This Platonic idea has such a powerful history that no modern school would risk discussing their particular form of education without claiming to have the means to ensure some form of academic learning, if not "excellence," for their students. We must consequently learn what Matthew Arnold (1896) later called the "best that has been thought and uttered in the world" (p. 82).

It is easy to recognize the influence of this idea in much of environmental education already. The debate between those who feel that if students only know the damage being done to the environment through their actions, they could not help but act differently, and those who advocate that students really need to know their living place and the interdependence within their bioregion and that then they will, of necessity, act in more environmentally appropriate ways are, in fact, both suggesting slightly different content for this same underlying idea. Teachers using the Platonic idea as a foundation are the wise possessors of the knowledge and, logically, it is they who must transfer it to the young. Often they are teachers concerned with getting the students involved in the "great conversation," of having them strive for "excellence," of supporting them to critique their worlds and look for ways to change it, and with getting them to a place where they have the knowledge necessary to make the changes that must occur. At the end of the day, when two exhausted environmental educators look at each other and say, "If only more people knew X [input you favorite piece of information about the environment here], then things in this world would change," they are only echoing an idea that was articulated powerfully more than 2,000 years ago.

The crucial feature of the Platonic idea, however, is that curriculum content is justified primarily in terms of the benefit it gives to the mind: helping the mind gradually become the organ that can thus see *the truth* about things, including environments.

Rousseau and Listening to Nature

The third of the big ideas of educational theory is probably the most prevalent in modern schools. Jean-Jacques Rousseau felt that the *Republic* was the best treatise on education ever written, but he was also convinced that Plato had missed a pivotal component and that the French educational and institutional establishments of his own historical period were hopelessly mired because of it. For Rousseau, the key to any successful education was to follow Nature's lead. This meant that the educator must listen carefully to the "path" chosen for the selected individual and do his or her utmost to protect the student from those who might influence them away from that particular path. On a more generalized level this meant that the educator needed to follow the distinct levels of development that all learners go through and use this understanding when seeking guidance as to what curriculum was most appropriate. Teaching and curriculum must conform itself to what students are capable of learning. Rousseau believed that all humans follow a natural process of development, and observation of the learners is critical in order to best know where they are developmentally. It is not just a more precise understanding of the developmental process that follows from Rousseau's ideas. We also need to understand more precisely the processes of learning itself—and motivation, development, and styles of learning—and anything that shows us how the mind of the student works, so we can then shape our teaching accordingly. Thus we need also to attend to our students' multiple intelligences, as these are features of our minds that will influence learning. Rousseau's influence can be seen deeply embedded in the work of Dewey and Piaget, and is reflected in educational language that focuses on student-centeredness and personal discovery.

The point for educators is that if students go through consistent stages of development, then there will be observable and recognizable signposts that indicate transitions between these stages, which in turn can act as means to better support the learning that is going on within the individual. As distinct from the Platonic teacher who holds particular kinds of knowledge to be most important, the Rousseauian teacher is a facilitator who shapes the environment and allows children to further their natural development through the use of the appropriate experiences, tools, or discussions.

The influence of these ideas on current environmental education practice is at least as pronounced as the Platonic influence. Practitioners regularly think of themselves as being "experiential" and argue that only if children were allowed to have ongoing relationship-building experiences with the natural world would they then be able to have the kind of connection to their environment that is considered necessary to becoming, for lack of a better descriptor, environmentalists. Theoretical examinations of the lives of famous environmentalists build upon Rousseau by suggesting educational trajectories for children in which age-based experiences parallel those of these same famous people. The best example of this is the work being done on both the definition and level of development involved that results in an ecological identity (Tomashow, 1996). In this case, when those same exhausted environmental educators say, "if only those kids were given the freedom to connect with the natural world without the trappings of our culture, and were allowed to discover their real, deeper selves," they are trying to push back on that corrupted human establishment which, as Rousseau pointed out, gets in the way of a much deeper and better plan. If we could only get out of the way and let it happen—is the common echo of Rousseau today.

The crucial feature of Rousseau's idea, then, is that it justifies practices in terms of the psychological development of the individual student, aiming to develop, through environmental education, the full potential of each student.

IN SEARCH OF THE RIGHT FOUNDATION FOR ENVIRONMENTAL CURRICULUM

Socialization for Environmental Change

> We must also turn to ourselves as individuals and as educational professionals to make change and develop a new ethic—a responsible attitude towards caring for the earth. (British Columbia Ministry of Education, 2006, p. 2)

At first glance it might be assumed that socialization has the most to offer environmental education. Here we have the big idea on which to build a curriculum that will result in the more caring, environmentally engaged, and active populace we are looking for. It even builds in the possibility for democracy and individuality within that larger framework of enlightened homogeneity. Would it not be nice if we could outline those characteristics of the environmentally aware citizen, clarify how we develop those characteristics, and then set about producing the finished product after 12 or 20 years of schooling? This, as explained previously, tends to be the language and even the modus operandi of socialization—sometimes explicitly, and always implicitly. Unfortunately, there are some challenges, beyond those frightening ones that immediately come to mind, when we propose environmental education in this way.

Socialization has a hard time operating on an agenda of unsure future aims. As offered in the manner just outlined, it is a way of bringing the next generation into what already exists, with only guesses about the future among the more enlightened educators. We want students to be able to communicate, to feel like they understand what is going on, to understand where they come from, and to maintain the knowledge and skills on which that understanding is based. The difficulty of socializing for a community that currently does not exist, and is not well represented through the media that impact so heavily on students' consciousness, and for the most part is out of the purview of our imaginations, is exactly the challenge of the unknown future. Socialization can only occur to what is already, and if it should happen that a more environmentally friendly, engaged, and active society requires a paradigmatic shift in worldview from the current modern western one (an argument that many have made; see, e.g., Evernden, 1999; Naess, 1990, 2002), then socialization becomes a big, but problematic idea. How could schooling possibly socialize the next generation into something that we cannot yet understand or conceive of?

The role that education continues to play in the socialization of children is somewhat contentious, however. As discussed earlier, the first difficulty for building curriculum theory for environmental education on a foundation of socialization rests on the seemingly oxymoronic idea of socializing for something that currently does not exist. If the point of socialization is to support the structure, values, and commitments of the society as it currently exists and to bring new members into the community by providing the necessary tools for making sense of the world they are encountering, it becomes difficult to see how those tools currently available—those same tools accused of causing the environmental crisis in the first place—might become the means through which the current western, modernist worldview might change. At a very superficial level (ignoring the layers of complexity involved in changing a paradigm), this would be like teaching the rules and culture of tennis in the hopes hockey will appear.

A second difficulty that socialization presents with regard to environmental education curricular theory is how these social structures and values are in fact transferred. There is a substantial amount of work that suggests much of this transfer occurs implicitly (Foucault, 1990; Peirce, 1998) and that it is very challenging indeed for any individual to ferret out all of their own implicit beliefs, values, and commitments, much less replace them with more environmentally engaged ones. Education uses the language of relationship, role models, unexamined positions, and "conscientization" to make this point and to claim that our primary socializer is in fact the situation in which we are immersed. The result is that even if the arguably impossible reality of a teacher having covered all the implicitly anti-environmental biases occurs, that singular and exceptional human must also replace those biases with pro-environmental tenets so as to put into place an environmental paradigm within each and every facet of her or his practice and, if teacher educators are to be believed, her or his existence as well. Beyond this, the students are still immersed in a "real world" that is fundamentally at odds with that particular teacher's daring curriculum and, as such, those students are receiving these conflicted messages with regard to the norms, values, and commitments of their society. If the goal of socialization is ultimately conformity and a homogenizing tendency toward the social norms of the culture and schooling is a key player in this process, then it is hard to argue that socialization is a viable means toward environmental goals, even the more minor ones, such as a greater sense of stewardship and care.

This is more certainly the case with the more complex goals advocated by some eco-ethicists, such as recognition of the inherent value in all living things. With this in mind we will turn our hopes to Plato and the possibility of Truth.

Plato and the Environmental Ideal

> Canadians of all generations and from all sectors of society should be given opportunities to engage in environmental learning within and beyond the classroom walls where critical questions can be asked and sustained and meaningful dialogue can take place. (British Columbia Ministry of Education, 2006, p. 2)

There seems to be little doubt that environmental educators currently create portions of their curriculum through the lens of Plato's big idea and that the focus on changing the world through critical engagement might offer an appropriate home for some of the goals of environmental education. Although it might be hard to learn all that knowledge stored in symbols and experiences available to children, it seems as though dedicated study and a good environmental education curriculum can carry children's confused minds to the truth about the environment and their place in it. But the problem is that some kind of magic (or technique we do not understand) is required to translate from this, potentially ancient, storehouse of knowledge that had significance when situated in other people's experience, and allow it to find new life in a new mind in a new situation in, likely, another millennium. But even if we can manage the pedagogical magic, even at its best, Plato's academic ideal cannot deliver on its promises.

Plato describes an educational program that will carry the mind from the confusions and illusions of the folk physics, folk psychology, and folk sociology learned effortlessly in our early years, through a curriculum of disciplined knowledge, to an understanding of the true nature of things. It is a program that requires the sacrifice of easy pleasures, and the deployment of our laborious general learning capacity to remake all our early false knowledge, converting our minds always toward rationality and truth, and away from the seductions of beliefs, myths, and superstitions. We are to climb beyond personal interest in looking at the world and to see it objectively. It is not clear if Plato's, or anyone's, curriculum can deliver these benefits. It is not clear if the products of high literacy include justice, objectivity, and truth. Plato believed these were the fruits of his educational program and justified the austere discipline necessary to gather them. It is probably a better educational idea than anyone before or since has had, but it is not adequate. The academic ideal of education is designed to achieve a kind of understanding it simply cannot deliver—its justification is an ideal that is unrealizable.

Even in the most gentle of environmental educational documents, the British Columbia Ministry of Education's (2006) Environmental Learning and Experience (ELE), this point is made: "we can no longer look to science and technology alone to solve these problems" (p. 2). In his essay "Wilderness as Home Place" Canadian ecologist Stan Rowe (2002) raises this very point and extends it in a way that makes Plato even more problematic to at least some environmental educators:

> The famous men we praise—the great theologians and philosophers, the eminent artists and scientists—with few exceptions shared one blind spot, one major intellectual defect. They knew practically nothing about the relationships of the human species to the Ecosphere. They conceived the Earth as resource not as source. Theistic or humanistic, but always homocentric, they speak to the human condition as it existed before 1950. They speak for a world that excluded the Real World. (p. 27)

For Rowe, as for many others, an anthropocentric worldview is not an appropriate place to base a curriculum theory for environmental education, and Plato took his anthropocentrism farther than most because he not only simply ignored the natural world but in fact viewed it with a deep suspicion. Theorists like Heesoon Bai (chap. 6, this volume) and David Abram (1996) argue that in part this detached intellectualization and dismissal of the sensuous experiences of lived existence is a profound if not fatal flaw. We can only hope that Rousseau's Nature holds more promise.

Rousseau and Nature

The first two big ideas seem not to offer the kind of support environmental education curriculum might need. However, Rousseau has Nature and children involved, so maybe his is the idea that can sustain environmental curriculum.

Unfortunately, several difficulties spring to mind almost immediately. The first has to do with what might be considered the fallacy of misplaced faith. An example of this faith, to be blunt, sounds like this: "All children who have a particular upbringing and the right set of experiences in and with Nature will build the appropriate relationships with the non-human world and as a result will not be complicit in its destruction. In fact, by following the development of children and allowing them to come to full adulthood they cannot help but be good people because everyone is if given a chance." But this faith is placed in an essentialist position that experience tells us is unsupportable. The ELE suggests as much when it quotes from the Proclamation of the United Nations Declaration for Sustainable Development (2005–2014), "*there is no universal model of education for sustainable development*" (British Columbia, 2006, p. 3). If the secret to curriculum design is simply to figure how humans develop and then add the correct components at age-appropriate times in order to get the environmentally responsible adults desired, why does the ELE insist on "locally developed frameworks for environmental learning" (British Columbia, 2006, p. 3)? The best example of Rousseau's influence in this direction is the developmentalism of Piaget that has for the last 40 years dominated much of modern schooling.

A second difficulty is that when environmental educators choose to use the word *nature* they may be using it in the colloquial way, meaning that which we find outside our doors or at the edge of our urban settings. At other times they are referring to that in which we are always immersed and with which we are in a constant state of interaction and on which we depend. Then, for those who have transcendental leanings, nature refers to that out of which we have created all civilizations, to paraphrase Henry Thoreau (1862). Nature is the means through which we genuinely understand what we are and in some cases should be as humans. However, when Rousseau is thinking of Nature, he is not using it in these ways. For him, Nature is like a script that has been written on the parchment of the universe. It is each individual human fulfilling the expectations that the divinity has for us in the best and most complete way we can. Connecting ourselves to our Nature is to act in the way that God has understood it and "planned" it. This notion seems to cause an unmitigated difficulty for environmental educators and theorists who have an understanding of the potential for self-deception and social manipulation that can and has occurred due to this kind of conceptual framework. This is especially true if those educators are aiming, as the ELE suggests, toward: (a) the promotion of respect for the dignity and human rights of all people throughout the world and a commitment to social and economic justice for all, (b) respect for the human rights of future generations and a commitment to intergenerational responsibility, (c) respect and care for the greater community of life in all its diversity that involves the protection and restoration of the earth's ecosystems and, finally, (d) respect for cultural diversity and a commitment to build locally and globally a culture of tolerance, nonviolence, and peace.

CONCLUSION: NOW WHAT?

In this chapter, we have shown that the "big three" educational ideas leave little room for a congruent and deeply rooted curriculum in environmental education. If the current theoretical tools available to us are incomplete and even incongruent with the purposes of environmental education, then what other areas of general educational theory are also limited with regard to those purposes (e.g., assessment, evaluation, subject matter, ethics, epistemology, etc.)? What alternatives can we turn to that are more adequate to the task? Well, if they are not at hand in the general discourse of education, then maybe we have to make them up ourselves. Of course, most people seem happy to try to deal in a straightforward pragmatic manner with the problems that face them, and just muddle forward as best they can. This does mean that the field does see some action and attempts are made to deal with our problems. This pragmatic muddling ahead, however, does not really offer us a solution, because it is a muddling that is, in turn, still tied up with the dominant ideas whose inadequacies we have attempted to demonstrate. Remaining largely unaware of the deep theoretical foundations of one's work, however, means that one is in fact captive to old theories that always constrain one's abilities to think effectively and imaginatively about problems.[3]

NOTES

1. "We" is meant to suggest the field that thinks of itself as being environmental education. The authors recognize that this field is large and spread across a quite disparate theoretical space. "We" might be better applied to those who argue that environmental education is not solely the narrow purview of a science curriculum and might even argue that the principles that underlie that narrow purview are potentially dangerous to what might be called the larger project of environmental education.

2. Although we recognize that environmental education is not a homogenous field of theory, we occasionally refer to a mainstream environmental education program, the recently approved British Columbia Ministry of Education document: Environmental Learning and Experience (ELE): An Interdisciplinary Guide for Teachers, as a standard that represents current mainstream environmental education.

3. We think we do have at least one fresh possibility that promises theoretical and practical support. The Imaginative Education Research Group (www.ierg.net) has been developing and working with a set of ideas and principles, and planning frameworks designed to engage students' imaginations in learning and in developing sophisticated understanding of curriculum material. Our future aim is to show how that approach can offer new hope in resolving the main problems of environmental education.

REFERENCES

Abram, D. (1996). *The spell of the sensuous.* New York: Vintage Books.

Arnold, M. (1896). *Discourse in America.* London: MacMillan.

British Columbia Ministry of Education. (2006). *Environmental learning and experience.* Victoria, BC: British Columbia Ministry of Education Integrated Resource Packages.

Durkheim, E. (1956). *Education and sociology* (S.D. Fox, Trans.). New York: The Free Press.

Egan, K. (1998). *The educated mind.* Chicago: University of Chicago Press.

Egan, K. (1999). *Children's minds, talking rabbits, & clockwork oranges.* New York: Teacher's College Press.

Evernden, N. (1999). *The natural alien.* Toronto: University of Toronto Press.

Foucault, M. (1990). *The history of sexuality* (R. Hurley, Trans.). New York: Vintage.

Havelock, E. (1963). *Preface to Plato.* Cambridge, MA: Harvard University Press.

Naess, A. (1990). *Ecology, community and lifestyle: Outline of an ecosophy* (D. Rothernberg, Trans.). Cambridge, UK: Cambridge University Press.

Naess, A. with P. Haukeland. (2002). *Life's philosophy: Reason and feeling in a deeper world.* Athens: University of Georgia Press.

Peirce, C. (1998). *The essential Peirce: Selected philosophical writings, Vol. 2 (1893–1913)* (Peirce Edition Project, Eds.). Bloomington: Indiana University Press.

Rowe, S. (2002). *Home place: Essays on ecology.* Edmonton: Newest Press.

Thoreau, H. (1862). *Walking.* Bedford, MA: Applewood Books.

Tomashow M. (1996). *Ecological identity: Becoming a reflective environmentalist.* Cambridge, MA: MIT Press.

The Place Where We Are Right
Yehuda Amichai

From the place where we are right
Flowers will never grow
In the spring.

The place where we are right
Is hard and trampled
Like a yard.

But doubts and loves
Dig up the world
Like a mole, a plow.
And a whisper will be heard in the place
Where the ruined
House once stood.

3

The Impossible Identity of Environmental Education

Dissemination and Emptiness

Edgar González-Gaudiano and Rosa Nidia Buenfil-Burgos

The main argument of this chapter is that the proliferation, ambiguity, and the very open-ended character of environmental education (EE) entails a productive political, ethical, and epistemic possibility for the permanent construction of its identity. To elaborate this argument, our text is organized into four sections. First, we present our theoretical perspective to examine the dominant discourses of environmentalism and their influence in the constitutive process of the field of EE in the context of current approaches. Second, we provide the area of dispersion of meanings of EE; third, we then try an analytical exercise of EE as an empty signifier; and finally, we offer some closing remarks to recapture the discussion of EE identity.

RECENT THEORETICAL APPROACHES TO ENVIRONMENTAL EDUCATION

EE research exhibits the influence of theoretical debates in a range of other fields such as philosophy, political theory, literature, psychoanalysis, and less so in anthropology and sociology. For example, there is interest in issues such as the critique of the Enlightenment, the linguistic turn, and their consequences in the ontological and epistemological assumptions at work in educational research. This interest was represented in the 1990s by those who engaged with theories of representation, by others who tackled it from a gender perspective and views concerned with an ethnic and racial focus, by those who were interested in a geopolitical view, and by others who emphasized the philosophical sources for the elaboration of EE theories (Peters & Irwin 2002; Sauvé 1996, 2005).

There are not only different focuses, but also different theoretical approaches to the field (see Scott & Gough, 2004). In this horizon of intelligibility, we place discourse theory and political analysis (Laclau, 1988, 1990, 1996, 2000; Laclau & Mouffe, 1985),[1] whose theoretical tools (e.g., concepts, logics and positions) draw on an articulation of philosophical perspectives that stress the political dimension of social practices, and who may provide inspiring possibilities for imaging the field in our contemporary conditions. In the early 1980s, this research approach "responded to the dissatisfaction with the dominant theoretical models of social explanation that existed . . . and it set out to elaborate an alternative approach to the understanding of the structuration of socio-political spaces by articulating a novel conception of discourse" (Laclau, cited in Howarth, Norval, & Stavrakakis, 2000, p. xi).

Discourse political analysis (Critchley & Marchart, 2004) is a qualitative perspective that does not involve one proper method of its own (Torfing, 1994), but according to the specific interest and the particular analytical unit chosen, it takes from a theoretical *toolbox* those that may be appropriate, provided, of course, that they are epistemically compatible. Here, however, only two of the possible theoretical corpuses are articulated: deconstructive reading (Derrida, 1967/1978, 1982) and pragmatist approaches to language (Wittgenstein, 1953).[2]

Discourse political analysis involves at least three clear theoretical components: an epistemic and ontological positioning, a conceptual body, and the specific type of logical connections between them. These three components and the plurality of theoretical contributions they combine, demand a specific epistemic alertness in order to avoid inconsistent eclecticism.[3] This is pursued via an ontological position that rejects essences in their different embodiments and, instead, emphasises the discursive, historical, and political character of Being (*ergo*, its contextual condition), and the epistemic adherence to the arguable character of knowledge (i.e., the Nietzschean [1907/1989] idea of "war of interpretations"), *inter alia*.

Two basic concepts equipping the theoretical *toolbox*[4] are discourse and hegemony. Our concept of *discourse* is constructed by means of the articulation of different theoretical matrices,[5] taking from them both the nonpositive character of language (i.e., its relational nature), and the possibility of expanding key concepts, processes, and the logics of language procedures to other fields of social relations. It involves linguistic and nonlinguistic signifying ensembles whose meaning is constituted in relations (difference, equivalence, antagonism, etc.) that it sustains with other discourses. Discourse is understood as a meaningful "totality," never complete or sutured but always exposed to dislocation due to the action of contingent external elements.

Hegemony does not mean a mere condition of domination and imposition: It rather comprises certain political practices (e.g., antagonism, articulation, and the definition of political frontiers whereby antagonistic identities are constructed). Other key concepts such as *empty signifier* are elaborated next in our analytical exercise.

Concerning what is meant here by *logics*, negativity together with *overdetermination*, *undecidability*, and *aporia* are among the key logics involved in discourse political analysis. Negativity introduces contingency, incompleteness, the failure, the gap, emptiness, the dislocation of harmonic and positive views of the social. When it is associated with something that has to be eliminated (scientific errors, morally unacceptable values, etc.), poor research benefits can be drawn from it; we rather sustain that it is important to scrutinise the way in which these logics operate (see recent debates in Benner & English, 2004). Overdetermination involves displacement and condensation. *Displacement* refers to the continuous circulation of meanings and identities between different signifiers (e.g., social movements, agents, and agendas). It shows that no identity is pure and uncontaminated, but always involves traces of other identities, thus displaying the relational character of the social. *Condensation* involves the precarious fixation that temporarily stops the flow of signification by fusing different elements in a single representation. Condensation thus helps us to understand that fixations are never definitive, but result from the welding of diverse elements into precarious units which do not completely eliminate the particularity of what has been condensed. Overdetermination is conditioned by a constitutive tension between necessity and contingency.[6] Undecidability (Derrida, 1982) points at the impossibility of fixating an identity, namely when one deals with frontiers, margins, boundaries, and limits, because these very notions show simultaneously the gap and the continuity between the two identities they differentiate. Frontiers then indicate the inside and the outside; however, the frontier itself—is it inside or outside? Aporia, another logic traditionally dismissed since it exhibits the impossibility of a final solution in a given opposition, shows the interminable possibilities to argue for the opposite reason or fact. This logic, however, is a condition for the proliferation of a multitude of alternatives that an alleged "final solution" precludes. Accordingly, this logic referring to the unsolvable tension between opposed tendencies represents a highly productive intellectual tool for our ends.

We have thus sketched the features of discourse political analysis that will operate in the exercise whereby our approach to the questions posed by the proliferation of meanings of environmentalism and EE will be presented.

Discourses of Environmentalism

Environmental movements are among the most recent phenomena to have appeared on the world stage on matters related to the organization of society and public policies. The varied ideological and political spectrums of the groups these movements comprise make them even more interesting as a topic of study. Environmentalism is an elusive notion, difficult to define as a discourse and even more so as a space of political action. Today, environmentalism addresses a wide arc of issues, thereby becoming an empty signifier, taking on different meanings depending on the signifier set from which affirmations and claims are made. However, it is precisely the fact that it can operate as an empty signifier that enables it to structure the field; that is to say, it can temporarily fixate a discursive field (like a nodal point).

Discourses of environmentalism have become established as meaningful wholes that go beyond the UN's declarations, giving birth to programmes that address certain issues and exclude others (e.g., war and militarism, government, discrimination and nationalism, refugees, gender) in accordance with the criteria and predominant forces.

In some discourses, ecologism is mentioned as being distinct from environmentalism and also from ecology. For Andrew Dobson (1997, pp. 21–22, 60) they "are sufficiently different for the confusion to become a serious intellectual error." They vary not only in degree, but also in kind, since environmentalism consists of "an administrative approach to the environment within the . . . current political and economic practices" rather than being a political ideology. Manuel Castells (1999), in opposition, argues that environmentalism is ecology in action.

Scientific ecology and militant ecologism have come into being during the last three decades; their coexistence has not been peaceful but has been subject to different levels of pressure from the complex spectrum of interests. Most of the ecologists base their holistic visions on the progress of science. The relationship of science to ecological discourse has been reviewed from the broadest range of analytical viewpoints. Guillermo Foladori (2000) states that ecocentrist and technocentrist currents have used science to bolster their positions, but that each of them has come to a different conclusion. Nevertheless, Yannis Stavrakakis (1997a, 1997b) adduces that green ideology offers us a fantasy construction, as the final solution to environmental and social dislocations. With this strategy, green ideology is attempting to rearticulate hegemonically the social field. Such a strategy rests on the reduction of the inherent original lack, around which the social field is always structured to a particular agent.

Thus, sociological and environmental studies have structured a new epistemic and political field, producing very distinct discourses that stem from dissimilar spheres and traditions. So, Ramachandra Guha and Juan Martínez-Alier (1997) provides a discursive approach centered on wealth and poverty based on a questioning of the origins and scope of current policies of the dominant environmentalism:

> The environmentalism of the poor . . . originate in social conflicts over access to and control over natural resources . . . Many social conflicts often have an ecological content, with the poor trying to retain under control the natural resources threatened by state take-over or by the advance of the generalised market system. (pp. xx–xxi)

These struggles of rural and Indigenous peoples have not been sufficiently acknowledged as environmental conflicts. The classic environmentalist metaphors are very transparent with regard to the diversity of existing positions on the current desperate situation. This situation is exemplified by the lifeboat metaphor used by Garret Hardin (1979): the boat already carrying the rich nations is surrounded by desperate swimmers, representing the world's poor, trying to clamber in. Hardin asks how many people should be allowed to get into the boat without risk of its sinking. What he does not ask was who decided that some would be in the boat and others in the water, and if those who are dry can feel truly safe even if no-one else is allowed to get in.

This metaphor is also linked to conservation policies, which explains why the conservationist elite is increasingly using the philosophical, moral, and scientific arguments concerned with wildlife habitat conservation, conferring on themselves the right to rule on the destiny of natural protected areas in the world and to expel the resident populations (see also Guha, 2000). Writing in a prestigious scientific forum, the *Annual Review of Ecology and Systematics*, Daniel Janzen (a prominent American biologist) argues that only biologists have the competence to decide how the tropical landscape should be used. As "the representatives of the natural world," biologists are "in charge of the future of tropical ecology," and only they have the expertise and mandate to "determine whether the tropical agroscape is to be populated only by humans, their mutualists, commensals, and parasites, or whether it will also contain some islands of the greater nature—the nature that spawned humans, yet has been vanquished by them" (cited in Guha & Martínez-Alier, 1997, p. 96).

Again, Guha and Martínez-Alier argue that these radical conclusions are unacceptable and intended to justify the idea that intervention in nature should be guided primarily by the need to preserve nature rather than by the needs of humans. The latter for deep ecologists is anthropocentric, the former biocentric. The authors suggest that such a dichotomy is, however, of very little use in understanding the dynamics of environmental degradation, because "the two fundamental ecological problems facing the globe are (a) overconsumption by the industrialised world and by urban elites in the Third World, and (b) growing militarization. Neither of these has any tangible connection to the anthropocentric/biocentric distinction" (pp. 94–95).

Despite their close links with ideological standpoints, as suggested earlier, the circulation of dominant environmentalist discourses has become globalized, spawning complex social (nongovernmental organizations [NGOs]) and political (green parties) movements. In the first case, a plethora of organizations with the most varied social and political affiliations has emerged, in league with different kinds of economic interests. The organization of society by environmental issues represents a new breed of phenomenon that is rapidly extending throughout the world, even though it faces serious challenges as to the legitimacy of its social representativeness. Timothy Luke (1998, p. xiv) states in relation to The Nature Conservancy that instead of ardently opposing the destruction of Nature in general, this organization seems content with conserving small pieces of undeveloped land to preserve tiny bits and pieces of habitat as precious containers of biodiversity. Building a nature conservancy by using capitalist strategies is more akin to maintaining a nature cemetery, than truly preserving nature from capitalism. That is why Victor Toledo (2005) says that assuming the conservation of biodiversity as a complex field of knowledge helps to highlight the limitations of "simplified thought," observed in many NGOs and even in an alarming number of scientists.

In other words, ideology, politics, economics, and the environment are spheres closely articulated. One example is the tuna fish embargo imposed on Mexico in 1990 and promoted by the U.S. environmentalist group Earth Island Institute. The embargo was connected to the commercial interests of U.S. tuna fish companies who charged almost $7 million per year through the Earth Trust Foundation for controlling the Dolphin Safe stamp. Environmental educators cannot ignore that constitutive articulation.

Finally, in the case of political movements, the platforms of green parties are also riddled with standpoints that vary greatly from country to country. The broad range of discursive positions on environmental issues underscores the diversity of existing interests associated with environmental management and public policies. The Mexican Ecological Green Party's main claims are cosmetic issues such as bullfights and grey whales advocacy, selected to get electors' attention. Their program is similar to neither *Die Grünen* in Germany, nor to the Green Party in Great Britain (eco-socialism and conservatism, respectively). Environmentalism occupies a growing political space because of the emergence of new groups and political organizations, and the inclusion of new matters on the political agenda of traditional political institutes that have been overtaken by social movements.[7] This new agenda, as Martí Boada (1998) says, is overloaded by a "babelism," which reveals not only the limitations of human knowledge, but also the proliferation of discourses and senses that make the world so complex and understanding of it uncertain.

Discourses of Environmental Education

The plurality of environmental discourses mentioned here exists in diverse relationships; some are antagonistic, each struggling for its own method of hegemonizing the environmental policy; some are sympathetic to each other because they eventually articulate a defence of a common advocacy; and in many cases they are indifferent to each other, because they do not defend shared environmental demands often enough.

As we have commented, environmentalist discourses pervade scientific agencies as well as political networks. Education has not been the exception to this proliferation. Lucie Sauvé's (1996) proposals have been analyzed to show how four different sustainable development concepts are associated with certain educational paradigms (González-Gaudiano, 1998). Furthermore, a similar analysis carried out the derivation of the educational strategies implicit in each of the five paradigms of sustainable development proposed by Michael Colby (1990). Behind each environmentalist discourse there is an ideology, and also an implicit or explicit pedagogical discourse.

However, it is frequently the case that the majority of environmental educators do not examine the ideological discourses underlying the educational projects they are putting into practice and, as a consequence, their daily work is governed by political inconsistency and immediatism. Generally speaking, two nonmutually exclusive approaches still prevail: One focused on conservation education (ecologism/biocentrism) and one on science education (technocentrism/anthropocentrism). The former evades the social components of the problem and may adopt extreme, radical conservation-related stances at any cost (e.g., Deep Ecology). The latter emphasizes mainly the technical solution of the problem in addition to also ignoring or reducing the social component, and the contents are usually organized in a school-like manner even for nonformal education projects. Such a constitutive bias shows an environmental education with little capacity to contribute efficiently to the complex challenge of environmental deterioration and to have its intrinsic social and political dimensions articulated.

An Exercise on Environmental Education

We have already sketched some lines of discourse political analysis to offer a different understanding of the field; then we presented an outline of the dominant approaches of EE. In the following sections we analyze EE as an empty signifier, in order to show the way in which our approach can work in the field.

As discussed in the second section of this chapter, "environmentalism" is an overdetermination of scientific knowledge, international agencies, agreements, public policies, and so on. Thus, the identity of EE embedded in the different views of environmentalism does not entail a pure, predetermined essence, but rather is a heterogeneous composite of different meanings, provided by conflicting approaches to define this identity.[8] Additionally, it has changed during the different phases of its institutionalization, and its articulation has been precarious (Fuentes, 2004; González-Gaudiano, 1998). This identity was constituted through successive processes of identification with images provided by different agents and struggles that have signified EE in specific contexts. It was constituted in a relation where a subject was negated by another; for example, within the environmental field, the conflicts between deep ecology and the environmentalism of the poor. In this antagonistic relation, a political frontier was established between two enemy perspectives. This identity, however, was also constructed by a sense of belonging to a similar social group (e.g., environmental educators and educators for sustainable development in dispute against climate change). This was possible through a hegemonic relation involving the construction of equivalencies among different social groups, all of which strategically signified their demands in a similar way. The very possibility of producing this sense of belonging emerges in the designation of a common enemy (e.g., overconsumption or toxic waste), and thus the shared construction of a plan to annul it, and a proposal to compensate for and heal its damaging effects. It entails an exclusionary system as a result of the struggle between competing views. There is a condensation of multiple meanings, institutions, and performative dimensions, none of which is the "true cause" but shows the relational character of all of them. Furthermore, there is also the displacement of these meanings and performativity throughout different agencies (i.e., their circulation and symbolic re-addressing from one to another social unit). Displacement and condensation operate as a mobile network through which power relations take place. Genealogically speaking (Foucault, 1977), one can visualize that environmentalism does not have a mystical origin but a contingent beginning, an emergence characterized by proliferation rather than unity or self-identity, by conflict and struggle instead of the pure and uncontaminated Being or metaphysical essence of nature, science, or the earth.

Environmental Education as a Nodal and Empty Signifier

Let us move now to another discursive angle of the same hegemonic practice, and relying on de-sedimentation (i.e., showing the area of dispersion of a signifier, as it was presented *supra*), and reactivation (suggesting other possible articulations), examine how the meaning of a signifier has been precariously fixed. Focusing on inclusion and exclusion, we search those power relations involved in the process.

EE has been constructed as a necessary tendency compelled by the intrinsic essence of the human being (Bonnett, 2002)[9] to be achieved by means of the curricula, or the desirable benefit to gain environmental justice and to preserve the integrity of ecosystems for future generations, and an alleged requirement to achieve a healthy capitalist development, among many others. It has been construed as a crusade against environmental degradation (as in the green ideology denounced by Stavrakakis, 1997a), and as a rational strategy that would allegedly guarantee conservation of natural resources (as in the technocratic view analyzed by Foladori, 2000). It is also viewed as the global move toward the mélange and pulverization of identities by means of media kits ruled by a capitalist market (Rolnik, 1997). It has been viewed both as a desired state of things, and as a compelling necessity by those who promote it and, paradoxically, as a minor issue by those who neglect it. This, of course, is not a matter of some lying and some others being truthful, but clearly is a matter of a proliferation of meanings (ordinarily understood either as polysemy or ambiguity). EE appears then as a signifier holding together and precariously fixing the disseminated field (i.e., operating as a *nodal point;* see Zizek, 1992).

In order to understand how EE has such a broad area of dispersion, the conditions for its polysemy and ambiguity are conceptually elaborated in two dimensions: first, to understand that the structure is neither preestablished nor has it a necessary unfolding, we comment on the concepts of contingent and undecidable structure; and, second, to understand why there is neither fixed nor full meaning, we draw on the concepts of floating and empty signifiers.

We have already seen how the meaning of EE flows, hovers, or floats in different directions depending on the speaker and the context, because there is no way in which one single meaning could exhaust all the possible uses this expression has. A partial emptiness of the signifier is a condition for its flotation and responds to the relational character of sign (de Saussure, 1959).

When EE is presented as an essential component of the human being, its meaning will be partially fixed because of its differential position and the contiguity it has with other signs in the same chain (e.g., environmentalism). However, as it is constructed as the *totalization of this society that the caring and preserved world wants to achieve,* equivalencies are then established with all the other components of this discourse. On the one hand, considering the internal relationship among elements constituting this discursive chain, EE is not synonymous with "science education," "human essence," or values promoted by UNESCO-UNEP in 1975–1995 in their environmental education programs (see footnote 1).

"EE" ≠ "science education" ≠ "human essence" ≠ "UNESCO-UNEP, 1975–1995 IEEP"

On the other hand, considering the relationship between this chain and other external significant chains, each one of these components—not being enclosed in itself—also works as an alternative equivalent name within this totality (e.g., someone who rejects science education can take it as an equivalent of EE, see Fig. 3.1), thus conferring its ideological dimension to this "environmental" discourse, as Stavrakakis (1997a) has studied. We must stress that the very contingency[10] in the articulation of EE, with either an ecocentric or a technocentric view, is what allows ethical and political action, some conviction regarding the social and historical benefits one or the other meanings of EE could bring about, and also the strategic discursive means to support one or the other.

In addition to its *floating* character, EE functions as an *empty signifier* because there is not one and only one meaning capable of filling it, and nonetheless, the signifier is able to articulate and temporarily fixate the field (just as a nodal point, see Zizek, 1992). The tendential *emptiness*

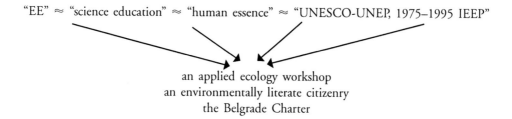

Fig. 3.1. Environmental education: Equivalence before external views.

of the signifier does not mean that the word is weakened or corroded. On the contrary, it is appealing and operates as a nodal point because it can accept many meanings; *ergo*, it is not and cannot be full.[11]

Both flotation and emptiness allow some signification of EE and simultaneously show that its full or final signification is structurally impossible (i.e., they are conditions of possibility and impossibility for the signification of EE). Two more dimensions of the same discursive operation can be considered. One marks the political *limits between inside and outside*.[12] This is evident in the confrontations taking place between precarious articulations of different environmental movements in a summit for instance, on genetically modified crops, where the enemy is clearly demarcated. The other functions as the foundation of the discursive system itself—which amounts to saying that it appears as if it had already been its core, basic nature, or its essence *from the very beginning*. These "essences," "primary origins," or "absolute foundations" can be embodied alternately by Nature, Science, Administration, and even mystical and esoteric assumptions (and their negative reversal, too). These alternate "essences" are, however, a space to be filled with some signifiers, none of which is isomorphic with one meaning (whichever it may be).

Now we can see that the "foundation" of the system of relational identities is not a positive core (e.g., the human essence) but the exclusion of the enemy's approach—an obstinate lack and an empty place that are endlessly "filled" with these and other meanings. Neither is the foundation a univocal or determined relation but, as we saw, an *undecidable* one. This leads to the ambiguous character of the signifier as a constitutive feature of the very system of signification. This impossibility, to neither infer nor determine once and for all a precise meaning (i.e., undecidability), is what has been approached (in the lines above) both as the *differential character* of an element of the system vis-à-vis the others within the system, and as the *equivalent character* of an element vis-à-vis the other elements of the same assemblage when they oppose a different discursive system. In this case, any of its elements represents the system *qua* totality (i.e., primacy of equivalence [$\approx$] over difference [$\neq$]).

In brief, we have thus far looked into the undecidable structure of the signifier and whether its articulation to one discourse or another is contingent. We have approached the principles ruling the floating character of EE and how this accounts for its differential and its equivalent sides. We have also looked on the exclusion operating as the *empty foundation* of a discursive texture: in this case, EE, finding that far from discovering a "necessary law" of Being, History, or the market, we have contingency and the undecidable structure of discourse. This is why even if we take a concept of EE within the same discursive context (e.g., social scientists) we find such a wide area of dispersion. This is precisely the constitutive ambiguity of the meaning of EE, a feature that widens the possibility for ethical, political, and epistemic intervention.

CONCLUSION

We have thus argued for the proliferation of views concerning environmentalism and the EE identity that is involved, the diversity of meanings in each language game. We have also tried an exercise to account for the outcomes of this proliferation when studied with the support of concepts, logics, and positionings taken from recent debates in the social sciences (i.e., discourse political analysis and a deconstructive reading). This exercise invites the reader to alternative constructions of EE that share some assumptions with postmodern research and also show their own political, ontological, and epistemic particularities.

Once one is suspicious of essences and rejects ultimate foundations, an alternate approach to be consistent with the former, and simultaneously remain distant from the alleged "relativist view where everything goes"[13] is needed (i.e., the assumption of the relational quality of identity, and the hegemonic character of those issues that operate as empty signifiers). Scrutinizing how those signifiers are open to a diversity of signifieds, while at the same time showing the capacity to articulate a field and temporarily fixate its meaning, seems to be a strategically convenient move. It serves both to show the historicity of signifiers and signifieds, and to argue in favour of a better project—one that is careful, sustainable, scientifically based, administratively feasible, and less oppressive—according to our beginning-of-the-21st-century context. Such a project will nonetheless have to be endlessly contested and improved or replaced in due time by another alternative. This, however, is the very possibility of keeping the ethical and political, as well as the epistemic discussion open to new positions.

Evidently, such an environmentally fair project is now far from being available and, although many international bodies have set agendas toward these ends, a much more strategically aware conversation (in Rorty's, 2006, sense) will have to take place before reasonable agreements are produced. Additionally, such understanding may have better chances of being realized if those involved in the conversation cease to adopt foundationalist and essentialist positions and abandon the belief that there is one and only one, true way of saving the planet. Instead, they can consider the possibility of hybrid agendas that may benefit from some caring traditions, from technological advances, from scientific studies and political approaches, from administrative awareness and aesthetic imagination, and from the local view as well as a planetary approach.

Therefore, the process of constitution of the EE field requires the construction of a new language that enables us to intensify the social dialogue and the debate on current educational practices and direct them toward research, because EE discourses are a varied set of intellectual traditions and currents of critical thought, having different degrees of contribution to the construction of a new social order. However, there are many largely unexplored intellectual avenues that might help shed light on the numerous opaque issues pervading the field—including the identity of the EE field itself—which refers to the articulation of other constituted disciplines and even educational processes in their broadest sense.

It has been our intention to contribute to this expansion through discourse political analysis, challenging some of the existing discourses and, more particularly, the concepts, assumptions, and visions underlying their particular approaches and the relationships they set up with the dominant perspective, and in turn, between societies and their environment. Language plays a substantive role in the material practices that shape subjectivity, which makes it important not to neglect those processes that tend to "normalize" our pedagogical relationships with the environment and to produce identities.

By means of institutionally legitimized, empirical research processes in EE, perspectives that tend to strengthen existing conditions have been promoted; this is because they do not question the existing mentality and political assumptions. In recent years, and more particularly since the 1990s, alternative forms of research have been encouraged that examine the epistemological, ontological, and ethical foundations of the Enlightenment, using qualitative or interpretative strategies, thus bringing about important advances in the field. However, while acknowledging these contributions, it must be said that approaches persist and prevail that still do not question the foundations that support the construction of knowledge.

As the foregoing arguments have shown, we are challenging these foundations by attempting to brush the cobwebs away from the conventional discourse of EE research, which has still not been able to break free of its Habermasian classification (empirical–analytical, interpretative, and critical). Our idea is to contribute to the construction of a postfoundational, discursive approach in EE research. We are attempting to decolonize our EE research strategies and locate ourselves in our experiences, redefining the frontiers and focuses of scientific and social inquiry, which, nonetheless, will just be other significations to be examined and contested in an endless war of interpretations.

NOTES

1. By 1975, the United Nations Educational, Scientific and Cultural Organization (UNESCO) and the United Nations Environmental Programs (UNEP) produced the International Environmental Education Programme (IEEP, 1975–1995) setting the agenda for this matter (see Buenfil, 1997, 2000, 2004; and in EE, Fuentes, 2004; González-Gaudiano, 1998).

2. The first, understood as a strategy for the desedimentation and reactivation of texts (text as textile, texture, weaving) in the search for reiteration, dissemination and de-centering of meanings; the second, understood as postfoundationalist approaches to *meaning as use in a language game* and in the search for family resemblance rather than literality, essences, or denotative meaning.

3. Some sort of eclecticism is always present in every theory (e.g., Marxism); however, it can be epistemically unaware and inconsistent, or it can be attentive and cautious in terms of what this eclecticism involves in the construction of knowledge. It is always present because no ultimate original thinking is possible. "New" ideas always have traces of old theoretical edifices; however, they can be resignified and articulated to other conceptual textures, by different logics and ontological assumptions. The point here is that eclecticism can be carefully scrutinized in search of consistency. In other words, eclecticism is not always ontologically incompatible as long as one takes epistemic responsibility for the implications it conveys.

4. We are taking the notion of theory as a toolbox from Levi-Strauss' *bricoleur* as discussed in Derrida (1967/1978) and as posed by Wittgenstein (1953).

5. For example, post-Heideggerian phenomenology, Gramscian Marxism, post-structuralism, and basic concepts such as *sign* and *signifier* (de Saussure, 1959); and family resemblance, *language game* and *use* (Wittgenstein, 1953).

6. By contingency, we mean, on the one hand, that the conditions of existence of any entity are exterior to it and that it is not possible to fix them with precision as a necessary and sufficient base; and on the other, that the link between the blocking and simultaneous negation of an identity introduces an element of radical undecidability in the structure of objectivity and an ineradicable impurity of the identity thus produced (Laclau 1990, pp. 19–21).

7. Let it be clear that we understand political spaces not by substantive definitions and defined borders, but as a space on several levels (a non-place) with blurred borders and porous surfaces.

8. The concepts of *identity* and *subjectivity* have already been challenged on different fronts: psychoanalysis, genealogy, and deconstruction *inter alia* (see Hall, 1996).

9. Bonnett (2002) claims that the essence of sustainability "is intrinsic to authentic human consciousness" (cited in González-Gaudiano, 2006).

10. The impossibility of finding an ultimate foundation on top of which the whole discursive edifice would be held together involves that the articulation of the signifier is contingent and unpredictable.

11. Every empty signifier is a nodal point; however, the opposite is not the case, because a nodal point is not necessarily one that accepts these many meanings.

12. For instance, how the signifieds connected to EE in an environment—neglectful discourse works as a constitutive outside of its critical counterpart (such as the discourse produced by the oil companies).

13. See Laclau (1990) for arguments concerning the rejection of this accusation.

REFERENCES

Benner, B., & English, A. (2004). Critique and negativity: Towards the pluralization of critique in educational practice, theory and research. *Journal of Philosophy of Education, 38*(3), 409–428.

Boada, M. (1998). *Medi ambient. Una crisi civilitzadora* [Environment: A civilization crisis]. Barcelona: Edicions de la Magrana.

Bennett, M. (2002). Education for sustainability as a frame of mind. *Environmental Education Research, 81*(1), 9–20.

Buenfil, R. N. (1997). Education in a post-modern horizon: Voices from Latin America. *British Educational Research Journal, 23*(1), 97–107.

Buenfil, R. N. (2000). Globalization, education and discourse political analysis: Ambiguity and accountability in research. *International Journal of Qualitative Studies in Education, 13*(1), 1–24.

Buenfil, R. N. (2004). Negativity: A disturbing constitutive matter in education. *Journal of Philosophy of Education. 38*(3), 429–438.

Castells, M. (1999). El reverdecimiento del yo: el movimiento ecologista. In *La era de la información. El poder de la identidad.* Vol. II. México: Siglo XXI.

Colby, M. E. (1990). *Environmental management in development: The evolution of paradigms.* Washington, DC: The World Bank.

Critchley, S., & Marchart, O. (2004). *Laclau: A critical reader.* Oxon: Routledge.

de Saussure, F. (1959). *Course of general linguistics.* New York: McGraw-Hill.

Derrida, J. (1978). *Writing and difference.* London: Routledge & Kegan Paul. (Original work published 1967)

Derrida, J. (1982). *Margins of philosophy.* Chicago: The Harvester Press.

Dobson, A. (1997). *Pensamiento político verde. Una nueva ideología para el siglo xxi.* Barcelona: Paidós Ibérica.

Foladori, G. (2000). El pensamiento ambientalista. *Tópicos en educación ambiental, 2*(5), 21–38.

Foucault, M. (1977). *Language, counter memory, practice.* Oxford: Blackwell.

Fuentes A. S. (2004). Constructing an identity: The environmental educators in Mexico. *Canadian Journal of Environmental Education, 9,* 163–176.

González-Gaudiano, E. (1998). *Centro y periferia de la educación ambiental. Un enfoque antiesencialista.* México: MundiPrensa.

González-Gaudiano, E. (2006). Environmental education: A field in tension or in transition? *Environmental Education Research, 12*(3/4), 291–300.

Guha, R. (2000). *Environmentalism: A global history.* New York: Longman.

Guha, R., & Martínez-Alier, J. (1997). *Varieties of environmentalism. Essays North and South.* New Delhi: Oxford University Press.

Hall, S. (1996). Who needs identity. In S. Hall & P. Du Gay (Eds.), *Questions of cultural identity.* London: Sage.

Hardin, G. (1979). Lifeboat ethics: the case against helping the poor. In J. Rachels (Ed.), *Moral problems.* New York: Harper & Row.

Howarth, D., Norval, A., & Stavrakakis, Y. (2000). *Discourse theory and political analysis.* Manchester, UK: Manchester University Press.

Laclau, E. (1988). Politics and the limits of modernity. In A. Ross (Ed.), *Universal abandon?* Minneapolis: University of Minnesota.

Laclau, E. (1990). *New reflections on the revolutions of our time.* London: Verso.

Laclau, E. (1996). *Emancipation(s).* London: Verso.

Laclau, E. (2000). In J. Butler, E. Laclau, & S. Zizek (Eds.), *Contingency, hegemony, and universality* (pp. 44–89). London: Verso.

Laclau, E., & Mouffe, C. (1985). *Hegemony and socialist strategy: Towards a radical democracy.* London: Verso.

Luke, T. (1998). *Ecocritique. Contesting the politics of nature, economy, and culture.* Minneapolis/London: University of Minnesota Press.

Nietzsche, F. (1907/1989). *On the genealogy of morals and ecce homo.* London: Vintage.

Peters, M., & Irwin, R. (2002). Earthsongs: Ecopoetics, Heidegger and dwelling. *The Trumpeter: Journal of Ecosophy, 18*(1), 1–17.

Rolnik, S. (1997). Toxicômanos e identidade. Subjetividade em tempo de globalizacão. In D. Lins (Ed.), *Cultura e subjetividade: Saberes nômades.* São Paulo: Papirus.

Rorty, R. (2006, February). *Putnam, pragmatism, and Parmenides.* Paper presented at Rorty in Mexico conference, México City.

Sauvé, L. (1996). Environmental education and sustainable development: Further appraisal. *Canadian Journal of Environmental Education, 1*(1), 7–34.

Sauvé, L. (2005). Currents in environmental education: Mapping a complex and evolving pedagogical field. *Canadian Journal of Environmental Education, 10*(1), 11–37.

Scott, W., & Gough, S. (Eds.). (2004). *Key issues in sustainable development and learning. A critical review.* London & New York: Routledge Falmer.

Stavrakakis, Y. (1997a). Green fantasy and the real of nature: Elements of a Lacanian critique of green ideological discourse. *JPCS: Journal for the Psychoanalysis of Culture and Society, 2*(1), 123–132.

Stavrakakis, Y. (1997b). Green ideology: A discursive reading. *Journal of Political Ideology, 2*(3), 259–279.

Toledo, V. M. (2005). Repensar la conservación: ¿áreas naturales protegidas o estrategia bioregional? *Gaceta Ecológica, 77*, 67–85.

Torfing, J. (1994). *Politics, regulation and the modern welfare state.* Unpublished doctoral dissertation, University of Essex, Colchester, UK.

Wittgenstein, L. (1953). *Philosophical investigations.* London: Blackwell.

Zizek, S. (1992). *The sublime object of ideology.* London: Verso.

Banksy, www.banksy.co.uk

Earth Democracy privileges diversity in nature and society in form and in function. When the intrinsic worth and value of every life form are recognized, biological diversity and cultural diversity flourish. Monocultures result from exclusion and dominance of species: one variety, one race, one religion, one worldview. Monocultures are an indication of coercion and loss of freedom. Freedom implies diversity. Diversity signifies freedom. (Vandana Shiva, at www.resurgence.org)

4

Playful Musement

Considering the Role of Optimism in Transformative Praxis for Environmental Education

Leigh Price

Given the absence of foundations in the post-positivist era, it is difficult for action-orientated educators, such as those working toward a healthy environment, to find guiding principles for their praxis. Somewhat unhelpful, the only thing that we can be sure about is that we cannot be sure of anything. Donna Haraway (1991) sums up this position: "In short, the certainty of what counts as nature—a source of insight and promise of innocence—is undermined, probably fatally" (pp. 152–153).

However, the alternative to this lack of a simple grounding of *truth* should not lead to cynicism. Haraway also says that "[t]he transcendent authorization of interpretation is lost, and with it the ontology[1] grounding 'western' epistemology. But the alternative is not cynicism or faithlessness" (pp. 152–153). Similarly, Patti Lather (cited in Gallaspie & Weems, 2003) states that the acceptance of a lack of foundations can lead to "a kind of cynicism which I think you have to be careful about." This chapter is my attempt to imagine an environmental education that avoids cynicism.

To begin with, I briefly overview some other educators' attempts toward optimism. For Thomas Popkewitz and Marie Brennan (1998), the optimistic solution to the problem is to alternate between foundationalism (naïve objectivity or positivism) and irrealism. Andrew Sayer (1999) calls this a "pomo flip" (p. 68). Using the work of Michel Foucault, Popkewitz and Brennan pragmatically make use of foundationalism in their assumption of power as *sovereignty*. Here, power is *something real* (an absolute) that people own and that can be redistributed. Popkewitz and Brennan then flip to irrealism with their understanding of power as *deployment* in which "the concern is not to find the origin of repressive mechanisms . . . [but to find] how 'sense' is produced through the complex inscriptions of power relations" (p. 19). Note that in Popkewitz and Brennan's conception of power as *deployment*, there is no recourse to truth, and reality is merely an artefact of power play.

Similar to Popkewitz and Brennan, and again influenced by Foucault, another example of a pomo flip is provided by Robin Usher and Richard Edwards (1994), quoting Cleo Cherryholmes:

Coercion appears to be necessary for emancipation while simultaneously subverting emancipation. The emancipation/oppression distinction thereby deconstructs and its deconstruction highlights an issue that critical educators keep at the margin of their discourse: which forms of domination (coercion, constraint) are justified in furthering which forms of emancipation. (p. 98)

Usher and Edwards' central commitment is to postmodernism. However, they insist that coercion is unavoidable. Thus, they flip between postmodern emancipation and a positivistic coercion, relying on a nebulous concept of "justification" to decide when coercion is appropriate. The sense that this flip is a necessary evil has been termed a "There-Is-No-Alternative" (TINA) compromise[2] by Ray Bhaskar (1993). However, even some of the proponents of TINA power play warn of its inherent *cynicism* (a word I use interchangeably with *skepticism* and *pessimism*). For example, Lather (cited in Gallaspie & Weems, 2003) is an advocate of Foucauldian, Machiavellian power play, which she describes as "training in the rhetoric of whatever the dominant discourses are. Learning to work them to your own purposes," but a few sentences later she warns, "[t]here is a kind of strategic mobilization of rhetoric as a skill, as training and skill. But I think more profoundly that can lead to a kind of cynicism which I think you have to be careful about" (n.p.).

One of Lather's (2002) alternatives to this cynicism is to suggest that we should follow Foucault's "absolute optimism" of "a thousand things to do" where our constant task is to struggle against the very rules of reason and practice inscribed in the effects of power of the social sciences. This option nevertheless seems pessimistic, since, in all the effort of 1,000 things to do, where do we find the time to act toward a common future? And, at the end of the 1,000 things to do, is there merely another 1,000 things to do? Sayer (1999) might describe this position, demonstrated here by Lather, as being the result of attempting to make a virtue out of the assumed lack of alternatives to irrealism by "arguing that answers cannot be expected, and all that one can do is persist with skeptical questioning." Bruno Latour (1999) also questions the optimism of people who hold this position of never-ending questions:

> Who can avoid hearing a cry of despair that echoes deep down, carefully repressed, meticulously denied, in these paradoxical claims for a joyous, jubilant, free construction of narratives and stories by people forever in chains? But even if there were people who could say such things with a blissful and light heart (and their existence is as uncertain to me as the existence of the Loch Ness monster, or, for that matter, as uncertain as the real world would be to these mythical creatures) how could we avoid noticing that we have not moved an inch from Descartes? (p. 8)

If interpretations of Foucault are unable to lead us out of debilitating cynicism, perhaps we might look to Jürgen Habermas' (1984) *theory of communicative action* for better guidance. This theory has been often been described by commentators as optimistic (e.g., Finlay, 1990; Flyvbjerg, 2000). Unfortunately, Habermas, influenced by the split reality of Kant, does not meet my criteria of optimism. This is because, similar to the pomo flips described earlier, Habermas flips between (a hidden) positivism and a kind of idealist Kantianism. In the words of Bhaskar (1993), Habermas "synthesize[s] hermeneutics with a still essentially unreconstructed empirical realism" (p. 375). The positivism (empirical realism) present in the work of Habermas has also been noted by Steven Levine (2006).

Habermas does not suggest that we need to use coercion, and neither does he disallow truth, and thus a way forward. However, his theory is unlikely to achieve its optimistic aims because positivism tends toward extreme oppositionals which lend themselves to violence. In the words of Zygmunt Bauman (1991), discussing the positivism of modernity, "The central frame of both modern intellect and modern practice is opposition—more precisely, dichotomy" (p. 14).

And this, he indicates, is linked to violence: "Invariably, such operation of inclusion/exclusion is an act of violence perpetrated upon the world, and requires the support of a certain amount of coercion" (Bauman, 2000, p. 2). The fact that Habermas' positivism is hidden—ironically, he is a strong critic of positivism—perhaps makes it all the more treacherous as it is less likely to be challenged.[3]

For the purposes of this chapter, questioning the optimism of such thinkers as Popkewitz and Brennan, Usher and Edwards, Lather, and Habermas and alluding to the difficulties in their positions is simply to introduce the need for an alternative. Early in my career as an environmental educator, I believed that positivism was synonymous with realism. I now realize that this was a simplistic but seriously misleading assumption. It was made possible by the parallel events of the critique of positivism and the linguistic turn, in which many practitioners "bracketed out" (Sayer, 1999) questions of reality. Jacques Derrida's statement that "[t]here is nothing beyond the text," was often used, some (e.g., Norris, 1996) claim inappropriately and contrary to Derrida's intention, to justify this questionable irrealism. As Bhaskar (1993) suggests, Derrida probably did not mean this or believe this and he almost certainly did not act according to it.

In rejecting positivism and its empiricism and actualism, which Bhaskar (1993) calls *ontological monovalency*, we do not need to reject realism. An alternative to rejecting realism is to argue that reality is stratified, such that some aspects of reality are real but not positive, including potentials or unexpressed tendencies. By *positive*, I mean present rather than absent. The aspects of reality that are real, but not positive, are the negative (or absent) aspects. Thus, in this conception, absences can be real. Bhaskar (1993) goes so far as to argue for "the positive as a tiny, but important, ripple on the surface of a sea of negativity" (p. 5). Acknowledging the reality of the negative also requires that we acknowledge the moment of transition, in which the negative becomes positive or vice versa. An example of *the moment of transition*, which is especially relevant to this chapter, is the process whereby we arrive at relatively new theories. Initially, there is the potential but still absent theory (negative valency); then there is the creative moment, or the moment of transition or musement (neither positive nor negative valency); followed by the presence of the new theory (positive valency). Taking the positive, the negative, and the transitional together achieves what Bhaskar (1993) calls *ontological polyvalency*. Assuming polyvalency gives us the layers of reality, which Bhaskar (1989) termed: the real, the actual, and the empirical (see Fig. 4.1).

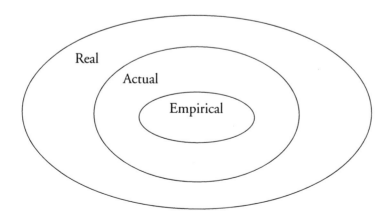

Fig. 4.1. Bhaskar's stratified reality: The real, the actual, and the empirical.

In this conception, what is real is not only what is empirical or positive. Some examples of real, causally efficacious things, which are nevertheless not empirical and/or positive, include the following:

- absences, such as the absence of health;

- potentials or tendencies, such as tendencies toward certain ways of being, which exist even if not expressed (e.g., the *potential* for climate change to further reduce biodiversity, or the *tendency* toward relationships of racism or sexism in society);

- events, such as the explosion of the nuclear warhead at Hiroshima (which actually happened but which we cannot now consider to be empirical because they are in the past); and

- aspects of our "selves," not currently expressed, such as the agent who, "*in virtue of being a stratified self,* no more has to forget her Nietzsche in untying a knot than lose her capacity to speak French in saying 'yes, please'" (Bhaskar, 1993, p. 149). Susan Leigh Star (1991) also explored the case for the reality of our multiple selves. She writes: "We are at once heterogenous, split apart, multiple—and through living in multiple worlds without delegation, we have experience of a self unified only through action, work and the patchwork of collective biography" (p. 29).

Nevertheless, to do justice to the important lesson of the linguistic turn, and thus to refuse to return to a primitive realism of the sort before we had science studies (Star, 1991)—or to the "illusion that there is no illusion" (Bhaskar, 1993)—it is necessary to acknowledge epistemological relativism (Bhaskar, 1989, 1993). This is illustrated by the signification triangle (Sayer, 1999), described in Fig. 4.2.

Signifier: the word/language used to denote/describe the referent (e.g., the words "oil spill")

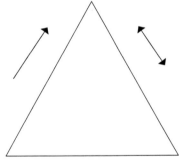

Signified: the meaning or interpretation attached to the signifier (e.g., just a necessary cost to the environment of economic activity versus an unacceptable natural disaster)

Referent: the thing itself (e.g., the oil spill itself)

Fig. 4.2. The signification triangle (after Sayer, 1999).

Here we see that although the signified is not the same as the signifier, there is a limit to unrestrained interpretation, imposed by the referent itself. Thus, there is not a simple, foundational relationship between the referent and the signifier, assumed by traditional western science; neither is the referent elided, as is the tendency in much post-positivist philosophy. Derrida's similar triadic approach to semiosis (cited in Borradori, 2003) can be seen in the following statement: "We can and, I believe, must (and this duty is at once philosophical and political) distinguish between the brute fact, the impression, and the interpretation" (p. 88).

The signification triangle allows pluralistic interpretations but avoids relativism because of the referent (roughly equivalent to Derrida's *brute fact*) whose acknowledged existence makes possible critique of signifiers (roughly equivalent to Derrida's *impressions*) and/or *interpretations*. This pluralistic approach to truth and reality seems similar to that held by Mohatma Gandhi, who spoke of "the doctrine of the manyness of reality" (cited in Richards, 1991, p. 3) but who nevertheless also mentioned *Satya* or *Truth*[4] (cited in Richards, 1991, p. 1). To hold both that there is a *Truth* and that there are *many truths* is not contradictory given the signification triangle because the referent *Truth* exists regardless of the fecund interplay of all three semiotic components (the referent, the signifier, and the signified).

The arrows included in the diagram of the semiotic triangle remind us that we know all things only through our relationships with them. As Haraway (1997) puts it, "[r]eality is the fruit of interaction, where material [world] and semiotic [word] apparatuses cannot be separated" (p. 116). Therefore, not only do we bring our social, cultural, and personal history into the dynamic, but we also change the *thing*. As such, all beings, human and nonhuman, language and nonlanguage, are variously, and to different degrees, co-constituted by each other in a complex web of interrelating. Another way to describe this complex web of interrelating is to say that all things are more accurately conceived as interactive processes. Perhaps it would be more accurate to use transitive verbs to refer to *things*, rather than nouns.

Most of the post-positivist environmental educators that I know intuitively use the signification triangle to avoid relativism in their teaching. For example, although they encourage plural interpretations, they guide learners away from misconceptions and toward reality congruence, if there is a discrepancy, by encouraging students to take another look at the referent, perhaps interpreted from a number of different perspectives. We could say that the referent is a sign that "speaks" for itself. Derrida's use of the term *brute fact* draws attention to its status as a sign, although in practice our knowing of the referent cannot be an innocent absolute. Nevertheless, the referent itself will refuse incorrect interpretations. For example, if I tried to call a tree (the *brute fact* of it) a handbag, then the tree itself would "insist" that this interpretation was incorrect; it would simply be nonsense.

However, the referent could not "insist" on one absolutely correct interpretation. Therefore, epistemological relativism would allow other kinds of interpretation to be attached to the tree itself, such as that: it is shade or firewood, an object to be preserved or a nuisance to be unrooted. Different interpretations would not necessarily be incommensurable. They could complement each other, for example: perhaps the tree is both shade and firewood; perhaps in some contexts it is a nuisance and in others it should be preserved; and a poet's "knowing" of a tree is not necessarily incommensurable with a biologist's "knowing" of the same tree, although it may not be reducible to it. Opinions that do seem incommensurable, given the existence of the referent and the optimistic assumption of a shared world of the different knowers, would provide motivation towards discussion and perhaps be a point of dialectical learning. However, cynicism with regard to the possibility of reaching a better interpretation of the referent (perhaps based on the cynical assumption that different epistemologies produce different knowledges which just *are* incommensurable) would tend to shut down the impetus towards exploration and learning.

An example of this kind of shutdown can be seen when it is assumed that scientific knowledge and Indigenous knowledge are incommensurable, thus diminishing the possibility that they learn from each other. I prefer to see western scientific knowing and Indigenous knowing as irreducible but complementary (Price, 2005).

Nevertheless, the idea that reality is stratified, the semiotic triangle, and the refusal of the mind–world split of Descartes, do not, on their own, fully overcome our heritage of ontological monovalence. There is also an absence in the inferential logic insisted on by ontological monovalence, which needs to be absented. Essentially, science in its traditional western construction sought certainty and foundations, and therefore could only allow the empirical to be admitted as real. This excluded much of what researchers found most interesting (recall the list of nonempirical things given previously). Science therefore concentrated only on inductive and deductive logic, proper to empirical investigations, although even inductive logic presented some problems for the empiricist (Popper, 1959). However, in our post-positive era, in which we are familiar with and expect uncertainty, the preconditions exist for us to deal with that which is nonempirical and can only be known uncertainly. This requires that we supply another inferential logic of inquiry in addition to deduction and induction, namely *retroduction*, but also called *abduction, pure play* or *musement*.

Musement belongs to a group of kinds of inference that move from observed to unobserved things (which includes the possibility of nonempirical things). Specifically, musement is the inference from actual phenomena to past (retro) structural causes. Induction is also one of these kinds of inference but it is the inference from past to future (the famous inductive inference being that if I have only ever seen white swans, then I can induce that all the swans are white).

Charles Sanders Peirce first described musement (Brent, 1993), and used the following example to distinguish between induction, deduction, and retroduction or musement (cited in Danemark, Ekström, Jakobsen, & Karlsson, 2002): Imagine that I have a bag of beans. I systematically take beans out of the bag, one at a time, and each time I do, the bean is white. After a time, I induce that all the beans in the bag are white. I then deduce that, if all the beans are white, then the next bean I take from the bag will be white, and this would be a falsifiable hypothesis. I then replace the beans in the bag and go out of the room. When I return, I notice that there is a white bean on the table next to the bag. I guess that the bean came out of the bag. This tentative guess, for which I have good reason, but no proof, is *musement*.

In terms of environmental concerns, although musement may not provide absolute certainty because the causes of the problem are not empirically measurable or testable, it does provide a "good enough" explanation of the global situation to allow us to decide on a way forward. The future of the planet perhaps depends on us taking our retroductively derived conclusions seriously. Nevertheless, because of the lack of certainty, our change in direction must be carefully monitored. Al Gore, in his film *The Inconvenient Truth* (Guggenheim, 2006), provides an example of musement with his story about a classmate who noticed the matching pattern of the shorelines of South America and Africa and theorized that they might previously have been joined. Likewise, Gore used musement to theorize about the existence of a causal linkage between the matching patterns of the earth's carbon dioxide levels and its surface temperature. Critics can correctly claim that such theories are untestable in contrived laboratory-like conditions, but in the approach advocated here a theory is not fatally flawed if it cannot be tested in a closed system or is otherwise unempirical. Notice also that a characteristic of musement, at least for the person engaging in it, is that it provides knowledge that was not known to them before; it is thus *surprising*. Furthermore, its validity lies in the testing of the claim's ability to explain the phenomena in question and in corroboration (Sayer, 1999).

Often, the testing of a theory achieved by musement lies in living one's life according to the actions suggested by the theory, and assessing its adequacy in explaining the consequences of the actions. For example, perhaps, like Star (1991), I notice I become ill after eating onions. I conclude via musement that I am allergic to onions, which suggests that I stop eating them, and therefore I do indeed stop eating them (test my theory in the way I live my life) and no longer become ill. This would provide some validity to the notion that I was allergic to onions, but would not be conclusive or absolute proof, because perhaps what I am actually allergic to is the pesticides added to the onions. Perhaps I would eventually work out, again through musement, that I am not allergic to organic onions, but the point here is that musement can provide good enough, if not absolutely certain, knowledge that is testable (although not in the strict western scientific sense).

Using the analogy of the story of being allergic to onions, and applying its central lesson to the relationship between carbon emissions and climate change, implies that we might usefully adjust our activities with regard to releasing carbon dioxide, despite the uncertainty of the information. The difference between the causal relationship between onions and allergies, and carbon emissions and climate change, is that it could be possible to isolate an extract of onion and carry out a laboratory experiment to test the theory empirically. In the case of carbon emissions, such a procedure is not possible and thus we must be content with testing our hypothesis through the living of our lives as humans on earth.

Optimism is a component of musement. This is because, specifically as it is here conceived, the precondition for cynicism is the assumption that our minds are in a vat (Latour, 1999) or separate from the world, and in its post-positivist form, this assumption is often related to an agnostic bracketing out of reality. Ironically, as Latour (1999) suggests, both positivism and postmodernism agree on the mind–body dualism of Descartes. In refusing this dualism and its scepticism of reality, we regain our optimism, since, if we are intimately connected to the world and all of its beings (human and nonhuman), we cannot *not* know them. Assuming that we are part of the world, or of the totality, closes the hermeneutical circle and thus texts and reality appear at least potentially intelligible to us (Bhaskar 1993), although this does not deny plurality of interpretation. Having optimistically retained our faith in our ability to know, we are able to engage, if not innocently, at least not cynically, in the process of musement. The key question thus changes from the cynical, "How can we know?"—rhetorically implying that perhaps we can never know—to the optimistic, "How can we not know?" Instead of considering "knowing" to be something that we impose, it becomes something that we allow. To put it another way, learning is absenting the constraints on our knowing. One of the ways that we absent the constraints on our knowing is through the creative process of pure play or musement.

For Peirce, the ability to Play required optimism, and because musement (Play) was a prerequisite for "the conduct of life," he thought of pessimists as perhaps not quite sane (Peirce, 1901, cited in Weiner, 1966). Latour also remarks on the link between insanity and cynical conceptions of philosophy. In his book *Pandora's Hope*, Latour (1999) describes the impossible bind that philosophers of the sceptical sort found themselves. "No wonder," he writes, "so many philosophers ended up in asylums" (p. 12).

Musement plays an important role in educational praxis because it is a key component of the dialectical process of explanatory theory development, which is necessary for guiding us in our attempts to address problems, or better, absences, in our world, such as the absence of clean water, or the absence of health. I prefer to talk about, for example, the absence of a healthy environment, rather than the presence of a degraded one, because a healthy environment is something that simply does exist if constraints to its presence are removed. In fact, a relatively healthy environment already exists potentially. Thus, transformative praxis toward a healthy environment is the absenting of absences that absent the healthy environment. Explanatory theory development is especially important for environmental educators because by definition we start from a problem, that of the environmental crisis. Bhaskar (1993) argues, optimistically, that it is possible to move from explanatory critique, towards a tentative suggestion towards removing whatever precondition was identified as making possible the problem, and from there toward action to remove the precondition. This movement, from critique to action, based on a conception of change as absenting, is what he calls radically transformed, transformative praxis. Previous formulations of praxis, based on Hegel, lacked a concept of lack and thus, instead of *letting* or *allowing*, they tended to be impositional and teleological.

Another argument for praxis as negative absenting is the idea mentioned earlier that process and relationships are ontologically prior to *things*, including, for example, oppressive systems. Changing *things* is therefore achieved by changing the relationships which form them, and since these relationships always pre-exist the thing and are sustained by the actions or *doings* of agents, praxis must necessarily involve negative *not doing*.

To explore this point about praxis further, one of the casualties of the linguistic turn was action. As Lather (1991) says, "The question of action, however, remains largely under-addressed within postmodern discourse" (p. 12). However, if as Latour suggests, we reconnect ourselves to the world, we discover that indeed the action was never missing, and that "we cannot not act" (Bhaskar, 2002, p. 252). This leads us to a conception of transformation as (un)action, since, given that we are always acting, to transform becomes an (un)doing or perhaps a change in direction rather than the creation of something new. Hence, we cannot avoid history and context, and our choice is not whether or not to act, but whether or not to reproduce or transform what already exists (Bhaskar, 2002).

I end this chapter by drawing attention to the similarities that I have noticed between optimistic transformed, transformative praxis and nonviolent nonconformance, or nonviolent action, which Gandhi also called *Satyāgraha* and which he defined as "the Force which is born of Truth and Non violence" (cited in Richards, 1991, p. 48). An extensive comparison is not the aim of this section; rather, I hope it offers an illustrative example.

I have already mentioned the similarities between Gandhi's ontology and epistemology and the ontology and epistemology that I argue for in this chapter, in terms of his commitment to the manyness of reality but also his commitment to Truth. That Gandhi tested his understanding of Truth in the living of his life (Richards, 1991, p. 1) is also perhaps evidence of a similarity between his understanding of knowledge and my understanding of musement.

Also similar to my position in this chapter, is Gandhi's assumption there is no mind–body duality and that ultimately all beings, human and nonhuman, are intimately connected. Glyn Richards (1991) states that: "It is this belief in the essential unity of life that underlies Gandhi's feeling of affinity with the animal kingdom" (p. 64). Furthermore, Gandhi's noncooperation, or his refusal to reproduce oppressive systems, is consistent with the concept of oppressive systems as being processes, such that change requires that we change our relationship with the system, which is in effect an (un)action, a (not)doing or simply *not cooperating*.

In this chapter, I have argued for a realist, but epistemologically pluralist, approach to environmental education, based on musement, which is a special kind of inference that measures validity in terms of the way we live. Another way to describe this process of musement is as a kind of praxis. My claim for this optimistic, transformed, transformative praxis is that it potentially avoids the coercive methods that it critiques. Furthermore, Gandhi's *Satyāgraha*, which explicitly encourages nonviolence, may be a useful inspiration as we attempt to explore what praxis, Peirce's Play, might mean in our everyday activities as environmental educators.

NOTES

1. Note Haraway's suspicions regarding the reality of ontology. However, I consider Haraway to be a realist, despite such statements. Her realism is noticed also by Sayer (1999, p. 103, n. 13), who writes: "Thus, despite Haraway's professed rejection of her realism, her discussion of objectivity and the situated and perspectival nature of knowledge is compatible with *critical* realism, and indeed helps develop it."

2. Bhaskar (1993, p. 116) obtained the idea of "There-Is-No-Alternative" (TINA) compromise formations from Margaret Thatcher's catch phrase "there is no alternative," which she used to describe her commitment to an antiquated monetarism. His aim was "to remind us of the fallibility of our claims to knowledge of [TINA formations]."

3. In my PhD thesis (Price, 2007) I gave a detailed explanation of the effect of pomo flips, TINA compromises, and hidden epistemological commitments on environmental education.

4. Some might object that Gandhi's *Truth* is a theological one. However, in the approach suggested here, this is not a limitation because all claims to truth, whether about material objects, relations, or God, are treated equally (see also Price, 2005). Therefore, unlike positivism and postmodernism, there are no prior expectations about the theological beliefs of practitioners and one could be a theist, an atheist, a polytheist, a pantheist, or agnostic and remain faithful to this position. Having said this, given my assumption of epistemological pluralism, fundamentalism or absolutism (whether secular or theological) are incompatible with the general tenets advocated here.

REFERENCES

Bauman, Z. (1991). *Modernity and ambivalence.* Cambridge, UK: Polity Press.

Bauman, Z. (2000). *Liquid modernity.* Cambridge, UK: Polity Press.

Bhaskar, R. (1989). *Reclaiming reality: A critical introduction to contemporary philosophy.* London: Verso.

Bhaskar, R. (1993). *Dialectic: The pulse of freedom.* London: Verso.

Bhaskar, R. (2002). *Meta-reality: The philosophy of meta-reality* (Vol.1: Creativity, love and freedom). London: Sage.

Borradori, G. (2003). *Philosophy in a time of terror: Dialogues with Jürgen Habermas and Jacques Derrida.* London: University of Chicago Press.

Brent, J. (1993). *Charles Sanders Peirce: A life.* Bloomington: Indiana University Press.

Danemark, B., Ekström, M., Jakobsen, L., & Karlsson, J. (2002). *Explaining society: Critical realism in the social sciences.* London: Routledge.

Finlay, M. (1990). *The potential of modern discourse: Musil, Peirce and perturbation.* Bloomington: Indiana University Press.

Flyvbjerg, B. (2000, April). *Ideal theory, real rationality: Habermas versus Foucault and Nietzsche.* Paper presented at the 50th annual conference of the Political Studies Association, London.

Gallaspie, R., & Weems, L. (2003). Conversation with Patti Lather. *The Initiative Anthology: An Electronic Publication about Leadership, Culture, & Schooling.* Retrieved December 7, 2003, from http://www.muohio.edu/InititaiveAnthology/.

Guggenheim, D. (Director). (2006). *An inconvenient truth* (Motion Picture). USA: Lawrence Bender Productions.

Habermas, J. (1984). *The theory of communicative action.* Boston: Beacon Press.

Haraway, D. (1991). *Simians, cyborgs, and women: The reinvention of nature.* London: Free Association Books.

Haraway, D. (1997). *Modest_Witness@Second_Millennium.FemaleMan_Meets_OncoMouse: Feminism and technoscience.* New York: Routledge.

Lather, P. (1991). *Getting smart: Feminist research and pedagogy with/in the postmodern.* New York: Routledge.

Lather, P. (2002, November). *Que(e)r(y)ing research/policy/practice*. Paper presented at the annual conference of the American Educational Studies Association, Pittsburgh, PA. Retrieved February 14, 2007, from http://www.coe.ohio-state.edu/plather/pdf/conferences/foucault.pdf.

Latour, B. (1999). *Pandora's hope: Essays on the reality of science studies*. Boston: Harvard University Press.

Levine, S. (2006). Review of truth and justification by Jürgen Habermas. MIT Press, Cambridge, MA and London, 2003. *Constellations, 12*(3), 437–444.

Norris, C. (1996). *Reclaiming truth: Contribution to a critique of cultural relativism*. London: Lawrence & Wishart.

Popkewitz, T., & Brennan, M. (Eds.). (1998). *Foucault's challenge: Discourse, knowledge and power in education*. New York: Teachers College.

Popper, K. (1959). *The logic of scientific discovery*. London: Hutchinson.

Price, L. (2005). Playing musement games: Retroduction in social research, with particular reference to Indigenous knowledge in environmental and health education. *Southern African Journal of Environmental Education, 22*, 87–96.

Price, L. (2007). *A transdisciplinary explanatory critique of environmental education (Volume 1): Business and industry*. Unpublished doctoral dissertation, Rhodes University, Grahamstown, South Africa.

Sayer, A. (1999). *Realism and social science*. London: Sage.

Star, S. L. (1991). Power, technology and the phenomenology of conventions: On being allergic to onions. In J. Law, *A sociology of monsters: Essays on power, technology and domination* (pp. 26–56). London: Routledge.

Richards, G. (1991). *The philosophy of Gandhi*. London: Curzon Press.

Usher, R., & Edwards, R. (1994). *Postmodernism and education*. London: Routledge.

Weiner, P. (Ed.). (1966). *Charles S. Peirce: Selected writings*. New York: Dover.

Until you dig a hole, you plant a tree, you water it and make it survive, you haven't done a thing. You are just talking. (Wangari Maathai, Nobel Peace Prize speech)

Enchanting Concrescence, Artin Lahiji

The Sensuous

5

Coyote and Raven
Talk About the Land/Scapes

Pat O'Riley and Peter Cole

curving shapes of canoe and paddle dance
with the reflection of snow-capped mountains
on stillness of water

coyote and raven are exhausted   from a long day's paddle
and head their canoe towards the shore
to rest for a bit on the cool moss
raven fluffs his feathers   fluttering   sighs
a cedar branch wavers in the last light

after taking a looong drink of water from the mountain stream
coyote rests against the roots of a thousand year old fir
you know   raven   we've been part of the land and sky
and other scapes so long and so intimately
that we don't often think about our relationship to them-it-those ones
since them-it-those ones was/is us
and us was/is them-it-those ones
without there ever being a twain to meet   or not

raven yawns   yeah whatever

it's like 'what's your relationship with your beak or your tail or your life?'
in this case the I's don't have it   'out of order!'   says the chief   justice
socratic syllogisms only   aristotelian analyses   platonic principles   reason rules!
no indian imaginings allowed   no loitering thoughts   no migratory metaphors

in coyote and raven's experience organic growth
in the form of linguistic and somatic rhizomatic dissemination
has been the shape and gesture of their enacted relationship
with the land and sky and with other otherthanlinguistic meaning

are you thinking rhizomatically coyote?

you mean as in gilles deleuze   french poststructuralist thought?

non   I mean as in picking *les mauvaises herbes* for 14 hours a day
as a fiveyearold under the vigilant parental eye
'And don't you miss (a) one!'   because one means myriad
rhizomes were either squarely in the weed category
or roundly in the flower category including water lilies
with a few ifs   lots of buts   and mostly maybes
with here and there a potato   trillium   ginger iris
there an arrowroot lily of the valley quack grass   hut two tree fore!
and using herbicides to eradicate (kill) them
which in turn causes a massive increase in artificial estrogens
in human bodies and a consequent increase in cancers
and other wasting diseases
poisoning the world poisons us   we are it   we are toxins
as we do so are we

I mean rhizome   raven   as in the geographization of language
and verse vice a   rhizome as in   the centre is everywhere   everywhence
hold two words   regarded from different angles at arm's length
mind's width   imagination's depth and slurry   do you picnic
as you might air photos (with or without the aid of a stereo/stetho/scope)
and you will notice their topologies rise to meet you
accelerate to impact you   urged on by your gravity
the weight of your thinking frameworks
the derivation from deleuze is evident!

évidemment to you perhaps from your locale and intellectual experience
but I had dirty fingers   all the way up   to my elbows   face and neck
for 10 years before the age of 14 and thereafter   thereduring
from working with rhizomes every day of the spring and summer
and many autumn days even until twilight   and just after
even after scrubbing with lye soap and pigbristle
not to mention 40 years of working as a landscaper
gardener   designer   clipping snipping digging edging
sodding seeding planting watering loving loaming looming

tell me coyote   does deleuze talk about tip layering
as in raspberry canes   where the growing tip becomes the root
which puts forth a growing tip
the growing tip being becoming
every/where/whence/will be will be was wert
in all tenses   and   conjugations   and in the case of slow verbs   declensions
find that in bescherelle   201 italian verbs   or arabic for beginners

you are speaking in abstractions   anti-western formattings
believing that you are thinking independently   postpositively
yet are deeply rooted in status quo   slaloming laterally
then moving in more straight lines   straight turns
machinemade rows monocrops cashcrops   selfdelusionings
your point of view petrified   fossilized   magmafied

the medusa syndrome   all that your methodologies touch
turn to reason   lined up for a community *coup de*   give me a break!

caw! wraaakk! harrrroooooo!   be careful coyote
you may be walking into linguistic quick/sand/lime
half a wit is not always better than none!
so don't argue with one

ha   more ravenings

exactly   where's the scholarship?

you mean western   scholarship?
out of evidence everywhere   wrakkk!   arroooo!
I'll second that devotion   harrroooo

so what's your vision coyote?
20:20:20   if you count my third eye
but that's mostly operational with my other two eyes shut
so I guess you could just call it 20   kilometres   give or take an m&m

I mean for education   for the upandcoming generations

respect   love   tolerance

that sounds like a good start

what about you?

aboriginal centred education   raven centred   earth centred   spirit centred
community centred   and I don't just mean human beings
earthworm centred   quack grass centred   or offcentred   camshafted
chaindriven   power takenoff

what about curriculum?

if we have a foundation of caring and respect   the rest will look after itself

how about the markets

farmers'?

no   stock   commodities   bond currency

what about them?

that's all   what about them

raven   education has to be relevant

but the agenda of respect and community will make them relevant

the agenda will? howso?   don't you mean speaking listening
with an open mind to it and similar agenda items
rather than the agenda *soi-même*

I agree but there are ministers of education and superintendents
and other administrators who want reason   logic   science

ohhhhhhh   my whole body aches when I say that word
but we can't pretend science
ohhhhhh
is of no value
what about value being   of no science
we're supposed to direct our abstract so that it coheres
use glue and clamps   maybe a have roll of duct tape will travel
duck tape   quack quack   somebody call   this is a wrap   rap!

looks like we'll have to go through this one again raven

until we can come up with reason and quantity and positivist principles

and vice principals

hmmm you're a troublemaker   go to the office right now

coyote remember the superintendent coming up home
with the guidance counselor
so   this is supposed to be an environmental education field trip
where's the lesson   what's the objective
who's on first   who will second it   all in disfavour
the lesson is the poop on your shoulder   guv the scuff on your shoes luv
the lesson is you are environment   billions of cells fall from you
in a constant rain day and night   are consumed by creatures
invisible to the common sight   creatures from this side
of science fiction   ah but which side are you
we are constantly   constant   ly consumed
breathing in creatures   in a continual wind tunnel
what was human 10 minutes ago is now part
of a creature for whom a grain of rice   is a mountain

who told you   you could teach this   rubbish
ah rubbish packaging waste superfluity
it is good to teach   teach about   the naming of
that which we discard   teaching about garbage
what is called garbage   this is very central to
teaching about the environment

garbage is in the air   we breathe it in   we become it
garbage is in the water   we drink it
it soaks into our skin as water vapour   as acid   rain
acid fog   acid mist   garbage   is us   are we

you're teaching this?   what are you?   who hired you?

I am from this land   of this land   this land

give me a break   with your pithiisms   your philosophic nonsense
you are here to teach a particular standardized curriculum

yes   I know   a prescribed curriculum
like a pharmacist doling out medications   fee   fee   fi fi fo fo fum
at the behest of members of the college of physicians and surgeons
to mask symptoms   to hold off the inevitable
to waylay the immediately probable

hey raven   this human being   the one in the suit
he wants a prescription filled   can you help him
and his silent friend   on a leash   give him a cattreat
that is very disrespectful talk   says the leashee   leashmite
I am charged with ensuring that the provincial curriculum
is advanced   is being taught and that a collegial structure   is maintained

okay teach I told him   give me the goods on ee
so that I might become a good citizen

and I   the feathered   one said you are a subject of ee   an object of discovery
you can't study yourself   if you are a primary source of data   for ee'ers
out of bounds   employees only

hmm   well that's a deep subject   digging down to the h two oh table
the knowledge we oh table   the practice table   the harvest table
witchwitchwitch digdigdig   draw and carry   yoked to reason
sustenance   is a very important part of environmental education
sustenance is what we give   so that there might be space
within us   to accept (understand) that which is offered us
raven   what are your earliest memories   with respect
to your environment?

earliest   well in that I did not come from a beginning
I'm not sure how to approach that thoughtscape
perhaps though   with crampons   pitons   biteons   phaetons
gideeyup   gideeyap   tsch tsch   get on up   like a teaching machine
I remember   as in member again   reconstitute   reassemble
when I was a ravenling   breaking out of the translucent   egg
it was getting cramped where I was so I just had to surge forward

and I did not even know that I was inside something
that I was inside an eggshell   it's like breaking out
of the sky   into another reality   shades of sky woman
I was a black hole antiparticle breaking into a white universe

yesyesyes   getonwithit willyou   what are   you onabout

so there I was   all covered with birthstuff   sticky wickety chickety
and needing to get on with it   not knowing though
what exactly it   was
whewwwwww   I felt both exhausted and exhilarated
wanting to sleep forever   but I knew I had a mission

so you were a missionary

well   I wouldn't put it that way
I had a mission   which I was not exactly of a mind
to share   in a missionizing manner

get on with it   bird

bird   I'm not bird   though I do have a bird shape
in fact   birds are not birds   though they have bird shape
I am I am ego ego e go egg o
waffles   toasted please with maple surple
so there I was with my 3 sisters and brother
in a nest   way up   in the ponderosa pine
opening our mouths anytime a shadow passed over us
eating something already semidigested
including the bodily fluids of our parents

I thought you said you had no beginning

oh   breaking out of the eggshell   wasn't a beginning
it wasn't even a continuing   it was just what it was
coming home while leaving home

oh that really makes a lot of sense

I'm sorry to hear that   I hadn't meant it to

what is with this indeterminable foreword
will you be getting to any point anytime soon
only three points in rapid succession   staccato   ellipses
terminal punctuation in triplicate   cc: bcc:
but which   is the original   and has it   an origin
has a moose an origin   is it born   in the eye   the ear   the mind
the nose   the mind   are we doulas   birth helpers   midwives
and which way   does birth happen

are we born old   filled with knowledge and experience
and spend our lives filled with ignorance

what has any of this to do with environmental education

look dr whatever   if you don't get it   you won't get it
so just relax   and stay out of the way of the children   the students
those for whom you are responsible

coyote   let's shapeshift   let's split   and so they did
into stones   butterflies   flowers   ants and sunbeams   moonshine
northern lights and tadpoles   mosses and mushrooms   and bear scat
sometimes they got stepped on   sometimes eaten   sometimes
they were loved   admired   accepted investigated
but always they foundcreated a prism through which
they were able to shapeshift into something understandable
for those for whom reason is not the only guide

hey where are your feathers   if you're a real indian
you're a fake   you're nothing but a   simulacrum   fakebread *miettes*
pass the bloodImeanwine

whatever that means   sure   you're just a puton
who is claiming to be an indian

I'm just saying I am from this land
and that my ancestors are buried for a thousand generations here

where is the environmental education   where?

I'm not sure   it's not spelled out
oh here here it is   what white indian expert folks are calling TEK
traditional ecological knowledge   our knowings
a quote from an unknown elder   by a well-known white academic

oh   who is the elder   is it auntie susie?   mmm?

it just says 'an unknown salish person'   a womanman

oh

what's the quote coyote?

I'm not sure   I don't speak ucwalmicwts that well
well what do you think it means?

means?   oh I don't know about that   I'm not sure

that our quotes actually   mean   anything

are they smalltalk then?

small   well I suppose given a choice between sizes
they could fit in pretty much anywhere

oh   it's there   to be found   discovered

is it wisdom then

I suppose it could be   but that's not what they call it the elders   I can't say
they'd refer to our knowledge as TEK traditional ecological knowledge

traditional?

you could call it that   not sure what the elders would say

remember raven how the superintendent was getting riled about all this talk
he yelled 'where is the environmental education in all of this?'
oh oh the super's blood pressure started going up
oh that's not so good   we have traditional medicines for that   ecological knowledges

don't say that raven   or they'll turn your talk into white knowledge

whiTEKnowledge

ahhhhhh   I've heard of that   it spreads
yes   it's quite virulent

so where were we
the super and the psycho   I mean guidance counselor
oh yes   gentleman   and lady   i7n a bi7t o7f a7 ru7sh a7re7n't the7y
I would say   and pardon the glottal stops
did you find out what you came for
they were speechless
that's a twist   witless too   I warrant
I got a witless   witless   witless

raven I told them environmental knowledge is the newest grail
mary magdalene had it   she took it with her to nice or was it massilia
in the form of salves potions   oils   harvesting methods

OH GIVE ME A BREAK!

you asked about environmental knowledge
ravens have it   coyotes have it   it's called following one's original instructions
doing what you do

so human beings have it too?

yes   of course   polluting the planet is a kind of environmental knowledge
not one which is particularly good for the tens of thousands
of species being extincted every year   or is it every day

you're not giving us a straight answer

I am not giving you any kind of answer   I am just talking

jump cut to eight hours later
the superintendent has torn some of his hair out
the guidance counselor has bitten her fingernails down to below her finger tips
they look frenzied and dishevelled   at wit's end   near corn wall
raven and coyote are having spruce tea and acorn cakes
zoom out and fade
iris shot opens slowly on forest clearing
enter coyote and raven

whewww that was a marathon   coyote
oh oh here comes a university dean   watchyerword manners

hiya

hiya?   what are you   a coaster   rockyfish trawler

intercoaster   actually   we travel hither and yawl

I hear you're giving the townie mates a bit of a hard time
with yer rural ideas about rigor

oh they're not rural   they're just not fenced in

and traditional   academic ideas are?   is that what you insinuate?

I think that insinuate depends on what side of the verb you are

raven   let's shapeshift

why   are you afraid of them

afraid   hm   I think as I get older I feel more cautious   at times
and don't give so much time to entertaining gladness foolishly

crossfade to desert warzone
coyote this is an   interesting environment   maybe we could learn something here

like survival

that's a good thing to learn   it's a kind of sustainability
but without investment and economic growth and

you mean except for the war industries

yes   and the clashes and the flashes are coming closer together
it's an environmental slide show   whatif whatif I'm the tallest thing
on the prairie   the most standing out person
in the thinkingplace relating to or of or about what's making everybody sick

it's words coyote   words are making people sick   heard words   internalized words
grinding words   selfimpaling words soundingwords
we make ourselves into word creatures then hurl clauses and petunias
aaaaaaa   aaaaa   aaaaaaaCHHHHOOO   pardon me   I'm allergic
to certain words   it's it's a kind of   symptom of
logojamorheia   environmental education is a biiiiiiig part of the jam
marmalade   jelly   preserve   reserve deserve   environmental racism
is a kind of passing on of knowledge   sustainability
talkingabout talkingabout about

is it necessarily a good thing

good   as in essentialist good   or good as in good

bytheway which one of us said that   what
those word molecules on the wind   just there   not sure
we'll find out when it's scripted   versed lined   and kerned   not that
it makes a whole   lotta difference   who or whom

good as in hey this is a beautiful earth and sky
let's look after them

kukwstum nia:wen

6

Reanimating the Universe

Environmental Education and Philosophical Animism

Heesoon Bai

If the doors of perception were cleansed, everything would appear to man as it is: infinite.

—William Blake (1958)

PRELUDE

Arne Johan Vetlesen, in his study of empathy and moral conduct, makes a compelling case that the most destructive kind of crime is not the crime of passion but of *psychic numbing*,[1] the inability to feel, especially the suffering and pain of others. Not being able to perceive and feel the humanity in the other, psychically numbed criminals technicize and industrialize killing to the point that killing becomes just a technical problem. Thus, Vetlesen (1994) reports, at its peak of "productivity" Auschwitz killed "more than twenty thousand Jews in one twenty-hour period" (p. 184). Compare this record with the current alarming rate of species extinction brought on by human beings' rapacious presence on this planet.[2] What we are witnessing is ecocide. Could it be that this ecocide is due to humanity's inability to perceive and feel the intrinsic worth of the other—in this case, nonhuman beings?

If, as Vetlesen argues, there is an essential connection between psychic numbing and the kind of numb indifference that is destructive to the world, this understanding would be a powerful interpretive lens through which to investigate our destructive attitude and treatment of the environment. The thesis that such ecological psychic numbing has become a pervasive condition in modernity has been put forth by a number of thinkers in our time. Thomas Berry speaks of our collective spiritual "autism" with respect to Nature,[3] observing that we have lost the ability to hear Nature. To our "deaf" ears, Nature is silent, and hence is the domain of dead matter. Raimundo Pannikar (1992), in outlining a nonary of priorities that challenge humankind today, names mechanistic and rationalistic worldviews as the topmost impediment to achieving an ecological renewal. He declares that "[n]o ecological renewal of the world will ever succeed until and unless we consider the Earth as our own Body and the body as our own Self"; and that "[t]he Earth is neither an object of knowledge nor of desire"; and that peace with the earth "requires

135

collaboration, synergy, a new awareness" (p. 244). Pannikar calls for a recovery of *animism*. I am profoundly moved by such a call, and this chapter is a response to his call. R. D. Laing (1980) is another thinker who points to the loss of "the *experience* of a bond between our experience and the universe of which it is a part, not apart" (p. 16). This loss precipitates in us an altogether instrumentalist mindset that "recommends [nature's] manipulation, control . . . exploitation and destruction" (p. 16). These atrocities are "not only allowable, not only barred by no prohibition, but gleefully and avidly pursued with self-congratulatory encomiums with the reckless abandon of extreme spiritual depravity" (p. 16). These are strong words, and we must take them like a strong medicine.

How can we reanimate our numbed perceptual consciousness so that the earth appears to us in full sentience and presence? How shall we recover the sensations and feelings in our numbed psyche so that we see, hear, feel the joy and pain, wonder and despair, in experiencing the earth and all its biotic communities? This is the quintessential question and quest that we face as we enter the *Ecozoic Age*, "the period when humans will be present to the planet as participating members of the comprehensive Earth community" (Berry, 1999, p. 8). It is not until we recover the faculty of animated perception, and experiencing the earth as an order of sentient beings that a fundamental change to our heedless and rapacious ways will take place. With this objective in mind, I first inquire how perceptual consciousness came to be de-animated in the first place. How did we become so numb, deaf, and blind when it comes to our perception of and feelings toward the earth community? Here, my aim is not a systematic examination, as such would take me deep and far into scholarship in archaeology and comparative civilization. Rather, I aim to work with a couple of diagnostic pulse points in the history of intellectual ideas, which gain us an insight into how we may address the problem. Such pulse points are, as shown here, Plato and René Descartes, the Grand Architects of western thought. I argue, along with other theorists, that Plato and Descartes made a decisive, immense, and enduring contribution to the creation of the disembedded and disembodied self and its attendant de-animated consciousness in the west.

Based on the insight gained from the first task, my second task is to explore a way to reanimate our disembodied perception. Can we *do* our perception differently so that the world may appear to us in its full intrinsic worth or, to speak in a more metaphysical language, in its numinous presence of Being? In answering this question, I suggest that the key to altering our normally disembodied perception is reversing the habitual superimposition of the conceptual over the perceptual. What could this seemingly esoteric sounding practice mean? A detailed explication of this practice awaits us in this chapter.

My hope is that this chapter helps environmental educators see that their fundamental task is to change, not just the content of our perception, but the very modality of perception. In his essay, *The Doors of Perception*, Aldous Huxley (1977) asks this rhetorical question: "[W]hen 'the sea flows in our veins . . . and the stars are our jewels,' when all things are perceived as infinite and holy, what motive can we have for covetousness or self-assertion, for the pursuit of power or the drearier forms of pleasure?" (pp. 27–28). I add: "and for the ecocide of the Earth?" William Blake (1958) says that "If the doors of perception were cleansed everything would appear to man as it is, infinite" (p. 101). When we can *see* the world as a sacred space, then it is most unlikely that we would violate and exploit the world. The question is: How do we cleanse the doors of perception?

DESCARTES' AUTISM

In my diagnostic palpation of our collective psychic numbing with respect to the earth, I start not with Plato, the customary starting point, but with Descartes. My reason for this order is based on a sound diagnostic principle: Start with observing the symptoms. Descartes is a full-blown symptom of Plato, and by clearly understanding how the Cartesian perception of the world operates and manifests, we shall be able to trace these symptoms back accurately to the defining features of Plato's philosophy that are responsible for the Cartesian perception.

It is true that Descartes bashing is quite fashionable these days. He is blamed for just about all the modern ills. In his defense, we need to see that, although undoubtedly a genius, he, too, was after all a symptom of his time. The idea of the clockwork Mechanical Universe was not his invention alone: It was part of the mechanical worldview then newly rising in 17th-century Europe. Descartes' decisive contribution, however, was his working out an ontology, and an epistemology to accompany it, that gave a philosophical justification for this worldview. In the present context, what I focus on is Descartes' theory of substance. This is how Descartes (1644/1985) defines substance: "By substance we can conceive nothing else than a thing which exists in such a way as to stand in need of nothing beyond itself in order for its existence" (p. 156). For Descartes, as for his and many of our own contemporaries, there are two fundamental substances in this universe: the mental or mind and the physical or matter. According to Descartes' understanding of substance, these two substances are completely independent of each other, meaning that they are separate entities and have nothing in common. In other words, whatever one is, the other is not that. Hence, the mental and the physical are mutually exclusive of each other. Given this absolute separateness of the two substances, Descartes had difficulty explaining how a human being was made up of both substances in a seemingly integrated manner. Such difficulty aside, Descartes' argument that human beings are made of two categorically separate substances was given ready and wide endorsement among leading philosophers of his day.[4]

The most disturbing implication of Descartes' theory of substances is just how degraded matter becomes when it is seen as having nothing to do with mind. When mind, or the mental faculty, is defined as the essence and perfection of humanity, it becomes therefore its most valuable possession. If matter is what mind is not, and mind is the only thing that has intrinsic value, then matter is just a stuff that has no intrinsic value and therefore has only instrumental value. This kind of degraded perception of matter is taken for granted in Descartes' ontology. Just how far Descartes took this degradation is seen in his formal definition of matter. He argued that "[t]he nature of body consists not in weight, hardness, colour, or the like, but simply in extension" (p. 224). What distinguishes matter is that it takes up space! Nothing else. He goes on to say that "[t]here is no real difference between space and corporeal substance" since "the extension constituting the nature of a body is exactly the same as that constituting the nature of a space" (p. 227). What Descartes did, with his theory of matter as extension, is basically stripping the object world of all qualities that make the world colorful and vivacious.

If we were confirmed and serious Cartesians, we would locate color, texture, and so on, in our perception rather than in the objects. Moreover, the qualities that would elicit and evoke our feelings of gratitude, respect, or even reverence, fondness, care, sympathy, and so on, do not belong to, are not part of, the objects themselves. All this has grave implications for the way we relate to and treat the world. When a person looks at his lover and thinks that the beauty that he previously thought belonged to his lover no longer does, and that it is he himself who is constructing his lover's beauty in his mind, would his admiration for his lover's beauty increase or decrease? Chances are that his lover would not appear so beautiful! The old saying that beauty is in the eyes of the beholder becomes a literal truth. To look at the natural world through the Cartesian lens is to see it stripped of sensuous qualities that have the power to profoundly move us emotionally. Berry (1996) rightly discerned the implications of Cartesian ontology when he vehemently cries out:

> In [a] single stroke [Descartes], in a sense, killed the planet and all its living creatures with the exception of the human. The thousandfold voices of the natural world suddenly became

inaudible to the human. The mountains and rivers and the wind and the sea all became mute insofar as humans were concerned. The forests were no longer the abode of an infinite number of spirit presences but were simply so many board feet of lumber to be "harvested" as objects to be used for human benefit. Animals were no longer the companions of humans in the single community of existence. They were denied not only their inherent dignity, but even their rights to habitat. (p. 410)

When I first read this passage, it was as though I suddenly gained some additional senses, by which I could see, hear, and feel, even if still somewhat inarticulately, the intelligible and animated presence of beings around me. The trees outside my window, the blue sky above, the air that I was breathing in and out: All these and everything else that entered my consciousness at that moment seemed to have been transformed from being hardly noticeable, matter-of-factly mundane stuffs to being extraordinarily alive beings, full of life and "magic" of their own. The Cartesian curse was broken for me.

The Cartesian Universe is inanimate. It is *merely* "a senseless, impersonal aggregate of matter in motion" (Kohák, 1984, p. 211). It does not speak to us, we do not hear it; it does not touch us, and we are not moved by it, at least not in the way of *biophilia* (Orr, 1994). Biophilia means the love of and appreciation for Nature or biosphere and all the beings it contains. When we look at the world through a biophilic view, trees, animals, streams, mountains, and all that exists in Nature elicits in us deep feelings of love, gratitude, compassion, care, and respect. We appreciate their aliveness, and are emotionally affected by their presence. We are enlivened and enriched by their flourishing presence. Or we are moved to pity and compassion for their suffering and diminishment. We are even moved to indignation and rage toward those who abuse and harm them. Our love and appreciation for the beings in Nature is not a different kind from the same toward fellow human beings. All earth beings, including humans, are fellow sentient and phenomenal beings. But the Cartesian reduction and devaluation of nonhuman beings does not inspire such emotions in us; rather it leaves us indifferent or, even worse, interested only in their utility to us. In other words, we value beings and things, if at all, for their instrumental worth, but not for their intrinsic worth.

The world we create is the outer reflection of our inner psyche. The Cartesian Universe is an incarnation of the alienated human psyche. When the mental and the physical are seen as two mutually exclusive substances, as Descartes argues, "man" is a divided being, alienated from within. One part is alive, which is the Cartesian *cogito*—mind that thinks, reasons, doubts, imagines, and so on. But the other part, the body, made of matter, has no life of its own. By itself, the body is as good as "dead." Dead flesh is called meat. Thus, the human body is basically no different from meat. It is in this vein that Marvin Minsky, a contemporary artificial intelligence guru, speaks of human beings as computers made of meat![5] Minsky may not be a self-avowed Cartesian, but his view of human beings surely qualifies him to be a Cartesian. In any case, my suspicion is that when a Cartesian looks at the world, it is not quite alive—not quite animated and enchanted—because he is looking at the world through eyes that are not animated and enchanted. Who are these Cartesians? They are *us*—most of us, more or less, insofar as we think and see that the world is largely made up of insentient and inanimate things and objects. And an important point of connection I am making here is that how the world appears to us has all to do with the state of our consciousness, or the quality of our being. In the same way that, to a tired person, the world looks tired and tiring, to a disenchanted person, the world appears disenchanted and inanimate. This should give us a strong clue as to what we must do to restore a vital and sacred perception of the world: We need to recover our own animism within (Bai, 2001). We need to become completely animated in our eyes, ears, skin, and so on, until every fiber of our flesh is charged with the vital energy of our carnality. However, there are serious obstacles to our becoming more animated. In the next section, I name the chief obstacle as the dominance of our conceptualizing mind, and trace its legacy to Plato's project.

PLATO'S LOGOCENTRICISM

If, as Berry accused, Descartes delivered a decisive last blow on Nature with a sledgehammer of philosophical argument, the first blow actually came much earlier—many millennia prior. Our perception of Nature had been losing its animation for a long time, and by the time Descartes arrived on the scene, Nature was already a reduced thing, stripped of her animating power. When did this de-animation start? Archaeological evidence, as interpreted by scholars like Marija Gimbustas (1991), seems to suggest that the beginning lies in prehistory, probably at the transition from a matristic to a patriarchal civilization, which is considerably earlier than the beginning of ancient civilization, such as Classical Greece. But because prehistory leaves no discursive texts behind, and because I am interested in philosophical arguments of the textual kind for my present analysis, I must turn to historical philosophical texts, for example, in Classical Greece. It is in Plato, the patriarch of western thought, that we indeed find an incisive philosophical argument that condemns the sensuous and animistic perception of the world that is achieved through the Homeric poetic consciousness. The Homeric poets appeal to the sensuous experience of the listener, and induces in the latter a trance-like hypnotic state in which the listener experiences an emotional identification or merging with what was presented to them through the poet's skillful performance. Tragic death stories enacted by the poet on stage left the audience weeping uncontrollably. Fearful stories inspired terrifying horrors in shrieking audiences, and so on. Plato's objection to the workings of the Homeric poetic consciousness is that the latter is not conducive to individuals developing their rational and analytic thinking. For the latter, one needs emotional dis-identification with the materials presented to one, and hence, requires a way to step outside the content of one's thoughts, perceptions, and feelings, and to coolly and calmly analyze the content. Plato's goal was to create a rational, as opposed to emotional, and a conceptual, as opposed to poetic, subjectivity. Plato's program was to create philosopher the thinker, as opposed to poet the bard. In short, Plato was heading a major epistemological revolution that changed the very texture, tone, and color of human consciousness: from the sensuous, emotive, empathic *participatory mind or consciousness*[6] to the conceptual, abstract, and analytic rational mind or discursive consciousness. Ever since Plato, we have been under the spell, not of the sensuous, but of the discursive.[7]

In *The Republic*, Plato (1965) waged a war against the Homeric poets, arguing that "all poetry, from Homer onwards, consists in representing a semblance of its subject, whatever it may be, including any kind of human excellence, with no grasp of the reality" (p. 331). When Plato speaks of reality, however, we have to know that he has a very particular qualification as to what counts as reality. What we encounter here is Plato's ontology (the question of what is real) and axiology (the question of what is worthy) that devalue the sensible, intuitive, and emotive, and privilege the conceptual, logical, and the abstract. To wit, that which is *perceptible* to the senses and arouses emotions is not real; only that which is *intelligible* to the rational faculty of mind is real. In other words, what we can know through the senses (and feelings and intuitions, too) is not real; whereas what we can know through the intellect—the faculty of conceptualization—is real. This is an astonishing notion that, we can well imagine, Plato had a hard time selling to his fellow Athenians who were still quite steeped in the tradition of the Homeric participatory consciousness. This kind of consciousness is prone to merge with anything presented to them through poetic rendition. Imagine being told that what you thought was very real was, in fact, unreal. What more devaluing can one face than being invalidated about one's sense of reality? Axiology is not separate from ontology. And ontology depends crucially on epistemology (the question of what one knows and how one knows), and therefore, axiology depends on epistemology. Change the ways of knowing, and we have changed both what is real and what is valuable. What Plato wanted was nothing less than a complete revolution of human consciousness, a radical turning away from the sensuous (sense-based understanding) to the intelligible (concept-based, discursive understanding) as the basis of knowing and acting.[8]

In Plato's appraisal, all arts, including poetry, are devoted to rendering matters perceptible to our senses and emotions. Hence, the arts are condemned as a shackle that prevents us from attaining our ultimate freedom, which lies on a higher plane of existence (the "noumenal" world). The well-known Allegory of the Cave in Plato's *The Republic* is an allegory of this situation of human entrapment. Humans are seen as literally trapped in their bodies and put under the spell of the senses. Philosophy alone is able to free the humans by opening their mind's eye, as it were, to the Real or the Supersensible. Given this notion, it is no wonder that the arts were considered inferior to philosophy. Plato explains that artists' and poets' specialty is simulation (*mimesis*), the art of presenting the subject matter in pictures and poetic words so as to arouse our senses and emotions. What is wrong with this? The Platonic answer, to put it succinctly, is that we cannot be independent and critical thinking persons when our senses and feelings are aroused and ready to do their trickery of distracting us from seeing and understanding things for what they *really* are, as well as distorting how they appear. Plato is determined to expose this deceptive artistry: "Strip what the poet has to say of its poetical coloring, and I think you must have seen what it comes to in plain prose. It is like a face which was never really handsome, when it has lost the fresh bloom of youth" (p. 331).

But, why, I have to ask, would anyone want to see the world without the "poetic coloring" which is like a "fresh bloom of youth"? Without such animating coloring, the world would appear drab and dreary: in short, a depressing place, would it not? Analogously, would one exchange one's color perception for black-and-white perception? Would any one in his or her right mind go for Plato's recommended perception of the world, one bleached of color and muted of sound (as well as drained of other sensorial qualities)? Why would we choose sensory and emotional deprivation? Plato's promise is that this sacrifice is made for a far more substantial reward. Plato has promised the potential followers of his epistemological revolution membership in the most powerful kingdom there is: that of Ideas, where there is no change, decay, and death, and there is only unchanging, imperishable Being, in short, Immortality. The way of the senses is perishable. Who can resist this incredible bargain of sacrificing the mere "poetic coloring" of the *phenomenal* world for the *noumenal* world of unchanging Truth, Beauty, Goodness? Insofar as all of us mere mortals are fearful of our mortal destiny of decay and death, and yearn for immortality, we are indeed tempted by Plato's persuasion. What we need to give up seems minimal compared to what we will gain.

Still, it must have been incredibly difficult to dissuade the common folk in Plato's Athens from giving up the way of the sensuous, which was the source of their feeling vitally alive and robustly real. Indeed, they were being continually well-fed and sustained on the rich diet of Homeric poetry. Plato alludes to a "long-standing quarrel between poet and philosopher" and mentions "countless tokens of this old antagonism" (p. 336). A long-standing quarrel implies that poets had been formidable matches for philosophers. The power of poetic reverie can easily rival the power of critical intellect, and the two wrangle interminably for an uncertain victory. Thinking like a strategist, I would say that, in light of this equal match of strengths, a way to win the battle without even needing to enter it would be most expedient. Hence (here, I am reading into Plato), Plato propagated the notion that the mimetic consciousness is developmentally inferior to the philosophical one. Poets for Plato are like children: in need of growing up. And being in the constant company of the poets (and, we could add, using today's lingo, "artsy" folks in general) infantilizes us. Here is Plato's advice: "Instead of behaving like a child who goes on shrieking after a fall and hugging the wounded part, we should accustom the mind to set itself at once to raise up the fallen and cure the hurt, banishing lamentation with a healing touch" (p. 336). Indeed, are not these words very familiar to all of us? Have most of us not heard them repeated to us at home, at school, and in playgrounds throughout our childhood? And many of us have repeated them back, in many variations, to our crying children and hurting students.[9]

Plato's stern advice contains two implications. One, the participatory consciousness rich in empathic emotions is childish. Two, the feeling way of life wounds us easily. Denying feelings and emotions and putting up a brave front with the help of the distancing rational mind seems to have been Plato's solution to the suffering that we sensitive and vulnerable humans are so prone to in life through change, decay, corruption, and demise. It seems that Plato equated learning to deny or suppress feelings and devaluing emotions through cultivating an abstract and discursive mind with humanity's growing up and entering adulthood. This is truly unfortunate. To connect back to the notion of psychic numbing that inspired me to write this chapter, I am suggesting that Plato's condemnation of poets and the poetic (participatory) consciousness, and his call for an epistemological revolution have had a profound influence on the direction of our civilization.[10] Hindsight is often perfect 20/20. In retrospect of history, we know better: The worst we can do to humanity is to suppress its capacity to feel and be empathic, for such is the *soul* of humanity. Destroy the soul, which creates a requisite condition for psychic numbing, and we can easily become inhuman, as Vetlesen, whom I quoted at the beginning of this chapter, amply demonstrates in his case study of the Holocaust. Extending Vetlesen's thesis, I am also suggesting that the soul destruction and consequent psychic numbing would also lead to the Holocaust of biotic communities. The soul destruction seems to precipitate soil destruction.[11] To note, I am not against Plato's project of promoting critical intellect and independent thinking. Critical intellect is a wonderful gift to humanity. My objection is to the privileging of critical intellect over and above, thereby devaluing another vital and precious gift to humanity: feelings. Moreover, I also object to the dualistic thinking that categorically separates intellect from feeling as if these are two separate entities or categories. We can think feelingly, and we can feel thoughtfully. For the well-being of our Planet and Humanity, we must cultivate this capacity more and more.

THE SPELL OF THE DISCURSIVE

From the colossal and lasting influence of Plato, a legacy that has endured for more than two millennia, we must conclude that his campaign for privileging the conceptual and discursive consciousness was quite successful. The Homeric empathy-based participatory consciousness has been largely supplanted under the philosophical persuasion of Plato and his successors. Today, in the spreading global civilization of late- or hyper-modernity (Borgmann, 1993), we all are, East and west, everywhere, children of Plato and Descartes. Our consciousness is dominated by the spell of the discursive, and by the time we are out of childhood and through formal schooling, most of us have largely disposed of the animated sensuous perception of the world. Many of us may recall how in our childhood the world seemed like an enchanted place, not because anything extraordinary and spectacular happened, not because we felt we were very powerful and could make things happen at will, but because we could feel the pulse of life and mystery of being in every thing and being that surrounded us. I recall one of my own childhood scenes. The very air that touched my skin was supercharged with an electrified sense of life; the droning, buzzing symphony of life from all the critters (especially the cicadas) inhabiting the grassy hill as I lay half-buried in the grass that summer's morning, many decades ago, was simply intoxicating and made me almost too dizzy to get up. And how breathtakingly blue that sky looked as I peered out of the grass walls pressed against the contours of my small body that made a depression in the grass. The blueness was so vivid and alive, and so inviting that I just wanted to dive in and disappear into the vast blueness. Today, I still hear the symphony of life, but only faintly most of the time, as though I am overhearing it from the next room, through a closed door. The air thinned out, too, and now hardly throbs. The sky is still blue and beautiful but I do not get that rush just from beholding it. Instead, I make a few pleasantries, to myself and to others, about the beautiful blue sky.

The spell of the discursive gets thicker daily. Everywhere, the abstract, conceptual, logical, and symbolic order of the world makes an increasingly larger claim on our consciousness. I invite the reader to closely examine his or her consciousness. What is it filled with most of the time? Ideas, concepts, notions, views, beliefs, stories, questions, arguments, plans, lists (most of all, interminably, to-do lists, shopping lists)—mostly in the form of words and numbers. One thought after another, they arise thick and fast, constantly and endlessly occupying the mind. Our mind is so preoccupied by the stuff of the symbolic order that there is hardly any room left for anything else, like *fully* seeing, hearing, feeling what meets our senses immediately, that is, unmediated, in the moment. When reality is heavily mediated by the symbolic and discursive order, we lose, however momentarily or minutely, the sense of Being, of Reality—that intensely "real," vivid, existential feel of being alive and seeing everything to be throbbingly alive. When we are gripped by such a sense, we often exclaim: "Unbelievable!" Indeed, inadvertently we are expressing the truth: that this experience of Being is not a matter of *beliefs*; that is, it does not belong to the conceptual, symbolic, and discursive order. The more our consciousness becomes entrenched in the conceptual and discursive order, the greater is our loss of this existential vivacity and of animism. When we become so entrenched in the discursive order that the conceptual functions as the real, what we have is, of course, *reification*: taking the abstract for the real. There are many common English expressions that describe this situation: "mistaking the map for the road" or "eating the menu instead of the food." This is not to say that reading state-of-the-art maps is not useful or very exciting, or that lavishly worded and pictured menus are not very handy or can nicely work up the appetite. Personally, I love maps and menus. But we would not want to substitute reading the road map for seeing what is on the road; or substitute reading the menu description and gazing at the picture for eating a real apple pie. And yet, incredulously, this substitution happens massively and constantly in our lives. As *homo symbolicus*, especially in the age of Media, we eat and breathe reification. And a diet rich in reification does not nourish us, and leaves us still hungry and thirsty—for the real.

Take the case of money. Money is an idea, a concept, as Derek Rasmussen (2004) reminds us. In itself it is nothing other than colored bits of paper, scraps of metal, or more commonly now, rapidly moving number figures in ones and zeros in cyberspace. Yet, as we are fond of saying, money rules the world. Money is fast becoming the ultimate human value, one that supercedes all others: therein lies the sickness of our age, our civilization. Complete monetization of the world and our lives, toward which our culture and society are rapidly evolving, spells the ultimate reification. That people should almost imperceptibly lose their health, happiness, relationships, friendships, connections with the land, and even their actual lives, for the gain of money, should tell us just how thick and sick the spell of the discursive that has been cast over us is. The story of King Midas' touch is an allegory of the deadly power of the discursive. The greedy King Midas makes a wish for everything he touches to turn into solid gold; then, in an unthinking moment, he affectionately embraces his beloved daughter, and to his absolute horror, the daughter turns into a lifeless golden statue.

Reification can de-animate us, in the way Midas turned his beloved daughter into a statue, by cutting us off from our source of vitality: the immediate, that is, in-the-moment, fully embodied, sensuous contact and connection with Being. The discursive content of the mind abstracts us from the in-the-moment sensuous experience that can have a most vivifying, enlivening effect on us. It is when we are fully and completely present in the moment to the phenomenal-material world that we are able to tap into what may be called the psycho-physical[12] energy of the universe. The latter is known in classical Chinese philosophy and practice as *qi*. Again, the fascinating theoretical inquiry into the nature of *qi* aside, what is of importance to us in the present exploration is the fact that when we become fully present to the sensuous reality before us, we feel extraordinarily awake and alive.

The world seen through this animated consciousness of *biophilia* is a very alive and enchanted place—a place that we want to fall in love with, rejoice in, celebrate, adore, hold sacred, and worship. In comparison, the world seen through the symbolically mediated and processed discursive consciousness is, however intriguing and stimulating to the intellect, pale and relatively lifeless. It thus fails to awaken the *Eros* in us that unleashes the urge to adore and protect, love and care. This is not to say that having a discursive consciousness is not useful to us. Rather, its over-usefulness has been the problem. We as a civilization have gone too far in the direction of the conceptual and the discursive. The result is a technologically very advanced engineering civilization that can divert a watercourse to erect a dam and blast a mountain to put in a highway but is unable to hear the water stream's love songs and the mountain's epic poems. To be able to think with concepts abstractly, logically, rationally is a useful thing, but not if it seriously interferes with the flow of empathy and sympathy in our intercourse with the world. The lasting legacy of Plato's epistemological revolution has been precisely this undermining of our ability to feel and commune with the physical world, resulting in varying degrees of psychic numbing with respect to the earth.

REANIMATION OF THE SENSES

It is not as though the spell of the discursive that Plato and others cast upon us stopped the operation of the senses. Our senses continue to operate and function: we still see and hear, feel and taste. But the mere fact that our physiological senses are working as they should tells us little about the qualitative phenomenological differences that exist in perception. The *phenomenological* quality of perception is what is at stake here. The discursive spell has thoroughly captivated perception to the point that much of our perception is an abstract conceptual exercise that bypasses the more sensuous experience of perception. Consider for a moment how we normally see. As our quick and sweeping gaze falls upon objects, we see "chair," "mug," "flower," "lamp," "sky". . . . Click, click. . . . Each perceptual frame, already labeled, flashes across our mental screens at lightning speed. This is the so-called pattern recognition, about which cognitive science theorizes endlessly. Besides these simple naming labels, our conceptual mind also "sees" use-and-profit labels in things and beings we encounter. Upon seeing a rose, I think: "Oh, what a nice centerpiece that would make for my table!" Upon seeing the rain outside, I think: "What a bother! The rain is spoiling the picnic!" In other words, we visually process things to recognize and label what they are (and what they are not) and what they mean to us in terms of utility, convenience, or other purposes we have in mind. In this sense, as David Appelbaum (1995) explains, sight has become a discursive exercise of comparative judgment. What does not happen is the more sensuous perception wherein we do not just conceptually process but attentionally engage with the sensory input. That the latter has a profound effect on the level of animism or vitality is a key point that I now wish to present and explain.

Let us start with a common observation: We experience fatigue when our mind is preoccupied and chased around by thoughts. There is no physical exertion, and yet we become very enervated when we experience mental exhaustion. Deep sleep is restful and restorative precisely because we are freed from this energy-draining activity of thought chasing, or more accurately, being chased by thoughts. Similar to deep sleep, a *thought-less* (which does not mean "thoughtless" in English) meditation is another way to experience restoration of energy. But how is it that the activity of thought, that is, conceptualization, is energy-draining? I find Appelbaum's phenomenological explanation most compelling and coherent with my experience. Appelbaum (1995) points to the vital source of animal, organic energy: the body, the fleshy "organic fold" that belongs to the unity of the phenomenal world. Using the figure of blind Sampson at the pillar, Appelbaum illustrates what it means to return to body, and therefore to the phenomenal world:

> Blind Sampson at the pillar is a man returned to his body, to corporeal existence. Inhabiting his organic fold, he no longer is a "thinking substance" but one that *resonates* with environmental tempos affecting him. His is a temporal existence, which means a tempoed one. As his hands grope to press the column, he gropes in his hands for the pressure of the *attention*. To accomplish this feat, he must occupy time *present*. The way time pulses in his fingertips is in tempo with the way it pulses through his whole body. Samson has returned to time from space that is separation, from distance that is *indifference*, cause and effect, dispersion, multiplicity. He has returned to the simple *unity* of life in time, in accordance with time, life no longer divided by desires, thoughts, and projects. (p. 30, italics added)

We can contrast what Appelbaum says about matter with Descartes' conception of matter. Descartes (1644/1985) defines *matter* as that which occupies space (extension). Space, however, creates distance and, hence, separation and, as noted above, indifference, and so on. It is time *present*, yielded by attention, which phenomenologically transforms inanimate and indifferent Cartesian matter into the body that pulses with life energy. Matter (which is etymologically related to *matrix*, *mater*, the womb) is the source of energy. The phenomenal world of matter of which one's individual body is a "fold," like a crease or bend in the fabric, is the source of our psycho-physical energy. But our access to this source of energy, which Appelbaum descriptively calls the "return," is not automatic. Just the fact of "having" the body does not guarantee this access. The access is attained through embodied awareness based on the practice of attention and presence.

What obstructs, distracts, and complicates our access to the source is—no surprise here—our habitual conceptualization. Habitual thought construction, "cut off from its organic context [the body]," disembodies us, that is, distracts, disengages, and abstracts us, from carnal awareness. We are, as it were, pushed out of the fleshy organic fold, which is the source of our energy, and we become drained of organic vitality. The animating, electrifying life-energy—*qi*, if you like—does not suffuse our being. Indifference sets in. Psychic numbness or indifference invades us. All these are phenomenological observations that can be easily validated by an individual who pays close attention to the quality of his or her experience. For example, notice how disembodied we become, that is, how we lose touch with the living reality of our bodies when we are engrossed in thought. Body awareness falls below the threshold of consciousness. This is a familiar phenomenon: When we are engrossed in reading a novel, we may not register sensations of discomfort in the cramped body. When we are engrossed in thinking while driving, we manage to autopilot around on familiar roads without being aware of consciously seeing anything. We wonder later when we come back to consciousness: "*Who* was driving the car?"

How do we interrupt habitual thought construction and return to immediacy? How do we return ourselves to the source of vitality? This is the work of attention. Attention breaks and stops the trance of thought construction, or "the rational automatism" (Appelbaum, 1995, p. 17), and returns us to the "present sensory experience" (p. 22). Calling this attentional work the *stop*, Appelbaum explained:

> To come *to* experience is always to come *from* a disembodied, disengaged state of thought construction. The first is the unhinging of the second, and the stop is the hinge. The stop is not the negation of movement. It is movement itself, a form of movement purer than that of body, mind, or feeling alone. It is movement away from entrapment of automatic and associative thought, just as it is movement toward an embodied awareness. The stop is a movement of transition. (p. 24)

What is the experience of the *stop* like? We have been talking about the impediment to experience, namely the habitual thought construction, and have indicated that a stop to the operation of thought construction is necessary for a more embodied experience. But what is this embodied experience like?

Again, Appelbaum has many insights to offer us. The *stop* halts the continuous, automatic leave-taking of the "percipient energy" that fuels "a conceptual frame that moment-by-moment constructs the world" (p. 77). In other words, "[t]he stop neutralizes a tendency of percipient energy to animate intellectual categories through which events are viewed" (p. 80). How I understand the explanation here is that thought-construction consumes energy, and takes this energy from the source—the body, which leaves the body so much more depleted. Put it another way, when the percipient energy no longer "escapes the fleshy folds of the body . . . it energizes the network of relations constituting the organism" (p. 77). Two points can be made about what happens here. First, feeling requires energy, and thus when there is no continual siphoning of percipient energy, more abundant and richer feelings become available. In other words, *perception becomes sensate or affective.* For example, eyes do not just see and record what is in their visual field, which is what objectification is. Objectification is indifferent seeing (hearing, touching, etc.). Seeing animated by percipient energy, however, becomes visual love-making. To see and hear the world through the *stop* is to make love to it. *Eros* regained.

The second point I make concerns the naturalistic nature, in contrast to the moralistic nature, of love that the stop engenders in us. What do I mean by this? In environmental education, as in moral education, there is an overwhelming tendency to prescribe and command respect, care, love, or what have you: "We ought to respect (protect, conserve, care about, love . . .) the environment." Invariably, we assume a moralistic tone. Apart from the usual annoyance and weariness that such a tone provokes in its listeners, the real problem is its ineffectiveness. If people could change just by being sternly but caringly told what to do or how to be, then learning and transformation would pose no problems and challenges whatsoever. Unfortunately or fortunately, this does not happen. At least, not usually. People are not programmable robots. They do not change just by being told, urged, scolded, or even threatened. Even if changes occur under external suggestion or duress, this creates more problems than it solves. It cripples the psyche and makes relational social life miserable. The solution lies elsewhere than moralistic persuasion. The solution is to learn to truly become the kind of consciousness that embodies respect, compassion, care, and love. Let the eyes, ears, mouth, skin . . . make love to the world! Transformation at the base of consciousness and at the heart of being is what we as educators are after here. It is not unless and until our whole being becomes respectfully and lovingly relational to the world that we can truly practice respect, love, and so on. And again, being relational is not the usual social, moral practice that tries to bind individual egos by obligations and considerations of various social norms. Rather, as Appelbaum shows, what we do is return to the *place* where all there is is relationality. This is the place of the *stop*:

> The return is to an organic, archaic level of experience. It is a return from a constructional, conceptual mind that predominates in the daily round. The return involves dwelling in the body as awareness while face-to-face with entrenched impulses to take flight. (p. 21)

Can we see this return as a critically important educational project today? Yes: very critical and very important. Although space does not permit me to fully explore the topic, this being a book that addresses the education community, I feel the necessity to at least put in a couple strong thoughts I have been having on education for participatory consciousness.

BEGIN HERE, AGAIN AND AGAIN

First of all, we start with an understanding that we humans have the native capacity for animism, that is, the capacity to be fully alive in the way that we sensuously participate in the phenomenological world of biotic communities. I believe that we are, in today's jargon, "hard-wired" for the capacity for participatory consciousness. It is a birthright of every child. The question of education then becomes not of how to create and inject a participatory consciousness into children (or anyone) but of how to protect, nurture, and expand the capacity that already exists and is ready to engage fully and grow, so that the capacity can manifest as full-blown experience and ability. The question also becomes one of asking how we may be vigilant and careful about conditions, circumstances, and structures that tend to dismiss, marginalize, "numb," and destroy this native capacity. Like the Hippocrates' injunction, we should think of education first and foremost in terms of not doing harm. Do not compromise and destroy children's native capacity for participatory consciousness—some call it the "aboriginal mind"—by forcing on them early, in the name of modern science education or progressive education, the mechanical worldview (Bai, 2001) that objectifies the world and sees it in mechanistic and quantitative terms. The initial damage to the Indigenous mind would be difficult to recover from and compensate for, even with high-quality environmental education. I feel very strongly about this point I am making here, having been put through a modernist education that nearly destroyed my own capacity for participatory consciousness or aboriginal mind. I am in recovery.

Second, recalling the connection I mentioned earlier among soil (earth), soul (the sensitive, empathic quality), and sole (the body and senses), I suggest that we provide ample opportunities formally or informally for students to make these connections themselves *experientially*. As it stands, in most conventional schooling experience, there is a relative paucity of opportunity for such connections. Our education marginalizes the embodied connection to soil, soul, and sole, by overemphasizing the discursive practices that not only crowd out such connections but also actively dismiss and discourage them. For example, conventionally, soil is considered worthless and dirty, and people who live close to soil are considered "primitive." Jobs that involve a direct contact with soil are less prestigious and important than jobs that require "brainpower." Given this bias, no wonder, then, there is little opportunity and encouragement in the curriculum to connect with soil: to study, work, worship, play, or, even more importantly, just *be with* soil. Why not, for example, grow vegetables and flowers in school gardens, keep beehives in schools, keep compost, and adopt a nearby stream, pond, or forest? There are 100 other projects and activities we can undertake in the way of study and practice to increase our contact and connections with soil. And more importantly, why are we not including in school curriculum a lot more time and mindful opportunities for students to be outdoors in direct contact with soil (and rocks, trees, water . . .) and be more curious and conscious about their connection to the earth? As David Orr (1994) condemns, "indoorism," and I would add, "cerebralization," are the mainstay for current schooling. It is not for lack of ideas that the studies and practices that connect us to soil are not taken up seriously but for the lack of understanding and recognition that these are critically important and worthy as educational objectives, and that a priority must be given to them on par with literacy and numeracy. In fact, if we were to take the contact and connection with soil very seriously, then we will have to be changing, and would be changing, the whole paradigm of schooling from the current goal—although no school mission statements put it quite this way—of producing workers who will perpetuate the current commodity consumption-based, corporatist, capitalist industrial civilization that is so destructive to the earth.

Recall the previously mentioned understanding that when soul goes, soil goes, and what connects soil to soul is, most prominently and not exclusively, the sole of feet that make contact with the ground. I suggest that this threefold connection is mutual—hence, interconnected—and not linear. Destruction of soil (biotic communities) impacts the viability of soul understood here as the sensitive, empathic, and resonating part of humanity. Use it or lose it: One's capacity and ability for something does not develop if it is not called on regularly to exercise itself in response. Our eyesight would dim and eventually disappear if there is no visible world to see. Likewise, with the diminished presence of the biotic communities all around and all their members in our lives, our soul's capacity atrophies. Species extinction is not just an event outside humanity. Part of our own humanity diminishes as other sentient beings disappear, leaving the earth less teeming with diversity of life. Hence, soil renewal is soul renewal, and every mindful contact we make with the ground restores humanity. Walking is not merely a locomotion practice—for those who cannot afford to drive a car!—that gets us from Point A to Point B. Walking is a sacred act of cultivating and expressing our deepest humanity through the embodied contact with the earth. Thich Nhat Hanh (1996), Buddhist monk and Nobel Peace Prize nominee, says it very simply: "Walking *mindfully* on the Earth can restore our peace and harmony, and it can restore the Earth's peace and harmony as well. . . . Whether the Earth is beautiful, fresh, and green, or arid and parched depends on our way of walking. When we practice walking meditation beautifully, we massage the Earth with our feet and plant seeds of joy and happiness with each step" (p. 15, italics added). This passage brings me to my third and final comment and suggestions about educational practice.

Walking is a supreme practice with many physical, emotional, and spiritual benefits, and I recommend it most highly as a main educational practice. Coincidentally (perhaps, I should mean, "not accidentally"), "pedagogy," the art and science of teaching, has its Greek origin in the meaning of "walking," as *paidagogos* were the trusted slaves in ancient Greek households whose job was to walk the master's children to school and also assist them with instructions.[13] However, going back to Hanh's passage, the most important concept here is not so much "walking" as "mindfully." Walking can be done in all manners, including manners that are hurtful, hateful, arrogant, disrespectful, and so on. It is not the activity *per se* that can do the great work of connecting us to the earth and reanimating us. It is the question of how: With what sort of consciousness do we approach and conduct whatever it is that we are doing or not doing? Curriculum designers and pedagogues (teachers) are prone to miss this critical point; so are students and parents. They think learning primarily in terms of particular subject matters, content materials, and learning activities. They ask: "So, *what* do we have to study, learn, and do to save the planet?" Mindfulness means the participatory consciousness of receptivity, embodied sensitivity, openness, and fully being present to what is here and now. And in the tradition of Buddhist meditation that Hanh (1996) and others practice, conscious breathing is the main "tool" with which we attain the consciousness of mindfulness.[14] Given just how foundational mindfulness is as a consciousness that supports our re-animation project, would it not make sense to practice it as the most basic—more basic than reading, writing, and math (and any other basics that the current culture supports)? The sign over Plato's Academy in Athens is said to read: "Let no man ignorant of geometry enter." My school, if I were to establish one, would have a different sign: "Breathe mindfully and enter."

It is the habit of our mind to take our perception to be the objective fact of the world. We project the content and the mode of our consciousness onto the world, and we then enact our projection as if that is the objective reality given to us. To the disenchanted, de-animated, objectified consciousness, the world is a place with corresponding characteristics. We then act out our perception and destroy the world, backwardly justifying that this soulless, machine-like world exists instrumentally as resources for our consumption. But to the consciousness that has been animated, that is, reawakened to its embodied participation in the world, this world appears numinously splendid and enchanted. St. Francis of Assisi (1182–1226) was one such consciousness:

> *Such love does*
> *the sky now pour,*
> *that whenever I stand in a field.*
>
> *I have to wring out the light*
> *when I get*
> *home.*
> (cited in Ladinsky, 1996, p. 48)

Rumi (1207–1273) was another:

> *On a day*
> *when the wind is perfect,*
> *the sail just needs to be open and the world is full of beauty.*
> *Today is such a*
> *day.*
>
> *My eyes are like the sun that makes promises;*
> *the promise of life*
> *that it always*
> *keeps*
> *each morning.*
>
> *The living heart gives to us as does that luminous sphere,*
> *both caress the earth with great*
> *tenderness.*
>
> *There is a breeze that can enter the soul.*
> *This love I know plays a drum. Arms move around me;*
> *who can contain their self before my beauty?*

Peace is wonderful,
but ecstatic dance is more fun, and less narcissistic;
gregarious He makes our lips.

On a day when the wind is perfect,
the sail just needs to open
and the love starts.

Today is such
a day
(cited in Ladinsky, 1996, p. 79)

NOTES

1. This term, *psychic numbing*, was coined by Robert J. Lifton in the context of his study of Hiroshima survivors. I came across this term for the first time in Vetlesen's work (1994), *Perception, Empathy, and Judgment,* and have since made it a central concept in my work about moral perception and action. To briefly explain this concept: Psychic numbing is the inability to feel and hence be affected by the sight of pain and horror associated with death, especially associated with brutality and injustice. The pain and horror is too great to bear for the witnessing person whose psyche then shuts itself off from the painful reality. In other words, it goes numb. In the context of Lifton's study, psychic numbing was a regular symptom among war and atrocity survivors, such as Hiroshima bombing survivors, Holocaust survivors, and Vietnam War veterans. I am extending the application of this notion to the context of our relationship to the biotic community and all its constituent sentient beings, which, of course, includes human beings.

2. According to Tuxill's (1999) report: "the natural or 'background' rate of extinction appears to be about 1–10 species a year. By contrast, scientists estimate that extinction rates have accelerated this century to at least 1,000 species per year. These numbers indicate we now live in a time of mass extinction—a global evolutionary upheaval in the diversity and composition of life on Earth" (p. 97). The estimate that I quote here is from nearly 10 years ago.

3. http://www.natcath.com/NCR_Online/archives/081001/081001a.htm

4. Just to name a few such thinkers: Leibniz in Germany, Malebranche in France, Spinoza in Holland.

5. http://content.cdlib.org/view?docId=ft338nb20q&chunk.id=d0e4891

6. Again, space does not permit me to explicate this notion of participatory mind or consciousness fully here; even so, a briefest possible explanation is due. Rational mind sees itself separate from, and stands outside of, reality it perceives and comprehends. As such, rational mind is basically an alienated consciousness in that it does not experience feelings of merging, uniting, intimacy, and collaboration with what it perceives: that is, feelings of oneness are not present. Participatory mind is the polar opposite to the rational mind in that it merges with its objects of perception and comprehension, and in the process, it feels intimacy and co-emergence. Skolimowski (1995) expresses it like this: "In beholding we are articulating. In articulating we are co-creating. In the act of articulation mind and reality merge; reality becomes an aspect of mind" (p. 31).

7. Throughout this chapter, I use the word *discursive* to mean both "pertaining to logic" and "pertaining to concepts." In my usage, "discursive," "conceptual," "logical," "rational," "abstract" are all related as cognates, and are used more or less interchangeably.

8. For an extended discussion of the psychology of poetic consciousness in the Homeric tradition and Plato's epistemological revolution, see Eric Havelock's (1963) *Preface to Plato.*

9. One variation I witness today in the academy is devaluation of arts-based and arts-related qualitative research. The latter is seen as being soft and "fluffy," and not hard and rigorous. My graduate students worry about appearing like "flakes" if they do any research that smacks of artistic expressions. As in Plato's epistemology, there is a hierarchy of academic research. At the top sits quantitative research

that deals with hard stuffs, like numbers, facts, and data. Empirical researches that work with hard data command the best attention and biggest funding. At the bottom of the hierarchy are, ironically (given Plato's legacy), conceptual researches that do not gather and work with data, like most of the researches in Philosophy of Education. Qualitative researches that gather data, even if of the subjectivist kind, as in interviews, fare better.

10. I do not wish to be misread and misunderstood here. Inasmuch as I single out Plato as a thinker who has had decisive and long-lasting influences, I do not mean to make him out to be solely responsible for shaping a civilization that privileges the intellect. Although we do not know the origin of Plato's Idealism (some suspect that it is related to Pythagoras), I doubt if he was alone, or unique, in struggling against the Homeric poets and their hold on the education and culture of the citizens. If he was alone, his call for demoting the poets as educators would have fallen onto deaf ears, ignored. This did not seem to have been the case. Skolimouwski interprets that Plato represents a transitional figure in the discursive trend from Socrates to Aristotle. By the time we come to Aristotle, systematization of intellectual knowledge becomes a strongly established pursuit.

11. Jungian analyst Robert Johnson (1987) mentions the connection between "soul" and "sole" (of feet): that the soul enters through the soles. My further elaboration on this takes me to connect "soul," "sole," and "soil." Our sentient connection to the earth (soil) is through our sensuous and empathic capacity (soul) that makes an embodied contact (sole) with the earth.

12. The word, *psycho-physical*, connotes nondualism of the mental and the physical. One of the most important contributions from Chinese culture and civilization is the philosophy of *qi*, vital energy or breath. According to this philosophy, the entire universe, that encompasses not only the material but also the psychical and spiritual realms, is composed of *qi*, and understands the multiplicity of phenomena and diversity of beings as due to modulations of *qi*.

13. Perhaps it is no coincidence that many *world teachers*, such as Socrates, Aristotle, Buddha, Confucius, to name a few, were almost constant and long-distance walkers, and often they conducted their teaching while walking with their students.

14. Space does not permit me to explain the more technical aspects of mindfulness practice and conscious breathing, and how such practice alters the consciousness. However, currently available are a whole range of mindfulness research studies and its applications, and interested readers are advised to do the literature search. This is a fast growing area of research. I myself have written about mindfulness and its application to education (Bai, 1997, 1999, 2001, 2002, 2003a, 2003b 2004, 2006).

REFERENCES

Appelbaum, D. (1995). *The stop*. Albany: State University of New York Press.

Bai, H. (1997). Ethics and aesthetics are one: The case of zen aesthetics. *Canadian Review of Art Education*, *24*(2), 37–52.

Bai, H. (1999). Decentering the ego-self and releasing of the care-consciousness. *Paideusis*, *12*(2), 5–18.

Bai, H. (2001). Challenge for education: Learning to value the world intrinsically. *Encounter*, *14*(1), 4–16.

Bai, H. (2002). Zen and the art of intrinsic perception: A case of haiku. *Canadian Review of Art Education*, *28*(1), 1–24.

Bai, H. (2003a). Learning from zen arts: A lesson in intrinsic valuation. *Journal of the Canadian Association for Curriculum Studies*, *1*(2), 1–14.

Bai, H. (2003b). The stop: The practice of reanimating the universe within and without, *Educational Insights*, *8*(2). Retrieved January 14, 2007, from http://ccfi.educ.ubc.ca/publication/insights/v08n01/contextualexplorations/bai/bai.html.

Bai, H. (2004). The three I's for ethics as an everyday activity: Integration, intrinsic valuing, and intersubjectivity, *Canadian Journal of Environmental Education*, *9*, 51–64.

Bai, H. (2006). Philosophy for education: Cultivating human agency. *Paideusis*, *15*(1), 7–19. Retrieved January 14, 2007, from http://journals.sfu.ca/paideusis/index.php/paideusis/issue/current/showToc.

Berry, T. (1996). Into the future. In R. S. Gottlieb (Ed.), *This sacred earth* (pp. 410–414). London: Routledge.

Berry, T. (1999). *The great work: Our way into the future.* New York: Bell Tower.

Blake, W. (1958). *William Blake.* Harmondsworth, Middlesex, UK: Penguin Books.

Borgmann, A. (1993). *Crossing the postmodern divide.* Chicago: University of Chicago Press.

Descartes, R. (1985). *The philosophical writings of Descartes* (J. Cottingham, R. Stootholff, & D. Murdoch, Trans.). Cambridge, UK: Cambridge University Press. (Original work published 1644)

Gimbustas, M. A. (1991). *The civilization of the Goddess: The world of Old Europe.* San Francisco: HarperCollins.

Hanh, T. N. (1996). *The long road turns to joy.* Berkeley: Parallax Press.

Havelock, E. (1963). *Preface to Plato.* Cambridge, MA: The Belknap Press of Harvard University.

Huxley, A. (1977). *The doors of perception & Heaven and hell.* London: HarperCollins.

Johnson, R. (1987). *Ecstasy: Understanding the psychology of joy.* San Francsico: Harper & Row.

Kohák, E. (1984). *The embers and the stars: A philosophical inquiry into the moral sense of nature.* Chicago: University of Chicago Press.

Ladinsky, D. (1996). *Love poems from God: Twelve sacred voices from the east and west.* New York: Penguin Compass.

Laing, R. D. (1980). What is the matter with mind? In S. Kumer (Ed.), *The Schumacher lectures.* London: Sphere Books Ltd.

Orr, D. (1994). *Earth in mind: On education, environment, and the human prospect.* Washington, DC: Island Press.

Pannikar, R. (1992). A nonary of priorities. In J. Ogilvy (Ed.), *Revisioning philosophy* (pp. 235–246). Albany: State University of New York Press.

Plato. (1965). *The Republic* (F. M. Conford, Trans.). New York: Oxford University Press.

Rasmussen, D. (2004). The priced versus the priceless. *Interculture, 147*(1), 5–38.

Skolimowski, H. (1995). *The participatory mind: A new theory of knowledge and of the universe.* London: Penguin (Arkana).

Tuxill, J. (1999). Appreciating the benefits of plant biodiversity. In L. Starke (Ed.), *State of the world* (pp. 96–114). New York: Norton.

Vetlesen, A. J. (1994). *Perception, empathy, and judgment: An inquiry into the precondition of moral performance.* University Park: Pennsylvania State University Press.

A few weeks before we made the rope swing, my tribe of friends and I had spent a ninety-degree afternoon on a stretch of river lower down the mountain, swimming in a gorgeous catchment pond below a waterfall. Not content with the languid inertia of a summer day, the men felt compelled to jump off the waterfall into the pool. The waterfall was fifty-five feet high.

A sun-fried brain or a bored ka propelled me to the top of the falls after they made their leaps. Treading water below, they yelled frantically. The roar of the water drowned out the meaning of their cries, which, I learned later, were cries of pain. They had jumped naked and were suffering scrotum impact problems. I knew the leap was scary but safe, so at the time I interpreted their screams not as a warning but as encouragement. They knew me to be reluctant and not enamored of danger, but thrilled once I crossed a threshold of risk, especially if it involved the river. "Your nerve endings are too close to the surface," they told me, which apparently accounted for both the fear and the exhilaration.

I waved at them and took position. Two black-chinned hummingbirds flitted out of a patch of manzanita and hovered at my fingertips, their needle bills poised at my turquoise ring, their emerald backs and obsidian and violet throats iridescent in the bright sun: gem clusters with wings and beating hearts.

The river threw itself off the precipice, as clear and slick as liquid glass, a mesmerising band of curving water. Below me the reassuring jewel-green of depth lay well away from the paler shallows and the surrounding shoulders of rock. Around me the mountains of my mother and grandmother and mothers before them rose high into the wide blue air, flanked with the blunt chaparral, then high timber and the keen polish of glaciers across their granite bulk. The sparest of the palette—emerald river, pale ecru stone, sapphire sky, and the unnameable color of their clarity—struck the deepest nerve. The ache of it all nearly made my knees buckle. I felt as if I was already beneath the waterfall, its weight pressing against my chest. "It is sheer beauty, so pure that it is difficult to breathe in," wrote poet Rupert Brooke, and there on the waterfall I had no breath. I knew the Sierra better than I understood love. The least precarious thing in my life was my appetite for the sensuous.

"I will do this once," I said aloud to no one. Just once.

Then I lifted my bare feet off the lip of flood-polished granite and plunging river, and I fell through the clear mountain air to a glittering pool of water the colour of a hummingbird's back. (Ellen Meloy, *The Anthropology of Turquoise*)

7

Birding Lessons and the Teachings of Cicadas

David W. Jardine

Last summer, some old friends and I went birding through the southern Ontario summer forests where I was raised, crackling full of song-birds and head-high ferns and steamy heat. It was, as always, a great relief to return to this place from the clear airs of Alberta where I have lived for 11 years—academic, Faculty of Education, curriculum courses, practicum supervision in the often stuffy, unearthly confines of some elementary schools.

As with every time I return here, it was once again a surprise to find how familiar it was, and to find how deeply I experience my new home in the foothills of the Rocky Mountains through these deeply buried bodily templates of my raising. It is as if I bear a sort of hidden ecological memory of the sensuous spells (Abram, 1996) of the place on earth into which I was born. How things smell, the racket of leaves turning on their stems, how my breath pulls this humid air, how bird songs combine, the familiar directions of sudden thundery winds, the rising insect drills of cicada tree buzzes that I remember so intimately, so immediately, that when they sound, it feels as if this place itself has remembered what I have forgotten, as if my own memory, my own raising, some of my own life, is stored up in these trees for safe keeping.

Cicadas become archaic storytellers telling me, like all good storytellers, of the life I had forgotten I had lived, of deep, fleshy, familial relations that worm their ways out of my belly and breath into these soils, these smells, this air.

And I am left shocked that they know so much, that they remember so well, and that they can be so perfectly articulate.

I became enamoured, during our walk, with listening to my friends' conversations about the different birds that they had been spotting. They spoke of their previous ventures here, of what had been gathered and lost, of moments of surprise and relief, of expectation and frustration. Their conversations were full of a type of discipline, attention and rich interpretive joy, a pleasure taken in a way of knowing that cultivated and deepened our being just here, in this marsh, up beside these hot, late-afternoon sun-yellow limestone cliffs.

Updraughts had pulled a hawk high up above our heads. We spotted a red-winged blackbird circling him, pestering, diving.

Sudden blackbird disappearance.

Hawk remained, over a hundred feet overhead, backlit shadowy wing penumbras making it hard to accurately spot.

Where had that blackbird gone?

"There. Coming down the cliff face."

Sudden distinctive complaint around our heads. He had spotted us as worse and more proximate dangers to this marsh than the hawk that had been chased far enough away for comfort.

My friends' conversations were, in an ecologically important sense, *of a kind* with the abundance of bird songs and flights that surrounded us—careful, measured, like speaking to like, up out of the hot and heady, mosquitoed air. And, standing alongside them there, sometimes silent, certainly unpracticed in this art, involved a type of learning that I had once known but, like cicadas, long-since forgotten.

I had forgotten the pleasure to be had in simply standing in the presence of people who are practiced in what they know and listening, feeling, watching them work.

I had forgotten the learning to be had from standing alongside and imitating, practicing, repeating, refining the bodily gestures of knowing.

I had forgotten how they could show me things, not just *about this place*, but about how you might carry yourself, what might become of you, when you know this place well.

Part of such carrying, such bearing, is to realize how the creatures of this place can become like great teachers (Jardine, 1997a) with great patience. Such a realization makes it possible to be at a certain ease with what you know. It is no longer necessary to contain or hoard or become overly consumptive in knowing. One can take confidence and comfort in the fact that this place itself will patiently hold some of the remembrances required: like the cicadas, patiently repeating the calls to attention required to know well of this place and its ways.

So we stood together in the bodily presence of this place. Listening, watching, waiting for knowing to be formed through happenstance arrivals and chance noticings. Seeking out expectant, near-secret places that they knew from having been here before, often evoking slow words of fondness, remembrance, and familiarity—intimate little tales of other times. Repeating to each other, with low and measured tones, what is seen or suspected. Reciting tales from well-thumbed-through books that showed their age and importance. Belly-laughing over the wonderful, silly, sometimes near-perfect verbal descriptions of bird songs: "a liquid gurgling *konk-la-ree* or *o-ka-lay*" for Roger Peterson's (1980, p. 252) version of the red-winged blackbird.

Then settling, slowing, returning, listening and looking anew. Meticulousness: "at the edge, below the canopy of the oak, there, no, left, there, yes!"

These are, in part, great fading arts of taxonomic attention, and the deep childly pleasures to be had in sorting and gathering and collecting (Shepard, 1996). There is something about such gathering that is deeply personal, deeply formative, deeply pedagogical. As I slowly gathered something of this place, it became clear that I was also somehow "gathering myself." And as I gathered something of the compositions of this place, I, too, had to become composed in and by such gathering. And, with the help of cicadas, I did not simply remember this place. Of necessity, I remembered, too, something of what has become of me.

A birding lesson: I *become* someone through what I know.

This little lesson may be the great gift that environmental education can offer to education as a whole. Coming to know, whatever the discipline, whatever the topic or topography, is never just a matter of learning the ways of a place but learning about how to carry oneself in such a way that the ways of this place might show themselves. Education, perhaps, involves the invitation of children into such living ways.

This idea of a knowledge of the "ways" (Berry, 1983) of things and the immediacy, patience, repetition, persistence, and intimacy—the "attention and devotion" (Berry, 1977, p. 34)—that such knowledge requires, is ecologically, pedagogically, and spiritually vital. It suggests that a knowledge of the ways of red-winged blackbirds is not found nestled in the detailed and careful descriptions of birding guides. Rather, such knowledge lives in the living, ongoing work of coming to a place, learning its ways and living with the unforseeable consequence that you inevitably become someone in such efforts, someone full of tales to tell, tales of intimacy, full of proper names, particular ventures, bodily memories that are entangled in and indebted to the very flesh of the earth they want to tell.

It was clear that my friends loved what they had come to know and what such knowing had required them to become. They took great pleasure in working (Berry, 1989), in showing, in listening, in responding to the simplest, most obvious of questions. There is a telling, disturbing, ecopedagogical (Jardine, 1994) insight buried here. Because a knowledge of the ways of a place is, of necessity, a knowledge webbed into the living character of a place and webbed into the life of the one who bears such knowledge, such knowledge is inevitably fragile, participating in the mortality and passing of the places it knows. A knowledge of ways then, must, of necessity, include the passing on of what is known as an essential, not accidental part of its knowing. It is always and already deeply pedagogical, concerned, not only with the living character of places, but with what is required of us if that living and our living there are to go on.

Another birding lesson: If this place is fouled by the (seeming) inevitabilities of "progress," the cost of that progress is always going to be part of my life that is lost.

Some days, it makes perfect sense to say that all knowledge, like all life, is suffering, undergoing, learning to bear and forbear. Because of this fearsome morality that is part of a knowledge of ways, we are obliged, in such knowledge, to cultivate a good, rich, earthy understanding of "enough" (Berry, 1987). We are obliged, too, to then suffer again the certain knowledge that in our schools, in our lives, in our hallucinations of progress and all the little panics these induce (Jardine, 1996), there never seems to be enough.

Sometimes, in bearing such knowing, I feel my age. I feel my own passing.

At one point we stood on a raised wooden platform in the middle of a marsh just as the sun was setting, and the vocal interplays of red-winged blackbirds' songs, the curves of their flights and the patterning of both of these around nests cupped in the yellow-and-black-garden-spidery bulrushes—audible but invisible sites bubbling full of the pink, wet warbling smallness of chicks—were clearly, in their own way, acts of spotting *us*.

"Ways" bespeaks a thread of kindredness with what one knows, a sense of deep relatedness and intimate, fleshy obligation (Caputo, 1993). But it betrays another little birding lesson: that we are their relations as much as they are ours, that we are thus caught in whatever regard this place places on us:

> The whole ensemble of sentient life cannot be deployed except from the site of a being which is itself visible, audible, sensible. The visible world and the eye share a common flesh; the flesh is their common being and belonging together. (Caputo, 1993, p. 201)

Or, if you like, a more drastic mosquito lesson about living relations: "flesh is . . . a reversible, just insofar as what eats is always edible, what is carnivorous is always carnality" (p. 200). So just as these mosquitoes eat up my sweet, sweaty blood skinslicked under the lures of CO_2 that drew them near, I get their lives in return, gobbled up into liquid gurgling *konk-la-rees*. This is the meaty, trembly level of mutuality and interdependence that crawls beneath all our tall tales of relations. This common flesh is the fearsome limit of our narrativity.

In a knowledge of ways, I do not simply know. I am also *known*. These cicadas and I turn around each other, each forming the other in kind, "both sensible and sensitive, reversible aspects of a common animate element" (Abram, 1996, p. 66). Even more unsettling than this, *as* we know this place, so are we known by it (Palmer, 1989). That is, the character of our knowing and how gracefully and generously we carry what we know reflects on our character.

One final birding lesson for now. Catching a glimpse of a blue heron pair over past the edge of the marsh, tucked up under the willowy overhangs.

Shore edge log long deep bluey sunset shadow fingers.

Sudden rush of a type of recognition almost too intimate to bear, an event of birding never quite lodged in any birding guides:

"It's *that* pair!"

What a strange and incommensurate piece of knowledge (Jardine, 1997b). How profoundly, how deeply, how wonderfully *useless* it is, knowing that it is *them*, seemingly calling for names more intimate, more proper than "heron," descriptions richer and more giddy than "Voice: deep harsh croaks: *frahnk, frahnk, frahnk*" (Peterson, 1980, p. 100). Such knowing doesn't lead anywhere. It is, by itself, already always full, already always enough.

Perhaps this irreplaceable, unavoidable intimacy is why our tales of the earth always seem to include proper names ("obligations require proper names"; Caputo, 1993, p. 201), always seem to be full of love and heart, always seem to require narrations of particular times and places, particular faces, particular winds, always seem to invite facing and listening and remembering.

It is squarely here that a great deal of my own work has come to rest: how to carry these birding lessons home, back into the often stuffy confines of elementary schools (Jardine, 1990a), back into the often even stuffier confines, for example, of elementary school mathematics (Jardine, 1990b, 1995), back, too, into the archaic, often literal-minded narrows of academic work and the forms of speaking and writing and research it allows (Jardine, 1992).

Just imagine: mathematics conceived as a living discipline, a living topography, a living place, full of ancestors (Jardine, 1997a) and kin and living relations (Friesen, Clifford, & Jardine, 2008), full of tales told and tales to tell. And imagine, too, mathematics education conceived as an open, generous invitation of our children into the intimate ways of this old, mysterious, wondrous place.

REFERENCES

Abram, D. (1996). *The spell of the sensuous: Language in a more-than-human world.* New York: Pantheon Books.

Berry, W. (1977). *The unsettling of America.* San Francisco: Sierra Club Books.

Berry, W. (1983). *Standing by words.* San Francisco: North Point Press.

Berry, W. (1987). *Home economics.* San Francisco: North Point Press.

Berry, W. (1989). The profit in work's pleasure. *Harper's Magazine*, March, 19–24.

Caputo, J. (1993). *Against ethics: Contributions to a poetics of obligation with constant reference to deconstruction.* Bloomington: Indiana State University Press.

Friesen, S., Clifford, P., & Jardine, D. (2008). Meditations on community, memory and the intergenerational character of mathematical truth. In D. Jardine, S. Friesen, & P. Clifford (Eds.), *Back to the basics of teaching and learning: Thinking the world together* (2nd ed, pp. 117–130). New York: Routledge.

Jardine, D. (1990a). "To dwell with a boundless heart": On the integrated curriculum and the recovery of the Earth. *Journal of Curriculum and Supervision, 5*(2), 107–119.

Jardine, D. (1990b). On the humility of mathematical language. *Educational Theory, 40*(2), 181–192.

Jardine, D. (1992). The fecundity of the individual case: Considerations of the pedagogic heart of interpretive work. *Journal of Philosophy of Education, 26*(1), 51–61.

Jardine, D. (1994). Littered with literacy: An ecopedagogical reflection on whole language, pedocentrism and the necessity of refusal. *Journal of Curriculum Studies, 26*(5), 509–524.

Jardine, D. (1995). The stubborn particulars of grace. In B. Horwood (Ed.), *Experience and the curriculum: Principles and programs* (pp. 261–275). Dubuque, IA: Kendall/Hunt.

Jardine, D. (1996). Under the tough old stars: Pedagogical hyperactivity and the mood of environmental education. *Canadian Journal of Environmental Education, 1,* 48–55.

Jardine, D. (1997a) All beings are your ancestors: A bear Sutra on ecology, Buddhism and pedagogy. *The Trumpeter: A Journal of Ecosophy, 14*(3), 122–23.

Jardine, D. (1997b). The surroundings. *JCT: The Journal of Curriculum Theorizing, 13*(3), 18–21.

Palmer, P. (1989). *To know as we are known: Education as a spiritual discipline.* New York: HarperCollins.

Peterson, R. T. (1980). *A field guide to the birds east of the Rockies* (4th ed.). Boston: Houghton Mifflin.

Shepard, P. (1996). *The others: How animals made us human.* Washington, DC: Island Press.

Untitled
Lorri Neilsen Glenn

You walked together into the open field of prairie
wool toward the ravine, its harvest

of old combines scattered, their rusted limbs
pocked and fixed, collapsed pliés of dancers

fired by the noon sun. And under here the grass
is flattened in the shape of animal's belly, and here

an owl bursts from under the metal to write
explosion in feathers against the hill. A mule fawn,

her ears like questions, her bounding
answer. The doe, and along the horizon, the stag,

alone and unreadable, a pale strutting ghost leaving
shelter in such a way you know he knows. And is

gone. Below, blooming: a member of the aster
family, one of you calls, as another stoops to look

at the pink, then the yellow, and the blue. It has become
a joke among you—the small encroachments

you make, words in cupped palms, allowing you to take
this image home, tuck it under the joists and beams

of language, safe, at least for now. A leaf,
a petal you can point to in a book, one of the asteraceae,

its twenty thousand species, surely it is listed
there. Near the flesh of your feet, the rubbed

grass, a badger hole, a magpie, its white flash against
black. An old story, and long: the prairie's sere

rough gospel, ragged, scrabbling, good news
that slips between the names.

8

Sitting on an Old Grey Stone

Meditations on Emotional Understanding

Bob Jickling

This is a chapter of resistance first written with students in mind. These students struggled with a teacher education system that pushed to the side everything that they most valued. They were a committed bunch: Some were outdoor educators, others environmental educators, and yet others were immersed in issues of social justice. All wanted more than they were experiencing. I shared their frustration. In this chapter, I reveal some of the issues underlying our frustration, and point in some directions for reimagining education.

I begin with William Wordsworth, and suggest that elements of his poetry are protests about what counts as worthwhile knowledge. Second, I take up Arne Næss's claim that the cognitive value of feelings is typically undervalued. This challenges ideas that emotional understanding should be separated from rationality and labeled *affective*, and/or separated into objective and subjective categories. I then discuss the epistemological importance of experiential and emotional understanding in education and relationships between these understandings and ethics. Finally, I suggest strategies that educators might use to resist marginalization of experiential-emotional aspects of cognitive understanding in formal and other educational settings.

ON EXPERIENCES

Think for a minute about your own education. What are the learning experiences that you remember best? Which have been most influential, or powerful, in shaping your life? Now think about their nature. Were they experiences that are common in schools and other educational settings? Were they experiences that are amenable to measurement and evaluation? Could they have been predicted in advance, or even found in the expected outcomes of a curriculum? During informal polls of groups that I have been with lately, the answer for many has been no.

These are admittedly broad questions and I have asked them to open a little space for reflecting on significant learning experiences that often seem to exist at the margins of mainstream education. I have also asked them because "understanding" in, and of, this chapter might require some reflection on past, and perhaps common, experiences. I wish to explore the nature of these experiences—some of them at least. And, I want to speculate about dangers in relegating them to the perimeters.

These thoughts and questions, and hence this chapter, were given more focus by a graduate student who asked me, "Why are students so happy when you take them outside somewhere for a field trip?"[1] I am sure that there are many reasons, some being more psychological. But it seems that these questions are too important to be left to psychologists alone; I think there are also reasons that lean more toward the philosophical, with important educational implications. With this in mind, I limit this chapter to those significant experiences that involve field-based, or outside of the classroom learning.[2] I begin with the assumptions that "field trip" learning is quintessentially experiential in nature, that these experiences enable an important way of knowing, and that this knowing is deeply personal, emotional in nature, and lies at the heart of our ability to be ethical beings. So, this chapter is about epistemology, emotions, and ethics and how they can be informed by experiential learning.

Although I understand that important educational experiences do not always take place in formal settings, I argue that we should make curricular space for the kinds of knowledge and/or experience that helps students conduct thoughtful lives. I am reminded of E. F. Schumacher (1977), who said the following:

> All through school and university I had been given maps of life and knowledge on which there was hardly a trace of many of the things that I most cared about and that seemed to me to be of the greatest possible importance to the conduct of my life. I remembered that for many years my perplexity had been complete; and no interpreter had come along to help me. It remained complete until I ceased to suspect the sanity of my perceptions and began, instead, to suspect the soundness of the maps. (p. 1)

I suspect that these words will resonate with some of you; they do with me. And they lead to another assumption. This chapter rests on the idea that ways of knowing that have the capacity to enhance abilities to be thoughtful and ethical beings deserve some space in school curricula (and in other learning settings). Put another way, Richard Peters (1973) once argued that it would be unreasonable "to deprive anyone of access in an arbitrary way to forms of understanding which might throw light on alternatives open to him [or her]" (p. 256).

Romantic Resistance

For me, a good place to start is with Wordsworth, a Romantic poet of the late 18th and early 19th centuries. To be clear, my interest in Wordsworth is not primarily as a nature poet, but rather as a social critic. As Neil Evernden (1985) interprets, these poets went to wild places, not because they were nature lovers, but because these places were thought to be less hostile to their task. In remote corners of England (and Europe) they pondered an emergent industrial revolution and the knowledge it rested on.

For industrialists, scientists, and technicians of the era a new and "enlightened" knowledge system was required. It was, as René Descartes (1637/1969) describes more than a century earlier, a system with a profound distrust of sensory experiences, "because our senses sometimes deceive us, I wished to suppose that nothing is just as they cause us to imagine it" (p. 127). And it was a system that privileged a particular form of reason:

> For finally, whether we are awake or asleep, we should never allow ourselves to be persuaded excepting by the evidence of our Reason. And it must be remarked that I speak of our Reason and not of our imagination nor of our senses. (p. 132)

For Descartes the purest form of reason was in the measurability and computations of mathematics. Obtaining measurement often requires reducing a phenomenon or an entity into measurable parts. Many (e.g., Evernden, 1985) call this process Cartesian reductionism.

Wordsworth also objected to another piece of this knowledge system: a radical separation between humans and other living beings. Whereas humans are capable of reasoning, Descartes (1637/1969) compared animals to automata, or machines. The inability to reason and communicate shows not merely that these "brutes have less reason than men, but that they have none at all" (p. 139). Having no reason, "it is nature which acts in them according to the disposition of their organs, just as a clock, which is only composed of wheels and weights, can tell the hours and measure time" (p. 140). Himself a busy vivisectionist, Descartes even doubted animal exclamations of pain, attributing them to mechanical events in mechanical creatures.

Against this backdrop, Wordsworth (1798/1959a), the social critic, rejected his friend Matthew's expostulation:

> Why William, on that old grey stone,
> Thus for the length of half a day,
> Why William, sit you thus alone,
> And dream your time away?"

Wordsworth's reply is defiant:

> The eye it cannot chuse but see,
> We cannot bid the ear be still;
> Our bodies feel, where'er they be,
> Against, or with our will.
> Nor less I deem that here are powers,
> Which of themselves our minds impress,
> That we can feed this mind of ours,
> In a wise passiveness. (p. 194)

For Wordsworth, important learning accrues through sensory experiences. He asserts that we are "fed" in important and wise ways by experiences on their own terms. And, he, thus, resists the privileged epistemology of his day.

Wordsworth (1798/1959b) also rejects prevailing discourse about the mechanistic nature of animals. In a companion poem to the one cited above, he boldly critiques the Cartesian legacy:

> Our meddling intellect
> Misshapes the beauteous forms of things
> —We murder to dissect. (p. 195)

In reading Wordsworth, I find his work is importantly about resistance—resistance to an epistemology that allowed no room for human senses, feelings, and even ethics.

Now, I ask myself: Can these comments be reflected in my own learning? And, if so, is there something about this learning that brings about happiness? Pondering these questions, I began to reflect on some of my own experiences—in this case they happened in wilderness (although they might easily have happened elsewhere). Could I test Wordsworth's claims through an exposition of my own experiences? Did my experiences lead to broadened possibilities for experiential understanding? For renewed relations with the more-than-human world? The result was the following reflection.

The Mountain River

On a river in northern Canada a canoe trip began. As the drone of the departing bush plane faded, we were left with piles of gear and canoes on boggy hummocks. We called this home for a few days. As on previous trips, we toiled to assemble everything on higher ground for camping. We did so with the acrid smell of smoke in our noses and its sting in our eyes. This year the north was on fire during one of the "worst" forest fire seasons in some time. Periodically, we looked up from our loads. Peering through the blue haze we tried to appreciate the magnificent vistas in the headwaters of an alpine river. Admittedly, we were disappointed. What would this all look like without the smoke? What a pity.

What a pity indeed—not because of the fires, however. We weren't looking at the vista through smoky lenses, but rather glasses tinted by the temper of our culture. This is normal at the beginning of trips to new places. We enjoy the immediate gratification of beautiful vistas—castellated ridges, and deep green valleys. And surely this is an important part of wilderness tripping. It is the first step in reconnecting us to the earth in a place. This time, with expectations a little thwarted, we moved slowly, even lethargically, while settling in. We longed for a clear day.

It doesn't have to be like this. When the forests last burned so vigorously and for so long, I travelled down Yukon's Snake River with long-time wilderness activist Dave Foreman. He revelled in the smoke. For him, forest fires were an act of wild defiance—something beyond human control. This is not to be confused with a callousness for those threatened by fires. Rather, it was the wonder of wildness in a world where humans normally strive to be in control. He felt the wildness in his eyes and his lungs, and it was something to celebrate, it had become part of himself—literally. A shift in perspective can make a difference.

Remembering Dave Foreman helped a little. So did walking in the mountains where we felt the ground beneath our feet, aching in our city-soft thighs, and the sting of hail pelting our shoulders. We walked to the river, too, and marvelled at a landscape where no human path showed the way. Yet there was something familiar about the landscape—beyond the resemblance with other mountainous headwaters. I *felt* it long before I understood it. It took me a few days to figure out the nature of this deeply embedded connection to this landscape. I felt something that transcended words and even memory. It was an embodied, know-it-in-your-bones kind of knowledge. In the end it was the Yellowlegs and their incessant lakeside chattering, a chattering familiar to all wilderness travellers in Northern Boreal Forests. It was this ubiquitous bird that reminded me of our essentially sensuous nature.

Still, why now? Why this bird? Its call so familiar, yet why did it stand out this year? And why did it bring such joy? I think I'd been missing it. It hasn't been so common in recent years. The joy of hearing it seemed to grow from felt loss. Perhaps this was, to borrow an idea from poet Dennis Lee (2002), an example of "kintuition"—or a kind of kinaesthetic intuition involving a capacity to register rhythm, in this case of the landscape, without any identifiable mediation. A recent conversation with a local ornithologist seemed to confirm my kintuition. Though "hard data" is still scant, there seems to be a marked decline in shorebirds in North America. Sometimes the witness of our experience precedes our understanding.

I recently learned that the Yellowlegs of my experience is actually the Lesser Yellowlegs. I take this refined understanding as a small measure of growing intimacy. And, it is the Lesser Yellowlegs that has taught me, in a deeply personal way, that a slow, grinding, incremental loss is affecting Canada's wildest places. The birds and the back eddies have helped me to understand that we are wild places and they are us. What I have come to understand is deeply experiential, embodied, and beyond my ability to put it into words.

Felt Learning And Feelings

For me, there are several interesting aspects to this story, and points of resistance. First, at its very core, the learning experience was felt—understood in a bodily and sensuous way. In the end it was also an emotional learning experience. It cannot be disproved or falsified. It just was. It was only later, upon reflection, that it included elements of abstraction. And second, the telling of this story resists separations of mind and body, and mind and landscape. In the end, I become more than my mind, more than my physical manifestation; I become a *field of self* (Evernden, 1985) that includes relationships between my physical being and my experiences. And, finally, I acknowledge that my pre-existing social constructions of wilderness experiences do shape these experiences; but, for the careful listener, more-than-human others, places, and experiences also contribute to the shaping of who we become. It is a multifaceted becoming.

There isn't space to thoroughly explore all aspects of this story. However, I would like to examine some questions that can have a bearing on schooling practices. How could one write a set of behavioural outcomes for this learning? How could it be reduced to measurable increments? Why is it that these embodied experiences can be so profound? And why can they bring happiness (sometimes, at least)? I think the answer to the last question lies in the impossibility of the first two. You just can't predict in advance what learning will take place within these kinds of experiential settings. And you can't measure it. Maybe that is part of the joy.

Some theorists remind us that many dominant types of analytic understanding rely on reason (Barry, 2002). But these are particular aspects of reason requiring particular outlooks—falsification in sciences, and scepticism in philosophy. Theoretically this makes some sense. If you have an idea and it can withstand the most intense scrutiny then chances are that it has some merit. And, granted, there can be a kind of pleasure (for some at least) in thinking through an elegant line of reasoning. But, for many such a nuanced, analytical reasoning can suck the joy and nourishment out of learning, especially when that's all there is. Put another way, Jan Zwicky (1992) describes thinking analytically as like going on a diet:

> Its aim is a healthy austerity of thought, a certain trimness of mind. But carried too far, we're only left with a skeleton. Carried too far too often, we lose the sense that something is amiss when the patient exhibits no life. We come to take pride in our cases of polished bone. (p. 154)

So complete is the loss of perspective, that educators can be awestruck by joy exhibited by students on field trips, freed from the constraints of structured and systematized learning (see also Price, chap. 4, this volume).

Personal experiential learning is different from the austere analytical thought Zwicky describes. You can know how an experience makes you feel. You can be thrilled to meet an old friend like the Lesser Yellowlegs, or a wolf, or a spider, or a penguicula, or Penguicula Creek. You can know the joy of watching a sunrise from a mountaintop or the pain of watching the destruction of a favourite haunt. You can feel anguish over a human's suffering and you can feel the ecstasy of success.

In each of these experiential instances, the ontological attention is, as Zwicky (2002) suggests, a response to a particularity: *this* Lesser Yellowlegs, *this* wolf, or *this* sunrise. She adds:

the phenomenal experience of *this*ness is not of a complex series of relations shading off into the temporally hazy distance. Rather, we are pierced. The *this* strikes into us like a shaft of light. . . . The phenomenal experience often includes an awareness of not being able to give an account of *this*—we can point, but not say. (p. 53)

In educational terms, the phenomenal experience will also be unaccountable in the language of learning outcomes or measurable educational achievements.

If you are Inuit, and live in Arctic Canada, you can marvel at the sight of a thrush with a red breast (a robin) but with no name in your Inuktitut language. And you can feel curious about that, all by yourself, before anyone tells you about global warming. These feelings are ways of knowing about the world. They are unique, deeply personal, and they exist, for some, in the language of gestalts. If these feelings and knowing are respected, they can be free from harassments and vexations like scepticism and falsification. They just are. They "don't have reasons: they announce themselves" (Zwicky, 2002, p. 92). And, just maybe this has something to do with why students can be so happy on field trips.

But experiential and emotional learning are more than tips to make students happy; they are profoundly important. As Aldo Leopold (1949/1970) once said, "We can be ethical only in relation to something we can see, feel, understand, love, or otherwise have faith in" (p. 251).[3] If we ignore these kinds of emotional understandings, and the kinds of experiential learning that can nourish them, we do so at our peril.

To be clear, I am emphatically not advocating abandonment of science or philosophical reasoning. And I am not suggesting that emotional understanding is infallible or sufficient. I can be mistaken when drawing inferences from this understanding, just as I can be mistaken when relying on scientific or other aspects of knowing. Yet, I do maintain that experiential-emotional understanding adds flesh and life to the bones so often polished smooth and white by analytical thought. In the interests of epistemological breadth, I am trying to create more space for experiential learning and all of the knowing and understanding that accrue in this way.

I am pondering emotional understanding—alongside processes of falsification and critical reasoning—and its importance in the conduct of our lives. For example, when making major decisions in life—about choosing partners, buying houses, caring for children—how many of us make decisions that are based on logic alone? What room do we make, and should we make, for more sensual, experiential, and emotional understanding? In what useful way can attention to these dimensions of our knowing and being add important "data" to our overall understanding?

I am also pondering the consequences on not paying attention. Perhaps this was illustrated in the senseless responses to Hurricane Katrina, where many residents of New Orleans felt ignored and abandoned by their governments, and their president, in a time of crisis. And here I mean that literally—senseless. When people are socioeconomically and racially separated, their sensual contact is diminished or impossible. The feeling, touching, seeing, smelling, and "walk-a-mile-in-their-shoes" knowing are absent. For each the "other" is an abstraction—perhaps even reducible to mechanistic others, the antithesis of the particularity of *this*ness. The others have no face (see Payne, chap. 18, this volume).

If this kind of experiential learning is so important, why does it generally seem to circle the perimeter of education? Why does it seem marginalized? Or, "othered"? Consider briefly a few possibilities.

First, a traditional scientific goal is to be objective; objectivity has been valorized. When we allow our work to be classified in the "lesser" category of "subjective" we are acquiescing to the language of the dominant cultural influences, the status quo, hegemonic forces. Perhaps we should seek other ways to talk about our work that doesn't place it in a position opposite to (and lesser than) "objective." Celebrating subjectivity might be one useful response, but I suspect that it would be worthwhile to reimagine other possibilities, too.

Second, we privilege particular aspects of cognitive learning but then hive off others into the dubious, and less prestigious category of "affective" learning. Perhaps as Næss (2002; Næss & Jickling, 2000) says, we do not pay enough attention to the cognitive value of feelings. Experiential and emotional understandings are not reducible to some dubious psychological category. As Robin Barrow and Ronald Woods (1982) argue, "there *are* uses of the word 'understanding' where the notions of feeling, emotion, attitude, empathy, etc., are involved" (p. 55).

Third, many dominant approaches to education do not seem to pay so much attention to those things that they cannot give an account of, or say, or measure—the things to which we can only point. It is interesting to consider that Benjamin Bloom and his team (Krathwohl, Bloom, & Masia, 1964), who coined the term *affective domain*, acknowledge this when they observed trends in the erosion of "affective objectives" in which:

> [T]he original intent of a course or educational program becomes worn down to that which can be explicitly evaluated for grading purposes and that which can be taught easily through verbal materials (lectures, discussions, reading materials, etc.). (p. 16)

Yet, they later argue, that if affective goals are to be realized:

> They must be defined clearly; learning experiences to help the student develop in the desired direction must be provided; and there must be some systematic method for appraising the extent to which students grow in desired ways. (p. 23)

It would be nice to think that the ideas of Bloom and his team are now a bit quaint and dated, but I do not see much evidence of this. It is not possible to effectively evaluate everything that is important; so let's just get over it.

And finally, when a bold idea comes along with potential to challenge the status quo, it is often dismissed as "romantic." But isn't that the point? Education needs bold ideas. I would like to take back the word romantic and make it a symbol of resistance. Or, at least, resist its use in a dismissive or otherwise pejorative way.

Given much said in this essay, it might be tempting for some to think that I am really talking about a version of "nature education" again. Emphatically no! When I think of the kind of learning that I'm talking about, I also think about Israelis and Palestinians who *work together*, with ontological attentiveness, trying to resolve water issues—issues that boil down to matters of conservation, justice, and equity (i.e., Haddad, Zuzovsky, & Yakir, 2000; Zuzovsky, 2000). I think about students being with one another in a multiracial educational setting in southern Africa during the dark days of apartheid. I see the understanding—carefully, emotionally cognitive—that occurred when people could be together for the first time in their lives. It is this ontological attentiveness and its relationship with epistemology in all settings—those more social and those more wilderness—that I am pointing towards.

I also remember Arne Næss. When asked if deep questioning was enough to explore difficult questions he replies:

> With deep prejudices you must use some examples of how you would behave in a particular situation. For instance, I was climbing a little with a strong supporter of Hitler in 1935. I had some pieces of bread and I said: "This was made by a Jewish girl. See if you can eat it anyhow." Then he admitted: "Well I do not mean that absolutely every Jewish person is a terrible so and so. There are exceptions." With reluctance he would then eat just a little of the bread.

But you see you have to, if you can, get into some practical situation—you start a walk
somewhere, do something together and then—bang—you have an example. (Næss & Jickling,
2000, p. 51)

The cynical person might say, "Well, that example didn't do very much to stop the Holocaust."
But the optimist might say, "Well, there weren't enough people 'sharing their bread.'" Seen another
way, Næss gave face to a particular Jewish girl through the gift of bread (see Payne, chap. 18,
this volume). The phenomenal experience of his climbing partner, expressed in the recognition
that not every Jewish person was terrible, didn't come with reasons; it just announced itself. Næss
had no simple recipe for communicating, no specific learning outcomes. He did, however, have
the wherewithal to point and hope (Zwicky, 2002).

It seems fitting to talk about resistance again, for surely that is another key part of Næss's
story. But Næss never looked for heroes, he has always advocated for little steps by many people—
for many people to "share their bread." So what about resistance? In the next section I point to
a couple of examples as starting points for you to think about your own resistance.

Bringing Resistance Home

My faculty recently commissioned a report about its evaluation practices (Crocker, 2004). It
found that, on average, our grades were substantially higher than in other faculties. There was
discussion about this and a number of recommendations for remediation. The recommendation
that interested me was that we should not give credit for attendance. Yet, for some kinds of
learning "being there" is the essence. If we don't acknowledge this in our course outlines, and
practices, then we are implicitly saying it isn't important.

I concede that "attendance" may not be the best word, but another term—maybe
"experiential learning"—would be more descriptive. But in the end it amounts to pretty much
the same thing. The important thing, for me, is to insist on having a little space to recognize the
learning that is embodied, experiential, emotional, personal, and that doesn't fit into traditional
evaluation schemes.

In another instance, I taught a graduate environmental education course at another
university that required instructors to include a "learning outcomes" grid on their course outlines.
This involved selecting from a Domain List a series of preapproved program goals and related
learning outcomes, and then lining these up with assessment criteria (Table 7.1). An accompanying
"Assessment" required breaking down assignment grading into weightings for each of the selected
learning outcomes (Fig. 7.1). Aside from not leaving much room for "just being" learning, it is
stunningly ironic that I can critique Cartesian reductionism in my classes but am required to
describe and assess this learning in such a reductionist manner.

So, why is this noteworthy now? Wordsworth critiques this same reductionism in 1798.
In 1985, Evernden acknowledges that Decartes' failings had already been amply discussed in
philosophical literature. And here I, together with several authors in this volume, raise this issue
again. Clearly, Cartesian thinking is remarkably resilient; it rests on assumptions so deeply buried
in cultural norms as to be virtually invisible. How else can I explain that the university program
just mentioned was guided by an eminent advisory group, and taught by experienced faculty,
with the collective experience of centuries—people who should know better (and likely do know
better)—yet it accepts planning and evaluation schemes as described in Table 7.1 and Fig. 7.1?
Evernden (1985) is as relevant today as he was more than two decades ago when he said, "we
must confront those failings, for they obscure the need for alternatives" (p. 54). In his analysis,

Table 7.1. Learning Outcomes

Domain	Learning Outcome	Assessment Criteria
Communication 1.1	Communicate effectively in writing using several media and techniques.	Well-written, coherent, skilled use of English language, APA formatted.
Communication 1.2	Communicate effectively in person using appropriate media and/or techniques.	Coherent oral presentation, thoughtful pedagogy, effective use of aids if and where appropriate.
Worldviews & Ethics 7.1	The extent to which practitioners possess an in-depth and systemic understanding of the range of worldviews and ethics, and their accompanying perspectives (e.g., attitudes and beliefs, values, ways of being, ways of knowing, and ways of looking at the world) toward the environment, the future, and human activity in the environment; and their implications for EEC programs and initiatives.	Demonstrate comprehensive understanding of topic at hand, coherent development of argument or story, effective use of course reading to enhance presentation and develop argument or story.
Worldviews & Ethics 7.2	The extent to which practitioners possess and can demonstrate an ability to respect, articulate and reflect critically on the range of worldviews and ethics, and their accompanying perspectives.	Demonstrate understanding of a range of extant perspectives and worldview related to the assignment topic, coherent development of argument or story, effective use of course reading to enhance presentation and develop argument or story.
Worldviews & Ethics 7.3	Explain how in a personal sense one forms an environmental view through perceptual, attitudinal, core knowledge sets, and values acquired in a unique blending of interaction with nature and culture.	Demonstrate reflection about personal dimensions of values and ethics in light of assignment topics, coherent development of argument or story.

Type	Due Dates	Outcomes					
		1.1	1.2	7.1	7.2	7.3	Total
Assignment #1 Paper	Aug. 1	4			3	3	10%
Assignment #2 Presentation and journal entry	Aug. 11	4	4		4	3	15%
Assignment #3	Aug. 4	5		10	5	5	25%
Assignment #4	Aug. 8	5		10	5	5	25%
Assignment #5	Aug. 12	5		10	5	5	25%
							100%

Fig. 7.1. Assessments.

the societal maps that perplexed Schumacher (1977) are "tracings from Descartes's original, a map which excludes concrete experience in the world in favour of abstraction" (p. 54).

In announcing that this is a chapter about resistance, there is, I suppose, an expectation that I should own up to my own resistance. Most apparently, I have written this chapter and I give it to my students. I may not live up to their expectations, but it is a start; I point with it and hope. I do credit participation, but I call it an "action project." I include items in my courses that defy reduction and evaluation and then grade these portions with a pass/fail system (playing havoc with standard deviations of mark distribution—for those who insist on caring about these things). And, I do field trips.

At another level, I have pointed to ways of knowing that cannot be said, and certainly not evaluated—to the happy learning that just announces itself. This is a kind of learning that is wrapped up in feelings—of joy, wonder, and sometimes anguish—and experience—especially in ontological attention and care for particulars. I have tried to write this chapter in a form that is consistent (even a little) with the functional need. If what is currently underrepresented, or absent, in education cannot be said, then it would be a misadventure to rely on an austere diet of analytic thinking and arcane theory. Zwicky (2002) experiments with metaphor to reach beyond skepticism and falsification as systems for determining knowing. Robert Bringhurst (2002) and Don McKay (2002) use poetry. Here, I point to experiences and have experimented with narrative accounts of these encounters—admittedly these accounts are just rough proxies for the phenomenal experiences themselves. Still I hope that when wedged between tidbits of residual academia, they will generate a glimmer of resonance.

In all, I haven't accomplished a lot; but, I'm not looking for heroes. For surely, a single person cannot reverse a way of thinking deeply embedded in educational policy. There can be room for all to engage in some resistance. We must! (It is doubtful that this kind of change will come down from above.) There will be many ways to do this. I also like to make a little room for curriculum theorist Elliot Eisner's (1985) "expressive outcomes." These are the consequences of activities that are planned to provide rich learning opportunities but without explicit or precise objectives.

The aim here is to shift emphasis away from evaluation and back to considering what good learning opportunities would look like—first and foremost. As Eisner (1985) says, "The tack taken with respect to the generation of expressive outcomes is to engage in activities that are sufficiently rich to allow for a wide, productive range of educationally valuable outcomes" (p. 121).

A key point is that we should pay more attention to providing worthwhile activities—as whole entities—and worry less about grids of objectives, and conjured goals and outcomes. Can you, as an individual educator, work in even a little room for something like expressive outcomes? A place where you can just point and hope. Perhaps we can all do a little to resist the tyranny of misplaced evaluation.

A FINAL THOUGHT

As I finish I want us all to remember that happiness, joy, and knowing are not mutually exclusive. Feelings are at the heart of the most important knowing; they are at the heart of our capacity to be ethical beings. And, I want to encourage us all to find a little time for ourselves, and our students, to go outside and sit for a while on an old grey stone, to awaken ourselves and themselves to bodies that "feel, where'er they be, against or with our will."

NOTES

1. This chapter does not focus explicitly on happiness, although this would make an important paper. Rather, I wish to draw attention to the ontological and epistemological conditions that may underlie experiences resulting in the notion of happiness described here.

2. However, as Anthony Weston (2004) points out, these experiences can take place inside, too.

3. There is not space to discuss this quotation at length. Although I acknowledge that some might draw on more abstract, or theoretical principles, for ethical inspiration, I maintain that Leopold's (1970) thoughts are relevant, important, and illuminating.

REFERENCES

Barrow, R., & Woods, R. (1982). *An introduction to philosophy of education* (2nd ed.). London: Methuen.

Barry, P. (2002). *Beginning theory: An introduction to literary and cultural theory*. Manchester, UK: Manchester University Press.

Bringhurst, R. (2002). The philosophy of poetry and the trashing of Doctor Empedokles. In T. Lilburn (Ed.), *Thinking and singing: Poetry & the practice of philosophy* (pp. 79–93). Toronto, ON: Cormorant Books.

Crocker, R. (2004). *Analysis of grading practices in the Faculty of Education at Lakehead University: A final report to the Dean of Education, March 31, 2004*. Thunder Bay, ON: Lakehead University, Faculty of Education.

Descartes, R. (1969). Discourse on the method. In M. D. Wilson (Ed.), *The essential Descartes* (pp. 106–153). New York: Meridian. (Original work published 1637)

Eisner, E. (1985). *The educational imagination* (2nd ed.). New York: Macmillan.

Evernden, N. (1985). *The natural alien*. Toronto, ON: University of Toronto Press.

Haddad, M., Zuzovsky, R., & Yakir, R. (2000). Water in an era of peace: A joint Palestinian and Israeli study on teaching for regional cooperation. *Canadian Journal of Environmental Education*, 5, 238–248.

Krathwohl, D. R., Bloom, B. S., & Masia, B. B. (1964). *Taxonomy of educational objectives: The classification of educational goals. Handbook II: Affective domain*. New York: David McKay.

Lee, D. (2002). Body music: Notes on rhythm in poetry. In T. Lilburn (Ed.), *Thinking and singing: Poetry & the practice of philosophy* (pp. 19–58). Toronto, ON: Cormorant Books.

Leopold, A. (1970). *A Sand County almanac*. New York: Ballantine Books. (Original work published 1949)

McKay, D. (2002). The bushtits' nest. In T. Lilburn (Ed.), *Thinking and singing: Poetry & the practice of philosophy* (pp. 59–77). Toronto, ON: Cormorant Books.

Næss, A. (2002). *Life's philosophy: Reason and feeling in a deeper world*. Athens: University of Georgia Press.

Næss, A., & Jickling, B. (2000). Deep ecology and education: A conversation with Arne Næss. *Canadian Journal of Environmental Education*, 5, 48–62.

Peters, R. S. (1973). The justification of education. In R. S. Peters (Ed.), *The philosophy of education* (pp. 239–267). Oxford: Oxford University Press.

Schumacher, E. F. (1977). *A guide for the perplexed*. New York: Harper Colophon.

Weston, A. (2004). What if teaching went wild. *Canadian Journal of Environmental Education*, 9, 11–30.

Wordsworth, W. (1959a). Expostulation and reply. In H. M. Margoliouth (Ed.), *Wordsworth: Selected poems* (p. 194). London: Collins. (Original work published 1798)

Wordsworth, W. (1959b). The tables turned. In H. M. Margoliouth (Ed.), *Wordsworth: Selected poems* (p. 195). London: Collins. (Original work published 1798)

Zuzovsky, R. (2000). Water in an era of peace: Teaching for regional cooperation in a multicultural setting. *Canadian Journal of Environmental Education*, 5, 213–237.

Zwicky, J. (1992). *Lyric philosophy*. Toronto, ON: University of Toronto Press.

Zwicky, J. (2002). *Wisdom and metaphor*. Kentville, NS: Gaspereau Press.

The Bellies of Fallen Breathing Sparrows
Don McKay

Some things can't be praised enough, among them
breasts and birds
who have cohabited so long in metaphor
most folks think of them as married.
Not only that, but
when you slide your shirt (the striped one) off
the inside of my head is lined with down
like a Blackburnian warbler's nest,
the exterior of which is often rough and twiggy
in appearance.
And as the shirt snags, hesitates, and then
lets go, I know exactly why he warbles as he does,
which is zip zip zip zip zeee
      chickety chickety chickety chick.
The man who wrote "twin alabaster mounds"
should have spent more time outdoors
instead of browsing in that musty old museum where
he pissed away his youth.

9

Education, Sustainability, and the Metaphysics of Nature

Michael Bonnett

It is perhaps now something of a commonplace to claim that our current global environmental predicament is such as to require for its amelioration not merely some amendment to certain aspects of human behavior, but a change in the ways we think of, understand, and relate to nature as a whole. Some of our most prevalent conceptions of nature, our sense of its value, and our resultant treatment of it, stand in need of radical review. What is sometimes less fully appreciated is the extent of the implications that follow from such an acknowledgment. I explore some of these here. In particular, I pursue the view that here we cannot be concerned simply with one relatively contained (if for some, very important) aspect of our lives—namely, our personal interactions with the natural world—nor, indeed, more broadly, with the consequences of our ways of living for the natural world. What is set in train by considering a review of this kind is—or should be—transgressional in a very basic sense. My argument is that because of the centrality of our idea of nature to our understanding of reality, any such radical reconceptualization of nature is indeed tantamount to a fundamental change of consciousness as a whole—that is, to the metaphysical space we occupy. I begin by illustrating what this means in more concrete terms by referencing that widely (indeed, almost universally) accepted response to our current environmental situation: the idea of sustainable development.

Certainly, at first blush, this idea appears to hold much promise. It gives the impression of creating a synergy between important (indeed, unavoidable) moral, political, economic, and conservational concerns that play into environmental issues. For example, considerations of social justice and the desire of developing nations to move large sections of their populations out of grinding poverty (and worse) are unrebuttable. Clearly, there can be no satisfactory moral or pragmatic resolution of environmental problems that does not take proper account of these social and political dimensions. Yet the ways in which these concerns are articulated, and the framework within which a balance is to be struck between differing demands and considerations, is key. That flower of the Enlightenment, which is the ascendance of a metaphysical framework of mastery, now dominates, and by its very nature must seek to dominate, mainstream thinking in our time. I argue that unless this is overcome, or at least attenuated, any such well-intentioned notion as sustainable development is doomed to destroy that which, for many, it had been framed to protect. Consider for one moment the highly anthropocentric nature of the much-used Brundtland Commission (1987) definition of *sustainable development* as: "development that meets the needs of the present without compromising the needs of future generations to meet their own needs." This definition has been influential for some two decades, having been officially consolidated into the education systems of the nations signatory to the Earth Summit's *Agenda 21* (UNCED, 1992). But clearly it exhibits a speciesism and instrumentalism of a pretty high order, and, arguably, such motives are precisely the ones that have been key contributors to the current state of affairs.

Of equal concern, is the high degree of ambiguity that the definition exhibits. In a situation of cultural and economic diversity that gives rise to expressions of varying and conflicting "needs," precisely whose needs, perceived and judged against what criteria, are to be given precedence? And, by implication, precisely what is to be conserved and over what time span? As things stand, such a policy expression of sustainable development is open to so many interpretations as to make it congenial to almost anyone, ranging from captains of industry to eco-warriors, or to any political institution or economy, ranging from subsistence to unbridled consumerist. Although some may seek to sustain the conditions necessary for the survival of an animal population or ecosystem, under the shared banner of "sustainable development," others, trading on such "green" connotations, focus on sustaining conditions for their own economic growth. Again, with the powerful combination of essential ambiguity and a global political climate increasingly dominated by the economics of the market and consumerism, it is difficult to avoid the conclusion that in all likelihood sustainable development will function as sanctioning precisely those motives that are a root cause of our current disastrous environmental situation. Thus, sustainable development easily becomes a net contributor to environmental problems rather than a savior.

Yet there is undoubted value and power in the notion of sustainability itself: the simple idea of leading a life that is truly sustaining of oneself, one's community, and nature. This, it seems to me, can lead to a fundamental reorientation from sustainability as a policy to sustainability as an essential frame of mind—a steady way of understanding and living in the world that lies at the heart of what it is to be human. In our postmodernist era the notion that there is such a thing as human essence is heavily contested or dismissed outright. And at some levels such radical questioning of the idea of a human essence is only to be welcomed. Reifications of what it is to be human that arbitrarily promote the interests of certain social groups by authenticating certain sets of power relations, set up as immutable what could be a matter of choice, and thereby close down our understanding of our own and others' potentiality, are indeed deserving of critical scrutiny. But there comes a point at which we come up against not only what is physically given—that can *sometimes* determine and often does condition aspects of our potentiality—but also the structure of the meaning-giving horizon against which it is possible to conceive of humanness at all. I refer here not to some set of fixed attributes, but rather an interplay of potentialities such as self-awareness, agency, concern, love, loss, mortality. And perhaps most fundamental of all—but also highly susceptible to distortion—the potential of humans, as centers of consciousness, to reveal things as they are, and to be sites of truth in the sense of being places where things themselves can "show up."

Here we have the most significant meaning of sustainability: human being that is sustained through its sustaining of things themselves. And of high importance among the things that we admit into the light of consciousness in this way are aspects of the natural (but not purely material) world, for, as I have argued elsewhere (Bonnett, 2004), these are deeply embedded in and constitutive of our sense of what reality is (and should be), either as instantiation or by juxtaposition. So conceived, sustainability as a frame of mind is not some bolt-on extra to being human, some sort of skill, strategy, or policy that we might adopt or exercise at will to get us out of a tight spot. It is the retrieval of an aspect of our essence that has been systematically dismantled and degraded by a modernist humanism that has led us to view the world ever more exclusively through the prisms of utility and consumption. This is the flowering of the motive for mastery that has long been on its way. Through the constant drive to organize and manipulate, a consequence has been, and always must be, an ultimate spiritual stultification and constipation. Things that are so processed lose their capacity to inspire and refresh, for they are no longer themselves.

So what, in detail, does sustainability as a frame of mind indicate as to how we should relate to the world? What does it mean to speak of revealing things themselves? If, as has been suggested, nature constitutes a primordial reality, what would be involved in allowing it to show up? To pursue this we need to address a prior question: What is nature?

There is, of course, an obvious answer to this question. Straightforwardly, nature is the world of earth, sea and sky, of animals and plants—locally, the "biosphere." But what is it metaphysically—what distinguishes nature from non-nature? In an analysis of the ancient Greek experience of nature, Martin Heidegger (1975, 1977) identifies the notion of "physis" as a central characteristic. "Physis": that which arises out of itself. It seems to me that although there are many senses of nature at play in our everyday discourse, this notion of nature as the self-arising is implicit in them all. Whether, to take just a few examples, it is nature conceived as the great scheme of things, as the innate, the wholesome, the nonartificial, a constant underlying idea is that of the autonomous and the essentially nonartifactual. Natural things befall us in their own manner and time. They do not compose themselves for our gaze; we come across them—if we allow ourselves to do so at all—as already there before us. I expand on this characteristic in terms of two closely related dimensions: nature's otherness and nature's mystery, for these well illustrate both what might be involved in knowing nature and how taking the issue of nature in environmental education seriously has fundamental implications for how we think of education as a whole, its "restorying."

Because it is not a human artifact, the post-Enlightenment Italian philosopher Giambattista Vico spoke of nature as being essentially unintelligible to us (see Berlin, 2000). We can never know natural things from the "inside," as we can ourselves, our culture, and its products. We can understand the origin and purpose of the things that we make, but whatever purpose natural things may have—and indeed whether they have any purpose, or are in any sense purposeful—is something that lies ever beyond us. This, not withstanding an almost ineluctable tendency to a beguiling anthropomorphism that tells us otherwise. Things of nature do not themselves participate in our intentional world in the way that we and our artifacts do, even though they may be seriously affected by it and react. Although we are the space where they come to presence and that space is culturally conditioned and structured, for example, by language, we have no authorship of them. Our concept of nature, like any other, can be regarded as a cultural product, and our perception of natural things, like everything else we perceive, occurs in the contexts of human significance and values. Yet our understanding and experience of them as not of our construction, but rather as essentially self-arising is not optional for us; this notwithstanding the fact that we can look past their self-arising presence, and that it can be overlaid.

It is my contention that this sense of the nascent other—the being that lies beyond the concept—is so fundamentally constitutive of our form of sensibility as to render this latter inoperable if somehow it were removed. This means that nature (and therefore the world) is inherently mysterious. The laws that science uses to describe and explain it say nothing of the sheer existence of things, their individual standing there in their suchness. They say nothing of the harmonies of the play of light on water, or of the rustling of leaves by a breeze, or the blue of the blueness of the sky—which they would ultimately transmute into a wavelength. We need to ask: what purpose is served by such a transmutation? What is gained and what is lost? Contrary to what conventional education would incline us to believe, the physical sciences do not give some privileged, more authentic, access to nature. The integrity and unity of nature does not consist in some set of abstract laws that ultimately can be expressed mathematically. Should it ever be achieved, any scientific grand unified theory—"the theory of everything"—would be a theory of nothing as far as nature itself is concerned.

In a different but related context, John McDowell (1996) argues that nature, as it has become to the gaze of the physical sciences, needs to be "re-enchanted," for if it is conceived as occupying the space of blind laws in which such science positions it, it becomes bereft of any capacity to play into the world that humankind occupies—a world where reason (in some very broad sense) operates. The two logical spaces are mutually exclusive, and thus our experience of nature as something that can validate empirical thinking and participate in our thinking about the world, requires that it be conceptual all the way down. There is no pristine sensory given that we somehow apprehend and *then* endow with significance. It comes *with* significance, is always apprehended *as* significant, and is experienced within a horizon of meanings and values (from which science then abstracts it). Although this clearly rescues nature in its essence from those kinds of science that condemn it to a world of blind laws—ultimately a dull and colorless world that consists in "merely the hurrying of material, endlessly, meaninglessly" as Alfred North Whitehead (1985) once said, it might also be seen at the same time to run against the idea of the "otherness" of nature as I have described it. If nature occupies the space in which reason prevails, if it is therefore susceptible to our reasoning, in what sense can it be so radically other? Here we are brought up against the issue of different *kinds* of reasoning and the possibility of a thinking that is nonpossessive and accepting of the strange in what might be the familiar and intimately known.

Something of the sense of the underlying mystery and fluidity of the world is nicely captured by Emily Dickinson (1957) where she writes:

> This World is not a Conclusion:
> A species stands beyond
> Invisible, as Music
> But positive as Sound
>
> It beckons, and it baffles
> Philosophy—don't know
> And through a Riddle, at the last
> Sagacity, must go

The seminal point here is that, ontologically, although our world is a world of significances, it cannot be thoroughly known. In nature there are events, profiles, histories, futures that we will never witness. And attempts at scientific explanation are not only quite irrelevant to the experience of the sheer existence of things, but can be distracting and sometimes destructive of it. Rather, what is required is a willingness to engage in a celebratory attitude that seeks receptive and responsive participation, and where the task, if any, is to find the language to do justice to what is before us, *les mots justes*. Rigor is the product of careful attention to a thing as it is in its relations to other things in each unique, unrepeatable moment. But this sense of transience and becoming is matched by a sense of the solid reality of the ever-changing cadences of things in their particularity. Both are often to be found in great art and literature. For example, they find eloquent expression in the poetry of Gerard Manley Hopkins (1979), such as in his celebrated *The Windhover:*

I caught this morning morning's minion, king-
    dom of daylight's dauphin, dapple-dawn-drawn Falcon, in
    his riding

Of the rolling underneath him steady air, and striding
High there, how he hung upon the rein of a wimpling wing
In his ecstasy! Then off, off forth on swing,
    As a skate's heel sweeps smooth on a bow-bend: the hurl and
    gliding
    Rebuffed the big wind. My heart in hiding
Stirred for a bird,—the achieve of, the mastery of the thing!

Brute beauty and valour and act, oh, air, pride, plume, here
    Buckle! AND the fire that breaks from thee then, a billion
Times told lovelier, more dangerous, O my chevalier!

    No wonder of it: sheer plod makes plough down sillion
Shine, and blue-bleak embers, ah my dear,
    Fall, gall themselves, and gash gold-vermilion.

Here, in addition to its religious connotations, the reality both of that which is elevated and that which is everyday—as when the working plough brings a lustre to the clay and decaying embers fall in, bursting into brief flame—is recognized, allowed to stand forth as worthy of remembrance. Additionally, we find elsewhere in Hopkins (1979) a strong sense of things in themselves and *for* themselves.

As Kingfishers catch fire, dragonflies draw flame;
As tumbled over rim in roundy wells
Stones ring; like each tucked string tells, each hung bell's
Bow swung finds tongue to fling out broad its name;
Each mortal thing does one thing and the same:
Deals out that being indoors each one dwells;
Selves—goes itself; *myself* it speaks and spells,
Crying *What I do is for me: for that I came.*

This notion of things in nature having their own integrity and fulfilment deserving of respect is a powerful motive in Romanticism as a whole. It reflects a general intuition that there is a sense in which nature has its own mysterious *telos* and that, although ultimately mysterious, we have a natural sympathy with it. Indeed, when not preoccupied with other matters, we can sense ourselves as a part of it and recognize its authority: it is part of *our* nature. And yet there are times when we override it; taken up with getting on in life, our sense of responsibility towards it can get left behind. Again, Hopkins (1979) speaks of this in his contemplation of the felling of *Binsey Poplars*:

O if we but knew what we do
When we delve or hew—
Hack and rack the growing green!
. . . .

After-comers cannot guess the beauty been.
Ten or twelve, only ten or twelve
Strokes of havoc unselve
The sweet especial scene . . .

I would like to dwell for a moment on these ideas of the "inscape" of natural things and the possibility of "unselving" them. Hopkins' poplars were clearly unselved in the obvious sense of being chopped down. Physically, they simply were no more. But such objective destruction is not the only way in which things become unselved—meaning by this the loss of their capacity to stand forth as the things they are in their unique integrity. Natural things do not exist in isolation. They are what they are in the context of an environment that they both constitute and are constituted by. But by "environment" here I do not mean the same thing that ecologists and natural scientists often mean by the term: some sort of causal network or system in which organisms are nested and on which they are biologically dependent. The nub of the issue is not that extracting living things from their natural environment will often result in physical harm or death, as, say, when a tree is removed to make way for a new road. It is that the tree, so displaced, has been withdrawn from the place that facilitates it in its occurring as the particular thing that it is.

It has been withdrawn from, say, the play of sunlight on its limbs and leaves, from its movement in the breezes that stir at that spot, from the fall of its extending and diminishing shadow, from its posture in relation to its neighbors, from the sounds and sights of the birds that visit or inhabit it, from the dance of midges beneath its canopy as evening closes; that is to say from its unique and infinitely manifold contribution to the precise ambience of its neighborhood. It holds this neighborhood together, contributes to the unique and ever-changing qualities of its space, and is held by it. In other words it participates in a *place-making*, and is constituted as itself through this participation. And perhaps what can be said here of a tree, in some respects can be said more forcefully of the unselving involved in removing sentient organisms from their natural environs, this denying the proper significance of their senses and movements: their essential adaptedness.

A key point here is that such unselving can be done in thought as well as in action—and perhaps even more insidiously. For example, what happens to the presence of the tree as it becomes installed into some database? As it is accounted in terms of some pro forma, here we "have" the tree neatly summed up in terms of prespecified and fixed objective properties that allow us to call it up at any convenient time; to classify, manipulate, and explain it, to bring it into an infinite range of relationships (e.g., those involved in processing it for some commodity) that are quite arbitrary from the point of view of its own living existence, as described earlier. In extracting it from its neighborhood in which it is physically and metaphysically rooted, in intellectually possessing it, we annihilate it, often without noticing.

Nature as revealed by science is at best highly partial and reductionist, and in many ways science misses the point altogether. Nature is not essentially an energy or information system, nor a deterministic causal network, nor an instantiation of abstract laws. It befalls us, is forever nascent, inherently ineffable, and in living interplay. The vital presencing of nature is imbued with a sense of the withdrawn—of that from which the thing arises, of aspects out of view, of what was and the expectancy of what is not yet. The presence of the withdrawn can sometimes be more sharply felt than that which seemingly is immediately present before us. It makes a call upon our thinking, leading it on, alerting it to the possibilities of an exploration of the unknown. Attendance to all this is thinking in a demanding sense, and sets the paradigm of the kind of thinking that education should cherish. For as we lose our sense of this particular presencing of nature, so do we lose touch with a reality that can inspire and spiritually sustain us.

In all, this perspective affirms a view of knowing that is not centred on a systematized, abstracting scrutiny, but rather a direct acquaintanceship with things. In part, this reaffirms the body as well as the intellect in the process of coming to know. For example, sensing the resilience of the grass underfoot, or the chill in the air and the brooding presence of storm clouds, and the knowledge that one acquires of the sheer power and sublime subtlety of wave and wind when helming a sailing boat—such sensings constitute an extensive domain of knowing that acknowledges and reveals the self-arising in all that is around us. It is most directly articulated in diverse outputs that are essentially poetic in character and that range from, say, a Hopkins poem to an oak table in which the maker has worked with the timber to reveal the figuring lying dormant within it. Such work participates in and celebrates aspects of things themselves, seeks to allow them to stand forth in their suchness. Here, masters of their craft exhibit a certain humility before the qualities inherent in their materials, one that is far removed from that mastery exhibited in the mechanical, and therefore essentially blind, processing of material according to some strictly pre-specified demand or blueprint. Here the making is not born of a respectful intimacy, but of a disengaged challenging, the ongoing quality of the working relationship between worker and material being of relevance only as it bears upon matters of efficiency and maximization of yield.

An intimate familiarity with the other that preserves its alterity can rightly be characterized as a kind of love. Iris Murdoch (1959) suggests that:

> Art and morals are, with certain provisos. . . . one. Their essence is the same. The essence of both of them is love. Love is the perception of individuals. Love is the extremely difficult realization that something other than oneself is real. Love, and so art and morals, is the discovery of reality. (p. 51)

I find seminal this idea of unpossessive love as the discovery of reality. From such a perspective, human flourishing consists neither in an insatiable mastery, nor in subordination to some great abstractly defined ecosystem, but in a genuinely creative receptive responsiveness to fleeting yet recurring occurrences; it is our essence, and can be our joy, to witness and allow such receptivity and responsiveness into the light of significance. Things and consciousness are entirely interdependent; each is nothing without the other. In attending to our responsibility to sustain natural things, we attend to our responsibility to sustain ourselves. Speaking from experiences of learning with Indigenous peoples, the environmental philosopher Jim Cheney (1999) writes:

> Missing in modern conceptions of knowledge is a sense of active and reciprocal communication with the nonhuman world. On an older understanding, knowledge emerges from a conversation between world and person, and our human part in the genesis of knowledge in its most essential aspect, is to prepare ourselves ethically and spiritually for the reception of knowledge. (pp. 141–142)

This affirms a somewhat less exploitative, arrogant attitude toward things. It requires the suspension of the mastery motive that perceives everything essentially as a resource and thereby turns touch into manipulation, sight into essential blindness, hearing into essential deafness. Something of this is graphically depicted in anthropologist Henry Sharp's (1988) description of White Canada's encounter with nature:

> White Canada does not come silently and openly into the bush in search of understanding or communion, it sojourns briefly in the full glory of its colonial power to exploit and regulate all

animate being. . . . It comes asserting a clashing causal certainty in the fundamentalist exercise of the power of its belief. It talks too loudly, its posture is wrong, its movement harsh and graceless; it does not know what to see and it hears nothing. Its presence brings a stunning confusion heard deafeningly in a growing circle of silence created by a confused and disordered animate universe. (pp. 144–145)

This issue of our underlying approach to knowledge that is raised by a different metaphysics of nature is of the highest importance to education as a whole. For example, it alerts us to the fact that many traditional subjects taught in schools arose historically in a social milieu that was not only largely innocent of environmental problems, but that also embraced motives of exploitation toward nature. Predominantly early-modern thinking perceived nature as something to be overcome. In addition, some relative newcomers to the curriculum (such as Design and Technology in the United Kingdom) may reflect even more remorselessly motives of manipulation and productivity—nature, now subdued, here being tacitly understood purely as a resource. Thus, it is important to consider the question of the projects toward reality that are implicit in the agendas and procedures of such subject areas and critically to review them in the light of this epistemology. Here we might embark on a restorying of education of considerable magnitude. We might seek to embed it in a narrative that ceased to characterize everything essentially as a resource and sought to reveal the truth of things in their self-arising. To do this, educators would need to be prepared to think in the demanding sense that breaks out of a superordinate defining conceptualization, and to allow ourselves to respond attentively to a sense of the withdrawn and to be held in the sway of the gods of the domain in which we are present.

To what such a restorying could amount is perhaps nowhere better illustrated than by the case of the teacher–pupil relationship. With the suspension of mastery comes the suspension of prespecification, and with this comes the possibility of respecting the self-arising in students and the world in which they are engaged. Instead of being a relationship whose *raison d'être* is the achievement of a set of externally imposed and predefined standards or targets (almost invariably defined in performative terms), it becomes an interplay that follows its own internal dynamic. Its precise direction and character is a function of a triadic set of relationships of teacher and learner, the learner to what calls to be learnt, and the teacher to what calls to be learnt. Here a voice is given to the "subject matter" itself—the world—and the need to listen and respond to what it calls for, rather than to manipulate and exploit. In such a "trialogical" relationship the mould of anthropocentrism is broken. It is the interplay of this set of relationships that essentially determines the roles and contributions of those involved, not some authority structure external to the site of learning. And actors will assume different roles according to the different positions in which they find themselves at different times: teachers becoming learners, learners, teachers, and so forth as they follow the call of the withdrawn wherever it leads.

Clearly, this conception of thinking as an open engagement imbued with a sense of the unknown has large implications for how we think about teaching. For example, it invites us to see the job of teacher as being less prescribed by either the logical structures of predigested knowledge or sets of external procedures or strategies to be applied to it. Rather a central role of the teacher will be to act as a guide and support in helping the learner cope with, and flourish within, the openness of the call of the withdrawn. That is to say, it will be concerned with supporting the *experience* of thinking rather than just the mechanisms: the constantly evolving courses of affective and cognitive responses involved in full engagement with content. Through drawing on his or her own knowledge of thinking from the "inside," the teacher may sustain the learner in staying alert to the call, sensitive to the pull of the draw, remaining within the ambience of what is withdrawn. This will often require the teacher to provoke and to challenge the pupil. Of such affective and cognitive careers that follow from this, some will be satisfying, some frustrating, some painful. All will involve risk. Some may disturb deeply held beliefs and aspirations that are constitutive of personal identity. Informed by her own experience of such engagement, the teacher can empathize with the courses of such emotions and encourage the learner to accept, for example, that confusion can be a necessary step to understanding, that what currently feels dead can, with suitable attentiveness, become enlivened, that which currently frustrates can become a source of enlightenment, that mystery and paradox may portend some greater truth—and that all such features are constitutive of the experience of thinking as it carries us in and out of them in ways that may on occasion astonish and mystify.

This all suggests a rather different conception of the enterprise of teaching from the currently dominant one that, at worst, still sees itself as predominantly transmitting prespecified information and, that at best, sees itself primarily as providing a universal kit of rules, strategies, and bolt-on skills that themselves are in serious danger of becoming mechanisms for the clinical dissection of experience and the ordering of thought in the pursuit of a sightless transparency—sightless, because such mechanisms are always looking past or straight through things themselves to some further goal. There is an important sense in which such teaching will be more a case of *letting* pupils think rather than *instructing* them. No one can understand for someone else, nor can understanding ever be commanded. These are two rather obvious truths that one could be forgiven for thinking had been forgotten in some teaching episodes driven by externally prescribed goals, where a regime of reinforcing the absorption of other people's ideas frequently stands substitute for providing adequate space for learners to think things through for themselves and genuinely to draw their own conclusions.

But "letting" here is not simply passive; rather it is responsive and challenging. It is harder for the teacher than for the learner, for the teacher has somehow to endeavor to be open—to think in the demanding sense—with regard to what is called to one's thought by both the subject matter *and* the learner. Neither can be turned into objects, prespecified. The teacher has to be held in, and maintain him or herself in, the draw of both. This means that the teacher is always very much a learner. This stance suggests a number of virtues, one of which is charity, in the sense of a disposition to entertain sympathetically another's thought, to be open to what might be worthy in it, to seek the most seminal interpretation, and to seek any important incipient element in it, rather than to "correct" it rapidly in line with some prespecified framework or agenda. Often it is an absence of such a spirit to thinking rather than a lack of relevant skills that is the greatest barrier to progress.

Here we have, then, a restorying that goes right to the heart of the enterprise of education, and that would clearly have significant implications for the school as a truly democratic community whose structures would need to be such as to enable respectful attention to the voices of all "parties," expressed in a variety of lexicons and grammars. Domination of nature and domination of humanity are kin. Both are sired by the desire for mastery, and this always brings with it enervating degrees of prespecification, abstraction, and control that ultimately are as stultifying for those ostensibly exercising the mastery as for those ostensibly under it. Both are caught up in a motive of which they are not themselves the master. I hope I have indicated how recognizing and responding to the self-arising in nature can cue us to a way of being in the world that would relocate education in a radically different metaphysical landscape.

REFERENCES

Berlin, I. (2000). *Three critics of the enlightenment.* London: Pimlico Press.
Bonnett, M. (2004). *Retrieving nature: Education for a post-humanist age.* Oxford, UK: Blackwell.
Brundtland Commission. (1987). *Our common future.* Milton Keynes, UK: Open University Press.

Cheney, J. (1999). The journey home. In A. Weston (Ed.), *An invitation to environmental philosophy*. Oxford, UK: Oxford University Press.

Dickinson, E. (1957). *The complete poems of Emily Dickenson*. New York: Little Brown.

Heidegger, M. (1975). *Poetry, language, thought*. New York: Harper & Row.

Heidegger, M. (1977). *The question concerning technology and other essays*. New York: Harper & Row.

Manley Hopkins, G. (1979). *The major poems*. London: J.M. Dent.

McDowell, J. (1996). *Mind and world*. Cambridge, MA: Harvard University Press.

Murdoch, I. (1959). The sublime and the good. *Chicago Review, 13*(3), 42–55.

Sharp, H. (1988). *The transformation of Bigfoot: Madness, power and belief among the Chipewyan*. Washington, DC: Smithsonian Institution Press.

UNCED. (1992). *Agenda 21*. New York: Author.

Whitehead, A. N. (1985). *Science and the modern world*. London: Free Association Books.

feeling is believing

Ricoeur tells us:
feeling is thought   *made ours*

the sublimating effect of   inhabiting
a body of words   where

we share icons   verbal
textures   of thought

that could be muddled by   an afternoon rain

or the way   a wing gathers
        into itself.

Frye believes:
the unity of a poem   *is the unity of a mood*

already the mention   of an egret
in water   is a way of touching

what cannot be   named
a way of carrying   across

      what resonates
        with the compelling voice of

           the image—

           its clarity.

by Daniela Bouneva Elza

III

Waves, Hybrids, and Networks

10

Remembering Our (Re) Source

Eastern Meditations on Witnessing the Integrity of Water

Claudia Eppert

> *Water, stories, the body,*
> *all the things we do, are mediums*
> *that hide and show what's hidden.*
>
> *Study them,*
> *and enjoy this being washed*
> *with a secret we sometimes know,*
> *and then not.*

—Rumi

In contemporary times we continue to witness dire environmental neglect, exploitation, and destruction, generally recognized as the legacy of a damaging western phallogocentrism. Our current social and educational challenge worldwide is to locate and support more responsive and responsible ways of engaging our natural resources. International educational inquiry is seeking to deconstruct the "west" (by which I mean less a geographical designation than a mindset) and to revive and/or envision and articulate alternate ways of being-in-the-world. Educators in different countries and communities are seeking wisdom and guidance in hopes of finding creative solutions for the many problems of today. Several are reaching for texts and practices composed and cultivated in ancient India and Asia, myself included.

Elsewhere I have begun to consider the implications of the wisdom residing in the canon of Eastern thought for scholarship and cultural endeavors concerned with the theory and educational praxis of "witnessing" (Eppert, 2008). Within the last decade, the language of witnessing is increasingly used to describe processes of working through the origins, dimensions, dynamics, and consequences of social suffering and trauma, and the possibilities for the creation of a more just and compassionate world. Our understanding of the ethical, hermeneutic, psychosocial, and political exigencies of witnessing, however, has yet to benefit from comprehensive consideration of environmental issues. This chapter consequently addresses environmental suffering through a study of select yet resonant Hindu, Taoist, and Buddhist perspectives and practices with a view to contributing to current rich dialogue about the complexities of witnessing and educational initiatives oriented toward personal and social (environmental) transformation.

More specifically, this chapter offers a meditation on two contrary relationships to "water." Within a western perspective, nature has long been regarded as exploitable. The water in oceans, rivers, streams has been drained, piped, hosed, bottled, sold, polluted, and purified. In economically affluent societies, it has been consumed daily and with relatively scant concern, until recently, as water scarcities are more and more becoming a global reality. Water shortages and water-related destruction exemplify the consequences of long-cultivated western consciousness. When we enter Hindu, Buddhist, and Taoist thought, however, we find expressions of a very different relationship to water. Water is perceived not as an object of control, mastery, and exploitation but instead more reverentially as a medium for educational insight. Much of this thought articulates the worth in remembering and becoming mindful of the properties and ways of water. From this natural resource, we learn possibilities for living with each other and with our environment, with integrity. In this chapter, I consider what it might mean to remember water, what such a process might teach us about well-being, witnessing, and the limitations of and potential for present social action. I proceed through an introductory discussion of water in two novels, followed by reflections on how we engage and exploit water today and how this human–nature relationship is embedded within western beliefs, investments, and the English language. I then examine Taoist, Hindu, and Buddhist discussions of water as an educational example of ethical living and acting. Finally, I return to a consideration of the implications of these insights for educational theory and praxis of environmental witnessing, emphasizing four themes: reconciliation, nonaction, integrity, and reverence.

LEARNING FROM WATER

I initially began pondering water and its educational possibilities while reading Leslie Silko's (1986) narrative, *Ceremony*, followed by Herman Hesse's (1999/2003) novel, *Siddhartha*. Each *Bildungsroman* describes the protagonist's search for significance, connection, and wisdom, and each compellingly deploys water imagery and stories in order to reflect the educational journey being undertaken.

Ceremony introduces readers to Tayo Couser, of mixed Mexican and Laguna ancestry, who needs to heal from the traumatic legacies of growing up Native on a North American Laguna Pueblo reservation following World War II. Within the larger framework of witnessing, Tayo engages in a process of what I've called "remembrance-learning" in which, through his teachers, he is slowly empowered to unlearn colonizing discourses, mourn their consequences, and reclaim ancestral ways of knowing and relating to self and world that he had abandoned or buried (Eppert, 1999, 2004). Remembrance-learning, as illustrated in much multiethnic witness literature, very generally involves the protagonist in a long process that includes facing rather than repressing or denying a traumatic past; engaging complex emotions, memories, and knowledge; the eventual mournful and transformational learning to live with loss, variously identified as loss with regard to lives and relationships, to concepts and idealizations, and to conventional self-understanding; a (re-)orientation to an ethics of relation and connection; and a developing commitment to the struggle for social justice/change (Eppert, 1999, 2000a, 2000b, 2002).

Tayo's journey results not only in his personal healing but also in new capacities for engagement and the collective "repair" of the witchery that the medicine men tell him has been unleashed on the world. Tayo is warned by one of his teachers, the medicine man, Old Betonie: "This has been going on for a long time now. It's up to you. Don't let them stop you. Don't let them finish off this world" (Silko, 1986, p. 152). The mountain woman/spirit, Ts'eh, echoes Betonie's warning, telling Tayo, "The destroyers: they work to see how much can be lost, how much can be forgotten. They destroy the feeling people have for each other" (p. 229). Unleashed witchery is evident not only in an extensive history of colonization, oppression, and violence but also in modern warfare and nuclear destruction, Tayo's southwestern U.S. home also being the site of the creation of the first atomic bomb. The effects of all this witchery are manifested in a dearth of rain that has been afflicting the Laguna region for 6 years. According to the holy men, the arrival of the White man disturbed the balance of the world, "bringing droughts and harder days to come" (p. 186). Tayo's Uncle Josiah remarks, "The old people used to say that droughts happen when people forget, when people misbehave" (p. 46). Tayo must not only remember his past but also learn how to remember in ways that are relational and responsive to the earth, having largely lost this capacity through his westernized schooling.

The narrative concludes with Tayo engaging in nonviolent social action and healing, coming to realize, "He was not crazy; he had never been crazy. He had only seen and heard the world as it always was: no boundaries, only transitions through all distances and time" (p. 246). It is a powerful vision and recollection of interdependence and impermanence. Reconciled, he returns home to pass on his story and its message to his community. The final verse of *Ceremony* reveals that the spell has been broken and that the witchery "is dead for now" (p. 261). Rain clouds are beckoning.

Whereas *Ceremony* frames the path from destruction to individual and communal healing and agency via drought and the ending of drought, *Siddhartha* describes river water as a primary site for remembrance-learning, reconciliation, and renewal. Toward the end of his journey, Siddhartha approaches a large river in the forest, the same one across which a ferryman had once ferried him when he was a young man still in the early stages of his (re)search concerning the mysteries of life. Newly awakened and gazing at the current, he feels that it has something special to tell him, and hears an inner voice invoking him to attend to its teachings: "Love this water! Stay with it! Learn from it!" (p. 89). He recognizes the river carries many secrets, but he has yet to be privy to more than one:

> He saw the water running and running, constantly running, and yet it was always there, was always and forever the same, and yet new every instant! Who could grasp this, who could fathom this?! He did not grasp or fathom it, he felt only an inkling stirring, a distant memory, godly voices. (p. 89)

Siddhartha continues his way upstream until he reaches the ferryman whom he befriends and who invites him to live with him in his hut. Siddhartha expresses his gratitude to Vasudeva for the invitation and notes how intently the ferryman listens to his passenger's life story:

> One of the ferryman's greatest virtues was that he knew how to listen like few other people. Without a word from Vasudeva, the speaker felt that the ferryman took in his words, silent, open, waiting, missing none, impatient for none, neither praising nor blaming, but only listening. Siddhartha felt what happiness it is to unburden himself to such a listener, to sink his own life into this listener's heart, his own seeking, his own suffering. (p. 92)

Siddhartha thanks the riverman for hearing him so well, commenting, "Rare are the people who know how to listen, and I have never met anyone who knew it so well as you. This too I will learn from you" (p. 92). But Vasudeva reminds him about the pedagogical injunction from the river:

> You will learn it . . . but not from me. It was the river that taught me how to listen. . . . The
> river knows everything . . . Look, you too have already learned from the river that it is good
> to strive downward, to sink, to seek the depth. (p. 93)

Learning from the river, Siddhartha comes to an insight shared by Tayo, about the fluidity of
time and space: "the river is everywhere at once [and] . . . has many voices, very many voices"
(p. 95).

In both narratives, water encompasses a resource for healing and awakening, and healing
and awakening mean relearning an intimate engagement with and reverence for the natural world.
As Tayo's Uncle Josiah asserts: "This is where we come from, see. This sand, this stone, these
trees, the vines, all the wildflowers. This earth keeps us going" (p. 45). Whereas Tayo's learning
in *Ceremony* is embedded in Native American spiritual understanding, Siddhartha's vehicles for
insight include the ancient *Upanishads* and a face-to-face encounter with the Buddha. *Siddhartha*
is the product of Hesse's own increasing involvement with Asian ideas during the war years of the
early to mid-20th century, and his awareness of the dire social need in the west for connection.
His river motif serves to illustrate the challenges and possibilities of passage, from west to east,
childhood to adulthood, human alienation to universal relation and reconciliation, from a cycle
of suffering (samsara) to nirvana and compassionate return. Both *Ceremony* and *Siddhartha* are
fiction. Yet they capture current realities and provocatively invite us to contemplate and creatively
re-envision our physical, psychic, and social landscape.

DROUGHT

If we subsequently put down these texts and take a moment to look at nature around us, we can
indeed readily observe literature in life and life in literature. Everywhere we can see the consequences
of western witchery on our water: pollution, diseased fish, ailing fauna, and so on. And it is
increasingly a time of scarcity and of global drought. A 2003 report commissioned by the United
Nations Environment Program maintains that current water shortages affecting at least 400 million
people today will affect 4 billion people by 2050 (http://www.usatoday.com/). The report cites
waste and inadequate management as the main cause for the current problem. Half of all coastal
regions have deteriorated through overdevelopment or pollution. Recently, hurricanes Katrina and
Rita flooded southern Louisiana and created devastation from which we have yet to be remotely
close to recovering. Part of what gave rise to the flooding was coastal erosion due to increasing sea
levels, navigation, land-building, and flood control projects. Indeed, according to the website of
the nonprofit group *Restore or Retreat*, since 1930, Louisiana has lost more than 1,500-square miles
of wetlands, and by 2050 it is estimated that 640,000 more acres will be under water. Globally,
coral reefs, mangrove forests, and sea grass beds face threats from overfishing, development, and
pollution. Oxygen-depleted seas, caused by industrial and agricultural runoff, could lead to fishery
collapses and "dead zones." The World Bank maintains that 80 countries currently experience water
shortages and 40% of the world lacks access to clean water and sanitation. Political conflicts and
hostilities over rivers that run across national borders and over scarce resources abound.

A growing world population is partly responsible for water shortages. Already at a taxing
6 billion, the population is expected to reach 9 billion in another few decades, and demands by
individuals, agriculture, and industry on water resources will be intense. According to the World
Bank, global demand for water is doubling every 21 years. At the same time, however, according
to the Worldwatch Institute's website: "since 1900, there has been a sixfold increase in water
use for only a twofold increase in population size" as a result of rising standards of living. Also,

approximately 95% of the world's cities still dump raw sewage into their waters. Climate change is also increasingly a factor in water concerns, as it is creating more severe droughts, declining water run off, rising sea levels, accelerated cycle of rainfall and evaporation, early snowmelt, and the melting of glaciers. The United States is one of the central contributors to climate change. While making up just 4% of the world's population, the United States produces 25% of the carbon dioxide pollution from fossil-fuel burning (http://www.nrdc.org/).

WITCHERY OF THE WEST

Efforts are underway to raise consciousness concerning our contemporary global water crisis. The United Nations has declared 2005–2015 the "International Decade for Action, 'Water for Life.' " Initiatives to achieve greater water sustainability are wide-ranging and include the promotion of more effective energy policies, better efficiency in irrigation, better management and distribution, cooperation across borders, careful land management, and community awareness and conservation, among many others.

Although there is no doubt that education and sociopolitical action are key, my concern here is the nature of this learning and action. I wonder how much can be gained from education and subsequent action if the action generated operates within the same consciousness as that which gave rise to exploitation and destruction in the first place. How much can be accomplished, for example, if we conserve and manage but more wholeheartedly continue to embrace and teach competitiveness, fear, consumerism, domination, the immediate fulfillment of individual and social desires, and so on? In other words, although education, conservation, and management efforts are undoubtedly vital, might there not be something deeper and necessary for fully addressing the challenges of environmental repair and renewal; namely, an *a priori* transformation in the "western" mindset that perceives, interprets, engages, and acts in the world in ways that cannot but threaten the environment? Surface endeavors, in other words, are bound to be insufficient unless we dig at the roots of what has gotten us in our contemporary situation.

Let us penetrate more fully the individual, communal, and collective consciousness that is endangering the earth and increasingly dominating the global public sphere. At its darkest, it is intensely technological and digital (out of touch with nature) and driven by competition, production, control, management, and consumption. All is an instant. Success is defined principally in economic terms, in terms of material acquisition and the view that "bigger is better" rather than less is more. Greed is a notion that is blurry round its edges and that continually threatens to eclipse honesty. Independence, autonomy, and freedom (understood as the unmitigated pursuit of the self's pleasures) are embraced and taught as unambiguous values. As such, self is fashioned against and over other. Other, whether animate or inanimate, is approached primarily in utilitarian terms, identified as exploitable and expendable, as existing for the self's consolidation. Echoes of this mindset can be read in the following response to a YouTube clip from a documentary about saving the arctic refuge. The commenter on the clip writes: "Think about what is more important: a pretty refuge and some oh so adorable animals, or a secure source of oil. . . . I am not hunter, I do not think killing animals for fun is by any means a noble thing, but I do not value the lives of a few animals above an American source of oil." Economic wealth, independence, and security are prioritized at the expense of wildlife and the preservation of the environment.

Many scholars have variously illustrated how we have inherited and developed our contemporary consciousness from western religious, economic, political, and scientific beliefs and interpretations, inventions, discoveries, and challenges. David Abram (1996), for instance, describes our present as an era of alienation and violence. In his view, western literacy is in part responsible. He documents how the Greek alphabetic script, with all its vowels, over time rendered mute an active interpretative and sacred relationship with the air and the breath. The term *psyche*, previously intimately connected with the sensuous world, became an abstract and rational phenomenon "now enclosed within the physical body like a prison" (p. 253). He further details how the New Testament, which was originally written in the Greek alphabet, thus came to ally religious doctrine with a dualistic linguistic sensibility. In the spreading of the Greek word, Christian missionaries were inadvertently cultivating among their pupils disassociation from the animate earth. Over time, the notion of an autonomous and sovereign self emerged, one that interacts with itself in virtual isolation. This new modern self has largely forgotten air, atmosphere, breath, and the "unseen depth between things—between people, or trees, or clouds" (p. 258).

REMEMBRANCE-LEARNING

Abram (1996) invites us to remember again, warning that "if we do not soon remember ourselves to our sensuous surroundings, if we do not reclaim our solidarity with the other sensibilities that inhabit and constitute those surroundings, then the cost of our human commonality may be our common extinction" (p. 271). Our future hinges on a critical unlearning and relearning, in recognition that remembrance is socially constructed and itself in part a product of hegemonic perspectives and practices (Simon, Rosenberg, & Eppert, 2000). I am reminded of a passage in the beginning of *Ceremony*:

> Tayo felt the old nausea rising up in his stomach, along with a vague feeling that he knew something which he could not remember. . . . [T]he feelings were twisted, tangled roots, and all the names for the source of this growth were buried under English words, out of reach. And there would be no peace and the people would have no rest until the entanglement had been unwound to the source. (p. 117)

Tayo suffers from a legacy of colonization and the long-standing denigration of his language and culture, and his remembrance-learning involves reclaiming his Native traditions and insights. This reclamation is a task particular to his context. At the same time, the responsibility Tayo comes to experience for ending the witchery is not his alone. The effects of western language and culture are everywhere evident—alienation, violence, and the slow obliteration of our earth—and call everyone to action, call everyone to confront the challenge of disengaging from destructive western sensibilities. Emotions (fear, anger, greed, and hatred) and beliefs (competition, aggression, autonomy, sovereignty, and consumerism) that have separated and are separating us from each other and from nature need to be unpacked and unwound to their source.

At issue is the willingness not to cover the past with convenient self-serving personal, communal, and national ideologies but instead to confront it, unearthing the physical and psychological losses that are the result of generations of environmental neglect and abuse (e.g., the extinction of species), and encountering and experiencing our loss of intellectual, emotional, and spiritual intimacy with self, other, and the natural world. As the remainder of this chapter emphasizes, the essence in this process is the slow, laborious, and painful mourning and letting go of attachment to a separate self, and the interminable cultivation of an interconnected, contemplative, creative, and fluid sensibility. In so doing, we undertake what Mary Doll (2000) describes as a release and "greening of the imagination . . . an ecological relationship between human and other myriad life forms in the cosmos" (p. 203). She elaborates that to green the imagination is to reorient us "to the sources and resources of life" and to creatively envision "new directions that reconceptualize the damaging ideals of progress and humanism" (p. 203).

Noel Gough (1990, 1991, 1993) situates the crisis and possibilities ahead specifically within our stories. He contends that the "global environmental crisis is in large part a direct consequence of western industrialized societies' cultivation of stories in which the earth (or 'nature') is conceived, and thus exploited, as an object of instrumental or intrinsic value" (Gough, 1990, p. 14). He asserts that education must support the criticism of such stories and of the myths and ideologies of the "cultivated" subject who transcends nature and can bend it to his will. Additionally, it is vital that Anglo-education encourage forms of storytelling that move beyond the conceptual and linguistic binaries, objectifications, and separations that are so deeply a part of English language and identity, and invite a sense of kinship with the earth. Gough refers to Aboriginal Australian stories as an example of deep ecological understanding. Such stories do more than entertain. They can invite the very critique of culturally embedded habits of consciousness that cause environmental destruction in the first place and awaken alternate understandings. At the same time, Gough is sensitive to issues of cultural appropriation. Like other writers, such as Joseph Campbell (1949), Joseph Campbell and Bill Moyers (2001), David Loy and Linda Goodhew (2004), Jacob Needleman (1976, 1994), Gough (1991) emphasizes the need for new "myths and metaphors that 'sing' the earth into existence in the conditions of urban and late industrial lifestyles" (p. 40).

Although activism concerning environmental issues is on the rise and conservation efforts are underway, the critical interrogation of destructive ways of seeing and engaging the world and the creation of alternate sensibilities and stories are, consequently, equally serious endeavors. As Heesoon Bai and Avi Cohen (2002) contend, "the task for us engaged in promoting the well-being of the planet and humanity is not to deliver moralistic injunctions and threats, but to introduce views and practices that will help people to inhabit a non-dualistic, intersubjective consciousness." It is the insight that directs this edited collection, and, to me, echoing Hesse, is part of what it means to "strive downward, to sink, to seek the depth" (p. 39). If we recognize our difficult task as one of untangling what we have created, remembrance-learning, and returning to our source, the questions that follow might include: But, how, more specifically, do we undertake this task? And, what is our source? The following discussion of Hindu, Taoist, and Buddhist views shed light on both these questions, showing how our common source is—water.

THE WAY OF WATER

Etymological inquiry reveals that the word water derives from the Sanskrit *ap*, which carried the meaning of water as "living force." *Apah* or *apas* reference the waters of space out of which the universe is produced. Water courses in and through everything. It is the universal softness and fluidity of water as well as its strength that has attracted the attention of sages. Indeed, it is fascinating how Taoism, Buddhism, and Hinduism speak of water. As Sarah Allen (1997) writes, in Chinese philosophy, "Water with its multiplicity of forms and extraordinary capacity for generating imagery, provided the model for conceptualizing general cosmic principles, principles which applied to the behavior of people, as well as the forces of nature" (p. 4). Although Allen primarily attends to Taoist and Confucian thought, this chapter draws brief attention also to the thematic presence of water within Buddhist, Vedic, and Hindu worldviews. Sages from all these traditions describe water's properties, its different manifestations, its interaction with the natural and the human in order to illuminate human capacities for insight, wisdom, and compassion, in order to teach an alternate ethics, and in order to address the possibilities of (social) action. Because the cosmologies embedded in these texts are complex and detailed, in what follows, I outline only select insights.

Water is centrally featured within Taoist philosophy, in such texts as the *Tao Te Ching*, compiled around the fourth century BCE. *Tao*, commonly translated as the "Way," represents cosmic unity and encompasses that from which all arises and to which all returns. The Way is within everything, is eternal and ineffable, unable to be rendered in language and only intuitively known. *Te,* apparently inordinately difficult to translate into English, denotes the "personal qualities or strengths of the individual, one's personhood . . . self-realization in relation to the cosmos . . . the embodiment of the Way" (Mair, 1990, p. 54). *Ching* translates as "classic," as in a classic text. The sum message of the *Tao Te Ching* is that human beings should align themselves with and follow the Way of the universe and, in the process, unite with their original Tao nature, which is obscured by the machinations of ego and society. Within Taoist philosophy, untangling to our source thus entails remembering and reconnecting with Tao. Water teaches us possibilities for re-engaging Tao. The *Tao Te Ching* emphasizes the power of water, and indicates that its vitality and invincibility comes from its fluidity. Chapter 78 states, "Nothing under heaven is softer or weaker than water,/ and yet nothing is better/ for attacking what is hard and strong,/ because of its immutability" (p. 54). Water is powerful not because it is tough and inflexible but rather the converse: It is soft, mutable, and always yielding, always following a path of least resistance. In this way, it overcomes all, even the largest and most solid of rocks. Taoist philosophy is embedded within an abiding respect for nature—for the organic, the simple, and the spontaneous—and calls on human beings to return to harmony with the natural world by aligning themselves and moving easily with rather than against the currents and rhythms of air and water.

This notion of flexibility and moving *with* rather than struggling *against* the forces of life is elaborated in the Taoist concept of *wu-wei.* It illustrates more the way of the way, drawing attention to how the natural world acts—without force and deliberation. *Wu-wei* literally means nonaction, understood more in the sense of the adage "going with the flow." Victor Mair (1990) emphasizes that *wu-wei* is not the absence of action but rather noninterference, of flowing in agreement with the natural and cosmic course of things. It is not passivity or withdrawal; rather, it is engagement that moves and transitions and gets where it is going, but it does so in a manner that is harmonious, yielding, gentle, accepting, and supple, rather than one that is resisting, forcing, controlling, dominating, and aggressive. It adapts readily to whatever is in its path, exactly like water. Patrick Bresnan (2003) says it well, "'Going with the flow' means far more than simply floating. Dead fish go with the flow; live fish swim against the flow, but they use the current to do it. *Wu Wei* is using the current to get where you're going" (p. 157). Bresnan elaborates with an apt example, distinguishing between a person sailing and a person in a motorboat. Both equally arrive at their destination, but the motorboat does so, perhaps more quickly, by plowing its way through and generating a great deal of noise and pollution. The sailboat, on the other hand, skillfully, silently, abidingly, and unobtrusively manoeuvres the sail in ways that are responsive to wind and water. For the Taoist, therefore, the how of things is central. It is better to arrive by having sailed. Indeed, particularly if one is talking about spiritual arrival, one cannot cross to the other shore with passage by motorboat.

The notion of *wu-wei* counters the common impulses of the ego, which inclines toward expansion rather than contraction, increase rather than decrease, investment rather than divestment. Much of ancient Eastern thought is linked in the insight that the ego's craving and insecurity is what causes discord, despair, and destruction. It is what blocks us from accessing and being at one with our true Tao nature. Thus, Mair translates lines from Chapter 38 of the *Tao Te Ching* as: "The person of superior integrity takes no action,/nor has he a purpose for acting" (p. 3). My interpretation of these lines is not that no action whatsoever is taken; rather, the action not taken is ego-based action—action driven by the purposes of the ego. Action in accord with the spirit of the Way is initiated, however. But, because it is so in harmony with Tao, is so a part of Tao, it does not appear as action. To draw on another common example—in windy weather the reed bends effortlessly; it is not trying to control or fight the wind through stiff resistance or attack but rather survives and is empowered through its swift and ready, intuitive adaptability to the forces of nature.

The Taoist sage Chuang Tzu, whose work preceded the *Tao Te Ching* but was composed in the same century, deploys water imagery to elaborate upon the difference between acting out of ego and acting from one's Tao nature:

> Water, if not mixed with other things, is by nature clear, and if it is not stirred up, it is level. However, if it is blocked and cannot flow, it cannot remain clear. This is like the Virtue of Heaven. It is said that to be innocent and pure, free from contamination, still and level, never changing, detached and acting without action, is to move with Heaven and to follow the Tao of sustaining the spirit. (Palmer, 1996, p. 131)

Te in *Tao Te Ching* is self-realization. A person of *te* is one who acts by releasing the blockages and contamination produced by ego-centered thoughts, emotions, and actions. Letting go is a discipline of gentle distillation. One becomes clear and calm like transparent and flowing water. Then one is connected with Tao. Such clearing does not mean repressing one's emotions or thoughts but rather not clinging to them such that one "acts out." A person of the Tao has distilled the everyday to its most pure, and lives simply and modestly, without interest in fame, power, or possession. He or she works naturally, harmoniously, and wholeheartedly—in tune with the Way, not seeking to bend the environment to his or her will, or own it, or stand out against it, but rather exercising his or her agency by blending in and becoming an integral caring part of the environment. Taoism thus offers a vision of "acting without action" in the world. This vision should not be misunderstood as easily attainable. Paradoxically, the ease being described here can only be attained with great effort.

ACTING WITHOUT ACTION

The concept of acting without action is similarly discussed in the ancient text the *Bhagavad Gita*, set within the Indian epic the *Mahabharata*, which was composed between the fifth and fourth centuries BCE and tells of (mythic) events that occurred in India between 1400 and 800 BCE. Indeed, Mair (1990) contends that the numerous affinities between the *Tao Te Ching* and the *Gita* are not incidental but rather the result of a history of intercultural exchange. He poses that the ideas expressed in the *Gita*, composed about one or two centuries before the *Tao Te Ching*, were orally transmitted to China where they were appropriated and transformed in response to Chinese philosophies and cultural investments. The *Gita* begins at that point in the *Mahabharata* in which two armies are preparing for battle. The battle can be read as an externalization of the war each of us engages within. Arjuna, the warrior prince leader of one of the armies, experiences angst in the recognition that he is about to slay former friends, teachers, and allies. The driver of the chariot that is to lead Arjuna into battle is Krishna, the incarnation of the god Vishnu. With the intent to motivate Arjuna and enable him to fight his inner demons, Krishna initiates a dialogue in which he teaches the yogas to his new disciple, recounting to him the characteristics of one who is spiritually awake.

Although a great deal is illuminated throughout the *Gita*, a recurring theme is that of action. Krishna does not accept Arjuna's sudden refusal to enter battle, and warns that there is nothing to be gained by avoiding action. Everybody is driven to action by their very nature. Important is the intent, nature, and manner of action. Krishna disavows action propelled by personal desire, greed, fear, revenge, and other selfish attributes of the ego. He asserts that the wise are those who act selflessly and for the welfare of all. Moreover, the wise, having renounced their separateness, act without attachment to results. Selfless action, or karma yoga, in Hindu terms, Eknath Easwaren (1985) notes, is the basic law underlying creation. Karma in Hinduism and Buddhism means deed or action and refers to the underlying dynamic of cause and effect that governs existence. Everything good or bad that happens to us is a result of prior good or bad actions. In order to escape the bonds of cause and effect one must engage in right action. Here we have echoes of Taoism in that right action is undertaken without regard for ego-driven motives, interests, and results. Action that is centered on self over and at the expense of the other, on personal rewards and on products of labor such as success, fame, and fortune, will likely produce negative karma, further entangling the doer in a cycle of suffering. In this regard, one's thoughts and mental disposition generally are integral to karma. As discussed in Taoism, the most natural and spiritual action is that undertaken with the ego forgotten, for example, like a teacher so engrossed while aiding a student that he or she momentarily lets go of self-centered thoughts and emotions. The process thus is essential; if the process is carefully attended to and the conditions solidly established, it is unnecessary to be concerned with the outcome and, indeed, the outcome is likely to be favorable, because the foundation was firm. So, in the *Gita,* Krishna maintains, "Those who are motivated only by desire/ for the fruits of their action are miserable, for they/are constantly anxious about the results of/ what they do. When consciousness is unified,/ however, all vain anxiety is left behind. . . . Actions do not cling to me because I am not/ attached to their results" (Easwaren, 1985, pp. 66, 86).

Furthermore, the *Gita* undoes the dualism of action and non-action. Krishna asserts, "The wise see that there is action in the midst/of inaction and inaction in the midst of action" (p. 87). In a way, this harkens back to Taoism, particularly the interplay between *yin* and *yang.* *Yin* is often identified as the soft, the weak, the feminine, the yielding, and the passive while *yang* is recognized as the hard, the strong, the masculine, the aggressive and active. But, as Hongyu Wang (2008) reminds:

> [W]e can see a light dot in yin and a dark dot in yang, signifying that yin and yang also are embedded within each other. Water itself is powerful because of its inner strength, even though this strength is constructed differently from the formation of stone. By the same token, there is a built-in vulnerability in masculine hardness. (p. 321)

In this sense, action and inaction are contained within each other. At the same time, the lines from the *Gita* emphasize that nonaction or actionless action is action done without the interference of the ego: hence, "even while acting . . . [the wise] really do nothing at all" (Easwaren, 1985, p. 87). They have gone beyond life's dualisms, and are not altered by success or failure. Easwaren writes "of persons so established in identification with the Self [i.e., true nature] that in the midst of tireless service to those around them, they remain in inner peace, the still witness of action" (p. 37).

STILL LAKE

Classical and contemporary Buddhist texts echo several of the themes and insights found in Hindu and Taoist literature. The importance of nonattachment to action, for example, is reiterated in such classics as the *Diamond Sutra,* composed in India in the fourth century CE: "bodhisattvas who achieve merit should not be fettered with desire for rewards" (Price & Mou-lam, 1990, p. 49). Abiding in Buddhism, Hinduism, and Taoism is the distinction between ego-consciousness and true consciousness, whether that is Tao nature as in Taoism, or Dharma nature as in Hinduism, or Buddha nature as in Buddhism.

Buddhist texts deploy the image of water to illustrate distinctions between ordinary/separated ego consciousness and awakened/interconnected consciousness. The former is likened to stormy and turbulent water, as a lake beset with clouds and wind, while the latter is deep, quiet, and peaceful. The ancient classical Buddhist text, *The Dhammapada,* describes how the minds of those who listen to the words of the dharma, "become calm and clear like the waters of a still lake" (Easwaran, 1985, p. 96). The clouds of illusion give way to inner clarity and peace. Coming to this point marks a process of passage and arrival. Hence, the *Sutra of Hui-neng* (or *Platform Sutra*), that is, the sutra of the Sixth Patriarch of Chinese Zen (638–713) maintains that:

> By clinging to sense objects, existence and nonexistence arises like the up and down of the billowy sea, and such a state is called metaphorically "this shore"; while by nonattachment a state above existence and nonexistence, like smoothly running water, is attained, and this is called "the opposite shore." (Price & Mou-lam, 1990, p. 81)

The passage resonates with not only Chuang Tzu's Taoist words but also with a passage from the ancient Vedic *Brihadaranyaka Upanishad,* in which the sage Yajnavalkya tells his wife Maitreyi what happens in realization: "As a lump of salt thrown in water dissolves and cannot be taken out again, though wherever we taste the water it is salty, even so, beloved, the separate self dissolves in the sea of pure consciousness" (Easwaran, 1987, p. 38).

Within Hinduism, far beneath the guise of individuality one finds *atman,* Self or Soul. *Atman* is the innermost essence or soul of life and of sentient beings, a unitive state of pure, universal consciousness. The discovery of *atman* is referred to as *moshka,* a journey to the still interior that may take life times (Bresnan, 2003, p. 215). If Hinduism emphasizes *atman,* Buddhism, however, posits a more revolutionary belief in the doctrine of *anatman,* or no Self. The Buddha maintained that there is no self or soul, no *atman* that can be found beneath the separate self, just impermanence (the Doctrine of *Anitya*) and various causes and conditions that bring things into and out of existence (the Doctrine of Dependent Origination). There is no doer, therefore, only the doing.

This prioritization of verb over noun is reflected in Japanese Zen master Dōgen's (1200–1253) Mountains and Water Sutra. In this sutra, written in autumn 1240, Dōgen studies the characteristics of water, noting, for example, that it escapes the bounds of either/or categorization:

> Water is neither strong nor weak, neither wet nor dry, neither moving nor still, neither cold nor hot, neither existent nor nonexistent, neither deluded nor enlightened. When water solidifies, it is harder than a diamond. Who can crack it? When water melts, it is gentler than mild. Who can destroy it? (Dōgen, 2000, p. 70)

The power of water emerges from its nondualistic, transitional nature; it is neither existent nor nonexistent but entirely dependent on particular conditions for its temporary form. Yet, this adaptability makes water not weak but indestructible, both when it is hard and when it is soft. Water is also not time-bound—not concerned with past, present, or future. It is only our perception of water that makes it appear as a static, stable entity rather than an ever changing composition of elements and conditions. Moreover, our perception is itself largely contextual and conditioned. Dōgen observes how some sentient beings perceive water as blossoms, whereas others see it as ornaments, and yet others envision it as fire and others as a palace and others as a forest: in other words, "water is seen as dead or alive depending on causes and conditions" (p. 70). Moreover, human beings often identify water as that which flows unceasingly and that which flows downward. Yet, in effect, according to Dōgen, water "flows on the earth, in the sky upward, and downward. It can flow around a single curve or into many bottomless abysses. When it rises it becomes clouds. When it descends it forms abysses" (p. 71). Finally, water is the effect of myriad conditions and causes—this is what Dōgen describes as water's "thusness"—its reality (p. 76). Water is not independent, not apart from but rather part and process of nature. He urges individuals to interrogate the "thusness" of water and of perception, and to come to recognize that there is "no original water" and no essential identity outside of conditions and causes: "water as earth, water, fire, wind and space realizes itself" (p. 71). Interrogating the realities of water and sentient perception, one comes to realize interdependence and impermanence as one's true nature: "Water also exists within the wisdom of realizing Buddha nature. . . . Buddha ancestors always take up water and make it their body and mind, make it their thought" (p. 72).

Closer study of ourselves and the environment shows, consequently, that we are part of universal processes of cause and effect, and are thoroughly interconnected. Contemporary Vietnamese Zen Buddhist monk Thich Nhat Hanh (1987, 1998, 2002) makes distinctions between the separate ego self and Buddha/no-self nature more accessible to understanding, particularly to western understanding. He frequently refers to a term in the *Avatamsaka Sutra* that he translates into English as *interbeing*. Interbeing is the awareness that we are not separate entities but rather that we are a composite of elements and conditions that we also share, water being one example. Our bodies are made of water. Water connects us with each other and with the universe. The reality of our existence, therefore, is not that we "are" but that we "inter-are."

In his *No Death, No Fear*, Hanh (2002) invokes an image of ocean waves in order to elaborate on distinctions between self and no-self. Individualism might be described as that of the wave; however, the reality is that the wave is part of the water that makes up the ocean. In ways that echo Dōgen's sutra, Hanh writes:

> When you look at the surface of the ocean, you can see waves coming up and going down. You can describe these waves in terms of high or low, big or small, more vigorous or less vigorous, more beautiful or less beautiful. You can describe a wave in terms of beginning and end, birth and death. That can be compared to the historical dimension. In the historical dimension, we are concerned with birth and death, more powerful, less powerful, more beautiful, less beautiful, beginning and end and so on.
>
> Looking deeply, we can also see that the waves are at the same time water. A wave may like to seek its own true nature. The wave might suffer from fear, from complexes. A wave may say, "I am not as big as the other waves," "I have been born and I have to die." The wave may suffer from these things, these ideas. But if the wave bends down and touches her true nature she will realize that she is water. Then her fear and complexes will disappear.
>
> Water is free from the birth and death of a wave. Water is free from high and low, more beautiful and less beautiful. You can talk in terms of more beautiful or less beautiful, high or low, only in terms of waves. As far as water is concerned, all these concepts are invalid. (p. 23)

Elsewhere, I detail how Buddhism cautions us to recognize the limitations of the mind which deploys the mechanisms of categorization, analysis, evaluation, judgment and so on in order to make sense of the world (Eppert, 2008). American Tibetan Buddhist monk Pema Chödrön (1997) points out how "all ego really is, is our opinions, which we take to be solid and real and the absolute truth about how things are" (p. 110). We are invited to dismantle preoccupation to our thoughts and thought processes, concepts, narratives, and ideologies. In so doing, we acquire insight into the true nature of water, experiencing how it cannot be contained by any such essentializing concepts as high or low, beautiful or ugly, birth or death.

Hanh (2002) similarly critiques conceptual understanding when he invokes water, as does Hesse in *Siddhartha*, in order to emphasize the nature of impermanence:

> When we bathe in the river today that we bathed in yesterday, is it the same river? Heraclitus said that we couldn't step into the same river twice. He was right. The water in the river today is completely different from the water we bathed in yesterday. Yet it is the same river. When Confucius was standing on the bank of a river watching it flow by, he said: "Oh, it flows like that day and night, never ending."
>
> The insight of impermanence helps us to go beyond all concepts. It helps us to go beyond same and different and coming and going. It helps us to see that the river is not the same river but is also not different either . . . Impermanence should be understood in the light of inter-being. (p. 40)

Hanh (1987) further asserts, "The Buddhist way of understanding is always letting go of our views and knowledge in order to transcend. This is the most important teaching. That is why I use the image of water to talk about understanding. Knowledge is solid; it blocks the way of understanding. Water can flow, can penetrate" (p. 43).

LOOKING DEEPLY: TOWARD A WITNESSING PRAXIS

The vision of human nature described by Hanh and others is, to me, refreshing, offering me opportunities to learn to regard myself and the natural world in mutually interconnected, supportive, and potentially healing rather than conventionally divisive ways. David Purpel (Purpel & McLaurin, 2004) writes that alienation "tends to produce a sense of life as empty, absurd, devoid of meaning, as well as an inability to identify with natural or social forces, which brings on feelings of anxiety, loneliness, and dread" (p. 66). In a similar vein, Abram (1996) contends, "A civilization that relentlessly destroys the living land it inhabits is not well acquainted with truth, regardless of how many supposed facts it has amassed regarding the calculable properties of the world" (p. 264). Theirs is an image of humanity gone awry, living in deception and illusion, far estranged from truth. What is this truth to which Abram refers? In this postmodern age the word *truth* is met with great suspicion. And a good deal of suspicion is warranted, as postmodernism has exposed the dangers of grand narratives and totalizing claims, and has recognized the partiality of language and thought. It asserts that there are no large truths, only local and subjective truths. What Abram describes *is* truth in a subjective, human, and lived sense; truth not as static fact, not as subject–object categorization, not as concept, but rather as "a quality of relationship" (p. 264). He elaborates, "A human community that lives in a mutually beneficial relation with the surrounding earth is a community, we might say, that lives in truth" (p. 264). Truth, then, is recognized as a lived and responsive/responsible relation of interdependence.

This chapter critiques a divisive mindset and considers the potential for embracing an interconnected relation to the world, long recognized by Taoist, Hindu, and Buddhist sages but largely disparaged by adherents to western perceptions and priorities. And so our waters are polluted. But, if we look at the true nature of clear running water, these sages remind, we can find an alternate way, one of interconnection. This intimate relationship between self and nature is illustrated in the myths and legends surrounding the Buddha's enlightenment. As Prince Siddhartha Guatama sits beneath the Bodhi tree in the final stage of his awakening, the demon *Māra*, lord of death and selfish passion, tries to tempt and terrify the soon-to-be Buddha from his goal of insight as to the nature of human suffering. However, in response to numerous dire temptations, the Buddha, with firm resolve, touches the ground with his right fingertip determined not to be swayed, whereupon the earth responds, "'I bear you witness,' with a hundred, a thousand, and a hundred thousand thunderous roars" (Smith & Novak, 2003, p. 10; Easwaran, 1985, p. 27). The Buddha's touching of the earth and the earth's answer underscores Shoshana Felman and Dori Laub's (1992) description of witnessing as a communicative act, only that the communication is not between human beings but between human beings and nature. The myth highlights a dialogical person–environment relationship of transformation. Awakening occurs in unison with an animated witnessing earth that thunders support and provides committed ground. The earth, by witnessing, enables the Buddha to become enlightened, to awaken. And, as Bresnan (2003) notes, enlightenment means healing: "That's what awakening is: getting well" (p. 213). In contemporary times, Mother Earth continues to bear witness to human endeavors, as is all too evident from the resources it yields and the mountains of refuse it continues to take and productively transform. Yet, by what measure are we reciprocally bearing witness to the earth and its current suffering?

At the beginning of this chapter, I introduced the notion of *witnessing*. Although scholarship on witnessing is wonderfully diverse and complex, we can identify some shared perspectives. Particularly writing informed by the framework of 20th-century philosopher Emmanuel Levinas, postmodernism, and psychoanalysis, communicates resonant insights concerning the challenges witnesses face. Very generally, these include: (a) figuring out one's relationships to the experience of the suffering of self, of another, of an event; (b) negotiating what is knowable with what is unknowable; (c) experiencing and working through difficult and conflicting emotions; (d) critically interrogating the personal and the political; and (e) opening oneself to the pedagogical possibility for deep transformational insight, one that potentially threatens the very psychological coherence of the "I" witness. A curriculum of witnessing that wrestles with these challenges (e.g., through the arts) sets the stage for the realization of a dire pedagogical hope among most educators; namely, that a deeper insight will emerge among witnesses, one which promises to translate into a positive transformation not merely of self but also of society. A curriculum and pedagogy of witnessing by and large is oriented to the seemingly impossible accomplishment of universal responsibility/responsivity and global peace and sustainability (Eppert, 2008).

In the final pages of this chapter, I consider more pragmatically what Eastern insights introduced herein might contribute to current reflection on the dynamics and educational possibilities of a witnessing praxis. Most centrally, as already discussed, these teachings connect witnessing with an endeavor of remembrance-learning oriented toward reconciling us with our "true" nature. Robert Hattam (2008) discusses the vital importance of reconciliation pedagogy in these unsettling times and the possibilities of Buddhism to "foster co-existence rather than promoting fear, anger, and revenge" (p. 112). Although he speaks of reconciliation pedagogy primarily in the contexts of national and social struggles to heal from oppression, violence, discord, trauma, it seems critical to also think of reconciliation and healing with regard to nature. To remember and reconcile ourselves to ourselves means painfully witnessing not only our separation from ourselves and from one another but also our alienation from the natural and spiritual world. Bill Devall writes, "[B]earing witness to our emotional wounds, our alienation from the rest of nature, we can move into healing relationships with a watershed, with our bioregion, with Gaia" (Devall, 2000, p. 390). Witnessing, as many have emphasized, encompasses endeavors of communities of learners to work through psychosocial experiences and manifestations of naivety, refusal, denial, aggression, silence, withdrawal, anger, guilt, shame, fear, apathy, indifference, melancholia, and disembodiment, and come to identify and embrace sites of personal and sociopolitical awareness, engagement, voice, mourning, healing, care, compassion, commitment, energy, and activity. It is an extraordinarily difficult nonlinear praxis that extends significantly beyond any predeterminable parameters of time and space, and defies external and internal impositions of uniformity.

But, more concretely, how do we go about addressing our emotional wounds in and through an awakening to and consciousness of source? Hanh (2002) states, "After you have touched the wave, you learn to touch the water" (p. 169). With contemporary life as it is, I venture that not only are we out of touch with ocean water (with intersubjectivity), but we have not yet even begun to touch the wave that is our subjectivity. Particularly in schools, in this current era of testing and accountability, which is valuing control and test scores more than inquiry, the emphasis is predominantly on the automatization of students, rather than on the exploration and learning of wave and water. Yet, witnessing calls for embodied reflection and contemplation, what Simone Weil (1951/1973, 1941/1997) describes as the cultivation of "gymnastics of attention." There are several opportunities and forms for such contemplative practice. The arts, for example, provide avenues for healing relationships. Richard Shusterman (2000) discusses the importance of somaesthetics, by which he means practices that support "awareness of our bodily states and feelings for the pursuit of central philosophical aims—knowledge, self-knowledge, right action" (pp. 268–267). He illustrates that although many ancient Greek philosophers emphasized the training of the body for the cultivation of wisdom and virtue, "a very sad curiosity of recent [western] philosophy is that so much inquiry has been devoted to the ontology and epistemology of pain, so little to its psychosomatic management, to its mastery and transformation into tranquility and pleasure" (p. 270). Although space and time are insufficient here to elaborate, suffice it to say that practices of yoga, tai chi, mindfulness, and meditation are centrally geared toward the accomplishment of such transformation, especially insofar as they are diligently motivated not by a spirit of capitalism and narcissism but rather by the journey for meaningful ethical engagement (see Eppert & Wang, 2008).

William Pinar's (1975, 1994, 2004; Pinar, Reynolds, Slattery, & Taubman, 2006) educational practice of *currere*, of "running the course," also offers prime opportunities for contemplative engagement. Participants immerse themselves in four stages of autobiographical writing: the regressive (an embodied remembrance of one's past), the progressive (a creative engagement with one's future), the analytic (an interpretative engagement with one's past, present and future), and the synthetic (an integrative exploration of experience in relationship with one's study of historical, political, social ideologies and contexts). In her book *Currere and the Environmental Autobiography*, Marilyn Doerr (2004) illustrates how *currere* can specifically foster ecological learning and awareness. She describes her teaching of an ecology class at a private all-boys college preparatory school through what she calls the students' production of an "environmental autobiography project" modeled on *currere* and also informed by Paulo Freire's notion of *conscientization*. The purpose of the year-long project was to encourage students to remember and reflect on how nature and geographical locale have helped shaped them, to connect students intimately and experientially with the physical environment in new ways, and to invite them to move from knowing and caring to become active agents of change. *Currere* inspired Doerr because it offers an alternative to the mere reading of ecological textbooks which, she observes, often resulted in students not connecting with the information articulated therein. She writes, "I am convinced that unless we get students to care, to feel, that the earth is in danger, the teaching of ecological principles will not transfer to living a life based on those ecological principles" (p. 96). Interestingly, one of her students, in his analysis, shares his love of water: "Water can relax me, excite me, and make me happy all at the same time. When I am in the water it is as if I am in a whole other world. I do not think about any problems I have, I simply enjoy the rush that water provides" (p. 46). Doerr comments how this student saw water as therapy and, indeed, his preservation. The project not only attuned him to his relationship with the environment but also transformed him: "it taught me to just go with the flow a bit more than I usually do" (p. 45). *Currere,* which Doll (2000), describes as a "coursing" like "running water," is learning to touch the wave, with the potential to remember and realize the wave is also ocean water. Reconciliation is returning to our source—water.

Second, scholarship on witnessing carries within it dimensions of relationship and the seeds of social change and action. The academic and cultural work that seeks to work through the psychosocial nature and possibilities of inciting social transformation is considerable and rich. We might also benefit from contemplating notions of nonaction as a means for social action. In contrast to much of western thought, here the path of human cultivation is not through action but rather through *wu-wei.* Contemporary western cultures commonly value productivity. There are pressures to continually do—engage in unceasing activity—which fosters competition, control, and causes the depletion of multiple resources (self, other, environment). There is a strong dualism between action and nonaction, and nonaction is perceived as inaction—as passivity or apathy. In current times, when social apathy is so prevalent, education toward action and social justice cannot be underestimated. Yet, we might also embrace balance and the possibilities of nonaction. John James Clarke (1997) writes:

> The concept of *wu-wei* . . . has proved difficult for Westerners to make sense of, for the ideal of nonaction, especially in the face of known evils or dangers, is contrary to an instinctive moral activism in the West. But as many commentators point out, this term does not imply moral indifference but rather a highly moral demand to work in harmony rather than in conflict with nature. (p. 202)

Nonaction is a rather uncommon perspective in today's economically obsessed world, and in this regard it too resonates with water. Chapter 8 of the *Tao Te Ching* says, "The highest good is like water, Water is good at benefiting the myriad creatures but also struggles to occupy the place loathed by the masses" (Mair, 1990, p. 67). Although this translation sounds rather arrogant, we might agree, for now, that in this economically driven climate, to take the way of nonaction, in several respects, to echo lines from a Robert Frost poem, is indeed to take the road less traveled.

I think about what nonaction might more concretely look like in the context of environmental social change. Rather than an emphasis on increase, would there not be an emphasis on decrease? With regard to environmental concerns, this might take the pragmatic form of consuming less, acquiring less, producing less, wasting less, and generally doing less of all those things that tax and drain us and the environment. Yet, nonaction cannot simply encompass conservation. As I hope this chapter illustrates, it demands of the self the very difficult and long-embodied effort of facing and detaching from destructive ego-based emotions, thoughts, and behaviors. Skill, self-discipline, and persistence are necessary for nonaction, for yielding, and for balance. Nonaction is not opposed to activism, but rather can productively inform it. In other words, activism is undertaken with nonaction as its spirit. It is thus guided by gentleness rather than violence, insight rather than confusion, calm rather than rage, humility rather than arrogance. Once again, we can learn from water. Philip Kapleau (1965/1980) in *The Three Pillars of Zen* reveals how Zen masters advise their pupils: "In all your activities you should move neither hastily nor sluggishly but naturally, like flowing water" (p. 203). He elaborates by quoting the 11th-century Taoist scholar Tao Chêng, who prosaically sums up several of the descriptions made in this chapter:

> Of all the elements, the sage should take water as his preceptor. Water is yielding but all conquering. Water extinguishes fire or finding itself likely to be defeated escapes as steam and re-forms. Water washes away soft earth, or when confronted by rocks, seeks a way around.

Water corrodes iron till it crumbles to dust; it saturates the atmosphere so that wind dies. Water gives way to obstacles with deceptive humility, for no power can prevent it following its destined course to the sea. Water conquers by yielding; it never attacks but always wins the last battle. The Sage who makes himself [herself] as water is distinguished for his [her] humility; he [she] embraces passivity, acts from non-action and conquers the world. (p. 361)

Acting from nonaction can support response rather than reaction to the world. Whereas reaction is the mode of engagement fueled by fear, anxiety, passion, arrogance, and greed, response is nonaction motivated by compassion, responsibility, equanimity, and wisdom.

Third, what seems so integral to these teachings of water, even though it is not foregrounded, is a notion of integrity, and in the west this seems an increasingly forgotten virtue. Clarke (1997) writes:

The confrontation between East and West is beginning to look fruitful insofar as it provokes fundamental questions about the underlying ethical assumptions of the West, and about the nature of morality itself. (p. 202)

Western ethical assumptions include a belief that we are sovereign and separate and that nature is ours to conquer, tame, and exploit. Because our ethical worldview issues from the center that is us and moves outward with dualistic and hierarchical expression, we consequently largely identify our moral imperatives in terms of the cultivation of values that are divorced from nature and cosmos. Honesty, responsibility, respect, and other such qualities are self-contained, located within the resources of the individual rather than within the individual who is inherently a part of and in harmony with the social and natural order. As Doerr (2004) points out, the transition to an ecological consciousness will "entail a resurgence of moral philosophy . . . virtue must be refound" (p. 117).

Mair (1990), in his translation of the *Tao Te Ching*, chooses the word *integrity* to describe *te*, rather than the more common word, *virtue*. He observes how, under Confucian influences, virtue carries the meaning of innate goodness or the foundation for ethical behavior but how in English it generally references a heavily prescriptive morality. Yet, he illustrates how an etymological study of the Chinese *te* in fact reveals that it refers to the entirety of what or who one is, whether positive or negative. Furthermore, it represents self-nature or self-realization understood in cosmic terms: "*te* is the embodiment of the Way [Tao] and is the character of all entities in the universe" (p. 135). Mair maintains that although integrity does not have the uniformly positive quality of the word virtue, it more fully describes the wholeness of interbeing reflected in *te*. When we think of water, for example, integrity does make more sense than virtue. The phrase "the integrity of water" more fully captures its fluidity and "thusness" than does the phrase, "the virtue of water," which also seems to anthropomorphize water.

Finally, the writings on water described in this chapter share a certain spirit of reverence. Reverence also strikes me as perception and practice that has much receded from the contemporary global economic and urban scene, forgotten in tandem with connections to nature. Paul Woodruff (2001) observes that English-speakers have the word "in our language, but scarcely know how to use it" (p. 3). He illustrated how a host of ancient Greek and Chinese philosophers and sages once held reverence as central to their discussions on ethics and politics. Referencing them, he describes reverence as beginning "in a deep understanding of human limitations; from this grows the capacity to be in awe of whatever we believe lies outside of our control—God, truth, justice, nature, even death" (p. 3). Along similar lines, Purpel (Purpel & McLaurin, 2004) maintains that we need to cultivate more humility in our educational institutions, and notes that "to be humble . . . is to be awed and amazed at the intricacies and complexities of what is being studied" (p. 64). But reverence is not merely a sense of awe in the face of our limitations. Rather, it more fully invokes capacities for a host of interlinked emotions and feelings, including respect and shame (Woodruff, 2001). Moreover, it is a response to the world that is not solely intellectual.

Reverence seems vital to witnessing and to actionless action. Woodruff imagines a confrontation between townspeople and a timber company that wants to cut the trees in order to bring in revenue, and environmentalists who want to preserve the forest. Each rational argument made by the environmentalists is refuted by the rational arguments of their opponents, who state their efforts of replanting and so on. Missing from both sides, he contends, is not the capacity to argue but rather a spirit of reverence: "the environmentalists should begin to feel the value of what their adversaries are trying to preserve. And the townspeople should conclude that they will be better people if they start finding in themselves, before it writhers away entirely, the power to walk reverently in the enormous shadow of the trees" (p. 25). If we reconsider the words of the YouTube commentator mentioned early in this chapter, who argues that securing American oil is more important than wildlife and refuge, we can recognize a language with little reverence. Woodruff adds that reverence is "often expressed in, and reinforced by ceremony . . . Ceremony is older than any surviving religion, and wherever there has been ceremony, there has been a way of taking ceremony seriously, and that requires reverence" (pp. 63, 54). This returns me to Silko's novel *Ceremony,* in which the spider Thought-Woman, co-creator and namer of all things, poetically remarks with regard to the witchery unleashed in the world: "The only cure/I know/is a good ceremony" (p. 3).

A contemporary lack of reverence is all too clear when we witness our engagement with water. This morning I heard on the news how the male fish in the waters off the coast of Washington were mutating and laying eggs like females because of their exposure to pollution. The relentless consumption and pollution of water betrays attitudes of greed, disinterest and lack of care, as does the general lack of ceremony with regard to water. In her testimonial, *I, Rigoberta Menchu* (Burgos-Debray, 1987), Guatemalan activist and Nobel prize winner Rigoberta Menchu tells of how her culture engaged in various rituals to honor the sacredness of water. I sometimes imagine what it might be like if reverence were collectively practiced by uttering a few words with each use of water. Perhaps it would usher in the memory that water comes from somewhere, and is a resource to care for rather than exploit. Thich Nhat Hanh offers a series of earth verses, one of which is precisely for daily water use: "Water flows from the high mountains./ Water runs deep in the Earth./Miraculously, water comes to us/and sustains all life" (Kaza & Kraft, 2000, p. 446). In times when there is so much conflict and politics, maybe this vision and practice of reverence, or even meditative interludes on returning to our source, will be perceived as far too idealistic. On the other hand, without idealism about what could or might be, what is there to reach for? The challenge seems to me one of openness, imagination, and fluidity with regard to unearthing and creating new possibilities, and the concurrent pragmatic undertaking of an embodied personal and sociopolitical educational journey toward healing that proceeds mindfully, arduously, step-by-step, individually and collectively, silently and dialogically, and is embraced as neither linear nor dualistic nor unilaterally prescriptive.

CONCLUSION: ON THE WAY TO RENEWAL

In conclusion, these meditations on water stand as a potential site of remembrance, of renewal, and of further global inquiry into and practice of possible paths other than the one toward devastation on which we are currently. Insofar as schooling and sites in the public sphere can offer access to these counterhegemonic meditations, inquiries, and practices, we can begin to recreate our world, and, in the process recover from the separation and destruction caused by western perspectives and priorities. Webster's dictionary defines renewal as restoring to freshness, making new spiritually, reviving, making extensive changes, replenishing. In contrast to a climate of conflict and destruction, the ending of western witchery and the ending of drought through the imaginative restorying of education and the public sphere might hold the realization of the following dream for the condition of our water, worldwide: clear and pure streams, rivers, and oceans, rich vegetation, diverse and thriving forms of water-life, clean tap water, abundant and protective coasts, plenty and balance. Time seems despairingly short, however, and loss piles daily.

REFERENCES

Abram, D. (1996). *The spell of the sensuous.* New York: Vintage.

Allen, S. (1997). *The way of water and sprouts of virtue.* Albany: State University of New York Press.

Bai, H., & Cohen, A. (2008). Breathing *Qi,* Following *Dao*: Transforming this violence-ridden world. In C. Eppert & H. Wang (Eds.), *Cross-cultural studies in curriculum: Eastern thought, educational insights.* Mahwah, NJ: Erlbaum/Routledge, Taylor & Francis.

Bresnan, P. S. (2003). *Awakening: An introduction to the history of Eastern thought* (2nd ed.). Upper Saddle River, NJ: Prentice-Hall.

Burgos-Debray, E. (Ed.). (1987). *I, Rigoberta Menchu: An Indian woman in Guatemala.* New York: Verso.

Campbell, J. (1949). *The hero with a thousand faces.* Princeton, NJ: Bollingen.

Campbell, J., & Moyers, B. (2001). *Joseph Campbell and the power of myth with Bill Moyers* (DVD Recording). Montauk, NY: Mystic Fire.

Chödrön, P. (1997). *When things fall apart: Heart advice for difficult times.* Boston: Shambhala.

Clarke, J. J. (1997). *Oriental enlightenment: The encounter between Asian and western thought.* New York: Routledge.

Doerr, M. N. (2004). *Currere and the environmental autobiography: A phenomenological approach to the teaching of ecology.* New York: Peter Lang.

Dōgen. (2000). Mountains in Water Sutra. In S. Kaza & K. Kraft (Eds.), *Dharma rain: Sources of Buddhist environmentalism* (pp. 65–76). Boston: Shambhala.

Doll, M. A. (2000). *Like letters in running water: A mythopoetics of curriculum.* Mahwah, NJ: Erlbaum.

Easwaren, E. (Trans.). (1985). *The Dhammapada.* Tomales, CA: Nilgiri Press.

Easwaren, E. (Trans.). (1987). *The Upanishads.* Tomales, CA: Nilgiri Press.

Eppert, C. (1999). *Learning responsivity/responsibility: Reading the literature of historical witness.* Unpublished doctoral dissertation, Ontario Institute for Studies in Education, University of Toronto, Ontario, Canada.

Eppert, C. (2000). Re-learning questions: Responding to the address of past and present others. In R. I. Simon, S. Rosenberg, & C. Eppert (Eds.), *Between hope and despair: Pedagogy and the remembrance of historical trauma* (pp. 213–230). Lanham, MD: Rowman & Littlefield.

Eppert, C. (2002a). Entertaining history: (Un)heroic identifications, *Apt Pupils,* and an ethical imagination. *New German Critique, 86,* 71–102.

Eppert, C. (2002b). Reading relations, loss, and responsive/responsible learning. In M. Morris & J. Weaver (Eds.), *Difficult memories: Talk in a post-holocaust era* (pp. 45–67). New York: Peter Lang.

Eppert, C. (2003). Histories re-imagined, forgotten, and forgiven: Student responses to Toni Morrison's *Beloved. Studies in Reading and Culture, 10*(2), 185–194.

Eppert, C. (2004). Leslie Silko's *Ceremony*: Rhetorics of ethical reading and composition. *JAC: A Quarterly Journal for the Interdisciplinary Study of Rhetoric, Writing, Multiple Literacies, and Politics. 24*(3), 727–754.

Eppert, C. (2008). Fear, (educational) fictions of character, & Buddhist insights for an arts-based witnessing cross-cultural curriculum. In C. Eppert & H. Wang (Eds.), *Cross-cultural studies in curriculum: Eastern thought, educational insights.* Mahwah, NJ: Erlbaum/Routledge, Taylor & Francis.

Felman, S., & Laub, D. (1992). *Testimony: Crises of witnessing in literature, psychoanalysis, and history.* New York & London: Routledge.

Gough, N. (1990). Healing the earth within us: Environmental education as cultural criticism. *The Journal of Experiential Education, 13*(4), 12–17.

Gough, N. (1991). Narrative and nature: Unsustainable fictions in environmental education. *The Australian Journal of Environmental Education, 7,* 31–42.

Gough, N. (1993). Environmental education, narrative complexity and postmodern science/fiction. *International Journal of Science Education, 15*(5), 607–625.

Hanh, T. N. (1987). *Being peace.* Berkeley, CA: Parallax Press.

Hanh, T. N. (1997). *Peace is every step* (VHS recording). Berkeley, CA: Legacy Media.

Hanh, T. N. (1998). *Teachings on love.* Berkeley, CA: Parallax Press.

Hanh, T. N. (2002). *No death, no fear: Comforting wisdom for life.* New York: Riverhead Books.

Hattam, R. (2008). Socially-engaged Buddhism as a provocation for critical pedagogy in "unsettling times." In C. Eppert & H. Wang (Eds.), *Cross-cultural studies in curriculum: Eastern thought, educational insights.* Mahwah, NJ: Erlbaum/Routledge, Taylor & Francis.

Hesse, H. (2003). *Siddhartha* (J. Neugroshel, Trans.). New York: Penguin. (Original work published 1922)

Issues: Global Warming. Retrieved 2007 from http://www.nrdc.org/globalWarming/f101.asp.

Kapleau, R. P. (1980). *The three pillars of Zen.* New York: Anchor/Doubleday. (Original work published 1965)

Kaza, S., & Kraft, K. (Eds.). (2000). *Dharma rain: Sources of Buddhist environmentalism.* Boston: Shambhala.

Loy, D. R., & Goodhew, L. (2004). *The dharma of dragons and daemons: Buddhist themes in modern fantasy.* Boston: Wisdom.

Mair, V. H. (Trans.). (1990). *Tao Te Ching: The classic book of integrity and the Way.* New York: Bantam.

Needleman, J. (1976). Psychotherapy and the sacred. *Parabola, 1*(1), 52–65.

Needleman, J. (1994). *The indestructible question: Essays on nature, spirit and the human paradox.* London: Arkana Penguin.

Palmer, M. (Trans.). (1996). *The book of Chuang Tsu.* London: Arkana Penguin.

Pinar, W. (Ed.). (1975). *Curriculum theorizing: The reconceptualists.* Berkeley, CA: McCutcuhan.

Pinar, W. (1994). *Autobiography, politics and sexuality: Essays in curriculum theory 1972–1992.* New York: Peter Lang.

Pinar, W. F. (2004). *What is curriculum theory?* Mahwah, NJ: Erlbaum.

Pinar, W. F., Reynolds, W. M., Slattery, P., & Taubman, P. M. (1996). *Understanding curriculum: An introduction to the study of historical and contemporary curriculum discourses.* New York: Peter Lang.

Price, A. F., & Mou-lam, W. (Trans.). (1990). *The diamond sutra & the sutra of Hui-neng.* Boston: Shambhala.

Purpel, D. E., & McLaurin, W. M. Jr. (2004). *Reflections on the moral & spiritual crisis in education.* New York: Peter Lang.

Robert Redford on Saving the Arctic Refuge. Retrieved 2007 from http://www.youtube.com/comment_servlet?all_comments&v=ewbHBJkhz6g&fromurl=/watch%3Fv%3DewbHBJkhz6g.

Shusterman, R. (2000). *Pragmatist aesthetics: Living beauty, rethinking art* (2nd ed.). Lanham, MD: Rowman & Littlefield.

Silko, L. M. (1986). *Ceremony.* New York: Penguin.

Simon, R. I., Rosenberg, S., & Eppert, C. (Eds.). (2000). *Between hope and despair: Pedagogy and the remembrance of historical trauma.* Lanham, MD: Rowman & Littlefield.

Smith, H., & Novak, P. (2003). *Buddhism: A concise introduction.* San Francisco: HarperCollins.

Wang, H. (2008). The strength of the feminine, the lyrics of the Chinese woman's self, and the power of education. In C. Eppert & H. Wang (Eds.), *Cross-cultural studies in curriculum: Eastern thought, educational insights.* Mahwah, NJ: Erlbaum/Routledge, Taylor & Francis.

Water shortages will leave world in dire straits. Retrieved 2007 from http://www.usatoday.com/news/nation/2003-01-26-water-usat_x.htm.

Weil, S. (1973). *Waiting for God* (E. Craufurd, Trans.). New York: Harper & Row. (Original work published 1951)

Weil, S. (1997). *Gravity & grace.* Lincoln: University of Nebraska Press. (Original work published 1947)

Woodruff, P. (2001). *Reverence: Renewing a forgotten virtue.* Oxford, UK: Oxford University Press.

11

Pedagogical Transgression

Toward Intersubjective Agency and Action

Marcia McKenzie

Discussing "parrots," "butterflies," and hybrid combinations of the two, in previous research I examine the links between students' articulations of their potential to affect change in the world and the sedimentation of earlier discursive practices and experiences. Interested in how students' understandings of their potential for agency are determined by various social and cultural discourses, practices, and conditions—such as friendship, family, media, schooling, class and cultural backgrounds, including the lessons of socio-ecological education programs specifically aimed at evoking agency and activism—this work suggests the overwhelming extent of students' constitution by the various influences they "parrot" (McKenzie, 2004, 2006).[1] In seeking ways forward in the face of ecological, social, and cultural injustices, and discomfort with education as merely another form of domination, here I ask what it can mean to proceed from a position of doubt about the potential of agency, as if agency and the means of encouraging it through education are indeed possible.

Joining others in countering "the argument that postmodernity leaves public education with two equally terrifying alternatives: performatization or anarchy" (Kiziltan, Bain, & Cañizares, 1990, p. 360), I undertake the theorization and practice of a contingent and intersubjective agency that aims to be a provocation to socioecological action.[2] This means exploring possibilities for education that enable us to consider our relationships with human and non-human others, in ways that do not suggest to have transcultural or transhistorical answers to questions about how we or others should live. Drawing on the work of Michael Foucault and a number of contemporary cultural and feminist theorists, as well as an ongoing study on teacher education, the chapter seeks to optimistically consider secondary, postsecondary, indoor, and outdoor educations that engage students in critical ontologies through experiences of to and fro movement at the limit. I begin with an exploration of Foucault's "limit-attitude" and related work on transgression, before turning to some possible pedagogical strategies towards agency and action.

CRITICAL ONTOLOGIES OF OURSELVES

Gogo: I am interested in, both in my classroom and in my students' classrooms, having them figure out ways to look at discourse, at the different and competing discourses that they function within.

Didi: I don't use the word "discourse" with them. It's a meaningful word to me, but when I'm talking about my teaching, I don't use that word generally—I think it scares students.

G: The word "discourse" is kind of hard to teach, really.

D: I mean, it's a very easy thing to read about, and it's kind of a difficult thing to unpack within the context of teaching.

G: I think about discourse as what occurs, the context—not so much in terms of how some people use it more literally, in terms of language.

D: You come to realize that there are a number of discourses at play all the time. They're never separate from one another. They're tangled up in each other, and we develop heuristics through language to be able to identify them and talk about them.

G: When I think about discursive practices it becomes engaged and involved with all of the tensions and contradictions and inner relationships between both what we think of as the material or materiality, and embodiment. So discourse still is impacted by the embodied notions of what's occurring, by reality, in a material sense. But there has to be connection to the sociopolitical and historical, in relation to how one understands. So discourse *is*, but it is because of how it continues to be in relation to all these other things.

D: It's understanding that all of us walk in the doors, or out the doors, having been embedded in particular cultural and historical contexts. We're marinated in a soup of assumptions, of wider societal assumptions.

G: I think as a society we don't do such a great job of revealing, or probing at, those assumptions, those discourses. How our assumptions about ourselves, about what it means to be a teacher, how all of those have been constructed.

D: We construct narratives for ourselves. And we live within those.

G: We engage in accordance with what we believe or how we've constructed ourselves.

D: And we make moral and ethical choices within that framework.

G: I guess I see part of my job as unpacking some of those stories, some of those understandings, some of those assumptions.

This text is part of a longer dialogue that consists of excerpts from interviews with nine teacher educators participating in the Discursive Approaches to Teaching and Learning Project (McKenzie, 2005–2008, www.otherwise-ed.ca/Projects/DATL/index.html).

Whether described as decolonization, deconstruction, excavation, or by other terms, the "unpacking" described by the educators in this dialogue is undertaken with an aim of examining those discursive understandings and practices that are viewed as contributing to socioecological injustice. By suggesting the culturally bound quality of knowledge and problematizing particular formulations of knowledge—those related to anthropocentrism, globalization, colonialism, racism, classism, heteronormativity, and so on—those educators using "discursive" and related pedagogical approaches seek to provoke reflection on what they view to be harmful understandings and practices. As in many articulations of critical approaches to education, this work of critique or decolonization seems to be understood largely as taking place in the cognitive realm, albeit in some cases with emotional investments and repercussions (Boler, 1999). For example, David Greenwood (formerly Gruenewald) (2003) suggests, this "means challenging each other to read the texts of our own lives and to ask constantly what needs to be transformed and what needs to be conserved" (p. 10): with "reading" and "asking" in this context suggesting conceptual tasks.

However, initiating this sort of critique, without simple indoctrination into merely another way of seeing the world, is complicated and to some extent impossible: We are all always "parroting" sociocultural norms and narratives, even when we seek to find agency within that (Butler, 2005; McKenzie, 2004). And, as suggested in the longer teacher educator dialogue from which this opening excerpt was taken, understandings of *how* one undertakes the *instigation* of this type of excavatory work are often more intuitive than theorized. While teacher educators in the study speak about using experiences of films, novels, outdoor settings, cultural difference, and so on, they do not articulate explicitly how these sorts of experiences function to enable students to engage in interrogating representations of subjectivity and society and in imagining and living other possibilities (Leitch, 1996). We are left with the question of how to enable transgression of the limits of our and our students sociocultural constitution in order to live in more sustaining and sustainable ways? Here we turn to Foucault for help.

First of all, it is useful to think further about what is meant here by *transgression*. Dictionary definitions point to two different understandings of the term: (a) to go beyond or over a limit or boundary, and (b) to breach (a gap or rift, the breaking of waves or surf, the leap of a whale from the water). The first is perhaps better suited to more emancipatory articulations of education, such as those of Paulo Freire (1970/2002) and bell hooks (1994), which can be viewed as seeking the "decodification" and righting of the world through "education as the practice of freedom." The second definition suggests something more tentative: a transgression that is a tear, a rupture, or, a spiral. Foucault (1963/2003a) writes,

> Transgression, then, is not related to the limit as black to white, the prohibited to the lawful, the outside to the inside, or as the open area of a building to its enclosed spaces. Rather, their relationship takes the form of a spiral that no simple infraction can exhaust . . . Transgression is neither violence in a divided world (in an ethical world) nor a victory over limits (in a dialectical or revolutionary world); and exactly for this reason, its role is to measure the excessive distance that it opens at the heart of the limit and to trace the flashing line that causes the limit to arise. (p. 447)

Transgression can thus be understood as not the opposite of limit, but rather as an attempt at "the illumination of limits" (Simons, 1995, p. 69; cited in Biesta, 1998). This is different from educational aims that suggest "the possibility or hope of authenticity and liberation, of arriving, at some future point, at some ultimate and fulfilling destination beyond power, structure, ideology, and even discourse itself" (Pignatelli, 1993, p. 416). It does not offer *freedom from* constituting understandings, or provide narratives of emancipation (Kiziltan, Bain, & Cañuzares, 1990). Rather, it suggests a tentative and limited *freedom to* undertake explorations of assumptions and understandings.

One can think about these sorts of practices as centering on a philosophical ethos that Foucault (1978/2003b, pp. 53–54) describes in his early work as a "limit-attitude" and as entailing a critical ontology of ourselves:

> The critical ontology of ourselves must be considered not, certainly, as a theory, doctrine, nor even as a permanent body of knowledge that is accumulating; it must be conceived as an attitude, an ethos, a philosophical life in which the critique of what we are is at one and the same time the historical analysis of the limits imposed on us and an experiment with the possibility of going beyond them. (Foucault, 1978/2003b, p. 56)

Foucault's later work on care of the self as a practice of freedom is more explicit on how this relates to considerations of the agency of the individual, suggesting the serious constraints of a critical ontology. Elaborating on his interests in how the subject constitutes him or herself in an active fashion through the study of ancient Greek and Roman life, Foucault explains how practices of the self are not something that the individual invents by himself. Rather they are patterns found in culture and which are proposed, suggested and imposed by culture, society, and social mileu (Foucault in Fornet-Betancourt, Becker, Gomez-Müler, & Gauthier, 1987). Thus, "freedom" in ancient times "means not being a slave to one's self and to one's appetites, which supposes that one establishes over one's self a certain relation of domination, or mastery" (Foucault in Fornet-Betancourt et al., 1987, p. 117). Despite this understanding of freedom or agency as highly limited by sociocultural contexts and as understood as "self-mastery," there is still spiraling, some breaching or de-breaching as the case may be; that goes beyond a discursive understanding of alterability,[3] of agency as merely action, to suggest the practice of something more intentional. In other words, self consciousness and self constitution are possible, if only through drawing on available discourses and practices.

As Bronwyn Davies (1990) suggests, the theoretical problem "is to understand how any desire can run against the grain of discursive practices through which that which is desirable is located/named/defined. From whence comes the struggle to redefine and resist?" (p. 345). Is it "a mere calculus of intersecting vectors, predictably resolved in the direction of the most forceful discourse?," or is an agentic "chooser" somehow born from these epistemic tensions (Zipin, 1998, p. 333)? Consciousness clearly can no longer be conceived as transparent, unmediated, or "the point of origin . . . from which a subject can observe and reflect upon representations it possesses in order to know and to act" (Pignatelli, 1993, p. 414). However negotiation, acceptance, or struggle is still possible (Nelson, 1999), and it is to some extent a strategic adherence to the notion of consciousness that becomes necessary (Spivak, 1988). Donna Haraway's (1997) figuration of the "modest witness" is helpful in imagining this further: "the notion of modesty as a form of accountability, open-ended dialogue and critical thinking that aims at witnessing . . . The 'modest witness' is neither detached nor uncaring, but a border-crossing figure who attempts to recontextualize his/her own practice" (Braidotti, 2006, p. 206). There is an ethic of discomfort, of risk, involved in this, that entails never consenting to being completely comfortable with one's own presuppositions: "There, at the transgressed limit, the 'yes' of contestation reverberates" (Foucault, 1963/2003a, p. 448).

Recommending that a critical ontology of ourselves be pursued in a thoroughly experimental way, Gert Biesta (1998) proposes it as a historical, practical, and nonuniversal test of the limits that are imposed on us, and an experiment with the possibilities of going beyond them. With the historical and sociopolitical considered as intersubjective forms of constitution, intersubjectivity can thus be understood as preceding subjectivity, not in "a deep truth human nature" kind of way, but in terms of understanding "the intersubjective as a space, unrepresentable in itself, from which any speaking about the subject and the world can only begin" (Biesta, 1998, pp. 10–11). This, Biesta (1998) suggests, "implies that education *and* politics will have to do away with the aims of autonomy, freedom, and rational consensus in so far as they are thought *against* intersubjectivity" (p. 12). Instead, he suggests, transgression, and an agency of sorts, is practiced through the examination of intersubjectivity and subjectivity via sociopolitical and historical inquiries.

The working theories of the teacher educators in the dialogue that began this section are certainly reminiscent of this type of approach, and we see in the articulations of their teaching methods an almost exclusive emphasis on sociopolitical and historical critique. As one of the educators explains:

I start with Neil Postman's notion of crap detecting and becoming critical anthropologists of our own culture. I ask [students] to look at the construction of ideas and values and cultural notions and ideology and what they've internalized in terms of stories or histories or popular histories that they've learned through curriculum, through culture, through all the institutions of culture—media, school, family, church, religion, etc. I introduce the question of why: "Why think about your world critically, what is to be gained from that?" I introduce the question of why these kinds of questions would be important to people who are going to be teachers and I say that the most important thing to me is for these pre-service teachers to be able to articulate their philosophy of teaching and that what's involved is a self-reflective journey about how they've come to have their values and cultural assumptions—both personally and in terms of social issues (race, class, gender, etc.)—and what that means for them as teachers. We proceed to have debate and discussion about where did they learn those [values and assumptions], what are the implications of those, what gets hidden, whose story is included, whose narratives are not held in those stories.

Mark Olssen (2006) suggests that this sort of critique is both personal and political and has as its focus the interactions between individuals and groups, as well as with, we might add, with other species and places. However, Olssen also indicates that critique in a Foucauldian sense is not a matter of simply "criticizing things as not being right as they are," but instead is *a consequence of problematization* (p. 259). In Foucault's (1988) words:

> [I]t is a matter of pointing out what kinds of assumptions, what kinds of familiar, unchallenged, unconsidered modes of thought the practices that we accept rest . . . Criticism is a matter of *flushing out* that thought and trying to change it: to show that things are not as self-evident as one believed, to see that what is accepted as self-evident will no longer be accepted as such. Practicing criticism is a matter of making facile gestures difficult. (p. 154, italics added)

What I focus on in the remainder of the chapter are the ways in which problematizations that instigate critique can be initiated. I suggest that intersubjectivity can be considered to precede subjectivity as that which provokes transgression at the limit, or in other words, as the enabler of Foucault's "flushing out." I discuss provocations of transgression that take place "on the borderline between oneself and the other" (Davies, 1990, p. 343), in the spiraling relationship with "other," here conceived as a range of experiences of dissonance and imagination. In other words, self and cultural critique cannot happen in a vaccum, but are always initiated through experiences that allow us to look at, or be in, the world differently. We are only able to open conceptual space at "the heart of the limit," through intersubjective experiences that enable us to imagine the world otherwise.

Described as a "poetic project," Kiziltan, Bain, and Cañuzares (1990) suggest that the difficulty of bringing a limit-attitude to education lies "in the failure and poverty of our . . . imaginations to begin to even conceive such a new arrangement in its bits and pieces" (p. 366). Likewise, Biesta (1998), indicates it "requires a new style of pedagogical imagination" (p. 13). Here I draw heavily on related work, on conversations with colleagues, and on interviews with other teacher educators concerned with similar problems in seeking to imagine education as if it can be "an ongoing individual and collective challenge to fabricate alternatives" (Pignatelli, 1993, p. 419).

STRATEGIES OF INTERSUBJECTIVE PROBLEMATIZATION

Talk of waves breaking, spirals, and borderline work offers a spacialized imagery that is helpful in considering practices of socioecological education as intersubjective problematization. Like Mary

Louise Pratt's (1999) "contact zone," where cultural understandings meet and grapple with each other, these are pedagogical experiences of interaction and possibly productivity. A contact zone can also be imagined as the intertidal or littoral zone between high and low water lines, with an ethic of discomfort found in the extreme conditions created by water movement up and down the shore. The materiality of these images is also a reminder of the ways in which spaces and places are infused with, and deployed by, discourse and culture—that meeting spots involve more than "epistemic tensions" of conflicting discourses or "intersecting vectors," but that these are overlaid onto real bodies and geographies. *How then do transgressive experiences of this interwoven matter/culture provoke "learning," understood as consciousness gained at the limit, as agency?*

Postcolonial, feminist, and technoscience literatures concerned with examining the meeting of different matter/cultures are helpful in thinking about this further. In her work on cyborgs and companion species, Haraway suggests that many of us now live in an intersectional world, "where people are made to live several non-isomorphic categories simultaneously, all of which 'torque' them" (Gane & Haraway, 2006, p. 138).[4] These conditions can be distressing, but also enabling of "restless imaginations" and so-called "world-making practices." These are the "promises of monsters," as Haraway (2004) describes those gestating in the belly of the "local/global monster . . . often called the postmodern world" p. 65). Cyborgs, coyote, humans: "all kinds of hybrids are being continually recast by processes of circulation within and between particular spaces" (Thrift, 2006, p. 139). Likewise, Homi Bhabha (1994) suggests that the "beyond" is "neither a new horizon, nor a leaving behind of the past . . . but a disorientation, a disturbance of direction, an exploratory, restless movement, a to and fro (p. 2). As Chapters 12 and 5 in this volume by Leesa Fawcett, and Pat O'Riley and Peter Cole suggest, interaction and hybridity, once upon us, can afford opportunities for feral imagination, for 20/20/20 vision.

Building on the "double consciousness" of W. E. B. DuBois (1903), postcolonial and cultural theorists outline the possibilities for in-between spaces that "provide the terrain for elaborating strategies of selfhood-singular or communal—that initiate new signs of identity, and innovative sites of collaboration and contestation" (Bhabha, 1994, p. 2). Outlining a consciousness of the Borderlands, a consciousness born of cultural hybridity, Gloria Anzaldúa (1990) writes,

> Like others having or living in more than one culture, we get multiple, often opposing messages. The coming together of two self-consistent but habitually incompatible frames of reference causes *un choque*, a cultural collision . . . The new *mestiza* copes by developing a tolerance for contradictions, a tolerance for ambiguity . . . Not only does she sustain contradictions, she turns the ambivalence into something else . . . That third element is a new consciousness—a *mestiza* consciousness. (pp. 378–379)

A number of educators have also written about how through experiences of various lived contact zones and cultural texts, teachers and learners may get glimpses of the multilayered and contradictory understandings that torque them and others, creating fertile grounds for critique as it functions as a consequence of problematizations (Olssen, 2006). In exploring curriculum as cultural practice, Yatta Kanu (2003), for example, advocates for an "alloyed" approach to education that is grounded in the reality of the hybridity of globalization and that enables knowledge production, representation, and circulation that escapes the monopoly and privilege of one group. Building on these sorts of circumstances, Henry Giroux (1999) has written of border pedagogies that allow "teachers, cultural workers, and students to not only recognize the multilayered and contradictory ideologies that construct their own identities but to also analyze how the differences within and between various groups can expand the potential of human life" (p. 175). Others also discuss purposefully creating contact zones through the use of literature or other arts to make the familiar strange, to suggest to students the ways in which knowledge and cultures shift, and to make possible new relationships with self and others (e.g., Kincheloe, 2003; McKenzie, Russell, Fawcett, & Timmerman, in press; Soetaert, Mottart, & Verdoodt, 2004). Chapter 14 in this volume by Rebecca Martusewicz, for example, suggests how bringing together cultural experiences of different generations, as well as experiences with the more-than-human, can enable ways of understanding and being in the world that are both new and old.

In Ursula Le Guin's (1987) story *Buffalo gals: Won't you come out tonight*, we see the difficult possibilities of in-between spaces between humans and other-than-humans; in this case the hybridized life of a human girl who comes to live for a while with Coyote and a range of other species. With two different eyes—one original and one given to her by her new companions—the girl who sometimes goes by Myra and sometimes by Gal, gains a different perception of the world. In reflecting on the story, Karla Armbruster (1998) writes,

> Ultimately, Le Guin's story provides us with a sense in which we can each act as conscious agents of political change. Through an openness to viewpoints and communities outside dominant human cultural experience, Myra . . . holds the potential for subverting dominant ideologies because her divisions and contradictions allow her to connect without oversimplifying her identity in ways that reinscribe those ideologies in new forms; such a self is the one Haraway describes as able to "interrogate positionings and be accountable, the one who can construct and join rational conversations and fantastic imaginings that change history. (p. 115)

Similar to Teresa de Lauretis' (1984) "eccentric subject," "displacement gives the subject a new perspective, highlighting the discrepancies and possibilities of meaning that allow for interpretation" (Armbruster, 1998, p. 111). One of the interviewed teacher educators illustrates her efforts to achieve this sort of dissonant experience of learning about the assumptions built into our relationships with others:

> We'll do an activity where I give them a slip of paper where they've got an identity— and I'll have a whole range of creatures as well as humans who might use the school yard, or the little woodlot beside the schoolyard. I'll have a kid, and a business person, and a homeless person, and then a whole variety of different creatures, including creatures who are demonized, like dandelions or snakes, and then some charismatic mega fauna like bears. So, all things that they might find there. I then have a series of questions, such as what does this place mean to you, why are you in this space, how did you get here, what do other animals or people think of you? And I just send them off to think about it. Then we take that up and we talk about the different meanings that particular spot has to a whole variety of people and creatures. And how do we manage or deal with the fact that there are multiple meanings here and that some of those meanings are contradictory? That the groundskeeper thinks about the land in quite a different way than, you know, the frog might.

Like the new eye that Myra gained through her time with various companion species (Le Guin, 1987), even minor experiences of dissonance such as this can suggest alternate ways of being in the world.

Greenwood suggests in Chapter 15 in this volume how culture and place are deeply intertwined, with places and geographies themselves also being potentially profoundly pedagogical. While our experiences with the more-than-human, or of places of matter/culture, are not precultural or presocial, but rather filtered through sociopolitical and historical understandings; we are none the less affected. In relation to thinking about experiences at the limit, we can thus see the transgressive possibilities of time spent in various novel and familiar places, combined with reflection on the ways in which "places produce and teach particular ways of thinking about and being in the world" (Gruenewald, 2003, p. 625). Instead of outdoor educations that focus on self-reliance and self-confidence, or seek to provide knowledge about our environments as consisting of static and knowable objects; these are pedagogical experiences that aim to highlight intersubjectivity and promote grappling with the ways in which we are both made by, and makers of, place. These places can include a range of geographies such as remote rivers, mountain valleys, oceans, and desserts, farms, banks, cemeteries, strip malls, gated communities, urban architecture, and schools. And whether it is visiting a cooperative recycling depot initiated and managed by those living on the streets, drinking safely straight from a stream, undertaking community mapping of a nearby mall area, or laying down in a field of green, experiences of place can serve as provocations to learning, and as problematizations productive to critical ontologies of ourselves.

Finally, testimony can also be a potential provocation to agency. As Claudia Eppert explores in Chapter 10, the paired events of traumatic testimony (of oneself or another) and a willingness to face or witness that testimony, ideally lead to "a (re-)orientation to an ethics of relation and connection; and a developing commitment to the struggle for social justice/change" (p. 192). Oral histories, literature, films, and other varieties of text and art which tell the stories of traumatic historical or sociopolitical events, or lives led, can all serve to initiate this sort of reorientation; as can exposure to the struggles of the earth and its many other species. An interviewed teacher educator indicates ways in which various autobiographical activities can function as forms of testimony:

> One of the things that I have used is looking at how different kinds of writing practices create different possibilities for [students] to imagine their lives. So, by doing different kinds of writing activities, they can see other directions, other possibilities, other ways of being. So this kind of work is connected to what I call the subjunctive space, and [involves] helping people look at possibilities and consider alternatives.

Paralleling the "ethic of discomfort" entailed in Foucault's limit-attitude, we see in the literatures on testimony and witnessing an emphasis on the emotional aspects of these sorts of pedagogical strategies. Shoshana Felman (1992) writes,

> I want my students to be able to receive information that is dissonant, and not just congruent, with everything that they have learned beforehand. Testimonial teaching fosters the capacity to witness something that may be surprising, cognitively dissonant. The surprise implies the crisis. Testimony cannot be authentic without that crisis, which has to break and to transvaluate previous categories and previous frames of reference . . . The question for the teacher is, then, on the one hand, how to access, how *not to foreclose* the crisis, and, on the other hand, how to *contain it*, how much crisis can the class sustain. (pp. 53–54)

Through the use of testimonial practices, Megan Boler (1999) likewise suggests that a "pedagogy of discomfort" can move students beyond passive empathy to the questioning of assumptions and understandings; while Deborah Britzman and Alice Pitt (2003, 2007) highlight the rich possibilities of learning "difficult knowledge."

Eliciting the crisis, discomfort, difficulty sometimes necessary for this type of reorientation, or to return to earlier language, to problematization and transgression at the limit; is, as Felman suggests above, a delicate balance. In response to the disorientation, fragmentation, and anxiety experienced by students following their viewing of a videotaped testimony of a Holocaust survivor, Felman (1992) assigned a paper:

> Many of you, indeed, quite literally said that they felt they *did not count* after the [videotape], that, had they been there in the camps, they are certain that they would have died. And I am

inviting you now to testify to that experience, so as to accept the obligation—and the right—to repossess yourselves, to take, in other words, the *chance to sign*, the *chance to count*. I invite you thus to write a paper on *your* experience of the testimony, and on your experience of the class ... I want you to work on precisely what you said was so difficult for you to achieve: you felt a disconnection, and I want you to look, on the contrary, *for the connections*. What has this experience taught you in the end? ... What I am suggesting is that you view this paper as *your testimony to this course*. (pp. 51–52)

Felman later writes,

Upon reading the final paper submitted by the students a few weeks later, I realized that the crisis, in effect, had been worked through and overcome and that a resolution had been reached, both on an intellectual and on a vital level. The written work the class had finally submitted turned out to be an amazingly articulate, reflective and profound statement of the trauma they had gone through and of the significance of their assuming the position of the witness. (p. 52)

Of course, things do not always resolve this smoothly. As interviewed teacher educators have suggested, and as is recounted elsewhere in the literature, the crisis of "recognizing one's own complicity" can result in paralyzing guilt or resistance that is not worked out within the timeframe of the course and which can leave instructors feeling incompetent or hopeless:

D: I don't see resistance as a bad thing. It's part of the journey. Shoshana Felman talks about learning as having to go through crisis. And I see that happens for a lot of students when they recognize their own complicity.

G: It's clear that the case for many of them that it's very uncomfortable to be asked to reflect on their values and their cherished cultural beliefs. For some students it's just really threatening. This is uncomfortable knowledge.

D: For some of them, it is the first time they've bumped up against some of these issues and ideas.

G: ... And then they have a tendency to go through all the things that people do when they start to think about these things.

D: They're stuck in guilt. Or there's a lot of resistance.

G: Or some combination thereof, right? It's not an either or thing.

D: Sometimes you just have a difficult class, you know? I've only had one really bad group, bad in the sense of it was just difficult for me. And I do remember that it really caused me to question myself in ways that weren't very helpful. It can really shake your sense of who you are as a teacher.

G: There have been classes where the student resistance is so high that I will come home and, you know, just break down. I'll just break down in grief and frustration and anger, and a lot of grief. And that's because these people are going to be teachers. I feel a huge kind of shock sometimes, to think that some of the views that are expressed are going to be taken into schools and passed on to students. I find that extraordinarily painful.

As Felman's recounting of her course illustrates, it is the pairing of dissonance and reflection, problematization and critique, intersubjectivity and subjectivity, that appears central to educative experiences of testimony and witnessing; and yet as interviewed teachers educators indicate, this is not always easy work.

ACTION

Intersubjective matter/culture experiences of hybridity, place, and testimony, instigating contestation at the limit, or the illumination of limits in a critical ontology of ourselves, offer suggestions of pedagogical strategies for intersubjective problematization. These are practices intended to elicit more intentional forms of agency and action. Parody, poetry, fabulation, media creation, friendship, and collaboration are but a few of many other possibilities for helping to "propel 'becomings' by bringing the unthinkable into representation" through dissonance and imagination (Gough, 2004, p. 256) (see McKenzie, 2008; McKenzie et al., in press).

In the context of socioecological education there are a range of possible outcomes of these types of practices. These include critical ontologies or practices of the self that perhaps too often involve minimal to and fro at the limit, difficulty, or accountability (Lousley, 1999; McKenzie, 2006). With increasing interest in issues such as climate change, sweatshop labour, and media literacy, many appear to be "becoming more personal, yet more global" in the actions taken in relation to socioecological issues (Magna Publications, 2005). Yet, everyday actions undertaken as practices of self (e.g., see Tanke, 2007, on vegetarianism as Foucauldian care of the self), while important, recall the political category of "everyday maker." As Henrik Bang (2005) suggests, this can be considered "a form of lay citizenship shaped by everyday experience," in which we refuse to take on "professional, fulltime nor strategic identity" but instead do things where we are, in our own ways, when we have time or feel like it (p. 5).

In considering additional possible outcomes of the sorts of pedagogical practices I have described, it is helpful to return to that which is most central to these considerations: the intersubjectivity that enables transgression at the limit. As Foucault suggests, it is relationships with others who tell us "truth," that cause us to encounter strangeness (Fornet-Betancourt et al., 1987, p. 118), or in other words, that initiate critique. Occurring from within discourses, practices, and spaces that are culturally constituted, agency can thus be understood as "an always incomplete and partial achievement brought about through networks of associations, capacities, and contestations that involve families, communities, language, technology, social institutions, resources of various kinds, and a wide range of discursive frameworks" (Knopp, 2004, p. 128). Ultimately, matter/culture provocations *to* agency can be considered a part of that agency (Cloke & Jones, 2004).

And so to hold hope in education in relationship to the socioecological, I am called to consider that, "the power of the subject in this context lies in creating affections and relationships" (Zembylas, 2007, p. 139). How and where we foster intersubjectivity—in geographies, local and global places and cultures, stories, art, friendship, collective spaces—is a matter of the previous provocations we are able or wish to build on,[5] and how we engage those; a matter of the spaces we are able to imagine for our students, and they for us and for themselves. We, as teachers and learners, enact these practices of the self in conversation, and in what can become "ensemble performances" (Lovell, 2003) of resistance and action.

NOTES

1. In the study entitled, *Parrots and butterflies: Students as the subjects of socio-ecological education* (McKenzie, 2004), I interviewed students and teachers from three programs in western Canada with a focus on global and environmental education. Ranging in age from 14 to 19, the students had a variety of class

and cultural backgrounds, with one of the three programs being an international school. The notion of students as parrots and/or butterflies came from students in the study, one of whom explained:

> I know one girl that for a long time did exactly what everyone wanted her to be, and now she's decided, it's like a caterpillar looks exactly like every other caterpillar, and then she gets the chance and she goes and her metamorphoses makes her turn into the most vibrant, crazy *butterfly* with like 10 wings and four proboscises, and every colour in the rainbow . . . or something like that, you know? . . . People in mainstream [classes] seem to be really, maybe they're not, maybe they like being like that, but they're kind of single minded in a way. Like, for instance, there's a lot of homophobia, and there's a lot of racism, and just because music, puts it in like it's an okay thing. They don't understand the connotations that go with the words that they're saying. They're kind of like *parrots*, you know?

Having participated in the Butterfly 208 project (www.bp208.ca), with its motto of "one flap, global impact," the butterfly seemed to be part of the language and collective psyche of students in this program. In the end it was in those students who perceived an inevitability to their own parrot-like constitution (the ways in which they were influenced by education, media, culture, and so on), who seemed to me to hold some promise for agency, for butterfly-likeness.

2. Mindful of those theorizations of so called "agency" which can be viewed as less optimistic in their expectations for the possibility of some degree of self-constitution (i.e., those that view constitution as something that only happens to, and not because of, the subject), I also think about how my own writings here can be considered as merely citations of agency thought as actions that institute education or educational theory (Hey, 2006). I produce or perform theories of agency and education with a self-consciousness about the discursive modes through which these ontological effects have no doubt been installed in me. It is thus helpful to be reminded that the "irritation of doubt is the only immediate motive for the struggle to attain belief . . . With the doubt, therefore the struggle begins" (Pierce, 1877, p. 67; cited in Green).

3. For example, see Judith Butler (1997) for an articulation of "agency" as alterability.

4. Chet Bowers (e.g., 2001) raises concerns regarding the modern root metaphor of continual "becoming" inherent in the change-oriented mandates of various critical pedagogies. Bowers suggests that in taking up post-Enlightenment understandings of "change as progress," critical pedagogy undermines forms of knowledge that value tradition and community continuity, and runs the risk of initiating students into a life of constant change with its related repercussions for loss of cultural and ecological diversity. Bowers advocates for educators acting as "gatekeepers" in deciding for students which ways of life are socio-ecologically harmful and therefore should be questioned, and which are healthy traditions and therefore, should be left unexamined and unchanged. In advocating the "promises of monsters" (Haraway, 2004), I am thinking of cultural contexts and locations where students are already experiencing torque. Facing, and implicated in, social, cultural, and ecological injustices, we are called to act as our own imperfect gatekeepers in examining the discourses we live by, including that of constant change. This is not meant to be a transcultural or context-less proposition, and as Patti Lather (1991) worries,

> It is important to take into account Foucault's warning of "the violence of a position that sides against those who are happy in their ignorance, against the effective illusions by which humanity protects itself" (1977:162). How do we minimize such violence by focusing less on disturbing cultural self-satisfaction and more on enhancing already there penetrations and frustrations? (p. 141)

5. See discussion regarding Bower's work above on the desirability of intersubjectivity and agency as contestation at the limit, and as suggested at the beginning of the chapter, it is also clear that the same modes and opportunities of agency are not equally available to all. It is critical to consider how markings and conditions such as class, race, and gender affect not only the issues we as consider important (Greenwood, Chapter 15, this volume), but also our potentialities for acting on the world and our understandings of these possibilities or lack thereof (McKenzie, 2006). In an interview shortly before his death, Foucault was asked, "Do not the practices of liberty require a certain degree of liberation?" To which he replied,

> Yes, absolutely. That is where the idea of domination must be introduced . . . There is a whole network of relationships of power, which can operate between individuals, in the bosom of the family, in an educational relationship, in the political body, etc. This analysis of relations of power constitutes a very complex field;

it sometimes meets what we can call facts or states of domination, in which the relations of power, instead of being variable and allowing different partners a strategy which alters them, find themselves firmly set and congealed . . . It is certain that in such a state the practice of liberty does not exist or exists only unilaterally or is extremely confined and limited. I agree with you that liberation is sometimes the political or historical condition for a practice of liberty. (Fornet-Betancourt et al., 1987, p. 114)

REFERENCES

Anzaludúa, G. (1990). *Making face, making soul/Hacienda caras: Creative and critical perspectives by feminist women of color*. San Francisco: Aunt Lute Books.

Armbruster, K. (1998). "Buffalo gals, won't you come out tonight": A call for boundary-crossing in ecofeminist literary criticism. In G. Gaard & P. Murphy (Eds.), *Ecofeminist literary criticism: Theory, interpretation, pedagogy* (pp. 97–122). Chicago: University of Chicago Press.

Bang, H. (2005). Among everyday makers and expert citizens. In J. Newman (Ed.), *Remaking governance: Peoples, politics and the public sphere* (pp. 159–178). Bristol: The Policy Press.

Bhabha, H. K. (1994). *The location of culture*. New York: Routledge.

Biesta, G. J. J. (1998). Pedagogy without humanism: Foucault and the subject of education. *Interchange, 29*(2), 1–16.

Boler, M. (1999). *Feeling power: Emotions and education*. New York: Routledge.

Bowers, C. A. (2001). *Educating for eco-justice and community*. Athens: University of Georgia Press.

Braidotti, R. (2006). Posthuman, all too human. Towards a new process ontology. *Theory, Culture & Society, 23*(7–8), 197–208.

Britzman, D. (2007). Teacher education as uneven development: Toward a psychology of uncertainty. *International Journal of Leadership in Education, 10*(1), 1–12.

Butler, J. (1997). *Excitable speech: A politics of the performative*. London: Routledge.

Butler, J. (2005). *Giving an account of oneself*. New York: Fordham University Press.

Cloke, P., & Jones, O. (2004). Turning in the graveyard: Trees and the hybrid geographies of dwelling, monitoring and resistance in a Bristol cemetery. *Cultural Geographies, 11*, 313–341.

Davies, B. (1990). Agency as a form of discursive practice: A classroom scene observed. *British Journal of Sociology of Education, 11*(3), 341–361.

De Lauretis, T. (1984). *Alice doesn't: Feminism, semiotics, cinema*. Bloomington: Indiana University Press.

DuBois, W. E. B. (1903). *The souls of black folk*. Chicago: A.C. McClurg & Co.

Felman, S. (1992). Education and crisis, or the vicissitudes of teaching. In S. Felman & D. Laub (Eds.), *Testimony: Crises of witnessing in literature, psychoanalysis, and history* (pp. 1–56). New York: Routledge.

Fornet-Betancourt, R., Becker, H., Gomez-Müller, A., & Gauthier, J. D. (1987). The ethic of care for the self as a practice of freedom: An interview with Michel Foucault on January, 20, 1984. *Philosophy Social Criticism, 12*, 112–131.

Foucault, M. (1988). Practicing criticism. In L. D. Kritzman (Ed.), *Politics, philosophy, culture: Interviews and other writings, 1977–1984* (pp. 152–158). New York: Routledge.

Foucault, M. (2003a). A preface to transgression. In P. Rabinow & N. Rose (Eds.), *The essential Foucault: Selections from the essential works of Foucault 1954–1984* (pp. 442–457). New York: The New Press. (Original work published 1963)

Foucault, M. (2003b). What is enlightenment? In P. Rabinow & N. Rose (Eds.), *The essential Foucault: Selections from the essential works of Foucault 1954–1984* (pp. 43–57). New York: The New Press. (Original work published 1978)

Freire, P. (2002). *Pedagogy of the oppressed*. New York: Continuum. (Original work published 1970)

Gane, N., & Haraway, D. (2006). When we have never been human, what is to be done?: Interview with Donna Haraway. *Theory, Culture & Society, 23*(7–8), 135–158.

Giroux, H. A. (1999). Border youth, difference, and postmodern education. In M. Castells, R. Flecha, P. Freire, H. A. Giroux, D. Macedo, & P. Willis (Eds.), *Critical education in the information age*. Lanham, MA: Rowman and Littlefield.

Gough, N. (2004). RhizomANTically becoming-cyborg: Performing posthuman pedagogies. *Educational Philosophy and Theory, 36*(3), 253–265.

Green, J. (2004). Critique, contextualism and consensus. *The Journal of the Philosophy of Education Society of Great Britain, 38*(3), 511–525.

Gruenewald, D. A. (2003). Foundations of place: A multidisciplinary framework for place-conscious education. *American Educational Research Journal, 40*(3), 619–654.

Haraway, D. (1997). *Modest_witness@second_millenium. Femaleman©_meets_OncoMouse™*. New York: Routledge.

Haraway, D. (2004). The promises of monsters: A regenerative politics for inappropriate/d others. In D. Haraway (Ed.), *The Haraway reader* (pp. 63–124). New York: Routledge.

Hey, V. (2006). The politics of performative resignification: Translating Judith Butler's theoretical discourse and its potential for sociology of education. *British Journal of Sociology of Education, 27*(4), 439–457.

hooks, b. (1994). *Teaching to transgress: Education as the practice of freedom*. New York: Routledge.

Kanu, Y. (2003). Curriculum as cultural practice: Postcolonial imagination. *Journal of the Canadian Association for Curriculum Studies, 1*(1), 67–81.

Kincheloe, J. (2003). Critical ontology: Visions of selfhood and curriculum. *Journal of Curriculum Theorizing, 19*(1), 47–64.

Kiziltan, M. U., Bain, W. J., & Cañizares M. A. (1990). Postmodern conditions: Rethinking public education. *Educational Theory, 40*(3), 351–369.

Knopp, L. (2004). Ontologies of place, placelessness, and movement: Queer quests for identity and their impacts on contemporary geographic thought. *Gender, Place and Culture, 11*(1), 121–134.

Lather, P. (1991). *Getting smart: Feminist research and pedagogy with/in the postmodern*. London: Routledge.

Leitch, V. (1996). *Local effects, global flows*. Albany: State University of New York Press.

Le Guin, U. K. (1994). *Buffalo gals, won't you come out tonight*. San Francisco: Pomegranate Books.

Lousley, C. (1999). (De)politicizing the environment club: Environmental discourse and the culture of schooling. *Environmental Education Research, 5*(3), 293–304.

Lovell, T. (2003). Resisting with authority: Historical specificity, agency and the performative self. *Theory, Culture & Society, 20*(1), 1–17.

Magna Publications. (2005, October 15). Student activism becoming more personal, yet more global. *National On-campus Report, 33*(20), 1–4.

McKenzie, M. (2004). *Parrots and butterflies: Students as the subjects of socio-ecological education*. Unpublished doctoral dissertation, Simon Fraser University, Vancouver, Canada.

McKenzie, M. (2006). Three portraits of resistance: The (un)making of Canadian students. *Canadian Journal of Education, 29*(1), 199–222.

McKenzie, M. (2008). The places of pedagogy: Or, what we can do with culture through intersubjective experiences. *Environmental Education Research, 14*(3).

McKenzie, M., Russell, C., Fawcett, L., & Timmerman, N. (in press). Popular media, intersubjective learning, and cultural production. In R. Stevenson & J. Dillon (Eds.), *Environmental education: Learning, culture, and agency*. Rotterdam: Sense Publications.

Nelson, L. (1999). Bodies (and spaces) do matter: The limits of performativity. *Gender, Place and Culture, 6*(4), 331–353.

Olssen, M. (2006). Foucault and the imperatives of education: Critique and self-creation in a non-foundational world. *Studies in Philosophy and Education, 25*, 245–271.

Pignatelli, F. (1993). What can I do?: Foucault on freedom and the question of teacher agency. *Educational Theory, 43*(4), 411–432.

Pitt, A., & Britzman, D. (2003). Speculations on qualities of difficult knowledge in teaching and learning: An experiment with psychoanalytic research. *Qualitative studies in education, 16*(6), 755–776.

Pratt, M. L. (1999). Arts of the contact zone. In D. Bartholomae & A. Petroksky (Eds.), *Ways of reading*. New York: Bedford/St. Martin's Press.

Soetaert, R., Mottart, A., & Verdoot, I. (2004). Culture and pedagogy in teacher education. *The Review of Education, Pedagogy, and Cultural Studies, 25*, 155–174.

Spivak, G. C. (1988). Subaltern studies: Deconstructing historiography. In R. Guha & G. C. Spivak (Eds.), *Selected subaltern studies* (pp. 3–34). Delhi: Oxford University Press.

Tanke, J. J. (2007). The care of the self and environmental politics: Towards a Foucaultian account of dietary practice. *Ethics and the Environment, 12*(1), 79–96.

Thrift, N. (2006). Space. *Theory, Culture & Society, 23*(2–3), 139–155.

Zembylas, M. (2007). A politics of passion in education: The Foucauldian legacy. *Educational Philosophy and Theory, 39*(2), 135–149.

Zipin, L. (1998). Looking for sentient life in discursive practices: The question of human agency in critical theories and school research. In T. S. Popkewitz & M. Brennan (Eds.), *Foucault's challenge: Discourse, knowledge, and power in education.* New York: Teachers College Press.

Manifesto (in progress):
J. B. MacKinnon

1. When we talk about "the system," it sounds like warmed-over Marx. But then, who can deny that there is "a system"? Am I right?
2. So, the system. The system can absorb almost every act of protest. Violence, for example. The system absorbs violence quite nicely, thank you. Almost without a bump.
3. Still.
4. The system is very poorly equipped to handle certain changes. Such as: it doesn't cope well with less.
5. That is, people who ask less, not more, of the system. People who do not contribute to "growth." Who don't go to the doctor that often, or take in a lot of movies, or consider a three-blade razor an improvement on a two-blade.
6. The act of asking for less, not more, is a radical act—far more radical than it's ever given credit for.
7. If you don't believe me, ask yourself why, after modern history's most appalling act of terrorism, the President of the United States of America would tell his people to keep on shopping or the terrorists win.
8. Here's why: consumption keeps the system standing. Take away consumption, and you need to come up with a radically different system.
9. That said, dropping out and joining a commune is volunteering to put your ideas in quarantine. And besides, communes tend to be a bit heavy on the rules. A tad monolithic.
10. We do not live in communes because we refuse to cede the culture. We prefer to be within the culture, a disturbance.
11. We are in the process of imagining the next civilization while living within the existing one. To use a short-memory metaphor, we are the digital revolutionaries tinkering in the garage in 1979. Not the guys who always dreamed of being what Bill Gates became, but the tinkerers who proved, again, that the key component of advance in any sphere—innovation—plainly does not depend on private interest and ownership and the exchange of paper money.
12. The on-line coupon salesmen and naked-on-my-webcam people came later.
13. So, we are inventing a way of life with less. We are asking the following question: Take away consumerism. What does the next culture look like?
14. To be honest, we don't have an answer. If this were the high-tech revolution, we would be at the stage, maybe, of the digital calculator.
15. Which is as good a time as any to explain what I mean by "we." We, I think, are the people who are rapidly losing the last remnants of interest in home theaters, multiple-car ownership, fast food, big-box retail, the Philip Stark toothbrush, all that. Or at least, most of it. We all have our small fetishes, our weaknesses, our chosen luxuries. Mine is travel. Yours, maybe, is your low-rider '82 Chevy Nova.
16. But I don't want to make this sound easy. This is not a lifestyle preference, though it is undeniably a life-style choice.
17. We are choosing, for example, to ride bicycles in a traffic system that threatens our lives, in weather that makes us miserable, over distances that make us tired. We do this because we are conscientious objectors to automotive culture and its environmental and social costs. When

enough people reject the auto-cult, a better system will emerge—public transport, cities with a smarter design. In the meantime, we ride our bikes whether we like to or not.

18. Except for the guy who can't give up his low-rider '82 Chevy Nova. But he's in a radical car-pool.

19. Another example. There is something called the pooh-rag system, in which you tear rags into small sheets to use in lieu of toilet paper. You place the used rags in a large jug of vinegar. When the jug is full, you take it to the laundromat and put the contents through a low-water wash cycle so the rags can be used again. There's nothing pleasant about this, but there's nothing charming about wiping your ass with old-growth forests, either.

20. Anyway . . .

21. . . . it isn't only about stuff. It's also about, say, living outside the entertainment pipeline of TV and Hollywood. Fumbling towards forgotten forms of leisure, or inventing new ones. Like protest.

22. Have you noticed? Many people in the mainstream media think global justice protests are just some kind of party.

23. They act like we should apologize for that.

24. Instead, the greatest danger is that we will let ourselves fall within their limits, their peculiar options for acceptable change, each one built on the idea of more—more for Bangladesh and Haiti, but more, too (and always, and ever-more), for Beverly Hills and Canary Wharf.

25. We say no. No thanks.

26. We say "no" with our selves. We are the people, sitting on a porch, sharing a meal at mid-day, asking a great deal from each other but little from the earth or from the state—less and less of its schools and shopping malls, its trade rules and tax regimes. We are the people who, as you walk by on your way to a job you hate, serve to remind that there are other ways to live, and that you can join in the imperfect search. And that searching itself is not a bad way to live.

27. In time, we will find signs and pointers towards a new culture, and we'll begin to live it from beneath, on the fringe, in the shadow.

28. A shadow culture.

12

Feral Sociality and (Un)Natural Histories

On Nomadic Ethics and Embodied Learning

Leesa Fawcett

In all the multiple sites and forms of environmental education, what is it that still motivates us imaginatively, ethically, and pragmatically? Feelings of deep social concern, sometimes bordering on alarm, quiet fury at the human ecological injustices we witness, and/or fear of loss of wildness in places, beings, and relationships. I move through these feelings as one who believes that theory and practice, thought and feeling cannot be pried apart. As Paul Ricoeur (1981) eloquently says, "Feeling is not contrary to thought. It is thought made ours" (p. 154). It is timely to reflect on our collective yet diverse work in environmental education. What are our strengths and weaknesses? Reflection always takes time, and time, especially contemplative time, is one of the rarest of things these days. If we do not look backward, forward, sideways, up and down, I fear our chances of transformative change will dwindle. We need a transformed ethics to guide us, to be our lifeguard in a sea of critical hope. Feminist Rosi Braidotti (2006) lends her hand:

> Ethics is rather a question of expanding the threshold of what we can endure and hence sustain, while not avoiding the effects of the crack upon the surface of our embodied selves. The crack is for Deleuze the indicator of poor health: the pain that necessarily accompanies the process of living under the overwhelming intensity of Life. (p. 213)

I suggest in this chapter that to address a transformative environmental ethics and education we need to greet and nurture feral creatures of environmental knowledge, creatures of hope and liberatory pedagogy. These creatures might live in a third space of feral sociality, and in the compost pile of ideas left by thinkers and activists such as Paulo Freire, and Gilles Deleuze and Félix Guattari.

To pursue the possibilities of a lively, liberatory environmental education and to realize the dreams of feral sociality oblige one to witness and practice educating for hope. This calls forth forms of imagining and seeking solidarity across contours of difference, including often polite yet treacherous disciplinary trenches. As Deleuze and Guattari (2002) assert, one plus one equals three, a new hybrid of its own. What wonderful hybrid creatures of environmental knowledge live in this third space, in the symbiotic interstices? Maybe lots of herbivores, parasites, carnivores, and love bugs.

Composting ideas of liberatory education (Freire, 1970/1984, 1994) with nomadic philosophy (Deleuze & Guattari, 2002) is one way to address environmental education and its possibilities in a globalized world having gross inequities. Throughout this chapter, I explore learning and teaching that offer promise for wild and feral narratives, ethics, and actions to emerge. I want to go beyond what Edward Said (1993) calls *counternarratives* to narratives that disrupt and transform the official natural histories, and question some of the reigning truths in environmental education.

Environmental education, as an outgrowth of the environmental movement and the deep desire for educational change, can be construed as an ally to social movements that question the status quo and nourish radical ecology (Merchant, 1992). Radical ecology is about a transformative politics and economics, and Carolyn Merchant (1992) places her "hope in social movements that intervene at the points of greatest ecological and social stress to reverse ecological damage and fulfil people's basic needs" (p. 13).[1] If educators think of their collective work as various social interventions in a civil society (i.e., through curriculum writing, teaching, learning, and community service), then it is important to examine our multiple locations, whom we represent, and what we hope for the future.

PEDAGOGIES OF HOPE, RHIZOMES, AND SOCIAL JUSTICE

Liberatory pedagogy has been critiqued for its fervent anthropocentrism and its modernist belief in the promise of science and technology. Deleuze and Guattari's (2002) meanderings on multiplicities offer a wilder, more ecological vision of the potential of ecological learning. In turn, Freire's (1994) pedagogies of the oppressed and of hope help address the often vague aspects of what one can do with Deleuze and Guattari's ideas; composting them together produces a rich, messy, third pile—one teeming with life.

In *Pedagogy of the Oppressed*, Freire (1970/1984) introduces his brilliant notion of dialogical, problem-posing education in opposition to the dominant model of banking education. In cultural action for domination (or banking education), ideology dominates science and sloganizing reigns; whereas in liberatory teaching, ideology is separate from science and problematizing is the modus operandi. Liberatory education or cultural action for liberation as he describes it is anti-hegemonic, spirited, and has faith in people, and their ability to thrive as subjects in history (Freire, 1970/1984). Regrettably, from an environmental standpoint, both sides of the dialectic largely held onto the domination of nature as one of their foundations. Cultural action for liberation partially redeemed itself by focussing on a love of life, in comparison to the more violent standpoints of cultural action for domination.

In his later work, Freire (1994) again rejects conservative and neoliberal forces, calling for public, social action in the belief that we need to actively educate for, and practice hope. It is not a naïve hopefulness he speaks of, but a pedagogy of hope born out of struggles and love. Freire (1994) maintains, "My hope is necessary but it is not enough. . . . We need critical hope the way a fish needs water" (p. 2). How does one learn to hope critically? To swim in a sea of critical hope requires a great deal of reimagining and restorying education. It also requires a few good lifeguards.

The two late French intellectuals and activists, Deleuze and Guattari offer a helpful methodological metaphor for imagining a critical education of ecological hope. Their work celebrates nature's agency: "Thought lags behind nature" write Deleuze and Guattari (2002, p. 5). I revel in the way they research and elaborate their ideas with examples from the natural world. The tree of knowledge so commonly used in education is, as Deleuze and Guattari (2002) remind us, the central western model of knowledge-making: "It is odd how the tree has dominated Western reality and all of Western thought" (p. 18). The erect tree of life, of taproots and dichotomous branches is a "system of thought that has never reached an understanding of multiplicity" (p. 5). Symbolically, one tree can reinforce notions of liberal individualism.[2] Instead Deleuze and Guattari take up the rhizome as a mode that illustrates nomadic thought that, "moves freely in an element of exteriority. It does not repose on identity; it rides difference" (Massumi, 2005, p. xii).

Rhizomes are a form of plant stem that spread horizontally, usually beneath the soil surface, in diverse, intentional directions: "Not all rhizomes run. Some walk, some crawl, some cruise.... gathering water from one place, nitrogen from another and sunlight from another," writes Dave Jacke (2005, p. 207), author of *Edible Forest Gardens*. Asparagus (*Asparagus officinalis*), a member of the lily family, is a rhizomatic plant and traditional medicine, full of vitamins A and C, and able to bear fruit for more than four decades. On Manitoulin Island, I mistook a rhizomatic beach grass for colored string. The plant ran along the sand beyond sight, each horizontal section an alternating shade of pink, yellow or green with flowering stalks popping up here and there in a seemingly chaotic order.

> A rhizome has no beginning or end; it is always in the middle, between things, interbeing . . . The tree is filiation, but the rhizome is alliance, uniquely alliance. The tree imposes the verb "to be," but the fabric of the rhizome is the connection, "and . . . and . . . and. . . ." (Deleuze & Guattari, 2002, p. 25)

Their rhizomatic model is about interconnection and interpenetration between beings and environments; it is about multiple "ands" that can be linked to critical education for social change. As Brian Massumi (2002), who translated *A Thousand Plateaus* by Deleuze and Guattari, writes in his foreword to the book:

> The question is not: is it true? But: does it work? What new thoughts does it make possible to think? What new emotions does it make it possible to feel? What new sensations and perceptions does it open in the body? (p. xv)

Nomadic thought and rhizomatic actions are about connection, and at the same time heterogeneity where multiplicities associate, extend or form rhizomes, and the rhizome is a map "entirely oriented toward an experimentation in contact with the real" (Deleuze & Guattari, 2002, p. 12). In the arena of environmental philosophy and education we need new thoughts and rhizomatic connections between teachers, students, and natures. If "the modus operandi of nomad thought is affirmation" (Massumi, 2002, p. xiii), what are the rhizomes affirming between nomadic and liberatory learning for hope?

To delve into this question, I find it helpful to cruise rhizomatically into the literature on new social movements to gather insights. In an article on reappraising social movement theory, peace activist Barbara Epstein (1990) differentiates between the early Marxist inspired communist and labour movements and the cultural radicalism of the 1960s civil rights, anti-war, environmental, women's, and gay and lesbian movements. These latter post-war movements for social change did not fit neatly into Marxist categories of working-class social protest and had more to do with a new politics of identity. So Epstein (1990) turns to Antonio Gramsci's influential argument that to sustain capitalist economies driven by the production of consumer goods meant that "force was no longer an adequate means of social control, that the working class must be brought to identify and cooperate with the system, and that therefore the realms of education, culture, consciousness were becoming increasingly important terrains of struggle" (p. 40). Gramsci's (1971) theory of hegemony explains the process of elite interests mystifying power relations and persuading the masses to consent to things that are not in their best interests. Nevertheless, as dian marino (1997) reminds us, the process of consenting is never 100%—there are always "cracks in consent" and "we have the choice of reorganizing or disorganizing that consent" (p. 14). We need to re/dis/organize our collective consent in environmental education. I maintain that educating about diverse forms of life, hope, and social justice is the most significant terrain of struggle we have to face at this time. There are no tidy answers, but at least in the compost pile of experiments we should hold on to Freire's struggles to unfetter learners, and to Deleuze and Guattari's multiple alliances as we watch new creatures arrive and get to work decomposing our mess.

WILD AND FERAL ETHICS AND POLITICS

To embody ecological learning from diverse ethical and epistemological standpoints, one has to remember, or learn anew, how to story it differently. Great stories and ethics require great imagination. As Richard Kearney (1998) says, the ethical potential of narrative imagination is its (a) testimonial capacity to bear witness to things; (b) empathic capacity to identify with different others; and (c) critical-utopian capacity to challenge official stories with unofficial or dissenting ones which open up alternative ways of being. The following recollection about salmon is in part a testimony to their resilience, an empathic identification with their feral differences and a story that challenges official natural histories.[3]

Feral Salmon

A very young boy ran into the house yelling incoherently that there were submarines coming up the river. He was in his fascination-with-all-things-military stage—tanks, stealth and bomber planes (clearly a parenting blip for a pacifist mother). Doubtful, I followed him to the shore. Before the first submarine appeared, I could hear fierce splashing around all the bends in the river, and the smell of stirred up mud, algae, and dying fish infused the autumn air. Lunging and surging up the Nottawasaga River were huge fish—two to four feet long, 20- to 40-pound fish. They looked like Pacific, ocean-going Chinook or King Salmon, known for returning to their natal rivers to breed in the fall. Their skin and scales were torn loose and raw from the rocky journey, but despite how battered they appeared, a number of them circled and fanned out areas with their fins to lay eggs in the loose underwater gravel. Oceanic Pacific salmon were spawning in our river.

About half a billion years ago, Hockley Valley was covered by a thriving sea, as the fossils we regularly find indicate. Today, we live on a freshwater river thousands of miles from any of Canada's three ocean fronts. These fish were definitely way out of place. So began numerous calls to fisheries biologists, including conversations that started with, "Lady, you can't have salmon in your river!" Aside from feeling that I was being treated like a dumb woman, I was pretty sure I knew what a salmon looked like in comparison to a trout, since I had been trained as a marine biologist. Until I told them about a neighbor who wrestled a 50-pound fish onto his barbeque, I didn't get very far. Finally, I spoke to a field worker who (a) believed me, (b) confirmed that others were seeing them too, and (c) wondered if they had escaped from fish farms. Eventually, a story began to unfold that Pacific salmon were introduced into Great Lakes waters as "farmed fish" and perhaps these fish were escapees. The word from the fisheries people was that these fish were "invaders, bad immigrants, stealing resources from the native fish." I was taken aback to listen to their rationale and speech so carelessly nestled within a xenophobic immigrant discourse.

Despite being described as "dumb, brain-damaged," farmed fish that did not belong anywhere, these fish had found a way to escape the global economy and survive "out of place." Bad immigrant salmon were not what we saw. What we witnessed were salmon swimming upstream and spawning. What we witnessed were feral acts of fish survival, breaking out of the official ecological stories.[4] There have been innumerable other stories spawned by these fish. One of my dear colleagues, originally from Europe, was so amazed when he first saw them, he remarked ironically, "How could anyone believe there is an environmental crisis, look at the size of these fish!"

In our quest to domesticate the planet, do we drive some beings into states of homelessness and then punish them for surviving and finding alternate ways to live?[5] In state apparatuses such as public education, the domination of colonizing discourses subtly governs the construction of subjectivity and belonging for diverse life forms. Both fisheries' experts and environmental educators described these feral salmon as "invaders and aliens" despite the fact that they were purposely introduced by other human beings in the first place. The reality is that these salmon persist and survive, so is it not the "epistemic responsibility" (Code, 1987) of environmental educators to consider them as feral citizens, not immigrants that need to be excluded? Ironically, these salmon seem like refugees from the relentless state of global economic maximization of flesh for growth and profit. Hatchery-raised salmon are a global commodity. Do they require protection from us?

Apparently, Scotland is also negotiating between their "alien" farmed fish and their wild ones. They are caught up in arguments about what counts as natural, appropriate, and technologically enhanced. For example, Christopher Bear (2006) points out that Scottish hatchery salmon now need "anti-predator and foraging training" in order to survive in the wild and replenish the declining rural stocks. In the making of monocultures of farmed fish, these fish are actually becoming deskilled in terms of how to actually live in the wild.

Salmon return every year to my backyard and spawn, some continuing further upstream to the headwaters, and others riding the current back towards Georgian Bay in Lake Huron. Originally, they came from wild stock, then some were domesticated, they escaped and became feral. Now their wildness has increased again. At the same time the complexities of releasing farmed salmon into the environment are vast, unleashing myriad vested interests and nature–culture–technology debates. Really, these salmon are cyborgs and they become feral cyborgs once they escape.

Feral Sociality (and Feminist Wanderers)

Nomadic thought that honours multiplicities and pedagogies of hope compares favorably with eco-feminist Vandana Shiva's (1995) notion of resisting monocultures of the mind, and Val Plumwood's (2002) anti-hegemonic work against homogenization of nature. Feminist scholars speak to the responsibility we have for the knowledge we make, the imaginings that empower us, our epistemic responsibility (Code, 1995). With the leadership of ecofeminist philosopher Patsy Hallen, I was honored to spend months in classrooms and various ecosystems in the Australian bush with postsecondary students from Murdoch University. Our purpose was to challenge the traditional official story about education with another way of learning, as Hallen (2000) explains:

> This move to take education outdoors flies in the face of long standing and deeply entrenched pedagogical and patriarchal traditions . . . When Phaedrus remarks on how awkward the citified Socrates is at being outdoors, Socrates replies: "You must forgive me, dear friend: I'm a lover of learning, and trees and open country won't teach me anything, whereas men in town do." (p. 161)

In an intense experiential and field-based course, we studied widely from Aboriginal philosophical texts, ecological and natural history sources, environmental phenomenology, and poetry. We read aloud to each other at dusk, hiked for weeks on end, swam naked in billabongs, ate meals together, slept outdoors nearby one another, and observed rituals that included lovely wake-up songs and silly bus songs. We disagreed, we were tired, mad, and silent at times, but we laughed a lot. Our shared laughter made learning from mistakes bearable, it healed rifts, and it was incredibly adaptive. As Shagbark Hickory (2004) wisely points out:

> Comedy surrounds us. It is abundant in our daily lives. It does not require rigorous spiritual discipline. It requires only that we remain the adaptive critters we are, that we appreciate the survival value, the power of comedy, that we not get caught up in the melodrama, the literally dead end of tragedy. (p. 73)

There is a very fine line between comedy, survival, and tragedy. In the Australian outback there are lots of reasons to be concerned for people's safety and well being, from poisonous snakes and scorpions to water shortages and sun stroke. The fear of these real but unrealized dangers can paralyze people into despair. As Freire (1994) cautions, "hopelessness can become tragic despair" (p. 3) and such despair when one is hundreds of miles from a medical center does not increase a group's chance of survival. Because humor exists in daily life we (un)consciously cultivated it, and this in turn nourished a diet of daily hopefulness among us.

Reflecting on where we had been together in western Australia, how our bodies related individually and collectively, one of the things I perceived was the intuitive knowledge and awareness we had constructed (implicitly and explicitly) of each other. An embodied knowing full of facial expressions, gestures, touches, postures, smells, walking gaits, energetic fields, laughter, hand, eye, and muscle movements. The knowledge we made with, through, and between our bodies was often an unspoken, yet noisy form of communicating: emotions, ideas, playfulness, intuitions, and the mysteries of being quite different people.

In learning, if one approaches the other differently, more attentively and openly, then transformed ethical views are possible. Jim Cheney and Anthony Weston (1999) differentiate an ethics-based epistemology from the more common western approach of gathering knowledge first and then forming an ethical stance. They argue that an epistemology-based ethics does not work on the grounds that the world is neither easily nor simply knowable; ethics is not extensionist and incremental, but pluralistic and dissonant; and because hidden possibilities surround us the task of ethics is to call them out, illuminate, and improve the world. Cheney and Weston's (1999) first step is not to gather knowledge, but to approach a situation ethically, respectfully and with a certain degree of etiquette. Through a shared purposeful stance of awareness and attentiveness, I felt that the bush group constructed a promising socionatural history of our (a) ecological surroundings, (b) embodied emotions, and (c) embedded community being, beyond individual selves into—a feral sociality. Inside spheres of feral sociality are unexpected surprises, tacit knowledge, humor, and intuitive leaps of faith into new learning. These days, this kind of being-together has become an (un)natural history because of its untamed feral characteristics and unpredictability.

Cultural phenomenologist Thomas Csordas (1999) questions and disrupts taken-for-granted bodily boundaries and fixed identities to problematize ideas about intersubjectivity. For example, Csordas (1993) discusses the phenomenon of *couvade* in Fijan culture in which "an expectant father experiences bodily sensations attuned to those of his pregnant wife" (p. 146). Resisting the medicalization of couvade, Csordas writes:

> Reconceived as a somatic mode of attention, it appears instead as a phenomenon of embodied intersubjectivity that is performatively elaborated in certain societies, while it is either neglected or feared as abnormal in others. (p. 146)

Csordas discusses the poverty of our vocabulary when it comes to understanding embodied knowledge, and "how imagination is discussed almost exclusively in terms of visual imagery, . . . Yet if we allow the other sensory modalities equal analytic status with the visual, an expanded concept of sensory imagery" (p. 148) would emerge into wider bodily potentials. Feral sociality has all the promise of a wilder, wider comingling of bodily beings and ecologies embedded in time and space.

This particular Australian teaching experience reconceptualized and reimagined environmental education and brought bodies back into learning together, bodies with all their differently abled sensory modes, quirks, and gifts. Walking together, blistered, grumpy and hungry helped me wander back towards the "environment" in meaningful, fresh ways. Until then, I had agreed with the abiding cynicism about how tiring the word *environment* had become: "Such a bloodless word. A flat-footed word with a shrunken heart" (Williams, 2001, p. 5). The company you keep and the walking you do are good for your heart in more ways than one. Nel Noddings (2005) believes that human interaction is the principal arena of happiness, and she writes that "A thoroughly relational view puts less emphasis on moral heroism and more on moral interdependence" (p. 35). It is difficult to be in wilderness areas without interdependencies of all kinds emerging.

Nevertheless, did we construct what Haraway (1991) calls "situated knowledge," or were we, like the salmon, out of place? In our case, we were a diverse ethnic group journeying, with permission from Aboriginal Elders, through a land wrought with competing claims by Aboriginal people and global mining companies. Together, we witnessed bounding rock wallabies, poisonous snakes, the wonder of rock paintings, emotional growth and emotional meltdowns. Afterwards, outside the classroom, long after the term ended people stayed in touch as they were flung out into peace marches, teaching, parenthood, environmental activism, love affairs, and more walking in the bush and around the world.

Our very act of bush walking was a kind of feral wandering that created a messy, fragile interdependence and political statement. In an original new work, Nick Garside (2006) elucidates how feral citizenship is a method, and "Wandering feral citizens create political moments and consider themselves capable of being *multiply political* (spectator, storyteller, and actor)" (p. 87). The actions of teachers and learners designing and attending a bush course can be seen as stark political resistance to the corporatization, social control, and commodification of knowledge that is besieging many universities. I envision an ad that says, "Wild domesticated woman waiting for the return of cyborg salmon and seeking feral sociality and citizenship. Looking for like-minded others." Just as the story of cyborg salmon releases the idea of nomadic thought and possibilities from uncolonized places, feral sociality can begin from deep within colonised spaces and discourses and find its way out to wander.

In Chapter 5 (this volume), Pat O'Riley and Peter Cole illustrate well the notion of a third eye:

Coyote what's your vision

20:20:20 if you count my third eye   but since it's mostly operational

with my other two eyes shut   I guess you could just call it 20

In this scenario one shut eye plus one shut eye equals one active intuitive eye. Both a third eye and the idea of a third space share a respect for cultural pluralism given the actuality of assorted ways of seeing. According to Ilan Kapoor (2002), postcolonial theorist Homi Bhabha coined "third space (1994, p. 37) as an in-between, incommensurable location in which minority or 'supplementary' discourses intervene to preserve their peculiarity" (pp. 652–653). Feral sociality is a peculiar form of affirming human sociality with all sorts of life, inside, outside, beyond the malls, at the edge of consumptive spheres.

ENVIRONMENTAL EDUCATION AND NOMADIC ETHICS

When Freire freed his theory of cultural action for liberation by focussing on a love of life, he refused to participate in a culture obsessed with death and how to avoid it at all costs. He also refused to be hopeless because he must have imagined that fixating on death "often produces a gloomy and pessimistic vision not only of power, but also of the technological developments that propel the regimes of bio-power" (Braidotti, 2006, p. 39). Instead, Freire affirmed life and the daily choices people make to live as best they can.

Braidotti, like Freire, is committed to emancipatory politics and education. Braidotti (2006) stresses an ethical responsibility that is based on the "generative powers of zoe" (p. 40), where "zoe refers to the endless vitality of life as continuous becoming" (p. 41). Her wonderful ideas about living/becoming resonate with my idea of feral sociality as she affirms:

> The subject is an ecological entity. . . . This mode of diffuse yet grounded subject-position achieves a double aim: firstly it critiques individualism and secondly it supports a notion of subjectivity in the sense of qualitative, transversal and group-oriented agency. (p. 41)

Subjects engaging in group-oriented agency can take innumerable forms, and feral sociality and friendship is one of them, as we continue to experience from the Australian bush class. On the lived animal continuum of captive–domesticated–feral–companion–wild, to imagine oneself as wilder, partly animal is to bust out of the anthropocentric humanist holding pen and into feral being. To decide to live simply and together, outdoors for weeks on end can nourish imaginations and nomadic ethics.

In the field of environmental education, friendships across various work terrains keep us enlivened and honest with each other, to shared histories and disparate efforts. Across national and international friendships, solidarity should be rhizomatic, respectfully connecting different projects. Vigilance is required always in our resistance to cultural domination in teaching and learning situations; such as the ubiquity of Eurocentric-only curriculum. Just as a "rhizome ceaselessly establishes connections between semiotic chains, organizations of power, and circumstances relative to the arts, sciences, and social struggles" (Deleuze & Guattari, 2002, p. 7), a revisioning of environmental education has to reach beyond academia and its disciplinary surveillance. Environmental education is not pure. It is much more interesting than any false notions of purity. It is a hybrid community of living beings sometimes learning from each other, sometimes socially feral, but always interdependent. We need to build rope bridges between environmental learning and other life-loving liberatory ways of being in the world. To be a successful transformative ally with other social movements, environmental education needs to increase its overall capacity to integrate lived theory and practice, honor diverse ideas and practices, and remain playful with an intact sense of humour.

Social movements suffer setbacks but like a rhizome they can set out again: "A rhizome may be broken, shattered at a given spot, but it will start up again on one of its old lines, or on new lines" (Deleuze & Guattari, 2002, p. 9). Actors in new social movements contend that conventional political institutions have not adequately listened to environmental issues. True enough, at least in Canada, but not an adequate reason to give up. As Braidotti (2006) says, "To be up to the intensity of life, the challenge, the hurt of all that happens to us entails great faith in the connection to all that lives. This is the love for the world that frames a horizon of sustainability and hence of hope" (p. 277). Nomadic ethics does not prescribe a path to follow but it does insist on wandering with others *and* forming nourishing alliances. Born from rhizomatic metaphors, nomadic ethics is all about the "and . . . and . . . and . . ." (Deleuze & Guattari, 2002, p. 25).

Nomadic ecological learning is somewhat like being an earthworm scholar. The majority of earthworms play an important role in soil ecology. By being continually loosened, stirred up, and aerated by the action of earthworms, soil is made more fertile and drainage is improved. Earthworms add their casts, decaying organic material to the soil, and form a source of food for others. They wiggle through the earth and "Burrows are (rhizomatic) too, in all of their functions of shelter, supply, movement, evasion, and breakout" (Deleuze & Guattari, 2002, pp. 6–7). Neil Evernden (1992) argues that environmentalists do not live in ivory towers but in ivory tunnels running underground full of societal effluent. Maybe it is time to tunnel together more conscientiously towards the light and away from the waste. It is always a day-by-day decision to feel the intensity of life, just as it is to hope.

ACKNOWLEDGMENTS

Portions of this chapter were originally presented at the session, "Re-imagining Ecological/ Environmental Education North of 49," organized by Marcia McKenzie and Heesoon Bai, with Paul Hart as the discussant, as part of The Ecological and Environmental Education Special Interest Group, AERA Symposium, Montreal, April 14, 2005. One of my favorite parts of the whole session was Paul Hart's riff rendition of the song, "My Bonnie Lies Over the Ocean," as follows: "My body lies over the discourse, My subject lies over the me. My body lies over the discourse, Oh bring back my body to me." I would like to thank Connie Russell, Michael Bach, and the reviewers for their helpful comments; and the salmon and the Murdoch University Eco-Philosophy class of 2003 for their inspiration.

NOTES

1. For example, Merchant (1992) discusses the following broad social movements: green politics, ecofeminism, sustainable agriculture, bioregionalism, restoration ecology, and so on.

2. Stand tall like an oak tree comes to mind. Of course, trees are full of diverse life, from the insects under their bark to the birds in their branches and the bacteria in their roots, but so often this interdependent community is not the focus. For example, if a tree dies the common practice is to cut it down right away despite the immense value it still has as a community of life.

3. I believe one of the implicit goals of this book is for educators to avoid alienation and "narrate our way into our collective strengths" (Fawcett, 2000, p. 145).

4. The problem of non-native and invasive species is a contentious one. See Evernden's (1992) ideas that weeds, like dirt, are contaminants, that go beyond moral pollution to become "dangerous matter, at least when out of place" (p. 5).

5. Desperately, issues of homelessness and its various repercussions affect humans and more-than-human beings.

REFERENCES

Bear, C. (2006, March). *Wild fish and alien fish: Negotiating nature in Scottish rivers.* Paper presented at the annual meeting of the Association of American Geographers, Chicago.

Braidotti, R. (2006). *Transpositions: On nomadic ethics.* Cambridge, UK: Polity Press.

Cheney, J., & Weston, A. (1999). Environmental ethics as environmental etiquette: Toward an ethics-based epistemology. *Environmental Ethics, 21*, 115–134.

Code, L. (1987). *Epistemic responsibility.* Hanover: University of New Hampshire.

Code, L. (1995). *Rhetorical spaces: Essays on gendered locations.* New York: Routledge.

Csordas, T. (1993). Somatic modes of attention. *Cultural Anthropology, 8*(2), 135–156.

Csordas, T. (1999). Embodiment and cultural phenomenology. In G. Weiss & H. F. Haber (Eds.), *Perspectives on embodiment: The intersections of nature and culture* (pp. 143–162). New York: Routledge.

Deleuze, G., & Guattari, F. (2002). *A thousand plateaus: Capitalism and schizophrenia* (B. Massumi, Trans.). Minneapolis: University of Minnesota Press.

Epstein, B. (1990). Rethinking social movement theory. *Socialist Review, 20*(1), 35–65.

Evernden, N. (1992). *The social creation of nature.* Baltimore: Johns Hopkins University Press.

Fawcett, L. (2000). Ethical imagining: Ecofeminist possibilities and environmental learning. *Canadian Journal of Environmental Education, 5*, 134–149.

Freire, P. (1984). *Pedagogy of the oppressed* (M. Bergman Ramos, Trans.). New York: Continuum. (Original work published 1970)

Freire, P. (1994). *Pedagogy of hope: Reliving pedagogy of the oppressed.* London: Continuum.

Garside, N. (2006). *Feral citizens, democratic ideals, and the politicization of nature.* Unpublished doctoral dissertation, York University, Toronto.

Gramsci, A. (1971). *Selections from the prison notebooks* (Q. Hoare & G. Nowell Smith, Trans.). New York: International Publishers.

Hallen, P. (2000). Ecofeminism goes bush. *Canadian Journal of Environmental Education, 5*, 150–166.

Haraway, D. (1991). *Simians, cyborgs, and women: The reinvention of nature.* New York: Routledge.

Hickory, S. (2004). Everyday environmental ethics as comedy and story: A collage. *Canadian Journal of Environmental Education, 9*, 71–81.

Jacke, D. (with E. Toensmeier). (2005). *Edible forest gardens: Volume one: Ecological vision and theory for temperate climate permaculture.* White River Junction, VT: Chelsea Green.

Kapoor, I. (2002). Capitalism, culture, agency: Dependency versus postcolonial theory. *Third World Quarterly, 23*(4), 647–664.

Kearney, R. (1998). *Poetics of imagining: Modern to postmodern.* New York: Fordham University Press.

Livingston, J. (1994). *Rogue primate: An exploration of human domestication.* Toronto: Key Porter Books.

marino, d. (1997). *Wild garden: Art, education and the culture of resistance.* Toronto: Between the Lines Press.

Massumi, B. (2002). Translator's foreword: Pleasures of philosophy. In G. Deleuze & F. Guattari (Eds.), *A thousand plateaus: Capitalism and schizophrenia* (pp. ix–xv). (B. Massumi, Trans.). Minneapolis: University of Minnesota Press.

Merchant, C. (1992). *Radical ecology: The search for a livable world.* New York: Routledge.

Noddings, N. (2005). *Happiness and education.* Cambridge, UK: Cambridge University Press.

Noske, B. (1989). *Humans and other animals: Beyond the boundaries of anthropology.* London: Pluto Press.

Plumwood, V. (2002). *Environmental culture: The ecological crisis of reason.* London: Routledge.

Ricoeur, P. (1981). *Hermeneutics and the human sciences* (J. B. Thompson, Ed. & Trans.). Cambridge, UK: Cambridge University Press.

Said, E. (1993). *Culture and imperialism.* New York: Knopf.

Shiva, V. (1995). *Monocultures of the mind: Perspectives on biodiversity and biotechnology.* London & Penang: Zed Books & Third World Network.

Williams, J. (2001). *Ill nature: Rants and reflections on humanity and other animals.* New York: Vintage Books.

David J. Nightingale, The West Wind

Who cyborgs will be is a radical question;
the answers are a matter of survival.

(Donna Haraway, A Cyborg Manifesto)

13

Network Logic

An Ecological Approach to Knowledge and Learning

Michael A. Peters and Daniel Araya

The concept of the network was developed in the 1920s to describe communities of organisms linked through food webs. Its use then became extended to all *systems* levels: cells as networks of molecules; organisms as networks of cells; ecosystems as networks of individual organisms (Barabasi, 2002; Capra, 1996). The network pattern is one of the very basic patterns of organization of all living systems whose key characteristic is self-generation—the continual production, reproduction, repair, and regeneration of the network. The notion of networks recently has been used to describe society and to analyze new social structures based on networking as an emerging form of organization (Castells, 1996, 2002). The question we are interested in here is whether there is a basic unity that integrates biological, cognitive, and social dimensions.

On the strong view, social networks are self-generating networks of communication that, unlike biological networks, operate in the nonmaterial realm of symbolic meaning. However, like biological networks, social networks form multiple feedback loops that become self-generating over time, producing a shared context of meaning that we call culture. It is through this networked culture that individuals acquire their identities as members of a social network (Bateson, 1972; Capra, 2002, 2004). Manuel Castells (1997) argues that the proper identification of an emerging global society is to be found in its *networked* social structure, both in terms of formal institutional organizations (including political organizations), and global and civil society more broadly. This chapter elaborates on these and related ideas and argues for an ecological approach to knowledge and learning from the perspective of systems theory. As anthropologist Gregory Bateson suggests, underlying the various domains of evolution, there is very likely a single ecological principle. We explore this perspective in the context of *peer-to-peer learning ecologies* and consider what implications learning ecologies offer to education, and more specifically, education concerned with the ecological.

SYSTEMS THEORY AND EVOLUTION

Rather than reducing phenomenon to their constituent parts, systems theorists endeavor to understand nature in terms of emergent wholes (Kauffman, 1996). From the perspective of systems theory, nature is seen as a complex system requiring discrete multilevel analysis. Taken as a whole, each level of nature—from atoms up through cells, molecules, organisms, and even social systems—demonstrates emergent properties that necessitate discrete laws and principles. A water molecule, for example, introduces emergent properties such as "wetness" that cannot be reduced or contained within the constituent elements of oxygen and hydrogen.

As Francisco Varela, Evan Thompson, and Elanor Rosch (1991) explain, this capacity for novel emergence appears to be found across all scientific domains, observing that in each case the network allows new properties to emerge. For systems theorists, the concept of emergent levels (i.e., levels arising from the combined interactions of constituent elements at lower levels) may offer a general theory capable of integrating the various branches of science into one framework. As Ervin Laszlo (1987) elaborates, evidence of regular patterns traced by evolution offers a glimpse into fundamental patterns of the evolution of the living world, of human social history and, indeed, the entire cosmos.

From the perspective of systems theory, we are beginning to understand that human beings and human societies are in no way separate from evolution but are directly embedded within evolutionary systems. Various scientific theorists of evolution are beginning to consider that the physical, biological, and sociocultural domains of evolution form a single continuum. Moving beyond an exclusively Darwinian framework, many theorists are now suggesting that evolution unfolds in punctuated stages:

> The results achieved in the [evolutionary sciences], even if occasionally controversial, furnish adequate proof that the physical, the biological, and the social realms in which evolution unfolds are by no means disconnected. At the very least, one kind of evolution prepares the ground for the next. Out of the conditions created by evolution in the physical realm emerge the conditions that permit biological evolution to take off. And out of the conditions created by biological evolution come the conditions that allow human beings—and many other species—to evolve certain social forms of organization. (Laszlo, 1987, p. 4)

Much like biological systems, human social systems can evolve into emergent features that transform human development. Castells (1996), for example, argues that the emergence of information and communication technologies (ICTs) underlies the rise of a new kind of socially networked economy and culture. According to Castells, information networks constitute "the new social morphology of our societies" (p. 469). Much as agricultural societies were transformed into industrial societies, today's industrial societies are being transformed into informational societies. As Castells (1997) writes:

> Our world, and our lives, are being shaped by the conflicting trends of globalization and identity. The information technology revolution, and the restructuring of capitalism, have induced a new form of society, the network society. (p. 1)

SOCIAL NETWORKS

In *social network theory* the focus is on patterns of relations and interactions among actors, where they can be both individuals and aggregate units, and on revealing the structure of the underlying network and the kinds of resource exchange that define the network and position actors. Relations are explored through mapping the exchange of resources, including data, information, goods and services, social support, and/or financial support. The strength of the relation is judged in terms of the number and types of resources they exchange, including the frequency and intimacy of exchanges between actors. In this context, we can consider social relations as complex, dyadic relationships characterized by sets of nodes and various kinds of ties that connect these nodes. Nodes might be persons, animals, or various kinds of collectivities, including all sizes and types of organizations, and even political units such as cities, nations, or entire societies. We can then think about relations among persons in terms of kinship, social roles, cognitive or affective relations, or simply in terms of interactions. In the context of organizations as networks, we might consider both formal relations (authority structures, task interdependencies, rights, and obligations), and informal relations (information sharing, trust, respect). In relationships among organizations more broadly, we might distinguish corporate links (financial transactions such as loans, investments, joint ventures, subsidiarity), and member links (interlocking directorates; Haythornthwaite, 1999). As Caroline Haythornthwaite suggests, individual, group, and organizational behavior may be more influenced by network relationships than by the attributes of the network components themselves.

The network perspective entails viewing natural and social systems as distributed networks: molecules as networks of atoms, brains as neural networks, organisms as networks of cells, organizations as networks of jobs, economics as networks of organizations, and ecologies as networks of organisms. Thus, it is not just the composition of elements of the system, but rather how they are configured and in what form relations exist. Network analysis, therefore, is nonreductionistic but focused on emergent properties. In this context, the structure of the system largely determines the outcomes or performance of the system, and the individual position in the system determines both the opportunities and constraints encountered. Against the mainstream, then, the network perspective is nonatomistic and relational, such that individuals are studied as both embedded in a web of social relations, and as having direct influence on one another.[1]

This approach lends itself to interesting applications in sociology and political economy. For example, Mark Granovetter (1985) argues that the concept of *homo economicus* in economics is extremely *undersocialized* because it ignores the importance of personal contacts and social networks (i.e., the embeddedness of economic transactions in social relationships). By doing so, economics ignores the incentives to mutual cooperation. More to the point, the focus on individualism in economics, based on rational choice theory, is unable to provide an analysis of the flows of information between actors—flows that are used to make decisions of mutual gain and are endogenous to the social network. Granovetter argues that "the behavior and institutions to be analyzed are so constrained by ongoing relationships that to construe them as independent is a grievous misunderstanding" (p. 481).

The assumption of fully rational agents pursuing their own self-interest must be embedded in the social networks in which they are involved and make decisions. Granovetter's point reinforces what has now become widely known, that many beneficial economic transactions are constituted by informal means involving trust, reputation, cooperation, and obligation. Thus, social scientists like James Coleman (1988) and Robert Putnam (1993) argue that social interactions and network closure—dense connections between network participants—are key determinants in fostering trust and cooperative relationships.

THE "NEW" SCIENCE OF NETWORKS

Helen McCarthy, Paul Miller, and Paul Skidmore (2002) begin their introduction to the *Demos* open access collection on *Network Logic* with the following:

> Networks are the language of our times. Think about Al-Qaeda. The Internet, eBay, Kazaa. The mobile phone, SMS. Think about iron triangles and old school ties, No Logo and DeanforAmerica. Think VISA and Amex, the teetering electricity grid, the creaking rail network. LHR to LAX. Think about six degrees of separation. Think small worlds, word of

mouth. Think about your networks. Your friends, your colleagues, your social circle. How new networks take shape through introductions at parties, over coffee breaks, via email. How your connections have helped you, supported you and hindered you. (p. 7)

One of their early conclusions is that "Networks are the language of our times, but our institutions are not programmed to understand them." The authors asserted that we simply do not understand their logic. They assumed, on the basis of strong evidence, that "Networks embody a set of fundamental principles for the ordering, distribution and coordination of different components, whether chemical, natural, social or digital." The authors' aim is to understand the logic and principles of networks in order to use them for organization and decision making, and to make possible better forms of coordination and collective action. They proceeded to interpret networks in relation to a set of key principles, including communication, transparency, knowledge, innovation, regulation, accountability, ownership, citizenship, and power.

In the context of communication, they argued that the dynamic of information is one of openness, and suggested that with the right kinds of transparency it is possible to rebuild trust in public institutions. The emergence of new communication networks permits increased capacity for high-level coordination such as that evidenced in the innovation-driven "open access" and "creative commons" movements. They tracked out implications for regulation, accountability, and ownership; and focus on "network citizens" who "participate in the creation of new decision-making capabilities as well as understand their informal power and responsibilities" (p. 19). As they acknowledged, the hardest nettle to grasp is the changing nature of power in a networked society. Following Castells (2002), McCarthy et al. (2002) suggest that power structures the contours of networks, determining the entry points and conditions that define structural advantage.

From another angle, other research has shown that complex networks display two important characteristics: They are scale-free and attributes are distributed according to nonlinear power laws. The study of the graph structure of the Internet demonstrates that nonlinear behavior is common to the Internet topology, the World Wide Web, and e-mail networks. Understanding the dynamics of complex networks can then, for example, enable the implementation of more efficient methods and algorithms of search on the World Wide Web.[2] As Watts (2003) explains, the development of the "new science of networks" builds on network analyses common to sociology and anthropology, as well as the history of graph theory in discrete mathematics, pointing out the interdisciplinary rise in social networks analysis in recent years. Watts (2003, p. 244) summarizes some of the features of "small-world" networks:

1. Real-world networks are neither completely ordered nor completely random, but rather exhibit important properties of both.

2. Some properties of these networks can be embodied by simple mathematical models that interpolate between order and randomness.

3. These properties can be quantified with simple statistics.

Watts clarifies that the term *networks*, although first used in 1979, was used and popularized by others to refer to networks with high local clustering and short global path lengths and was tested in relation to three network datasets—the affiliation network of movie actors, the power transmission grid of the western United States, and the neural network of the nematode *Caenorhabditis elegans*. He also suggests how network structures influence their dynamics, even to the degree that subtle modifications, perceptible only to local participants, can result in significant changes in the dynamics of the system.

In reviewing networks and collective dynamics, Watts points out that the success of network exchange theory demonstrates that individual outcomes depend not only on intrinsic factors but also on network embeddedness. At the collective level, for example, the nature and arrangement of network ties may play an important role in fostering the global spread of information and disease (Boorman & Levitt, 1980; Rapoport, 1963), or facilitating collective action (Granovetter, 1973). There is no space here, for example, to go into detail about mathematical epidemiology and disease spreading, or indeed, "node failure." What Watts (2003) clearly demonstrates is that the "new" science of networks borrows from or is similar to well-established work in mathematics, economics, and sociology. He characterizes *the new* in the following terms: by saying that it is similar to previous work but has a rapidly emerging, interdisciplinary grouping of analytical techniques, much greater computing power, and vastly more empirical data.

Although the *new science* is led by mathematicians and physicists, Watts argues that it will need the guidance of other disciplines such as sociology in, for example, interpreting both empirical data and theoretical models with respect to policy applications, and in suggesting solutions relevant to existing problems. Gestalt psychology, and the European structuralism that spawned relational systems and genetic epistemologies, also offer not only a relational account of structures (of the whole and its parts), but seem to offer the possibility of accounting for the genesis and transformation of structures, and provide epistemological status to network theory.

In short, network theory is pictured as attaining the status of a mega-paradigm in the social sciences as a form of social theory and analysis. Thomas Kuhn (1962) is highly regarded for his work on the idea of periodic re-constructions of the scientific worldview, and today, the influence of systems or network theory on science is widely viewed as such a *paradigm shift* (Wilensky & Resnick, 1999). Impacting disciplines as disparate as biology, business management, and history, systems theory has emerged as a dynamic research paradigm. Yet the tangled genealogies of the emergence of the field are difficult to describe and there is doubt as to the degree that we might consider the different strands of network theory comprising a coherent program or even sharing similar epistemological assumptions.

This first flush and "infatuation" with networks in the social sciences has also recently been questioned. Hannah Knox, Mike Savage, and Penny Harvey (2006) suggest that in the context of social network analysis, network thinking marked "a critical engagement with mainstream social science's individualistic assumptions and championed a kind of structuralism" but that in social anthropology "it marked a critical engagement with structural functionalism and signaled a recognition of fragmentation and complexity" (p. 133). Their conclusion is that network thinking "does not offer a coherent or convincing theoretical foundation for itself, and we should be cautious of attempts to suggest it offers an easy interdisciplinary resolution to deep-seated disciplinary differences" (p. 133).

With these cautions in mind, the central question of this chapter is whether there is a basic unity that integrates biological, cognitive, and social dimensions of networks. The strong view clearly evident in the work of Bateson—although not brought to fruition in his lifetime—is that there is a basic unity between nature and mind. We argue that like biological networks, social networks form multiple feedback loops, which become self-generating over time, producing a shared or common context of meaning that we call *culture*. We now turn to Bateson's work in order to provide a suggestive account of these *learning ecologies* based on what we call the strong view.

LEARNING ECOLOGIES

Bateson's (1972) *Steps to an Ecology of Mind* is a work well before its time. In it, Bateson draws on his early anthropological work in New Guinea and Bali (Bateson, 1965; Bateson &

Mead, 1942), along with his work in psychiatry and communication (Bateson, 1961; Ruesch & Bateson, 1951), and combines insights from these fields in his search for a unified theory of mind and nature.

In a paper presented at a conference on mind–body dualism in 1976, Bateson indicates that " 'Evolutionary Theory,' 'epistemology,' 'Mind-Body,' 'cybernetics,' 'ecology;' and, indeed, 'theology' and 'ethics' are labels for different paths that all lead to the same problematic mountain," and enumerates five common aspects of these various fields. These include that phenomena are commonly linked in recursive systems, that energy available in such systems is triggered, and triggered by events whose force might vary (e.g., *differences* in the biosphere) with the differences sensed through epistemology—the way of knowing, that these events act as triggering mechanisms such that differences are always "at one remove" from the events in which they are immanent, and finally that the epistemic way of knowing through the senses is dependent on the location within the ecosystem of the person sensing. Bateson says that "A description of the behavior or anatomy of a living thing (say a starfish) should relate—be a bridge between—our way of knowing and the way of the system which we are describing," meaning that there should be a connection between our epistemic outlook of the starfish and the morphogenesis of the starfish itself.[3]

Bateson's work predates complexity theory, yet his interweaving of ecology and cognitive psychology provides a basis for the notion of human rationality and learning in terms of networks, and the development of the concept of "learning ecologies" as a means for analyzing differences between ideal (normative) rationality and "adaptive rationality." These commonalities, these principles, we take to be the basis for what we have called *ecologies of learning*. Bateson was, of course, famous for his antireductionism and compelling account of mind. As his daughter, Mary Catherine Bateson, points out in her foreword to the 2000 University of Chicago Edition of her father's writing, all of his work pointed to a strongly coherent single theme:

> It was not clear for many years, even to Gregory, that his disparate, elegantly crafted and argued essays, the "steps" of this title, were about a single subject, but by the time he began to assemble the articles for this book, he was able to characterize that subject, the destination of forty years of exploration, as "an ecology of mind." (M. Bateson, 2000)

John Brockman (2004) also points to this singularity of purpose and the driving theme of a necessary unity between mind and nature in Bateson's thinking (see Bateson, 1979). It is worth quoting Brockman at length:

> In *The Evolutionary Idea*, a proposed new book, he planned to gather together those new advances to present an alternative to then current orthodox theories of evolution. This alternative view was to stress the role of *information*, that is, of mind, in all levels of biology from genetics to ecology and from human culture to the pathology of schizophrenia. In place of natural selection of organisms, Bateson considered the survival of patterns, ideas, and forms of interaction.
>
> "Any descriptive proposition," he said, "which remains true longer will out-survive other propositions which do not survive so long. This switch from the survival of the creatures to the survival of ideas which are immanent in the creatures (in their anatomical forms and in their interrelationships) gives a totally new slant to evolutionary ethics and philosophy. Adaptation, purpose, homology, somatic change, and mutation all take on new meaning with this shift in theory." (n.p.)

Clearly, Bateson was grappling with a fundamental idea concerning information and its central role in biology. Yet, considered in terms of today's scholarship in biology, the concept is still open to interpretation even though its role is critical. There is also a technical dimension to information in biology that requires careful scrutiny. João Queiroz, Claus Emmeche, and Charbel Niño El-Hani (2005), adopting a semiotic approach, reassess and reconsider the role of information in living systems, pointing out that information as a biological concept has generated considerable interest in recent years, as has the evolution of these information systems—to the point where "information" can be seen as a major force in the history of life. Others, aware of Bateson's work and following his general theoretical direction, still want to take issue with him (e.g., McWhinney, 2005).

It is not our purpose here to ascertain the correctness of Bateson's characterization, but only to recognize the underlying logic of his position as representing what we have called the strong view, based on a unity of nature and mind, and to use this conception as a basis for *learning ecologies*, a concept that may have more analytical power than that of a simple metaphor. John Seely-Brown (1999) formulates the same concept but without the biology. His account of how he arrived at the concept and its application to knowledge and learning is also worth quoting at length:

> I became interested in *learning ecologies* because of their systemic properties. We need to view higher education from a systemic perspective, one that takes into consideration all of the components—K–12, community colleges, state and private colleges and universities, community libraries, firms, etc.—that make up a region. This, in turn, raises additional questions about how we might create a regional advantage such as in the Research Triangle in North Carolina or in Silicon Valley. For example, is there a way to extend science parks that typically surround universities, into also being learning parks and from there into being learning ecologies by combining the knowledge producing components of the region with the nearly infinite reach and access to information that the internet provides? And, if so, might this provide an additional use of the internet in learning—one besides just distance learning. But first, let's consider what the Web is and see how it might provide a new kind of information fabric in which learning, working and playing co-mingle. Following that we will then look at the notion of distributed intelligence which has a great deal to do with the social basis as well as the cognitive basis of learning, and how those fold together. Then we will look at the issue of how one might better capture and leverage naturally occurring knowledge assets, a topic as relevant to the campus as to the region or to the firm. Finally, we will come to the core topic of how all this folds together to lead to a new concept of a *learning ecology*. (n.p., italics added)

Note here that Seely-Brown's formulation, drawing on cybernetics of the Web, is constructed entirely in social terms that give no emphasis to either biology or culture (in the anthropological sense). Seely-Brown defines a learning ecology as an open, complex, adaptive system comprising elements that are dynamic and interdependent and although this clearly draws on a biological metaphor, it does not squarely face the question of the strong view or indeed the unity of mind and nature in the same way as does Bateson. George Siemens (2005) picks up on Seely-Brown's analysis, suggesting that learning ecologies possess numerous components; he lists them in terms of a set of socialized network characteristics:

- Informal, not structured. The system should not define the learning and discussion that happens. The system should be flexible enough to allow participants to create according to their needs.

- Tool-rich. Many opportunities for users to dialogue and connect.

- Consistency and time. New communities, projects, and ideas start with much hype and promotion, and then slowly fade. To create a knowledge sharing ecology, participants need to see a consistently evolving environment.

- Trust. High, social contact (face-to-face or online) is needed to foster a sense of trust and comfort. Secure and safe environments are critical for trust to develop.

- Simplicity. Other characteristics need to be balanced with the need for simplicity. Great ideas fail because of complexity. Simple, social approaches work most effectively. The selection of tools and the creation of the community structure should reflect this need for simplicity.

- Decentralized, fostered, connected; as compared to centralized, managed, and isolated.

- High tolerance for experimentation and failure. (Siemens, 2005)

Siemens focuses on design, utilizing aspects of learning ecologies as a means of improving the overall spatial learning environment between "gurus" and beginners; as means of self expression (blog or journal) or debate and dialogues (listserv, discussion fora, open meetings); as means of searching archived knowledge (portal, website); as means of structuring learning (courses, tutorials); and, as means of communicating new information and knowledge indicative of changing elements within the field of practice (news, research). He explains the notion of a network with respect to the concept of *ecology*, providing an environmental view of learning and technology that questions how designers might approach learning, where a critical approach involves linking social and cultural change with ecology-designed learning. Nodes of learning communities, information sources, and individual people link together in networks to share resources. This is how we organize our personal learning nodes into ecological, networked communities.

The work of Seely-Brown and Siemens on learning ecologies highlights the issue of technology design based on ecological (i.e., networking) principles, yet it fails to draw on or match the insights of Bateson's work. Bateson provides an integrated and unified approach that raises deeper questions about the underlying coherence of the social mind and its characterization in terms of *learning ecologies*. Bateson's views stand up remarkably well to the most recent conceptions of information in the biological sciences, and hold considerable promise for further experimental work. An ecological approach to learning and knowledge, based on Batesonian assumptions, permits a more rigorous concept of learning ecologies, rooted in the biology of open networks and anchored in the strong program that asserts a unity between biological and social networks. However, to understand learning ecologies in concrete terms, let us consider the dramatic growth of peer-to-peer (P2P) social networks.

PEER-TO-PEER LEARNING ECOLOGIES

Both an emergent technology and an emergent social practice, P2P represents a sophisticated example of network ecologies. In simple terms, the principle behind P2P is the voluntary collaboration between *equipotent* partners (Bauwens, 2005). Collaborating across distributed information networks, P2P communities form robust globally distributed social structures that eliminate the need for intermediaries. This is seen, for example, in the context of P2P file sharing, grid computing, and instant messaging. Unlike the structural vulnerability of centralized command-and-control systems, P2P networks are highly organic (the Internet being the most obvious example of this). In P2P network ecologies, any computer node can directly connect to any other. Unlike traditional client/server modes of networking, P2P networks operate independently of any single Web server, all resources (including storage space and computing power) are provided and maintained by individual users at the "edges" of the Internet (Berman & Annexstein, 2000).

The success of P2P projects in the production of Open Source Software (OSS) has provided a dynamic model of shared production that is influencing many other fields. The collaborative online encyclopedia, *Wikipedia*, for example, is emerging as a dynamic tool for researchers and layman alike. Carrying the slogan "The Free Encyclopedia that anyone can edit," Wikipedia is the first collaboratively constructed encyclopedia built on a democratic network structure. What makes P2P ecologies specifically different from other modes of social and economic collaboration is that they do not rely on monetary incentives or fixed, hierarchical organization. Instead formal authority is "organic," emerging and receding with the domain-based expertise needed to complete specific tasks. It is literally "person-to-person" production that depends on the voluntary participation of partners. As an emergent mode of production, P2P not only "flattens" the organizational pyramid, it creates an ecology of exchange without recourse to higher authority at all. Moving beyond the one-to-many logic characteristic of industrial manufacturing, P2P introduces *network logic*.

In both the public and private domains, P2P has become an essential infrastructure because of its global reach. In the field of education, P2P is emerging as a promising framework as well (Berman & Annexstein, 2000). *Helpmate*, for example, is a Web-based P2P environment designed to allow educators to share and modify documents in real time from anywhere in the world. *Edutella*, another strong example, is a software-enabled P2P resource for highly distributed query processing, and is specifically designed to enable free collaborative support for a global-learning community. In using P2P educational resources like Helpmate and Edutella, university instructors and students are able voluntarily to share their latest research across widely distributed regions of the globe.

Perhaps the most ambitious P2P project for academic collaboration is *LionShare*, an open source environment that uses a mixed open–closed architecture that combines P2P file exchange with a user authentication system (LionShare White Paper, 2004). The stated goal of the LionShare project is to enable students and researchers to participate in the worldwide exchange of knowledge. While "PeerServers" are deployed for centralized support in LionShare, peer nodes are free to share files throughout the entire academic network. LionShare utilizes the same open source protocol as the popular file-sharing application *Limewire*, allowing anyone to contribute to the development of the LionShare network.

The value of distributed P2P ecologies like Wikipedia, Helpmate, Edutella, and LionShare, is that anyone who cares to contribute to ongoing development can do so. Wikipedia, for example, currently has more than 2.5 million articles, in several languages and is constantly growing in size and quality. As the number of contributors to Wikipedia increases, the total capacity of the Wikipedia encyclopedia increases as well. To realize this same dynamic in the context of education could be hugely beneficial. The possibility of enabling shared customizable resources in support of collaborative learning ecologies could have revolutionary implications for knowledge and learning around the world.

AN ECOLOGICAL WORLDVIEW OF KNOWLEDGE AND LEARNING

As we have endeavored to show, the key to an ecological worldview is understanding the dynamic nature of self-organizing systems. Even while matter forms its base, nature is not constrained by entropy but functions as an *open system*, "importing" energy across system boundaries. In nature, the distinction between open and closed systems lies in the permeability of a system's boundaries. It is the capacity of an open system to self-organize by exchanging matter and energy with its surrounding environment that enables it to evolve. This capacity for "autopoiesis" (Varela, Maturana, & Uribe, 1974) is precisely what gives ecological networks their incredible capacity for growth. When this system permeability is translated into the context of social networks such as Wikipedia, it manifests in the mass importation of ideas and labor.

Henri Bergson (1944) once said that there are two tendencies to the universe: a reality that is making itself within a reality that is unmaking itself. For the past two centuries, western civilization has developed within a worldview shaped by a mechanical understanding of the universe. This worldview is changing. As Margaret Wheatley (1998) observes:

> For at least 300 years, Western culture has been developing the old story. I would characterize it as a story of dominion and control and all encompassing materialism. This story began with a dream that it was within humankind's province to understand the workings of the universe and to gain complete mastery over physical matter. This dream embraced the image of the universe as a grand, clockwork machine. As with any machine, we would understand it by minute dissection, we would engineer it to do what we saw fit, and we would fix it through our engineering brilliance. This hypnotic image of powers beyond previous human imagination gradually was applied to everything we looked at: Our bodies were seen as the ultimate machines; our organizations had all the parts and specifications to ensure well-oiled performance; and in science, where it had all begun, many scientists confused metaphor with reality and believed life *was* a machine. (p. 341)

In the place of this "old story," Wheatley believes that an ecological worldview is emerging. Advancing on contemporary biology, she argues that modern institutions must begin to be modeled on biological systems. Organic evolutionary growth, she explains, is fundamental to human society and its development. This is clearly the case for the institution of education, as well. Our contemporary industrial model of knowledge and learning is incompatible with an evolutionary worldview. An age of collaborative networks requires an ecological model of education. With the emergence of network ecologies like P2P comes the slow unfolding of a new logic and architecture to support the needs of this new age.

So, among the new stories generated by those already immersed in relational ecological form, as Pete Reason and Hilary Bradbury (2001) describe this new worldview, comes a reimagining of what we have called *environmental education*. Could we suggest models of "nature-rendered self-conscious" where networking forms unimagined relational links with the potential for addressing environmental concerns through more imaginative and collaborative educational forms? Could we suggest network ecologies as generators of questions of relational practice that encourage different forms of environmental education? Perhaps these questions of significance invite us to connect our stories in ways that attend to quality of interaction that is, after all, what education imagines.

NOTES

1. This basic description is taken from http://www.analytictech.com/networks/topics.htm.

2. See the comprehensive course offered by I.A. Boudourides at http://nicomedia.math.upatras.gr/courses/mnets/index_en.html.

3. http://www.oikos.org/batdual.htm. Accessed 23 November, 2005.

REFERENCES

Barabasi, A-L. (2002). *Linked: The new science of networks*. New York: Perseus.
Bateson, G. (Ed.). (1961). *Perceval's narrative: A patient's account of his psychosis, 1830–1832*. Stanford, CA: Stanford University Press.

Bateson, G. (1965). *Naven: A survey of the problems suggested by a composite picture of the culture of a New Guinea tribe drawn from three points of view* (2nd ed.). Stanford, CA: Stanford University Press.

Bateson, G. (1972). *Steps to an ecology of mind: Collected essays in anthropology, psychiatry, evolution and epistemology*. New York: Chandler.

Bateson, G. (1976). Invitational Paper. Mind/Body Conference, at www.oikos.org/batdual.htm.

Bateson, G. (1979). *Mind and nature: A necessary unity*. New York: E. P. Dutton.

Bateson, G., & Mead, M. (1942). *Balinese character: A photographic analysis*. New York: New York Academy of Sciences.

Bateson, M. (2000). Foreword. In G. Bateson, *Steps to an ecology of mind: Collected essays in anthropology, psychiatry, evolution, and epistemology*. Chicago: University of Chicago Press. Retrieved November 1, 2005, from http://www.oikos.org/stepsintro.htm.

Bauwens, M. (2005). *P2P and human evolution*. Retrieved November 1, 2005, from http://www.networkcultures.org/weblog/archives/2005/03/michael_bauwens.html.

Bergson, H. (1944). *Creative evolution* (A. Mitchell, Trans.). New York: The Modern Library.

Berman, K., & Annexstein, F. (2000). *A future educational tool for the 21st century: Peer-to-peer computing*. Retrieved November 1, 2005, from http://www.ececs.uc.edu/~annexste/Papers/EduP2P.pdf.

Boorman, S., & Levitt, P. (1980). The comparative evolutionary biology of social behavior. *Annual Review of Sociology, 6*, 213–234.

Brockman, J. (2004, November 24). About Bateson. In *Gregory Bateson: The Centennial 1904–2004, Edge, 149*. Retrieved November 1, 2005, from http://www.edge.org/documents/archive/edge149.html#ab.

Capra, F. (1996). *The web of life*. London: HarperCollins.

Capra, F. (2002). Living networks. In H. McCarthy, P. Miller, & P. Skidmore (Eds.), *Network logic: Who governs in an interconnected world?* Retrieved August 19, 2005, from http://www.demos.co.uk/files/File/networklogic02capra.pdf.

Capra, F. (2004). *Hidden connections*. London: HarperCollins.

Castells, M. (1996). *The rise of the network society*. Oxford: Blackwell.

Castells, M. (1997). *The power of identity: Economy, society and culture*. Oxford: Blackwell.

Castells, M. (2002). Afterword: Why networks matter In H. McCarthy, P. Miller, & P. Skidmore (Eds.), *Network logic: Who governs in an interconnected world?* Retrieved August 19, 2005, from http://www.demos.co.uk/files/File/networklogic17castells.pdf.

Coleman, J. (1988). Social capital in the creation of human capital. *American Journal of Sociology, 94*, S95–S121.

Granovetter, M. S. (1973). The strength of weak ties. *American Journal of Sociology, 78*(6), 1360–1380.

Granovetter, M. S. (1985). Economic action and social structure: The problem of embeddedness. *American Journal of Sociology, 91*(3), 481–510.

Haythornthwaite, C. (1999). *A social network theory of tie strength and media use: A framework for evaluating multi-level impacts of new media*. Technical Report UIUCLIS—2002/1+DKRC, Graduate School of Library and Information Science, University of Illinois at Urbana-Champaign, Champaign, IL. Retrieved November 25, 2005, from http://people.lis.uiuc.edu/~haythorn/sna_theory.html.

Kauffman S. (1996). *At home in the universe*. New York: Oxford University Press.

Knox, H., Savage, M., & Harvey, P. (2006). Social networks and the study of relations: Networks as method, metaphor and form. *Economy and Society, 35*(1), 113–140.

Kuhn, T. (1962). *The structure of scientific revolutions*. Chicago: University of Chicago Press.

Laszlo, E. (1987). *Evolution: The grand synthesis*. Boston: New Science Library.

LionShare White Paper. (2004). *Connecting and extending peer-to-peer networks: LionShare white paper*. Retrieved November 1, 2005, from http://lionshare.its.psu.edu/main/info/docspresentation/LionShareWP.pdf.

McCarthy, H., Miller, P., & Skidmore, P. (Eds.). (2002). *Network logic: Who governs in an interconnected world?* Retrieved August 19, 2005, from http://www.demos.co.uk/files/File/networklogic01intro.pdf.

McWhinney, W. (2005). The white horse: A reformulation of Bateson's typology of learning. *Cybernetics & Human Knowing, 12*(1–2), 22–35.

Putnam, R. (1993). The prosperous community: Social capital and public life. *The American Prospect, 13*, 35–42.

Queiroz, J., Emmeche, C., & El-Hani, C. (2005). Information and semiosis in living systems: A semiotic approach. *The SEED Journal (Semiotics, Evolution, Energy, and Development)*, 5(1), 60–90. Retrieved November 25, 2005, from http://www.library.utoronto.ca/see/pages/SEED%20journal%20library. html#5_1.

Rapoport, A. (1963). Mathematical models of social interaction. In R. Luce, R. Bush, & E. Galanter (Eds.), *Handbook of mathematical psychology* (Vol. 2, pp. 493–579). New York: Wiley.

Reason, P., & Bradbury H. (Eds). (2001). *The handbook of action research*. London: Sage.

Ruesch, J., & Bateson, G. (1951). *Communication: The social matrix of psychiatry.* New York: Norton.

Seely-Brown, J. (1999, March). *Learning, working and playing in the digital age.* Paper presented at the meeting of the American Association for Higher Education Conference. Retrieved November 25, 2005, from http://serendip.brynmawr.edu/sci_edu/seelybrown/seelybrown4.html.

Siemens, G. (2005). *Learning development cycle: Bridging learning design and modern knowledge needs.* Retrieved November 25, 2005, from *elearnspace* Web site: http://www.elearnspace.org/Articles/ldc.htm.

Varela, F., Maturana, H., & Uribe, R. (1974). Autopoiesis: The organization of living systems, its characterization and a model. *Biosystems, 5,* 187–196.

Varela, F., Thompson, E., & Rosch, E. (1991). *The embodied mind: Cognitive science and human experience.* Cambridge, MA: MIT Press.

Watts, D. (2003). *Six degrees: The science of a connected age.* New York: Norton.

Wheatley, M. (1998). What is our work? In L. Spears (Ed.), *Insights on leadership: Service, stewardship, spirit, and servant-leadership.* New York: Wiley.

Wilensky, U., & Resnick, M. (1999). Thinking in levels: A dynamic systems approach to making sense of the world. *Journal of Science Education and Technology, 8*(1), 3–19.

Images from Detroit. Rebecca A. Martusewicz (2007)

14

Educating for "Collaborative Intelligence"

Revitalizing the Cultural and Ecological Commons in Detroit

Rebecca A. Martusewicz

Several years ago, I was invited to join a group of neighborhood people and community activists in a cleanup project on Wabash Avenue in Detroit, Michigan. A former factory site was being used for illegal dumping and the residents wanted to make it clear that this was their children's playground, and no place for the industrial debris being left there in the dead of night. Initially, I went thinking that it would be a commitment of a few weeks and a chance to see how such groups worked. I was not prepared for the overwhelming kindness, love, and spirit of regeneration among the people there, many of whom are facing incredible poverty, violence, and political neglect. I kept going back. Over the next several years, I found—among a rich tapestry of relationships and activity—a powerful process of education. This education entails teaching and learning relationships that pay attention to what is needed for community well-being, both among the humans themselves and between humans and the larger ecosystem. In this chapter I argue that such educational relationships grow out of and nurture a "collaborative intelligence" necessary to both human cultures and all living systems. I look closely at how the work I witnessed in Detroit—a set of practices, relationships, and accompanying language patterns that I identify as the cultural and environmental "commons"—provides openings toward the recognition of our dependence on, and interaction with, such a system of "intelligence" and thus for healthy sustainable communities. The chapter begins with a discussion of the theory defining this system, specifically through the work of Gregory Bateson, moves into a discussion of what we mean by "the commons and their enclosure" and how these concepts express either openings for understanding collaborative intelligence or barriers to it. Using these discussions, I then characterize the Wabash Avenue residents' efforts to revitalize their cultural and environmental commons in Detroit as a beacon of hope and possibility emanating from what might seem the most unlikely of places.

LOCATING COLLABORATIVE INTELLIGENCE: BATESON'S "ECOLOGY OF MIND"

I begin with the idea that intelligence, even knowledge, is not born of the human capacity to think or make sense of the world alone. Rather, it is the result of a collaborative endeavor among humans and the more-than-human world. In this sense, as human communities are nested within a larger ecological system, we participate in and are affected by a complex exchange of information and sense-making that contributes to the well-being of that system. Borrowing the term from Susan Griffin (1996), I call this exchange of information *collaborative intelligence*, a concept that shares important qualities with Bateson's (1972) notion of an "ecology of mind."

What could it mean that intelligence or knowledge, or perhaps even wisdom, comes to us from our participation in a larger ecological system? This is a difficult idea when we are used to thinking of such concepts as essentially human qualities. The following example helps explain what I am getting at: I am a gardener. In my garden I pick up a handful of soil, squeezing it in my fist. The force I apply sticks the matter in my hand together; it holds, and its very elasticity sends me a strong message about its possibilities. But what is going on here? The specific relationships between all of the various elements in the soil—the water content, the specific minerals, the humus, and the microorganisms—work together to create a particular response in my hand and, mediated by the language that I use to interpret it, tell me something about what it can do for the plants growing there. And if I raise the soil to my nose and breathe in deeply, another whole set of messages are sent via the odors that this specific elemental combination creates. All these elements are in a particular *differentiating relationship* to each other, and to my own senses and prior knowledge about soil. That is, they form a differentiating system of communication that sends messages to me and to other elements in the garden, the plants they feed, for example. I say *differentiating* here because they are in relationships that *make a difference* in terms of what they form together; it is the very differences among them, those spaces of relationship, that create the specific quality of the soil as a whole, and eventually of the plants they feed. Any change in those relationships would make a definitive *difference* in the makeup of the soil and its possibilities for the plants, and eventually the quality of the food I might eat from them. We could say that these changes would be *differences that make a difference*. They would create the meaning in the system that creates all possible changes creating life.

Intelligence, then, involves a process of collaboration among all these elements as they combine and communicate with one another, as well as with me, via their differences. In fact, *what I know* (or think I know) is only possible because of the whole system as it engages this communication process among differences making differences, and is, thus, much more than just the operation of my own cognitive abilities.

This way of thinking about intelligence is at the heart of the work of Bateson, an English biologist and psychologist. Described by philosopher Morris Berman (1981) as the epistemologist of the 20th century, Bateson produced work that converges with what poststructuralist theorists call the postmodern "decentering of the human subject," and many other ideas within poststructuralist philosophy concerning the operation of difference (see, e.g., Deleuze, 1994; Derrida, 1974). Countering the usual anthropocentric notion (anthropocentrism is the idea that humans are superior to all other creatures in the natural world) of a dominating human rationality that is objective and separate from body or from "nature," Bateson refers to an "ecology of mind," to explain the human relationship to other living systems as a living, communicating, and generative whole, all set within a limited earthly context.[1] In this sense, the autonomous thinking "self" (the "I" in the example given earlier) is a fiction, or a human social convention. Rather, for Bateson, "Mind" (or what I refer to as "collaborative intelligence") consists of a complex interactive system of communication and transformation where information is created and exchanged as various elements enter into relationship with each other.

Rather than thinking in terms of energy exchange as mainstream biologists generally do when thinking about how life is created, Bateson sees communication among elements in a life-system where elemental differences come into relationship with each other (think back to my soil example). These differences are not static: they impact and change other elements, creating other differences that trigger yet other differences and so on.[2] This series of communicating relationships creates a system of differentiation—it is how things are transformed, or become different than they were, and how we notice that they do this. For Bateson, this whole exchange of information—this "intelligence" or Mind—including our perception and interpretation of the world through our use of language, is at the heart of what we mean when we say we live in an interdependent relationship with the natural world.

THE MAP IS NOT THE TERRITORY

Furthermore, as the differentiating world impacts us (communicates to us), humans map that world with our discursive (linguistic, textual, and other symbolizing) forms (which poststructuralists tell us are also differentiating forms), and thus we build powerful epistemological patterns and practices—including our words, our knowledge, indeed, our culture. As generations pass in any given culture, the interpretive, sense-making processes become deeply embedded and layered cognitive patterns that are created and recreated via specific language patterns. We encode the world via our linguistic forms. It is important to note here, as Daniel Nettles and Suzanne Romaine (2000) point out, that there still exist across the planet at least 5,000 different languages that correspond to different cultural systems and also to specific bioregions where they originated. Thus, there is an important relationship among linguistic, cultural, and biological diversity that creates different maps or ways of seeing and behaving relative to the natural world as well as toward other humans. All cultures use words and other symbolic forms to respond to the world that touches us. When we organize those interpretations into knowledge, we give them status, and they become ways of defining our relationships and behaviors toward the world. As many of these 5,000 languages across the world are threatened by the demand for adopting particular languages as global languages—English especially—so too are the diverse cultural knowledges and the biological diversities they represent and protect.

For some, in particular in the west, the ways of encoding the world that have been handed down and reinterpreted over many generations may actually blind us to the fact of our immersion in this wider living system, and at the same time, allow us to confuse the maps we make for the territory in which we are standing. When we are touched by something in the world, we apply our words to try to explain it—differences in the natural world become differences (words, concepts) in our languaging system. We call this process "knowing the world" and, framed by a set of assumptions that defines us as separate from and superior to that world, we assume we are thinking it "ourselves," apart from the world itself, and that our words are a direct translation of that world, that they are even the world itself. Yet, Bateson teaches us that although one may imagine that humans are separate from, and "know," the world as an objective observer capturing the truth, one is never really "outside" that world at all. The processes that we use to understand that which we perceive as outside, are the same differentiating processes that produce the contexts we are in. Culture is not the same as the natural world, but difference as a creative, transformative effect cuts across these lines nonetheless.

Blinded by the hubris of hyperseparation and a faith in our own rational superiority, we too often miss, forget, or deny the ways our perceptions and the words we use to record or communicate them, are all part of the differentiating system itself. And yet, Bateson warns, the map is not the territory. His epistemological project thus carries a strong ethical imperative, not necessarily as a particular set of answers, but rather as a plea to us to recognize the larger world we live in as we pose our questions and construct our maps. If our maps make it difficult or impossible to see our interdependence with the natural world, we may act in ways, and through beliefs, that harm it and thus ourselves. But, if we open ourselves to the recognition that intelligence is much bigger than our own minds or words, then we may begin to understand our specific dependence on that which we currently treat as outside or Other. For Bateson, the first step in creating social well-being is systemic wisdom. That is, social well-being among humans depends upon understanding that we are dependent on, and participants in, a larger communicating and living system that operates via what I am calling here collaborative intelligence. We do ourselves and others great harm when we fool ourselves into thinking otherwise. "Lack of systemic wisdom," writes Bateson (1972) in *Steps to an Ecology of Mind*, "is always punished" (p. 440). Any creature that imagines itself outside of or superior to this system of intelligence will wreak havoc on it and ultimately upon itself.

So, we might ask, for example, which different cultural practices matter more to maintaining collaborative intelligence and sustaining life? What are the natural limits of the system to which we must attend? What in our day-to-day lives or in our political and economic practices needs to be conserved, and what changed? These are questions that call us toward recognition of, and conscious participation in, a collaborative intelligence—that is, a dependence on a living system, where everything including our knowledge is created within an interactive web of communication, an ecology of mind.

INTELLIGENCE AS REASON IN MODERN INDUSTRIAL SOCIETIES

Clearly, this is not the form of intelligence that we have inherited as a "modern" industrialized culture, where along with certainty and predictability, human-centered rationality is considered superior to all other forms of relating to and knowing broader living systems and their creatures. As part of this thinking, the land and creatures within the more-than-human world are at our mercy as resources to be turned into commodities. The "market" and consumerism supersede community. As Val Plumwood (1993, 2002) shows, reason and associated terms such as *intelligence* and *mind*, tend to be understood as exclusively human qualities, legitimating our definition of that which is not human as an objects of exploitation. Such an orientation to the world can be traced as far back as Plato, through the "age of reason" in the work of René Descartes and other Enlightenment thinkers, and into the modern world. Specifically, we have inherited and internalized a form of thinking that divides the world into a naturalized system of hierarchical oppositions—man–woman, reason–emotion, body–mind, culture–nature—where the first term in the pair not only has more value, but is given the "natural" right to define, control, and even exploit the other. There is no interdependence among these terms, only dependence of the second "weaker" term upon the first.

Ecofeminists recognize this ideological foundation as the basis for the oppression of women and other marginalized groups who are represented within western discourses as either part of nature or closest to it. Thus, we see close ideological ties in this mindset, among anthropocentrism, patriarchy and ethnocentrism. All interweave via these dualistic assumptions mapped onto our consciousness through our daily conversations, and within our cultural institutions to form a deeply embedded set of assumptions that underlie and lead to both the ecological crises and social crises plaguing our communities. These are our particular "maps" handed down over many generations, and we have learned to use them to exploit and control each other and the natural world, leading to disastrous results.

As the "maps" of western industrial culture are globalized in the name of modernity, development, and civilization, diverse and centuries-old patterns and practices that acknowledged ecological limits and human interdependencies with natural systems are swept aside, defined as primitive or "undeveloped," in favor of the "technological efficiency" of industrial methods. Monoculturalization and market-based relationships are replacing what were once rich relationships nurturing community along with biological and cultural diversity (Mander & Goldsmith, 1996; Pollan, 2006; Shiva, 1993). We live in a culture that presents these problems as inevitable consequences of human "progress." As C. A. Bowers (1999) points out, such a mindset is the result of deeply embedded and discursively reproduced ideological forms that represent modern industrial processes as the most "evolved" even while they are killing us: "A form of cultural intelligence that ignores how toxins introduced into the environment disrupt the reproductive patterns of different forms of life jeopardizes its immediate members as well as future generations" (Bowers, 1999, p. 169).

In contrast to this degrading form of cultural intelligence, what I am talking about is the need for recognizing the existence of an interwoven system of intelligence, a system of life-creating processes. This system that Bateson describes as a differentiating communication system, or Mind, is not *right* or *wrong*. Rather, it is what *is*. And, we can either recognize it or deny it. If we deny it, we will create a particular set of maps and consequences; recognizing it leads to another set. These are the choices that have critical moral implications. If we fall short of understanding this, we threaten the possibility of collaborative intelligence and the possibility of our own survival. If we poison the natural world, we poison our own bodies; however, if we nurture the places where we live as part of our own communities, our own families, our own bodies, we protect our children's futures and we knowingly enact and protect the living systems we need. That is, if we understand that we are part of a larger living system, not in control of it, or superior to it, we will protect it, and we will surely do this via different "maps" than the one industrial cultures in the west have created.

Although it should be clear by now that I see these particular maps as destructive, I must emphasize that I am not advocating for one right map, or way of seeing. Indeed a wide range of diverse cultural responses to the natural world organized via diverse cosmologies and articulated through different languages can be found across the planet. Many of these embrace and protect their embeddedness with the natural world and thus nurture the collaborative intelligence needed to maintain living systems. Examples of these can be found among the Ladakhi people of India (Norberg-Hodge, 1991), among the Quéchua in the Andes (Appfel-Marglin, 1993), among the Apache of North America (Basso, 1996) and many other Indigenous cultures around the world (Grim, 2001). These cultures have developed diverse systems in close recognition of their interdependence with living systems. These diverse cultural maps or cosmologies create important *differences that make a difference* among humans and the ecological systems on which we depend. But the point I want to make in this chapter is that such possibilities also exist within our own industrial culture where groups of people are beginning to reclaim ways of knowing and living that also open them to recognizing the needs of the larger system and their reliance on it. The example I investigate below gives us hope that we can shift our cultural maps, that ways of seeing and knowing exist among us that can help us stem the tide of community and ecological destruction that we currently face.

I tell the story of Detroit, Michigan, where despite the detrimental effects of more than 50 years of economic, political, and cultural "enclosure"—outsourcing of work, increasing unemployment, food and water insecurities, housing crises, urban violence—there is strong evidence of an emerging effort to revitalize what I identify as "commons-based" practices and relationships among neighborhood and grassroots groups. I argue that these practices, and the educational relationships used to reproduce them, tune into, and are thus able to nurture, an essential collaborative intelligence. Thus, the work they do creates specific differences that make a difference—in this case it is a difference that moves residents toward survival and flourishing, even as they are surrounded by violence.

As is seen here, the people working to revive their commons in Detroit are beginning to work with a different map, one that comes to them from both old intergenerationally transmitted knowledge and from current grassroots interpretations of what is necessary to live well together. I argue that their work together and the language that they use to frame and interpret what they do opens them to the workings of collaborative intelligence: that is, to a connection with the processes of the natural world and the needs of their community that help to maintain life. In order to put this work in a larger context, I turn first to a discussion of what I mean by the commons and their enclosure.

THE COMMONS AND THEIR ENCLOSURE

In the analysis that follows, I use the "cultural and ecological commons" (Bowers, 2006; Cavanaugh & Mander, 2004; The Ecologist, 1993; Shiva, 2005) as a concept that can help us pay attention to the nonmonetized relationships and practices that people across the world use to survive and take care of one another on a day-to-day basis. The "commons" is a concept that allows us to recognize both the interactions between cultural and ecological systems, and the ways that certain practices, beliefs, and relationships are oriented toward the future security of both. These include non-money-based economic and social exchanges including work-for-work; strong communitarian beliefs, practices, and relationships; alternative forms and spaces of education and democratic decision making; and efforts to create more sustainable, ecologically sound relationships with natural systems. Aimed at protecting the ability of both human communities and natural systems to live well together into the future, these are the sorts of day-to-day relationships and practices that function to nurture the larger communicative system of intelligence—or Mind—to which Bateson refers as essential to life. What we are interested in then, are the specific practices that open us to an awareness of, and promote the nurturance of, collaborative intelligence, as well as those enclosure practices that become barriers to such an understanding, and may thus damage living systems, including human communities.

The most basic concept and practice of the "commons" dates back to ancient English law, where peasants shared land for grazing their animals, as well as decision-making practices for how to do so without overtaxing the land and thus degrading it for future use. Although we may borrow this concept—"the commons"—from that ancient time and place, diverse cultures across the planet have also developed ideas and practices designed to protect what they need from the natural world to survive: gathering, developing, exchanging, and protecting seeds for future planting, protecting water sources, nurturing and protecting forests, caring for and protecting the soil and biodiversity more generally. These forms we refer to as the environmental commons (Bowers, 2006).

Key to defining the commons is an understanding that (a) they are not owned. They belong to everyone, and thus, (b) they do not require money to be accessed. Fundamentally, when the cultural and environmental commons intersect, our practices are aimed at protecting the larger life-systems we need and thus we are actively engaging and protecting collaborative intelligence. This includes an acknowledgment of the vital nature of each and represents our attention to security, to social and ecological well-being. The purpose of education within this context is thus systemic wisdom where learning is oriented toward understanding and acknowledging of the ways in which we interact with, depend on, and impact a larger system of intelligence. Such educational processes are visible, albeit in diverse ways and via diverse languages, wherever communities are depending on commons-based practices for survival.

The cultural commons may include food cultivation and preparation, medicinal practices, language and literacy practices, arts and aesthetic practices, games and entertainment, craft and building knowledge, decision-making practices, and so on. These practices are generally very old, dating back in modern western cultures to a time when our economy was based primarily on small self-sufficient farms, organized around agrarian values that protected the land and its creatures, and when our economy was more community-based. For many of us in the west, our commons have been so eaten away by processes of commodification, that it may be difficult to identify them as still existing (Bowers, 2006). And yet, as the story of Detroit will demonstrate, they do exist as nonmonetized assets, forms of wealth in the community (sometimes seemingly in the most unlikely places) that help to nurture our relationship with life-giving systems and thus awaken us to a conscious participation in the collaborative intelligence surrounding us.

Enclosure

Woven into the long history of the world's diverse ecological and cultural commons, and now causing severe threats to the sustainability of diverse ecosystems, is the practice of enclosure, which privatizes and commodifies what was once freely shared, and cuts people off from the life-giving relationships offered by the commons. Founded on deeply embedded cultural assumptions that define humans as in charge of and outside of all natural systems, and cultural progress as a creation of autonomous individuals seeking material accumulation, this practice claims everything and anything to be up for grabs for the market and private profit. When the commons are enclosed by processes of privatization, they are no longer available to people who need them to survive unless those people can pay. If the people cannot pay, they are generally blamed as deficient in any number of ways, and left to fend for themselves. Enclosure is thus a process of exclusion created, and kept in place, by a complex cultural mindset that presents hierarchical relationships of value as natural.

It is important to keep in mind that enclosure practices are founded on very old ways of thinking that, going back to Bateson again, are mapped onto our consciousness via the language and interpretive practices that we use, and thus function ideologically as "natural" so that we are not able to think in terms of the systems on which we depend. To summarize, these include the belief that (a) people and human relationships are more valuable than nonhuman creatures or relationships between humans and nonhumans; (b) human nature is fundamentally based on the self-interest of autonomous, atomistic individuals; (c) that some individuals are more deserving of the goods and services needed to live than others; and (d) that this system of value is most efficiently articulated by processes of exchange governed by private ownership of the means of production, and the exchange of money as representative of relative worth in the system. Thus, individualism, meritocracy, ethnocentrism, and anthropocentrism form a primary ideological foundation encoded, articulated, and exchanged in our very linguistic system and reproduced in our institutions (Bowers, 1997; Prakash & Esteva, 1998). Erroneously assuming these ideologies to be natural human characteristics, Garret Hardin (1968) famously refers to this process as "the tragedy of the commons." In truth, as many authors have pointed out, what Hardin identifies is the tragedy of enclosure (Cavanaugh & Mander, 2004). And as the work of Bateson demonstrates, such practices *are* tragic, indeed ultimately suicidal, because they cut us off from systemic wisdom: recognizing and protecting the living patterns and relationships that embed us in a necessary system of interdependence.

Practices and ideologies of enclosure do not arise from some part of humans' essential individualistic "nature." They are culturally created and maintained, and they contradict those collaborative interdependent relationships that help us to survive. Yet, as some neighborhoods in Detroit are demonstrating, when push comes to shove, people turn to commons-based relationships and practices that reinvigorate and demonstrate Bateson's idea of systemic wisdom. In Detroit, in fact, there is strong evidence of a return to age-old patterns of relationship precisely based on understanding the need to nurture community and the forces of life among humans and the more-than-human world that hold communities together. The educational relationships that I witnessed in the Detroit commons are based on the development of this understanding.

DETROIT'S STORY

In the 1920s and 1930s the rapid growth of Detroit's automobile industry as the primary economic force, brought hundreds of thousands of European immigrants, sparking the growth of a rich variety of Hungarian, Polish, Jewish, English, and Scottish neighborhoods. Additionally, Blacks migrated from the American south looking for jobs and a better life. Although they found work in the auto factories, Black families also found a city of profound racial conflict and discrimination as they were excluded from decent housing, education, health care, and higher paying jobs. Following World War II, their situation worsened radically when manufacturing plants began moving outside the city, spurring White flight in the 1950s and 1960s and a rapid decline in the city's tax base. Although Whites in the surrounding suburbs took economic security, good schools and safe neighborhoods for granted, the Black population was systematically cut off from the surrounding White suburbs by redlining at the hands of banks and real estate companies, combined with a lack of public transportation. This isolation doomed Blacks to high rates of unemployment, declining educational quality, poverty, and violence.

Today, Detroit is one of the world's "shrinking cities" as people continue to leave. The population is 83% Black, about 5% Latino, and approximately 11% White. According to statistics from the 2000 U.S. Census, the level of education within the Black community ranges from 32% having completed high school to 1.4% having achieved a graduate or professional degree. One trend reflecting the lack of employment opportunities is that of young people leaving the city and their families: 55% of grandparents are taking on a role as the primary caregivers of children. Household incomes also reflect a degree of poverty not found in other regions of the country. For example, 39% of households have an income of less than $10,000 per year, with 11.7% having incomes between $10,000 and $15,000 per year. The number of households with an income above $35,000 falls off dramatically. In 2003, 41% of children under the age of 18 were living below the poverty line, whereas another 22% were classified as living in low-income families. Given such entrenched desperate conditions, it is not surprising that violent crime in the city is more than three times the national average.

In a very real way, people in this city have been forced into a subsistence mode of life resembling what many Americans would identify with so-called third-world communities and cultures. The city's once majestic homes and architecture that were built as part of the rise of industrial culture are now mostly crumbling or already torn down, leaving more than 40,000 empty lots across the city. People live in houses that may or may not have roofs or windows. Children play in lots where factories once stood, on concrete or where the soil is likely contaminated with lead and other toxins. The city's Welfare Rights Organization and other community groups struggle against the privatization of water as all utility prices continue to rise, causing thousands of shut offs every year which in turn cause families to lose their children to social services. Grocery stores are almost nonexistent (there is one major chain store within the city limits), but liquor stores and fast food restaurants are found on every other corner. Obesity is a problem among teenagers, diabetes is on the rise, and the elderly are finding it increasingly difficult to find sufficient food. People are literally starving and freezing to death, and yet the city bureaucrats continue to invest in stadiums, theaters, casinos, and other downtown entertainment facilities that primarily serve residents of the White suburbs. To say that people are living in a day-to-day survival mode here is an understatement for many.

But this is not the whole story. Although it may seem an odd way to view their situation, this subsistence mode of existence is exactly what has opened a crack of hope in the otherwise dismal situation for many people in Detroit. As Detroit journalist Matt Borghi (2002) says, "There's no question that parts of the city, many parts in fact, are still very dangerous and hostile, but things are different now. The dynamic in Detroit is different now. The city is growing spiritually, and almost away from its industrial roots" (para. 26). In the last 5 years or more, I have had a big helping of that spiritual energy—nothing less than love, really—and that is the story that I want to tell here.

LIVING BATESON'S EPISTEMOLOGY IN BURNED-OUT BUILDINGS, BROWN FIELDS, AND BIG HEARTS: EDUCATING FOR COLLABORATIVE INTELLIGENCE

One spring day about 5 years ago, I got in my car and headed east on I-94, a knot of anticipation wedged solidly in my chest. A good friend and colleague had invited me to join him and a small group of other people in a neighborhood cleanup effort on the street where he grew up on the west side of Detroit. I had been hearing about this and similar efforts in the city, where civil rights activists were joining with ecologically minded community builders and neighborhood groups to take back their city. I was to spend the day working on a brownfield cleanup in the heart of a Black neighborhood, joining others there in the hope of making a safe play area for their children. Driving through the neighborhoods, I was shocked at the decay, neglect, and overall poverty along once-grand boulevards. It looked like it had been bombed.

When I arrived at the address given to me, Charles, a long-time civil rights activist, journalist, and resident of this very neighborhood, greeted me with his customary big smile and welcome. Along with his greeting came handshakes and hellos from a handful of other people. Some were members of a small group called the Committee for the Political Resurrection (CPR) of Detroit, an organization that Charles founded and co-chaired with two women a couple of years earlier. Others were residents of Wabash Avenue and were Charles's neighbors. Some were children ranging in age from around 5 to 15 or 16. Holding shovels or rakes and wielding wheelbarrows, they had stopped just long enough to welcome me, and were now getting back to the impossible work of moving rubble off a big lot strewn with piles of broken up concrete, bricks, rocks, old tires, and other debris. "Mostly left here illegally by construction companies that find it cheaper to just dump their trash on us, than to take it to a landfill where they have to pay!," one man told me as he wheeled his load by. He pointed up high where I noticed signs posted on telephone poles that said, "Don't Dump on Us!" Charles handed me a shovel and said that CPR believes that if they clean it up, the dumping will stop and the trucks will go someplace else.

CPR Detroit organized with the mission to "advocate a grassroots movement that would fight for neighborhood empowerment, community control of schools and police, and support existing social and environmental justice organizations" (Simmons, 2002, p. 1). Delineating as its primary focal points the privatizations of city agencies and services, fair wages for workers, and community control of neighborhood development and land use, the group set to work to re-invigorate Citizen District Councils and to demand that the city begin to include local people in its decision-making processes. CPR even ran a political campaign supporting Charles for City Council. He lost, but it invigorated the group.

In Charles' neighborhood, where their work was focused at that time, a factory had been illegally torn down by thieves who were after the steel support beams holding up the century-old abandoned factory building. The building collapsed into the street, making it impassable and dangerous. Local families became concerned for their children who played nearby. After 2 years of struggling to convince city officials that the building had indeed been knocked down, neighbors on Wabash Avenue, supported by CPR, finally succeeded in having most of the rubble removed from the street and adjacent lots. That was their first victory.

Next, a basketball court was planned on the remaining concrete floor, and there was talk of starting a community garden. In taking back their neighborhood from criminal activity (mostly drugs and prostitution) and reclaiming it for their children as a healthy place to grow up, the residents were also teaching their children how to do that, and why it was important. I began showing up each Saturday morning, joining the others in the joyful work of moving bricks and dirt, and building hope in this neglected, but resilient neighborhood. I was welcomed and charmed, cajoled, and wooed by the generosity, care, and good will generated by the residents. That was probably the most powerful part of the lessons being exchanged there. Love was always in the air. It showed up in people's faces, in their words, in the kindness of their gestures, and the gentle seriousness with which they approached this work. I was being introduced to a particular language, framed by metaphors of community, mutuality, and simple kindness. An old map, but shockingly unfamiliar to me.

Once in a while a screeching sound would come from some bushes nearby and my raised eyebrows were met with grins by some of the residents, and shrugs by others. "We have interesting new neighbors," one said. After a while, I caught a glimpse of one strutting across the lot: a big male pheasant who also claimed the place as home, having been expelled from the ever-developing suburbs a few miles to the west. With so many empty lots turning to green space and naturally reforesting, Detroit has become good habitat for pheasants, coyotes, and other wildlife. And the attitude of the people here was to welcome them with a certain amount of wonder and delight.

This was my introduction to a larger movement coming to life across the city. A network of people across the city were working to take back their neighborhoods by growing gardens that fed their families, creating public murals, converting abandoned storefronts into studios, shops, and educational facilities. They worked in small independent groups to revitalize their commons often through barter relationships, or giving work for work, and all the while educating each other in the process. I heard Charles offer a young man the use of his car if he would roof his house in exchange. It was actually more than an exchange: it was a lesson in basic neighborliness from the older man to the younger. Charles mentored no fewer than 20 young men in this neighborhood and across the city. In a variety of circumstances and venues across the city, I watched older men teaching younger men the art of the commons: how to wire a building, or fix plumbing, lay concrete, or build a stage for local musicians and poets in exchange for whatever might be needed at the time. I listened as women shared stories about, and techniques for, food cultivation and preparation, or tended each others' children, or talked to me about what herbs to look for if I was feeling this way or that way: "Honey, sounds like you need some *chlorophyll* in your blood!"

These exchanges, in all their specificity in terms of language, intergenerational knowledge, and the circumstantial needs of these neighborhoods, were and are an essential characteristic of rebuilding the cultural and environmental commons of Detroit. Although there was not 100% participation, Charles often cajoled people to leave their porches and come help. There was a spirit of neighborliness that I found infectious. Some people held paying jobs, but most were unemployed. Make no mistake: Detroit is a desperate place in many ways. Suffering from years of high unemployment, there is a well-developed and violent "underground economy" based primarily on drug trade and prostitution. Young men die almost on a daily basis in war-like situations. But, that said, even the "gang-bangers" who lived on Wabash knew they were part of a community. Charles told me a tale of two young men who lived on the block known to be part of a gang dealing drugs. They were also relied on to take care of his auntie while she was ill. "They'd check on her and bring her groceries. They even cashed her social security checks for her and brought her the cash."

Quite poignantly, people here have been forced to return to older ways of doing things, and ways of being together. I heard many talk at length about knowledges, attitudes, and practices that their parents, aunts and uncles, and other mentors in their lives passed on to them regarding caring for each other and protecting their families and community. One of the women who worked with us was also especially known for taking care of a number of elderly residents on the street in addition to caring for her own children and grandchildren. She also grew a gorgeous garden in her postage stamp backyard and fed her family and many of the neighbors from it. I heard her talking about medicinal properties of some of the plants she grew, and of the "weeds" in the cracks of the cement in the old factory site. "That plant in my yard, that's comfrey? . . . great for poultices."

While some talked about knowledge that had been passed down since the days of slavery, others talked of highly politicized learning, gleaned during the early years of the civil rights movement, and aimed at gaining access to the system of domination that was undermining those very values that their parents and grandparents understood.[3] But much of this particular education was also about how to live well despite the racist context of Detroit, and how to hold their lives together in spite of the economic disruptions characteristic of their context.

> My daddy always taught me to work hard and to stand up for myself as a strong, capable, good person and to help others do so. It's about security and love. We lived in a very diverse neighbourhood, and all got along and helped each other in spite of the racist policies and practices that were happening all around us. That's what I learned, and that's why I am an activist for this city. (Harris, personal communication, July 2005)

Probably the most powerful educational processes that I observed were organized around the production of food. The CPR-sponsored Wabash project joined more than 150 community gardens in the city, supported by a growing network of community organizations, but especially by the Detroit Agricultural Network (DAN), the Greening of Detroit, and Earthworks. All of these were food security-oriented organizations operating on shoestring budgets and by sweat equity to help neighborhood folks grow the food they need to feed themselves. Here commons-based education was directly related to supporting collaborative intelligence as people shared knowledge of ancient ways of cultivating, harvesting, preparing, and preserving food. Guided by master gardeners and supported by the food security organizations, they taught each other how to build and maintain compost bins, they exchanged seeds and seedlings, they volunteered to work in any of the neighborhood gardens needing help, they plowed, they planted, they harvested, and they ate together. On any given weekend especially during the growing season or harvest time, there are still DAN-sponsored festivals and potlucks that bring people together to celebrate and partake of the fruits of their work together. And through all of this, a very important process of re-education is going on that is shifting the value system of the people involved from a need to participate in the consumer economy, to one of appreciating and protecting their community, including the land.

As Brother Rick Samyn, a Detroit-based Capuchin monk who founded EarthWorks writes: "As a society, we have become dangerously disconnected from the land and the sources of food that sustain life. We have detached ourselves from the real source of wealth . . . a respectful and reverent relationship with the land" (Samyn, 2007, para. 1). Thus, emphasizing the importance of relationships across human and natural boundaries, he works within a network of grassroots activists toward what he called "interactive green-space" providing both food for the hungry but also an important educational opportunity for local neighborhood families. "People desire wholesome, healthy food. So why not start with food?" (Samyn, personal communication, July 2004).

Adding to the informal mentoring of the neighborhoods, nonprofit organizations like Earthworks were systematic in their educational strategies; offering workshops, summer institutes, and lots of hands-on work with kids that developed a wide array of skills from building bikes to composting to painting complex civil rights and historical community-based murals. Their work together and the relationships, practices, and values being acted and reenacted, although they may not be recognized as such, are reasserting an ancient map composed of a specific language, the language of collaboration, mutuality and support. And while this language and these practices may have their own place-based specificity, they belong to an order of life experienced around the world as basic to community survival. Reading Bateson back into this setting, what we can see on a more micro-level is that these people were engaging the differentiating system, creating collaborative intelligence, opening themselves to something bigger than themselves via practices and relationships necessary to sustain life, creating differences that made a difference by nurturing their connections within a living system rather than enclosing or exploiting it. The work to which I bear witness with this writing includes an ethical/educational process that has its own peculiarity made of the particular history of the people there and the land itself, of the tragedy of neglect, of suffering, and the determination to live.

All this occurs while gang violence rages on and city government and local developers continue their quests of enclosure. While the city claims eminent domain on tax-delinquent properties, the Greening of Detroit is hard at work negotiating with city officials for an official designation of green spaces, pathways and protection of community gardens. While the city shuts off the water supply to those who can no longer afford rising prices, organizers of a local water activist group teach people how to use pipe wrenches to turn their water back on. And while the city shuts down 52 public schools, local grassroots organizers join teacher Paul Wertz at Catherine Ferguson Academy to mentor pregnant and parenting girls in caring for animals, building barns, renovating houses, growing fruit trees and gardens, and making decisions that will ultimately nurture their unborn and young children as well as themselves.

CONCLUSION

My work in Detroit began as a volunteer position on a brownfield on one little street with a handful of people. What I encountered there on Wabash and across the city was something that I did not anticipate, but it is something happening all over the world. That is, people are organizing themselves around ways of thinking, ancient in reality but unfamiliar to and often devalued by those of us in industrial and postindustrial cultures. These ways of thinking, organized into what I have been referring to as commons-based practices, require teaching and learning that are constantly framed by questions of community well-being, and ethical connections made to life-nourishing forces—differences that make a difference. Theirs is an education that is enacted in the very fabric of their lives, and is about life itself. But this is not a way of thinking that is currently being discussed in many education courses. For many of us, caught as we are in "high-status" and "high-stakes" notions of education, it may not even be identifiable as education.

And yet, perhaps this is precisely what we need to learn ourselves. Recognizing intelligence as an ecology of mind necessary to stem the tide of destruction in an overcommodified world is a moral responsibility we have to our children's futures. It requires that we—educational theorists, teachers, teacher educators—begin to take seriously our dependent relationship on the larger ecological system, and how our own ways of thinking interfere with such systemic wisdom. Whether in schools or in grassroots relationships, taking the notion of collaborative intelligence seriously means that we teach our children and our neighbors as future and current citizens, important ethical choices and responsibilities that recognize those practices that contribute to sustainable healthy communities of life, and those that do not. We must be willing to teach and argue for the purpose of education as just this, to develop the systemic wisdom in future generations that will allow us to make choices that allow life's generative forces to flourish. This is the legacy of Bateson's epistemology. Learning to make such choices collectively is what educating for collaborative intelligence means.

Such learning cannot happen if we place ourselves over and above or outside this system of collaborative intelligence. Those hierarchical cultural assumptions that define human life as superior to other life forms, and some humans as superior to others are ultimately destructive of the relationships fundamental to life itself. And education, not schooling necessarily, but education as the willingness to engage with questions around the common good, around what sustains life and what we need to do to honour life, is at the heart of maintaining such relationships. This means that we need to pay attention to the wisdom within our communities, and to those engaging in mentoring others around such ways of thinking that bear witness to the passion and connection—the embodiment of collaborative intelligence—that nurture this spirit. Children in our communities, teachers in our schools and universities, and leaders in our organizations need to learn to identify and protect and teach toward those ecological and cultural commons that maintain life as a matter of responsibility toward their communities.[4] Alienated youth (both those in urban centers where money is scarce unless obtained through illegal drug trade involving high levels of youth mortality, and those in the suburbs who are immersed in a materialist culture) can clearly be brought to see meaning and purpose in their lives that are otherwise dominated by hyper-consumerism.

The examples of commons-based education and relationships found in Detroit and around the world help us to understand the interconnected nature of culture and the more-than-human world, both in terms of the damages being done by a hyper-consumer market liberal mindset, and the possibilities alive in more ecological—collaborative—ways of thinking. I learned that in the most unlikely of places, where the pheasants and coyotes dart in and out of concrete and rubble-strewn lots, to reclaim life with the people of Detroit in these urban fields of green.

ACKNOWLEDGMENT

I thank Marcia McKenzie, Gary Schnakenberg, Johnny Lupinacci, and Chet Bowers for their close readings and insightful comments on this chapter.

NOTES

1. It is important to note that Bateson's work, steeped in, yet critical as it is of the science of western culture, comes very close in sensibility to many of the cosmologies of Indigenous cultures where a relationship with the land, and kinship with the spirits and living creatures of the natural world compose

community, and human life is dependent on what humans learn from the more-than-human world. The Quéchua people of the Andes, for example, use the term *chacra* as a central unifying concept that means both the patch of land that each family cultivates, as well as the responsibility "to nurture" one another in a community that includes the earth (Pachamama) and all of her creatures and spirits. The land nurtures the community, as the people take care of the land. See Apffel-Marglin (1998) and John Grim (2001).

2. In *A Recursive Vision: Ecological Understanding and Gregory Bateson*, Peter Harries-Jones (1995) translated Bateson's insight this way: "If information is considered as variety, and if the information event is some type of selection of form in variety, the 'form' of the form is triggered by difference. An information event in the natural order was triggered by form interacting with form, the interaction itself generating a contrast or comparison, which, in turn, embodied a difference, much as in any other type of communication" (p. 173).

3. For a more in depth analysis of this, see Bowers (2006).

4. For a direct discussion of how this relates to teacher education in particular, see Martusewicz and Edmundson (2004).

REFERENCES

Apffel-Marglin, F. with PRATEC (Eds.). (1998). *The spirit of regeneration: Andean culture confronting western nations of development.* London: Zed Books.

Basso, K. (1996). *Wisdom sits in places: Landscape and language among the western Apache.* Albuquerque: University of New Mexico Press.

Bateson, G. (1972). *Steps to an ecology of mind.* New York: Ballantine Books.

Berman, M. (1981). *The reenchantment of the world.* Ithaca: Cornell University Press.

Borghi, M. (2002). Black history in Detroit: From GM to Motown take a journey through Motortown's past. Retrieved July 4, 2007, from http://www.urbanmozaik.com/2002.january/jan02_fea_detroit.html.

Bowers, C. A. (1997). *The culture of denial: Why the environmental movement needs a strategy for reforming universities and public schools.* Albany: State University of New York Press.

Bowers, C. A. (1999). Changing the dominant cultural perspective in education. In G. A. Smith & D. R. Williams (Eds.), *Ecological education in action: On weaving education, culture, and the environment* (pp. 161–178). Albany: State University of New York Press.

Bowers, C. A. (2006). *Revitalizing the commons: Cultural and educational sites of resistance and affirmation.* Lanham, MD: Lexington Books.

Cavanaugh, J., & Mander, J. (Eds.). (2004). *Alternatives to economic globalization: A better world is possible.* San Francisco: Berrett-Koehler.

Deleuze, G. (1994). *Difference and repetition.* New York: Columbia University Press.

Derrida, J. (1974). *Of grammatology.* Baltimore: Johns Hopkins University Press.

The Ecologist. (1993). *Whose common future? Reclaiming the commons.* Gabriola Island, British Columbia: New Society Publishers.

Griffin, S. (1996). *The eros of everyday life: Essays on ecology, gender and society.* New York: Doubleday.

Grim, J. A. (Ed.). (2001). *Indigenous traditions and ecology: The interbeing of cosmology and community.* Cambridge, MA: Harvard Press for the Centre for the Study of World Religions, Harvard Divinity School.

Hardin, G. (1968). The tragedy of the commons. *Science, 162*(3859), 1243–1248.

Harries-Jones, P. (1995). *A recursive vision: Ecological understanding and Gregory Bateson.* Toronto: University of Toronto Press.

Mander, J., & Goldsmith, E. (1996). *The case against the global economy, and for a turn toward the local.* San Francisco, CA: Sierra Club Books.

Martusewicz, R., & Edmundson, J. (2004). Social foundations as pedagogies of responsibility and eco-ethical commitment. In D. Butin (Ed.), *Teaching context: A primer for the social foundations of education classroom* (pp. 71–92). Mahwah, NJ: Elrbaum.

Nettles, D., & Romaine, S. (2000). *Vanishing voices: The extinction of the world's languages.* Oxford: Oxford University Press.

Norberg-Hodge, H. (1991). *Ancient futures: Learning from Ladakh.* San Francisco: Sierra Club Books.

Plumwood, V. (1993). *Feminism and the mastery of nature.* London: Routledge.

Plumwood, V. (2002). *Environmental culture.* London: Routledge.

Pollan, M. (2006). *The omnivore's dilemma: A natural history of four meals.* New York: Penguin Press.

Prakash, M. S., & Esteva, G. (1998). *Escaping education: Living as learning within grassroots cultures.* New York: Peter Lang.

Samyn, R. (2007). *EarthWorks welcome page.* Retrieved July 4, 2007, from www.earth-works.org/Welcome_Page.html.

Shiva, V. (1993). *Monocultures of the mind.* Penang, Malaysia: Third World Network.

Shiva, V. (2005). *Earth democracy: Justice, sustainability, and peace.* Cambridge, MA: Southend Press.

Simmons, C. (2002). *First report to Detroit residents from CPR-Detroit.* Unpublished manuscript.

IV

Geographies and Place-Making

15

Place

The Nexus of Geography and Culture

David A. Greenwood (formerly Gruenewald)

Writing about the significance of place to culture, anthropologist Clifford Geertz (1996) observes, "no one lives in the world in general" (p. 259). That is, our cultural experience is "placed" in the "geography" of our everyday lives, and in the "ecology" of the diverse relationships that take place within and between places.

In the last two decades, the terms *multiculturalism*, *diversity*, and, more recently, *culturally responsive teaching* have been used frequently by educators concerned with equity, social justice, and democracy, and who are working to undo the damage perpetrated in schools by all forms of oppression. These culturally loaded terms, I argue in this chapter, need to be contextualized in order to avoid the abstraction that often accompanies their institutionalization and decontextualized overuse. Indeed, "no one lives in the world in general," and the concept of place can help to make concrete the cultural thinking promoted by many progressive and critical educators. By focusing on place and place-based cultural thinking, I hope to invite educators committed to social justice, anti-oppression, and the non-neutrality of teaching into an expanded conversation about *why* educators must be responsive to culture and diversity and *how* we can be responsive through local inquiry and action.

Since I began teaching in the 1980s, diversity issues and multicultural education have been two of the most visible themes promoted in the schools and universities in which I have worked, eclipsed only by the themes of "standards, testing, and accountability." In my current role as a faculty member in a college of education, I hear and see these words constantly. I am even evaluated each year, in part, for how I include "diversity" in my teaching, scholarship, and service. No other word holds such power in the evaluation process or in the culture of my department and college. Like many colleges and universities, mine also offers various courses on diversity, convenes several diversity committees, and staffs both a multicultural center and a center for equity and diversity. Quick searches for any of these terms on our website's homepage will net tens of thousands of hits. Clearly, multiculturalism and diversity are important to educators, and for good reason. Once institutionalized, however, these terms are used with such frequency that their meaning and purpose have become unclear.

My treatment of *diversity*, *identity*, and *difference* in this chapter is far from complete. I focus on these and related concepts to call their meanings and educational usefulness into question, and to suggest the appropriateness of place-based pedagogy as one pathway toward clarifying and expanding some of the common aims of critical, multicultural educators in diverse places.

DIVERSITY AND THE INSTITUTION OF SCHOOL

The language of educational theory, practice, and policy includes many clichés—"leave no child behind," for example. Often these terms, such as *democracy, social justice, equity*, and *diversity* are used as if they are unproblematic and universally understood and accepted. Who would want to leave a child behind? Who wouldn't want to "increase achievement for all kids" or "close the achievement gap"? Yet, through sheer repetition, such slogans and words such as *diversity* have been reified—that is, their everyday use now suggests a taken-for-granted concreteness and righteousness, when, in fact, such words and slogans are rhetorical abstractions that can only be understood by analyzing the contexts in which they are used and the purposes to which they are put.

Responsiveness to diversity, cultural competence, or culturally responsive teaching have become nearly ubiquitous phrases in the education literature, popular especially among progressive and critical teacher educators. To be responsive to diversity in education generally means that one understands how the power dynamics of difference in race, class, gender, sexual orientation, ability, and other forms of "otherness" play out in schools and classrooms, and that one has the skills or the cultural competence to teach for equity, social justice, and democracy. These are important ethical goals that exist in education because people from oppressed groups have taken the political action necessary to influence the policies and discourses around the historically colonizing practices of schooling. A key reason for attempting to train teachers for cultural competence in the United States is that although the teaching force remains overwhelmingly White, students are increasingly diverse in terms of race, culture, ethnicity, nationality, and language. Without teachers who are sensitive to and knowledgeable about differences among individuals and groups, "other people's children" can be marginalized, neglected, undervalued, poorly served, and even greatly damaged by their experience of school (see, e.g., Delpit, 1995; Gay, 2000; Ladson-Billings, 1995, 2001).

Teaching "diversity" to predominantly White teachers and teacher education students is a delicate challenge that is often met with resistance, especially by some White students who frequently believe that racism and prejudice are ancient history. Diversity lessons and field experiences designed by teacher education faculty can have a transformative impact on some students and help them understand the political dynamics surrounding other people's experiences. These same lessons, however, can raise the defenses of other students and cause them to become even more dismissive of differences in educational or social opportunity based on race, class, gender, or sexual orientation. But underneath the unresolved pedagogical challenge of how to teach White teachers about diversity, a more serious problem looms: Once diversity discourse is institutionalized in schools and universities, its meanings become standardized, shaped, and absorbed by the institutional culture.

In my own institution, *diversity* has become a code word that, paradoxically, is not at core about diverse cultural perspectives and diverse cultural ways of being. Instead, the word represents the progressive project of addressing inequality by providing greater support and institutional access to individuals from cultural groups that have suffered institutional violence. For the most part, the code word diversity is simply the safer substitute for the word race, although it also sometimes means class, gender, or sexual orientation. In teacher education, the standard or common definition of a culturally competent and responsive teacher is one who can help an individual from one of these "othered" groups succeed in schools or universities. This is an important goal that I fully support, especially when connected to the goal of raising teachers and students' "sociopolitical consciousness" (Ladson-Billings, 1995, 2001) of the cultural and institutional practices that help to maintain oppressive relationships. However, the complex and contested issues surrounding "sociopolitical consciousness," or what Paulo Freire (1970/1993) calls *conscientization*, is often reduced in schooling and other institutions to the issue of individual and group access to opportunities that have been denied. Greater institutional access does not equate to greater cultural diversity; indeed, institutions like schools, universities, and governments, through their assimilating regimes of standardization and power-laden rituals of credential-granting, have proven remarkably good at epistemological homogenization and the creation of a global monoculture.[1]

Moreover, the emphasis on diversity in the paradoxically prescriptive path toward teacher certification has focused teacher education faculty and students' attention mainly on classroom interactions between teachers and students. This focus tends to deflect attention away from a larger analysis of political economy, diverse cultural ways of being and knowing, and the relationship between education and specific geographical/cultural communities—places. When diversity issues are framed as classroom problems instead of cultural problems, the purpose of cultural competence can be reduced to "leaving no child behind" or "closing the achievement gap." In the institution of school as a whole, such noble rhetorical aims currently manifest in tightening regimes of standardization, test preparation, and remediation—each of which works against the elusive value of diversity.[2]

PUBLIC EDUCATION OR HOMOGENOUS SCHOOLING?

As a White, male, educated-class heterosexual, I am wary that problematizing diversity may be misunderstood as intolerant, uninformed, or racist by some educators working to improve the experience of students from diverse cultural backgrounds within the existing educational system. My purpose is not to discredit diversity as an important educational term, but to describe the relevance of place to critical, multicultural educators committed to diversity issues. Three key assumptions about public schools underlie my argument. First, I want to acknowledge the fact that most conversations about public education, critical or not, are actually conversations about schooling. Because schooling is only one aspect of the much broader field of education, terms such as "educational research," for example, are remarkably misleading. In everyday use, the proper term should be *schooling research*, a narrower, specific, and institutionalized form of education limited by countless taken-for-granted rules and conventions. The fact that education and schooling are confused, even by those who identify as critical educational researchers, reflects the power of institutions to shape our language practices and confine our thinking to the usual acceptable categories. My first assumption, therefore, is that the broader field of education should inform the narrower subfield of schooling. Currently, the narrower subfield of schooling dominates and distorts the broader fields of educational research, theory, and practice.

My second assumption, which follows from the first, is that most critical educational research, when primarily focused on schooling, reinforces the power of school discourse to limit educational discourse. There are good reasons for the focus on schooling. Schooling as a whole is an exceedingly expensive and inequitable enterprise that, according to most critical educators, privileges some and disempowers others. Within the framework of schooling, this is obviously the case. Even the No Child Left Behind Act is premised, at least on the surface, on equalizing educational opportunity and outcome. Critical educators do try to go much further in addressing inequities than what is required by current legislation. In response to the multiple ways that schools enact violence on identities and communities, critical educators seek to acknowledge and redress the multiple imbalances of power endemic to schooling. Although I fully support and embrace this goal, my second assumption is that conversations about diversity and schooling, once institutionalized, fall short of questioning the educational value of schooling itself and its relationship to specific communities—human and nonhuman. In efforts to close the achievement gap, the underlying structure and purpose of school, which can be described as meritocratic competition for scarce social and economic rewards in a capitalistic society, remains largely unchallenged. For the most part, critical educators have been successful at establishing diversity as a construct important to the discourse of schooling, at least at the level of rhetoric. However, in their effort to promote changes in schooling practices, educators committed to diversity often get trapped in what David Tyack and Larry Cuban (1995) call "the grammar" of schooling. This grammar or logic, focused as it always has been on efficiency and short-term thinking, and more recently on efficiency, short-term thinking, and standards and testing, has tamed the conversation about diversity into one about equity and access within the grammar of schooling. What is often missing is an open challenge to the grammar of schooling and critical questions about the meaning of school success and achievement in the wider context of the communities and cultures in which education, and schooling, take place.

My third assumption is that there is a sad and difficult irony surrounding the continuing push to acknowledge and teach for diversity in schools: that is, schools as public institutions are some of the least diverse places imaginable. What is the meaning of diversity when the basic grammar of schooling segregates children by age and regulates them by the hour and minute for 12 to 16 years or more? What is the meaning of diversity when the only adults students typically see in schools are official representatives of the institution, the very custodians of its grammar? What can diversity possibly mean when school curriculum is unabashedly standardized and managed as official knowledge? What becomes of diversity when schools isolate—by law and often by lock, key, and sometimes barbed wire—teachers and learners from the wider community of which schools are only a small and homogenous part? Although the ethical project to respond to diversity and teach for equity and social justice is a noble project that I support and embrace, the piece I want to add to the puzzle is that from a structural, organizational, temporal, spatial, architectural, cultural, intellectual, and ecological perspective, schools lack diversity big time. This *fundamental lack of diversity*, the isolated, regulated, and narrow nature of schooling, its disconnection from and disregard for community life—these are issues that critical educators need to take seriously.

PLACE, EXPERIENCE, AND POLITICS

Public education in the United States has always been synonymous with state-controlled schools and regimes of standardization that work against cultural diversity. It is therefore necessary to look outside of schools and classrooms in order to find the actual diversity that has become so important to educational discourse. Places are a good place to begin.

Place has in recent decades become a powerful theoretical construct in many disciplines, including philosophy, literature, environmental science, health, geography, history, human ecology, and many others (Casey, 1997). Philosopher Bruce Janz's website, Research on Place and Space, is a growing catalogue of thousands of articles and books on the topic (Janz, 2005). Gary Snyder (1990) sums up well why so many academics, writers, and cultural groups embrace place: "the world is places" (p. 25). That is, places are where people and other beings live their lives. The concept of place, especially when informed by this multidisciplinary scholarship on place, can potentially concretize the notion of culture and cultural difference in the lived experience of people in their diverse and unique environments (see, e.g., Harvey, 1996; Massey, 1994, 1995).

The movement for place-based education has only begun to borrow from this rich reservoir of place-consciousness in politics, aesthetics, geography, philosophy, cultural studies, anthropology, sociology, architecture, and so forth. For the most part, place-based educators use the term *place* synonymously with *community*. Indeed, both place-based and community-based educators advocate using diverse communities as "texts" for curriculum development and engaging teachers and learners in direct experience and inquiry projects that lead to democratic participation and social action within the local environment. However, unlike community-based education, and unlike much of the literature around place and space, the literature around place-based education is self-consciously nonanthropocentric.[3] For many place-based educators, place also signifies what social and cultural theory, as well as diversity advocates, most often overlook: "the land," "the natural environment," and "the nonhuman world." Place is essential to education, then, because it provides researchers and practitioners with a concrete focus for cultural study, and because it expands a cultural landscape to include related ecosystems, bioregions, and all the place-specific interactions between the human and the more-than-human world.

Place-based educators are especially interested in the power of place as a context for diverse experiences that do not and probably cannot happen in the institution of school. It is diverse places that make possible diverse experiences and diverse cultural and ecological formations. The attention to experience in place-based education locates its pedagogy in the broader traditions of experiential and contextual education and in the philosophical tradition of phenomenology. Places, and our relationships to them, are worthy of our attention because places are powerfully pedagogical. Edward Casey (1996) writes, "To live is to live locally, and to know is first of all to know the places one is in" (p. 18). Such an idea may seem obvious. But when considered against the background of standardized educational practices or the homogenizing culture of global capitalism, claiming the primacy of place is revolutionary: It suggests that fundamentally significant knowledge is knowledge of the unique places that our lives inhabit; failure to know those places is to remain in a disturbing sort of ignorance (see Gruenewald, 2003b).

As long as there have been cultures, cultures and their related politics have been entwined with places. Thus, places are far from strictly geographical locations; they are not precultural or presocial; places are at least partly social constructions or cultural products. Writer Terry Tempest Williams (2001) formulates this equation: "Place + People = Politics." People, in other words, are not only shaped by places, but we are place-makers, and what we make of our places, and the character of the places we leave behind over generations, reflects much of our political and cultural lives, as well as our theories of knowing and being. But to call people "place-makers" is to invoke an incredible responsibility on every human community, every member of the species *Homo sapiens*. It is also probably a dangerous kind of hubris to assume the godlike role of place-maker. This is so because, although humans are only one species among many, we have the power to make any place, or the planet itself, unsuitable for particular forms of life, and also unsuitable for particular (culturally diverse) ways of belonging to human communities.

Recognizing that people and cultures are place-makers suggests a much more active role for schools in the study, care, and creation of places. Educationally, this means developing connections with diverse places that allow us learn from them. From the perspective of democratic education in diverse societies, schools must provide more opportunities for students to participate meaningfully in the processes of coming to know places and shaping what our places will become. Educational disregard for places works against diversity and democracy, and makes unlikely the cultural competence sought by many multicultural educators.

RECONNECTING CULTURE AND ENVIRONMENT IN PLACES

Conversations about diversity, culture, and schooling, focused as they often are on race, class, gender, and so on, make it very difficult to talk about "the land" or "the environment"—*all the diverse ecological places that make possible any cultural formation, any identity, and any idea.* Somehow the natural environment or even the physical environment, in which the culture environment is *always* embedded, continues to be neglected in most cultural and educational theory. Within schools and universities as a whole, environmental studies remain a subfield of various sciences, and are rarely the concern of those focused on diversity and the conflicts of cultural politics. In schooling, environmental education itself is rare, and rarely intersects with culturally responsive teaching. Place helps to bridge this culturally constructed epistemological divide.

When I was a graduate student trying to bring a passion for the land into a cultural studies program, I initially met resistance from faculty and students focused instead on issues of race, class, gender, identity, difference, and other forms of anthropocentric "othering." I remember being challenged by one of my professors over wine at Thanksgiving dinner. With his usual passion, he asked me point blank: "How can you talk about 'the environment' when people in South America are killing stray cats for dinner?" His question baffled me. I did not yet have the intellectual experience needed to articulate the many ways that killing cats for food exemplifies the intersection of culture and environment. I remain grateful to my pre-ecological professors for introducing me to several critical traditions through which I am beginning to make sense of people's different cultural experiences of their different environments, or places.

Recently in my seminar on environment, culture, and education, a doctoral student studying communications reminded me again of why so many people are reluctant to allow "environmental" discourse into the cultural conversation. The student, who describes himself as an African American/queer community activist put it pretty plainly: "It's hard to be concerned about 'the environment,'" he said, "when someone's foot is on your neck."

Without question, the word *environment* has taken on many connotations from White, middle-class environmentalism; for some people, such connotations diminish the word's power to describe contested cultural situations. For many educators advocating cultural responsiveness, environment is not a high-priority concept and is, in fact, often ignored or resisted. A broader view of the environment, however, one that is informed by the traditions of environmental justice (e.g., Bullard, 1993), social ecology (e.g., Luke, 1999), ecofeminism (e.g., Warren, 2000), Indigenous knowledge (e.g., Cajete, 1994), and ecojustice (e.g., Bowers, 2001), recognizes that the poverty and violence described by my former professor and student are environmental problems. Poverty and the violence of exploitation and racism have for hundreds of years been connected to patterns of colonization that impact people and their geographical-cultural environments. Talking about the cultural constructs of racism and poverty without talking about geography and environment is to abstract these concepts from where they have been constructed and experienced. Still, arguing that the environment is a critical cultural construct is difficult work in social and institutional contexts such as schools and universities, probably no less difficult than arguing the enduring significance of race. As a critical cultural and educational construct, place can be described as the nexus of culture and environment; places are where we constantly experience their interconnection. We only need to learn to pay attention to see that the distinction between things cultural and things environmental is artificial. No one lives in the world in general.

RECOVERING RELATIONSHIP AND INTERDEPENDENCE WITH LAND

Each one of us is a product of a lifetime of environmental and cultural education that includes our embodied experience of places. When David Orr (1992) said, "all education is environmental education," he may as well have said "all education is cultural education." Whether we are conscious of it or not, environmental and cultural education is happening to all of us, all the time. There are, however, important differences in the core foci of cultural and environmental studies. Central to environmental education are the concepts of *relationship* and *interdependence*. The science of ecology is about studying the relationship and interactions between different parts of a system, and the interactions between systems. Although there are undoubtedly great differences between people and cultures, from an ecological perspective, people, cultures, and places are inescapably interconnected in relational systems. In cultural studies, these systems are sometimes described as a "political ecology"[4] of power relationships that privilege some groups or individuals over and at the expense of others; the result is the many "faces of oppression" (Young, 1990) experienced today and throughout human history. However, the exercise of power, colonization, imperialism, and exploitation have always involved people *and* land, culture *and* the places that make culture possible. To borrow postmodern geographer Edward Soja's (1989) phrase, we need to "reinsert" the land into our critical educational theories.

I acknowledge that for some people, because of differences in experience, because of differences in race, class, and gender and other categories of otherness, there is a hierarchy of appropriate entry points into conversations about people, place, culture, and education. It really is hard to talk about the environment when someone's foot is on your neck. Critical race theorists, Marxists, and gender studies people all have their own literatures and their own agendas. These agendas are crucial to understanding identity, difference, culture, and education—and they help to explain the neglect, the marginalization, and the atrophy of ecological attention. As important as cultural studies is, in its various incarnations, to theorizing education, the silence in this field toward ecological reality can only be described as a kind of intellectual hegemony, a disciplinary practice, and an egregious act of institutional, biological, and cultural violence.

Cultural studies as a field is concerned with the production of discourses, and the power of these discourses to shape and limit our thinking and experience. If there is a dominant, or hegemonic theme in the cultural studies literature that informs schooling, that theme is *difference*. Broadly speaking, cultural studies, cultural politics, and cultural thinking (the kind that is currently in vogue among educational theorists) is about deconstructing and reconstructing identities and communities through the construct of difference. This is an incredibly important, powerful, and complex project: How can we better understand ourselves, one another, and our differences? How can we act on these understandings? If cultural studies are concerned with deconstructing and reconstructing identities and communities through the construct of difference, I would argue that ecological studies are concerned with deconstructing and reconstructing identities through the construct of *relationship*.

Perhaps for good reason, the idea of relationship in cultural studies is looked upon with great suspicion. How can you know me when your experience is not mine? The related literature of postmodernism and postcolonialism are full of words to warn off the concept of "sameness" (which is not the same as relationship): The last thing you want in a cultural studies environment is to be accused of utterances that are totalizing, homogenizing, universalizing, or essentializing. Phrases like "common humanity" and even the word "we" have become taboo; the idea of *difference* is privileged over the idea of *relationship*. The result is that there is very little ecological or relational (not to mention species-level) thinking in cultural studies, or in educational discourses informed by cultural studies perspectives. Difference, rather than relationship, has become what Michel Foucault (1980) calls "a regime of truth" or what is often referred to among critical theorists as "official or high-status knowledge." Thus, it is possible to speak of the "hegemony" of cultural studies, and its own "totalizing" discourse that has "marginalized" ecological thinking and has in many cases "disqualified" the very idea of relationship or of the human family.

As "ground zero"—where culture and environment come together—place can help to reclaim the idea of relationship and interdependence between different parts of the cultural/ecological system. Place-based pedagogy, then, offers two key challenges to the discourse of culturally responsive or relevant pedagogy. The first is to inform the concept of cultural relevance with place-specific cultural and ecological study. This means expanding the focus of cultural competence well beyond classroom interactions between White teachers and non-White students. Without a focus on a diversity of places, and the relationship between them, the sociopolitical consciousness-raising important to diversity advocates will lack specific and diverse cultural grounding. The second challenge, if we are to live together peaceably on a finite planet, is to seek more balance between the concept of *relationship* and the concept of *difference*.[5] The privileging of the discourse of difference in cultural study reinforces an anthropocentric stance that obscures the relationship between all people and the land, between all cultures and the diverse environments out of which all cultures emerged. The great irony here is that the discourse of diversity in cultural studies and schooling neglects biological diversity, the vast "diversity of life" (see Wilson, 1992) that makes all life possible and worth living. The ecological reality and cultural necessity of biodiversity can remind educators and cultural theorists to pay more attention to relationship. Educators concerned about culture and the possibilities for democracy need to continue to work to understand our differences, our relationships, and our interdependence. This does not mean advocating "one world" thinking. It means acknowledging that we live on one world. Despite our differences, the process of learning cannot be limited to individualistic political claims between me and you. It needs to be about us—and we are only one species among many.

A CRITICAL PEDAGOGY OF PLACE: CULTURALLY AND PLACE-RESPONSIVE EDUCATION

The phrase "culturally responsive teaching" begs an important question that needs to remain open: that is, to what in culture should educators be responsive? Diversity educators have successfully foregrounded one answer to this question: Culturally responsive educators must be responsive to differences among students so that no child is left behind. I have argued that this response, as important as it is, tends to trap classroom teachers in the grammar of schooling and limit the role of teaching to a relatively narrow set of increasingly prescribed classroom interactions. Place-conscious educators propose a different but related focus for educational attention and cultural responsiveness: the cultural/ecological places common to the lived experience of learners (see, e.g., Bowers & Apffel-Marglin, 2005; Cajete, 1994; Gruenewald, 2003a, 2003b; Hart, 1997; Lai & Ball, 2002; Prakash & Esteva, 1998; Reisberg, Brander, & Gruenewald, 2006; Smith, 2002; Sobel, 2004; Theobald, 1997). A focus on the lived experience of place puts culture in context, demonstrates the interconnection of culture and environment, and provides a locally relevant pathway for multidisciplinary inquiry and democratic participation.

This is not to say that all examples of place-based education successfully integrate all of these possibilities. Much place-based education continues to foreground local environmental study while neglecting the more politically charged cultural environment. However, place-conscious or place-responsive education proposes fertile ground for educators dedicated to diversity or cultural competence.

I have previously proposed the phrase "a critical pedagogy of place" to signify the potential confluence of cultural and ecological thinking in the emerging discourse of place-based education (see Gruenewald, 2003a). Although critical pedagogy has been challenged by C. A. Bowers (1991, 2003, 2005), Bowers and Frédérique Apffel-Marglin (2005), and others as nonresponsive to diverse cultural ways of being, the intent of the phrase, "a critical pedagogy of place," is to combine the critical tradition that has historically been concerned with human oppression, difference, and radical multiculturalism with geographically and ecologically grounded (i.e., place-based) cultural experience. A critical pedagogy of place posits two fundamental goals for education: decolonization and reinhabitation. Decolonization roughly equates with the deeper agenda of culturally responsive teaching: to undo the damage done by multiple forms of oppression. Reinhabitation roughly equates with the deeper agenda of many environmental educators: to learn how to live well together in a place without doing damage to others, human and nonhuman. Pedagogically, these two interrelated goals translate into a set of questions that can be put to any group of learners on any place on earth: What is happening here? What happened here? What should happen here? What needs to be transformed, conserved, restored, or created in this place? How might, as Wes Jackson (1994) asks, people everywhere learn to become "native" to their places?[6] Such questions provide a local focus for socioecological inquiry and action that, because of interrelated cultural and ecological systems, is potentially global in reach. In other words, place-consciousness suggests consciousness not only of my place, but of others, and the relationship between places.

Obviously, these inquiry questions point to a very different kind of school experience than what is typically assumed by multicultural education or culturally responsive teaching. These questions turn one's gaze outward from schools to the culturally and ecologically rich contexts of community life. This does not mean abandoning the classroom, but rethinking its relationship to the wider community. The institution of school and the space of the classroom cannot be expected to solve cultural or ecological problems. This is especially so when schools remain disconnected from actual communities outside their own institutional boundaries. The juxtaposition of culturally responsive and critical, place-based pedagogy suggests several additional focusing questions important to the development of place-based education:

- To what in places should teachers and learners be responsive?

- What forms of cultural, economic, and political colonization impact multiple places?

- To what forms of grassroots resistance and reinhabitation might educators pay attention?

- What is the role of Indigenous knowledge in reinhabitation and decolonization?

- How can a focus on the local also provide opportunities for intergenerational, interregional, and international communication and collaboration?

- What kinds of experiences are needed for people to learn how to perceive, critically analyze, and act on their human and nonhuman environments and relationships?

One of the main goals of place-based education is to expand the landscape of learning opportunities among and between students, educators, and community members. It may be that culturally responsive teaching in diverse communities is only possible when students and teachers encounter the cultural and ecological diversity that is threatened or extinct in schools, but still endemic to places.

NOTES

1. The then-current Bush Administration, for example, could boast the most diverse Cabinet in the history of the American presidency. Yet, the members of this Cabinet speak in the White voice of the political right wing.

2. This does not mean the discourse of diversity or cultural responsiveness always gets reduced to classroom interactions between teachers and students for the purposes of closing the standardized achievement gap. The work of the Alaska Native Knowledge Network (1998), The Coalition for Community Schools (2005), and the Rural School and Community Trust (2005) are notable exceptions. Their publications on culturally responsive teaching, schools, curriculum, and communities are fundamentally concerned with the relationship between culture, education, and place. Other exceptions include Stephen Haymes (1995), bell hooks (2003), and Eric Gutstein (2003).

3. See Bowers (1993, 1995, 1997) for a discussion of anthropocentrism as one of the "root metaphors of modernism."

4. The appropriation of the word *ecology* can only be seen as ironic whenever it neglects nonhuman systems and interactions.

5. The converse of these challenges also holds true: Culturally responsive pedagogy challenges place-based pedagogy to pay more attention to classroom interactions and to difference.

6. Increasingly, I am convinced that, despite problems of appropriation, Native, Indigenous, First Nations, and Aboriginal educational processes and epistemologies need to be at the center of place-based, culturally responsive teaching. Only through studying Native experiences will educators understand the enduring legacy of colonization and the possibility for diverse cultural ways of being.

REFERENCES

Alaska Native Knowledge Network. (1998). Alaska standards for culturally-responsive schools. Anchorage, Alaska: Alaska Native Knowledge Network. Retrieved October 12, 2005, from http://www.ankn.uaf.edu/.

Bowers, C. A. (1991). Critical pedagogy and the "arch of social dreaming": A response to the criticisms of Peter McLaren. *Curriculum Inquiry, 21*, 479–487.

Bowers, C.A. (1993). *Education, cultural myths, and the ecological crisis*. Albany: State University of New York Press.

Bowers, C.A. (1995). *Educating for an ecologically sustainable culture: Rethinking moral education, creativity, intelligence, and other modern orthodoxies*. Albany: State University of New York Press.

Bowers, C.A. (1997). *The culture of denial*. Albany: State University of New York Press.

Bowers, C.A. (2001). *Educating for eco-justice and community*. Athens & London: The University of Georgia Press.

Bowers, C.A. (2003). Can critical pedagogy be greened? *Educational Studies, 34*, 11–21.

Bowers, C. A. (2005). How Peter McLaren and Donna Houston, and other "green" Marxists contribute to the globalization of the west's industrial culture. *Educational Studies, 37*, 185–195.

Bowers, C. A., & Apffel-Marglin, F. (Eds.). (2005). *Rethinking Freire: Globalization and the environmental crisis*. Mahwah, NJ: Erlbaum.

Bullard, R., (Ed.). (1993). *Confronting environmental racism: Voices from the grassroots*. Boston, MA: South End Press.

Cajete, G. (1994). *Look to the mountain: An ecology of Indigenous education*. Durango, CO: Kivaki Press.

Casey, E. (1996). How to get from space to place in a fairly short stretch of time. In K. Basso & S. Feld (Eds.), *Senses of place* (pp. 13–52). Santa Fe, NM: School of American Research Press.

Casey, E. (1997). *The fate of place: A philosophical history*. Berkeley: University of California Press.

The Coalition for Community Schools. (2005). Retrieved October 12, 2005, from http://www.communityschools.org/.

Delpit, L. 1995. *Other people's children*. New York: New Press.

Foucault, M. (1980). *Power/knowledge: Selected interviews and other writings* (C. Gordon, Ed.). New York: Pantheon Books.

Freire, P. (1993). *Pedagogy of the oppressed*. New York: Continuum. (Original work published 1970)

Gay, G. (2000). *Culturally responsive teaching*. New York: Teachers College Press.

Geertz, C. (1996). Afterword. In S. Feld & K. Basso (Eds.), *Senses of place* (pp. 259–262). Sante Fe, NM: School of American Research Press.

Gruenewald, D. (2003a). The best of both worlds: A critical pedagogy of place. *Educational Researcher, 32*(4), 3–12.

Gruenewald, D. (2003b). Foundations of place: A multidisciplinary framework for place-conscious education. *American Educational Research Journal, 40*(3), 619–654.

Gutstein, E. (2003). Teaching and learning mathematics for social justice in an urban, Latino school. *Journal for Research in Mathematics Education, 34*(1), 37–73.

Hart, R. (1997). *Children's participation: The theory and practice of involving young citizens in community development and environmental care.* London: Earthscan, Unicef.

Harvey, D. (1996). *Justice, nature, and the geography of difference.* Malden, MA: Blackwell.

Haymes, S. (1995). *Race, culture and the city: A pedagogy for black urban struggle.* Albany: State University of New York Press.

hooks, b. (2003). *Teaching community: A pedagogy of hope.* New York: Routledge.

Jackson, W. (1994). *Becoming native to this place.* Lexington: University of Kentucky Press.

Janz, B. (2005). Research on place and space. Retrieved October 12, 2005, from http://pegasus.cc.ucf. edu/~janzb/place/geography.htm.

Ladson-Billings, G. (1995) Toward a theory of culturally relevant pedagogy. *American Educational Research Journal, 32*(3), 465–491.

Ladson-Billings, G. (2001). *Crossing over to Canaan: The journey of new teachers in diverse classrooms.* San Francisco: Jossey-Bass.

Lai, A., & Ball, E. (2002). Home is where the art is: Exploring the places people live through art education. *Studies in Art Education: A Journal of Issues and Research, 44*(1), 47–66.

Luke, T. (1999). *Capitalism, democracy, and ecology: Departing from Marx.* Urbana: University of Illinois Press.

Massey, D. (1994). *Space, place, and gender.* Minneapolis: University of Minnesota Press.

Massey, D. (1995). *Spatial divisions of labor: Social structures and the geography of production.* New York: Routledge.

Orr, D. (1992). *Ecological literacy.* Albany: State University of New York Press.

Prakash, M., & Esteva, G. (1998). *Escaping education: Living as learning within grassroots cultures.* New York: Peter Lang.

Reisberg, M., Brander, B., & Gruenewald, D. (2006). Your place or mine? Reading art, place, and culture in multicultural children's picture books. *Teacher Education Quarterly, 33*(1), 117–133.

The Rural School and Community Trust. (2005). Retrieved October 12, 2005, from http://www.ruraledu. org/.

Smith, G. (2002). Place-based education: Learning to be where we are. *Phi Delta Kappan, 83,* 584–594.

Snyder, G. (1990). *The practice of the wild.* New York: North Point Press.

Sobel, D. (2004). *Place-based education: Connecting classrooms and communities.* Great Barrington, MA: The Orion Society and The Myrin Institute.

Soja, E. (1989). *Postmodern geographies: The reassertion of space in critical social theory.* London: Verso.

Theobald, P. (1997). *Teaching the commons: Place, pride, and the renewal of community.* Boulder, CO: Westview Press.

Tyack, D., & Cuban, L. (1995). *Tinkering toward utopia: A century of public school reform.* Cambridge, MA: Harvard University Press.

Warren, K. (2000). *Ecofeminist philosophy: A western perspective on what it is and why it matters.* Lanham, MD: Rowman & Littlefield.

Williams, T. T. (2001). *Red: Passion and patience in the desert.* New York: Pantheon.

Wilson, E. O. (1992). *The diversity of life.* Cambridge, MA: Harvard University Press.

Young, I. (1990). *Justice and the politics of difference.* Princeton, NJ: Princeton University Press.

The Greater Common Good
Arundhati Roy

> *"If you are to suffer, you should suffer in the interest of the country."*—Jawaharlal Nehru, speaking to villagers who were to be displaced by the Hirakud Dam, 1948.

I stood on a hill and laughed out loud.

I had crossed the Narmada by boat from Jalsindhi and climbed the headland on the opposite bank from where I could see, ranged across the crowns of low, bald hills, the tribal hamlets of Sikka, Surung, Neemgavan and Domkhedi. I could see their airy, fragile, homes. I could see their fields and the forests behind them. I could see little children with littler goats scuttling across the landscape like motorised peanuts. I knew I was looking at a civilisation older than Hinduism, slated—*sanctioned* (by the highest court in the land)—to be drowned this monsoon when the waters of the Sardar Sarovar reservoir will rise to submerge it.

Why did I laugh?

Because I suddenly remembered the tender concern with which the Supreme Court judges in Delhi (before vacating the legal stay on further construction of the Sardar Sarovar Dam) had enquired whether tribal children in the resettlement colonies would have children's parks to play in. The lawyers representing the Government had hastened to assure them that indeed they would, and, what's more, that there were seesaws and slides and swings in every park. I looked up at the endless sky and down at the river rushing past and for a brief, brief moment the absurdity of it all reversed my rage and I laughed . . .

16

"My Father Was Told to Talk to the Environment First Before Anything Else"

Arctic Environmental Education in the Language of the Land

Derek Rasmussen and Tommy Akulukjuk

Derek Rasmussen and Tommy Akulukjuk are friends. Tommy was born in Iqaluit Nunavut, and grew up in Pangnirtung, including many seasons spent out on the land with his family. After 2 years of college and 2 years working as an environmental researcher in "the South" (Ottawa), he returned North to "Pang" to hunt with his father. At the time of editing, Tommy was advising the territorial government on the new Inuit Cultural School for Nunavut. Derek lived in Iqaluit, Nunavut, from 1991 to 2001, and he worked as a policy advisor to Nunavut Tunngavik Incorporated (NTI), the representative body for the Inuit of Nunavut Territory in Canada. Derek advised NTI on economic and social policies, including education policy. The following exchange between Tommy and Derek is compiled from their conversations, e-mails, and telephone calls over the past 2 years.

Hi Tommy:

It seems to me that if we're going to talk about environmental education then we ought to be asking what language the environment speaks (and whether students, teachers, researchers, and scientists speak the environment's language).

In Nunavut, the land speaks Inuktitut.

What I mean is that the land (and sea) evolved a language to communicate with (and *through*) human beings, namely an Indigenous language that naturally "grew" in that area over thousands of years of interaction between the elements, and the human and plant and animal beings. Now, this might sound like an obvious point for Inuit to discuss, but it isn't that obvious to most folks like me who grew up in the South without any intimate or necessary interaction with the nonhuman environment. Instead, we southerners usually take for granted a view of language as a dislocated phenomenon that develops in an isolated way inside the brains of human beings without any necessary influence from their environment (Rasmussen, 2000).

What environmental vocabulary and grammar arose from the Indigenous interaction with the land? I recall that when I first started working with NTI, the then-executive director, Hagar

Idlout-Sudlovenick told me of an Inuktitut program with the elders of her hometown, Pond Inlet. The twist in this program was that the elders would only teach Inuktitut out on the land—not in a classroom. The elders from Pond said that too many of the Inuktitut terms were disappearing, and that the only way to resuscitate the appropriate vocabulary was out on the land where the objects to be named could be found.[1]

The elders know the wisdom encoded in the environment; they speak the language that evolved there. They know that "nature [is] the very source of voices" (Kane, 1998, p. 190). Shouldn't environmental studies at universities be teaching the languages and epistemologies of the people Indigenous to the particular biocultural region under study? In fact, doesn't it seem odd that this isn't already an automatic practice in environmental education? Doesn't it seem odd that a biologist would want to study "arctic char reproductive stages" and not first make an effort to learn the words and stories relating 4,000 years of teaching about char encoded in the language and knowledge systems of Inuit? Why is it an anathema to suggest that the "hard" sciences (biology, geology, chemistry, and environmental studies) should learn the language of the eco-culture system? The hard sciences seem to insist on the universal ability of English, French, Spanish, German, and Mandarin to provide complete explanatory frameworks for every event and context in the Arctic, but Indigenous languages that evolve in particular biocultural regions have nuances and explanatory power superseding the globalizing languages.

Studying the languages and epistemologies of the Indigenous people is deeply sensible, because "languages encode a culture's way of understanding relationships and attributes of the participants in both the human and natural communities, [therefore] maintaining the diversity of languages is essential to preserving the renewable characteristics of local ecosystems" (Bowers, 2005, p. 7). For example, linguist Tove Skutnabb-Kangas says that in Finland, "fish biologists have just 'discovered' that salmon can use even extremely small rivulets leading to the river Teno as spawning grounds—earlier this was thought impossible." Pekka Aikio, the president of the Saami Parliament in Finland, told her that "the Saami have always known this—the traditional Saami names of several of those rivulets include a Saami word which means 'salmon spawning-bed.' This is ecological knowledge inscribed in Indigenous languages" (Skutnabb-Kangas, 2002, p. 13). Moving from the Arctic to the tropics, the professor warns that "nuances in the knowledge about medicinal plants and their use disappear when Indigenous youth in Mexico become bilingual without teaching in and through the medium of their *own* languages—the knowledge is not transferred to Spanish, which does not have the vocabulary for these nuances" (Skutnabb-Kangas, 2000, p. 13; also Maffi, 2001).

According to the Tucson Biodiversity Institute, "about 50% of all humans speak and think in one of ten globally dominant languages. That means 0.2% of languages hold sway over 50% of the human species and likely upwards of 85% of the globe's land surface" (Suckling, 2000, p. 19). The institute's director, Kieran Suckling (2000), points out that "these are the language cultures primarily responsible for the global extinction crisis and the eradication/assimilation/marginalization of Indigenous cultures. One percent of the human race, meanwhile, speaks 50–60% of all human languages. This one percent and all its wealth of knowledge is being driven to extinction at an unprecedented rate" (p. 19). Watching Indigenous languages disappear is like watching someone set fire to half the world's libraries. Environmentalists should be on the front lines, protecting and resuscitating the languages that are deeply woven into the land.

This should hold special importance for environmental educators: for biodiversity and linguistic diversity are intertwined. "If you've got a society that has lived in the same place for hundreds or thousands of years, they'll be changing the species composition by selective hunting and use of plants," says conservationist David Harmon from Terralingua:

Because humans modify their environment as they adapt to it and *then transmit their knowledge through language, ecosystems and languages co-evolve*. In turn . . . when indigenous languages die out, there's a self-reinforcing downward cycle: The language is not spoken, and people are not as intimately involved with the local biodiversity. So they are not going to take care of it and value it the way they did, and it will be more vulnerable to development. (Harmon, 2004, p. 43. See also Harmon, 2002; Muhlhausler, 1996)

Indigenous "languages represent vast reservoirs of intellectual knowledge stretching back thousands of years," says B.C. Shuswap chief Ron Ignace, adding that "the English language is an infant relative to our languages. In my view, the loss of these languages in our country will rival the great ecological disasters of the world, such as the destruction of the rainforest. It has that potential" (Philip, 2000, p. 1). Bowers, an education professor from Oregon, says that if we are going to find solutions to the climate change crisis we'll need environmental education that "understands the vital connections between linguistic diversity and biodiversity" (2005, p. 5). This is what Bowers calls "ecojustice education" because it "highlights the connections between viable interdependent ecosystems and viable interdependent communities—and that our future depends on maintaining the widest possible diversity in cultural approaches to sustainable living" (p. 148).

The southern scientific obsession with protecting and studying the nonhuman animals and environment need not deafen us to the language of the land—spoken through the culture and language of the humans who have lived there for thousands of years (Rasmussen, 2002). Culture is the canvas, language is the paintbrush; together they display the ecological intelligence of a place.

—Take care, Derek

Hey my white Bro,

I feel like a real Eskimo this spring, finally with a great tan with a raccoon face. Finally this year, the name of my tan is not a farmer's tan—wooo hoo! I'm having a great spring.

Anyhow, I think it's a great idea that we talk about the lack of Inuktitut in any science or biology courses. These subjects talk the most about the environment around us and how it supposedly works. These subjects shape the attitudes we have towards the place we live in.

The Qallunaat (European-Canadians) have a strange concept of their environment. For instance, the term "wildlife" is used to separate themselves from their home and separate their community from the natural environment. They do not realize that they're part of the wildlife; They were wild once and will be part of the wild forever, but they like to exclude themselves from anything the natural world provides. Inuit do not have such a word in their language, we are part of nature and cannot be excluded from it. (The word "Inuit" itself means "living beings"; it does not connote any sense of superiority.)

Sometimes southerners describe the Arctic regions as "daunting" and they write about how Inuit survived in the "inhospitable" Canadian north. I don't think there is anything daunting about where I'm from. I think this paints a bleak picture of Inuit, as if we are always struggling to survive. I have never heard my father talk about "survival" and he's practically a full-time hunter; he doesn't think of himself as "surviving" when he is out hunting, it's just what he does. Actually it's not nature, but the dominant southern culture that threatens our survival as Inuit, with its insistence that education exclude the use of Inuktitut in the so-called "hard sciences," whether or not Inuktitut offers valuable information. What threatens our survival is the manner in which English is treated as the only legitimate way of describing the works of nature.

The English language is a language of money and economics. Most Indigenous languages are languages of interacting with their environment. When I went home to Pangnirtung this spring,

I realized Inuktitut, the language I hadn't used for a while, was so sophisticated in describing its surroundings. I forgot many of those words. I had to keep asking my father what he really meant when he would explain the whereabouts of an animal. Even the names of different animal parts I forgot (that was embarrassing). Inuktitut, when spoken, is so descriptive. . . . Students should learn as much of the material that is being taught to them through actual experiences and actions, rather than through theory. When I was hunting this spring, I felt something that I had been missing—to be part of the environment and the food chain again, to feel that human beings are not superior in this world but are just part of it like any other being.

Going back to Pangnirtung, I had seen the cycles of nature again and how good it felt. Inuit do not have four seasons; we have many seasons. To many southerners, it may seem that there are just two seasons in the arctic: winter and a brief summer. But in Inuktitut there are many seasons: winter, before spring, spring, summer before fall, fall, before winter, and winter again. I am sure that an elder could explain it better, but that is what I learnt when I was growing up. I remember when one of our schoolteachers asked us what was our favourite season. What is an English word for "just before the actual summer"? These are the words you learn when you are immersed in the language of the environment; these are the words that help you appreciate nature and wildlife.
Take care,
your brown brother.

Hi Derek,
While I was reading the e-mail, I thought of how the names of animals, especially birds, are after the sounds they make, not after some guy who wrote about them in a book or after the area where they live. Take, for example, the Canada Goose: it is called nirliq. Next time your see one, listen carefully to the sounds it makes, and you'll notice that it sounds like it is saying "nee-r-leek." You see, when Inuktitut is spoken, the emphasis seems to be more on the feeling of the senses, like what the person felt when he went to a place, or how it looked when he went through there or how it looked when he shot the animal. Like Ross (1996) says, native languages are more energy-based. And I have to say too that when my father or other hunters describe an experience, they never make it feel like it only happened to them, even if they have never seen anyone do the same thing; they always leave room for someone else and the possibility that someone else can do the same thing.
I think one of the huge differences between young Inuit and older Inuit now is that we, the younger generation, have been taught that Inuktitut needs rigid guidelines or things to follow. We have become more dependent on books, and, how to say, Inuktitut is put into books—taking away the real essence of the language. Imagine: my father learning everything through listening and experiences of his language, never being told that the language is supposed to be this way. And here I am, just one generation away, having been taught through books and instruction about the workings of my language. Through southern eyes, I am supposed to be better educated and have more knowledge because I was taught through something they consider solid, but if an Inuk compares my language with my father I am at an infant level. Taking away kids from their parents into schools for most of the day to teach Inuit Inuktitut has eroded the actual language and made it into phrases and small talk rather than being the teacher of senses and experiences like the real language is. (This is what the elders in Pond Inlet are realizing: It is losing the real essence of the language.) Inuktitut, to me, is to feel the workings of nature; through Inuktitut I can feel the weather, the warm sun, and describe it that way.
When I had to translate the TV weather forecast for my father, it really made me feel that I was taking away the feeling of the weather, instead putting it into numbers ("it's going to be this warm . . . its going to have this much wind," all associated with numbers). All these questions about the weather and nature and the world are supposed to be answered by TV, by an electronic item, which gives us an impersonal and such fake feeling for the world. And the weather forecasters only welcome the weather

when it is going to be sunny and warm, and they are usually negative about it when that doesn't happen. Back home most of these questions are answered differently. I was living in "the south" for a few years; but I come from a small, scenic community of 1,200 in Nunavut: Pangnirtung. I'm proud to say that I grew up in the great outdoors. Since birth, I have been interacting with the environment; my father's generation even more so. My father grew up in an isolated camp with no playgrounds, no television, no VCR, no DVDs, and no negative discussions about his surroundings. His playground was the environment around him; his television, VCR, and DVDs were his family and the activities they did. He is aware of his surroundings; with his keen ability to see the intricateness of the weather; it allows him to see the big picture. He looks at the clouds, snow, water, the horizon, and he feels the temperature, wind speed, the texture of the ground that he walks on, and he can predict what nature is trying to say to him. When he—my father—was growing up, he was told to go outside his dwellings as soon as he woke up: talk to the environment first before anything else. As he was growing up, his elders would talk generally about the environment, not as if it were disconnected from their lives, but as if it was part of their everyday lives. He was not shown numbers, he was not shown pictures of snow, or rain, he was not shown how long it might last nor how much wind, snow, or rain it was going to be. (Again, I think this connectedness is what the elders in Pond want to produce after a successful outing.)

My father had to learn the complicated weather system, how it behaves in different seasons, how much it affects snow and ice, what different cloud shapes and colours mean, and many various subjects about the weather. Not only that, he had to apply his knowledge to his hunting skills to feed my siblings and our extended family. Which means he had to follow the seasons, not in terms of migrating to different places, but in terms of watching the environment closely; so that he would know: When is the snow going to start melting? And when it does melt, what is the texture of the snow, and when and what kind of snow is safe to drink? When he travels on the ice, he has to know where the shoals are, to predict where the ice is going to be rough, and where it might be thin. Whenever he has to cross Cumberland Sound, he has to look far to the horizon to predict if it is going to be safe to boat. He knows what the colors of the clouds mean and what kind of snow, rain, or wind they might bring. He doesn't look at all these things as if they are all separate links, but as connected links: whenever something behaves this way, it might be that way over there. He has to know when the tide goes up and down, and how much. When he sees an animal, it is not just food, but it also tells you the state of the surrounding environment. How is that seal acting on top the ice sunbathing? And does the color of this caribou skin seem different from the year before? These observations are essential for "survival," but they also give a person a glimpse of the connectedness of animals, humans, and the environment to themselves. (Which impatient scientists miss often, when things have to be waited out to get the correct results. A hunter/"understand-er" has to be patient.) To my father, weather is life: It restricts him, but it also makes him excel in hunting when the weather is right. In certain seasons, the weather acts like this and that, and if the weather changes, it is going to affect the animals; so it is important to know and learn the weather, not through TV or other sources of communication, but to interact with it, be one with it.

Having said that, Inuktitut should be the main vehicle of teaching in all the schools if we are to have a culture of our own. Unfortunately, we can turn Inuktitut into a language of English. What I mean is that we can use the workings of English and have them translated into Inuktitut, but are they really Inuktitut words, or are they just a transfer of English into Inuktitut phrases and sounds? Is it really Inuktitut? Do the words really capture the language and the feeling of what is being said? My father made predictions of the weather that I would have never thought of, and that goes for all the Inuit hunters; they can make predictions that I'll never fully understand. It is their understanding of the world around them that makes them Inuktitut professors. They understand more about their environment than any scientist will ever know: the intricate workings of the environment complement their language and vice versa.

To use English as the main language in schools will further erode our culture and take away the importance of our language. Inuktitut has strong roots in describing the workings of the natural environment around Inuit. English has strong roots in detaching the student from their environment and putting them into a hypothetical environment. English, to me, was a language of imagining, not a language of action. When we were taught any subject in school, they took us into a fantasy place and made us imagine what it would be like there. Inuktitut, when it is spoken, takes you to the place, and the sounds of those words make you feel as if you belong there. (In school, through school, trying to understand such concepts and ideas, thinking becomes troublesome and hard to the imaginer without the correct tools of Inuktitut to help fix it. The more the imaginer has trouble, the more he/she is going to have a hard time remembering the words in Inuktitut.)

I remember when we had science projects in school, we never really studied Inuit science, maybe because we were never taught that there is such a thing; but we always had projects about tornadoes, formation of mountains, etc. It is as if we neglected our culture and traditions because the language of the science projects was always in English, never in Inuktitut. No wonder Inuit felt inferior in front of English-speaking teachers; English has strong commanding words that infer that there is no other good language to teach how nature works. Even the word "theory" is completely different from the way young Inuit see it and understand it. Theory (as most young Qallunaat students know) is theory, something not really proven. In my classes, theory was something that couldn't be changed. For us it was hard to challenge a theory—maybe it had something to do with our strong-headed teachers that couldn't really take criticism about their knowledge. To me, that is what English brings: the feeling of inferiority. And just imagine all those young Inuit students that don't have a good footing in any language. They fail because English makes them scared. (In turn we become subject to "dominant" English words and phrases, further eroding the real essence of our language.)

Hi Tommy;

Unfortunately (as you know) Inuktitut is taught in the formal school system only up until Grade 3; then children have to switch to English. This means that they don't get a good grounding in any one language and so Inuit children usually do not end up with very good skills in English or in Inuktitut (Berger, 2006). In fact, even though 75% of Nunavut residents list Inuktitut as their mother tongue, there is no K–12 schooling in Inuktitut anywhere in Nunavut. It's all English (except in Iqaluit where there is a new $7-million French school). Even though Canada's Nunavut Act of 1993 requires the new territory to function in three languages, Inuktitut gets nowhere near the same level of funding and protection as English and French: $3,480 is spent per every francophone (600 citizens) in Nunavut, versus $48 for every Inuktitut-speaking person (23,000). In other words, the francophone community receives twice as much money from the federal government than the Inuktitut-speaking community, even though the Inuit outnumber francophones by 40 to 1.

But it's funny how governments never seem short of money to translate from English into Inuktitut, to "help" equip Inuktitut conceptually to describe economics and technology—money for translating "important" words from English into Inuktitut—words like *satellite, computer, and accounting.* And yet I am not aware of a single government dollar going into translating Inuktitut into English (to try to illustrate/illuminate the beauty and the uniqueness of it), or of a single program to celebrate the breadth and utility of Inuktitut to Inuit and European Canadians.

Now, obviously terms like "kayak" or "igloo" are just what they are; there's no need to replace them with clumsy expressions like "covered canoe" or "snow house." But what other Inuktitut terms and concepts might enrich our understanding of the world, if only we chose to ask?

I remember hearing Norman Hallendy on the radio telling a story of his conversation with Kenojoak Ashevak, the great printmaker in Kinngait (Cape Dorset). The gist of it was that they had a long chat (through translation) about art, but when he asked her to write the word for "art" in Inuktitut syllabics, she said she couldn't, because there was "no word for 'art' in Inuktitut." Admitting to some frustration, he then asked "what was it that we've been talking about?" Kenojoak answered (through translation): "that which takes something real and makes it more real than it was before."

Isn't that beautiful and clear? I've mentioned that phrase to art teachers at several universities and they all think it is one of the most succinct definitions they've ever heard in any language. The gift of Inuktitut thinking.

I think this could be the other benefit of braiding Inuktitut into environmental education: helping the dominant society appreciate the Indigenous concepts and attitudes that grew from these lakes and lands.

Hi Derek,

I think you are absolutely right that governments are spending a huge amount of money on translating English words into Inuktitut. The official translations that the government did on climate change (Inuktitut Climate Change Glossary) which seem to point that out, are a good example of this. The work was done over a couple of years with consultations with elders all over Nunavut and many Inuktitut translators participating. I don't mind the book that they produced, what I dislike is that the words are from English. The term in English is given first and then they translate it into Inuktitut. It's as if they didn't trust what Inuktitut can say about the change in the environment and then translate that into English with all its meanings. I don't think Inuktitut is given the room to make some new words of its own. Inuktitut, and Inuit as well, has always been seen as the poor cousin by many languages, especially European-derived languages. Little do they realize that Inuktitut has the full ability to make sense in this so-called modern world of ours.

Inuktitut captures what nature has said to Inuit. Even what seems to be a simple word in Inuktitut is so difficult to translate into English, like the word kajjarniq. *Kajjarniq means "to reflect positively about our surroundings."[2] We usually use that word when we like the weather. And because people like all sorts of weather, we say kajjarniq to refer to different kinds of weather. It can even refer to indoors, when people experience what they remember and have that positive outlook on it. I guess it's like nostalgia.*

And I don't think we can really understand a language through books only. Books are very far from our actual feelings and senses. To know a language is to be immersed in it and take part in it. Languages are not about books—they're about feelings and experiencing what those feelings bring to the individual. To understand an environment, a person has to understand the language of the environment.

An Inuk (well actually any human being should feel what it is to have such a wonderful body) has to become a person first, before you put stuff inside him or her with school. With school, they start filling you up with things, thoughts, ideas, but you're not even a person yet (not a full person yet, you are still realizing what your body can do and feel). You need time to become a human being, to just feel what it's like to have fingers (to have ears, taste, and see), to have senses—to know what it's like to touch this table right now, you know what I mean? To feel the edge of the table on the ridges of the skin of your finger—that's amazing! How much time do we spend actually learning this—watching—paying attention to this? To what it feels like to have a human body? (I wish that I could feel what my ancestors felt when they went outside first thing in the morning wearing only skin clothing.) And then what it feels like to be in the cold, or in the weather, in the environment, out on the land, to eat certain foods, to be happy (to be thankful that we have such a life, no matter how hard it gets). Just to notice these things.

Instead the School tries to fill us up with history about Napoleon and so on—things, "facts" that don't really mean anything to us—things that aren't necessarily helpful—when we haven't even had the time to become a Person yet. To become a Person we need time: time with our family, time with our elders and community, time out on the land, and time with ourselves—to reflect on our actions. Instead, the Qalunnaat government puts us in school—away from the land, away from our family, our community, our elders. In many ways school takes away the very thing it is to be a human being: to feel and love the earth and what it provides. (But the more we learn western ideas, the more our feelings become inferior to the extraction of resources in our lands.) Instead it makes us look forward to an artificial world of economics. Makes us think about what job we want, how much money we want. In many ways, we look forward to an uncertain future, full of doubts about what we are capable of. When I think about Inuit long time ago, they knew what they could do and how much strength they had, they knew what their bodies could do. One needs a lot of knowledge about one's abilities to wait patiently for hours by a seal hole just to hear a seal breathing and splashing in that tiny hole. When I think about it, it is like meditating—focusing on yourself and the environment around you to accomplish a task.

My mother always says that the best therapy is to be out on the land, to clear your mind and think positively about yourself. She can let her negative feelings out by just being on the land. To be out on the land is to let civilization's materialism out of our bodies, to let the burden of trying to make a living go out of your body—to put it simply—to be free. (To know what your body is capable of is a huge stress-reliever because the body acknowledges the environment around you and it does the same to language, they embrace each other. A great big symbiosis!)

Hi Tommy,

Do you remember when you and I and David Joanasie went to see beluga (*qilalugaq*) in the aquarium in Vancouver? I remember there was a biologist there, a beluga expert, she was so proud of these animals in their enclosure in the aquarium. I remember when you and David talked to her, I think the first thing you said was how seeing beluga made you hungry. ("The sweet taste of *maktaaq* is unforgettable after the first bite. To explain the texture of *maktaaq* would be to give away the magic of the whale.") She seemed to get pretty upset by that; she seemed to be quite keen on separating beluga from their environment. In a way, she could have asked you guys so many questions (like asked her)—but she didn't—after all, you've seen beluga in their environment. And those of us who've eaten beluga (you more than me) are—in one way of speaking—part beluga: we have beluga inside us, in our cells. Talking to you guys is like being able to talk to beluga, in a way; but the biologist didn't show any sign of knowing that, nor any interest in that. "Eating confirms my selfness with what I consume" is the way historian C. L. Martin puts it (1992, p. 86). There's a beautiful one-sentence explanation that I once heard Louis Tapardjuk (now the Nunavut Minister of Culture, Elders, and Youth) deliver to a room full of wildlife biologists in Iqaluit: "It's wildlife that manages Inuit, not the other way 'round." George Wenzel, one of the few southern scientists I know of who speaks Inuktitut, used to quote Ortega y Gasset's statement, "I am I and the environment," as a synthesis of "the kind of meaning Inuit impart when they speak about *niqituinnaq*—a unity of environment, community, and human identity" (Wenzel, 1991, p. 191). Wenzel (1991) says "harvesting is not just the means by which food is extracted from the natural environment, but also the critical medium through which the human and animal communities are joined together" (p. 137).

Scientists and experts, however, tend to prefer "locationless logic" because it "makes societies legible" (Mitchell, 2002, p. 15; Scott, 1998, p. 2). In the Yukon, the Kluane people complain that "Biologists, at least in their official capacities, talk about animals as 'things.' They are not interested in individual moose but only in 'moose' in general . . . [F]or them, moose are not individual beings with thoughts and feelings; they are merely representative instances of an abstract quantity" (Nadasdy, 2003, p. 111):

Though no biologists would ever suggest using these techniques (aerial surveys, radio-collaring) to learn about people, they have no qualms about using them on animals, whom they do not view as persons but simply as objects of study, as non-sentient beings with whom social relations are impossible. Many Kluane people, however, refuse to make such a distinction between the proper treatment of animals and people. Unlike biologists, they are very concerned with what animals think and feel in response to such treatment. One man summed up his concerns by stating that he would like to collar all the biologists and watch what they do for a while. Then, he said, they would know what it feels like to be treated that way. (Nadasdy, 2003, p. 110)

Perhaps making Inuktitut a co-requisite for environmental study and research in Nunavut would help scientists appreciate "the size and importance of the gap between general knowledge and situated knowledge" (Scott, 1998, p. 318). Maybe another way of talking about this is what Bowers (2005) calls the difference between "low-context" knowledge, and "high-context" knowledge (p. 147). High-context knowledge includes traditional oral wisdom, the type of wisdom that Cruikshank (2002) calls "sentient knowledge"; wisdom that doesn't try to "pry nature away from culture and fragment it into data," but rather a wisdom that permeates a person only after a long immersion in the local context (pp. 12–13).

Unfortunately, schools tend to teach us that any knowledge that you can't write down or externally record in some way is "low status" knowledge—including hunting and navigation, and "personal talents and skills expressed in communal activities ranging from growing, preparing, and sharing food . . . to musical performances, healing, and repairing the material forms of culture [tools] . . . encompassing the organic complexity of orally based cultures" (Bowers, 2005, pp. 146, 155). While this knowledge is situated in context it is unremarkable, but remove it from context and record it on paper or audiotape and you convert it to "high status" knowledge in the eyes of the formal school system (de Castell, 1990, p. 30; Steele, 1999).

For 16 years, the federal government's Northern Science Award, for example, was always given to researchers from Southern universities. Finally, in 2000, Igloolik's Inullariit Elders Society received it for their audio recording of traditional knowledge. They didn't win the award for developing traditional knowledge (for 4,000 years), or for speaking it, but for *recording* it (for 10 years). During those 10 years of recording, 30 of the elders recorded on the tapes have died. This is the urgency: The older generation has learned out on the land, the youth have learned in the classroom. We have to build a bridge (oral, experiential) before the gulf between generations becomes too wide to span. We can taperecord knowledge all we like, but as James Hillman says: "Nature dies *because* culture dies" (Hillman & Ventura, 1992, p. 238). Building this bridge between the generations could be as simple as insisting that Inuktitut be made one of the school and college requirements for environmental education in Nunavut.

Perhaps if there were a requirement that Inuktitut fluency and training be part of the licensing of research in Nunavut, then more Inuktitut-fluent Inuit would be hired onto research teams. And if a significant portion of Arctic environmental education was required to be conducted in Inuktitut, that would probably precipitate a sharp rise in Inuktitut-speakers entering the environmental programs (as well as generally increase the respect for Inuktitut within Nunavut). Environmental education conducted in the language of the eco-culture system would also likely involve more elders and increase the recognition of, and respect for, elders' knowledge and land-based learning.

—Regards, Derek

Hi Derek,

I keep forgetting to write about how important it is for environmental educators, scientists, and biologists to affiliate with Inuit organizations. This should be a central objective researchers and scientists alike. Curricula, course materials, reports, and documents should be communicated in Inuktitut first and foremost. Inuit organizations are representatives of their Inuit beneficiaries in their regions and provide a connection to each community. With affiliations to Inuit organizations and Inuit communities, teachers and researchers gain a certain respect, and a better response from the community is likely to be given. Inuit hiring priorities should be established by environmental education programs to help them better represent the environment and its inhabitants. Hiring more Inuit researchers would help the researcher publish more accurate reports of their findings; and reports should be reviewed by the communities first, before they are released to the public, as the people being researched have a huge stake in these studies. And if a scientist wants to research in the Arctic, wants to study the Arctic, then to make valid conclusions, he or she has to be part of the natural Arctic environment and not consider themselves apart from what they are studying. The scientific research done by most researchers is not accurate as they are not one with the environment they study. Inuit know that this world is not to be owned, and my guess is that the scientists who come up here think that they own the animals and plants and they own the world and that is why I think many Indigenous people do not like or trust scientists.

Scientists and biologists say they do their job because they care for the plants and animals to save them. (Why is "saving" something always part of western culture?) But if they have that goal, then why do they do things like tag animals and interrupt their natural behaviour. If my father sees a scientist tagging a polar bear or any other animal, he feels sorry for the animal, and he asks questions like: "Why are they doing that?" He never understands: If they are trying to help them, then why are they hurting them? I agree with the Kluane people that biologists don't seem to think animals have feelings, but they really do. My father always told me that when I hunt that I should never show disrespect towards the animals in any way; or else, he said the next animal I try to catch will know that I did something bad to another animal and won't allow itself to be caught. We know that animals have feelings just like us. Respect for any animal is paramount in our culture. We can feel it when we skin or eat a caribou: they know they are helping us Inuit. Knowing these small things about the environment gives us human beings a better understanding of our world, and it allows us to respect and to love the world the way it is, and to accept that animals move and that they never stay in the same area. To accept that some animals will never be here in the same condition. We have to be educated in Inuktitut and through Inuit so we have a better understanding of this world.

Today, as I occasionally do, I was reading John Amagoalik's (1977) essay "Will the Inuit Disappear From the Face of This Earth?" This is a very serious question for any Inuk. This question scares me everyday, and I deny the question and never want to hear it verbally, although reading the question seems to be acceptable and does not sound so strong. John A (as he is known) says: This question brings a great sadness to me. To realize that we Inuit are in the same category as the great whale, the bald eagle, the husky and the polar bear brings me great fear. To realize that our people can be classified as an endangered species is very disturbing. Is our culture like a wounded polar bear that has gone out to sea to die alone? What can be done?

These words were written in 1977 by a very intellectual Inuk, called, by some, the "Father of Nunavut." The first paragraph speaks to me like an elder does when they tell their grandchildren myths and legends. Even today, the question would still scare Inuit (many of them elders), maybe even more than it scared them in 1977. I think many of us do not realize that adjusting to a dominant society has its limits. At what point do we know that we have lost most of what is precious to a strong culture? An Inuit identity is on the line: a way of life and a language so unique that it is in its own league.

I wish that Inuit had the opportunity to document their ways not through paper but by listening to their elders and to people who want to make a difference. I say now that the sound of our mouths has a huge effect on the state of mind and heart. Orality is important for my culture, but I am also the tool that is taking that away.

As I write these papers, I realize that I am also part of the system that produces papers and documents. The more I write, the more I realize that I go against what I have written so far about the degradation of a culture by an onslaught of "paperistic" materials. I am a tool in the documentation of our world.

I feel guilty in a way that I was taught English. I wish that I were uneducated, unable to write, but instead traditional in the sense of the word. I want to be a traditional Inuk—ESKIMO.

But what is an uneducated human being? Is "uneducated" the right word to use; to explain that I want to contribute traditionally to the Inuit worldview? I am haunted by the fact that I advocate for a traditional way of life, but I am unable to realize that I am not traditional. To be uneducated means that I do not know the world: to not have knowledge and a sense of going forward. But I have to say that there is no such thing as an uneducated being. Animals learn to live by being educated by their environment and after all, are we not animals?

To educate through books about the environment is to belittle the environment, to make it less than us: and it makes us think that we are the kings of this world and we hold the fate of this world. Little do we know that the environment holds us rather than us holding it.

I love education and don't take me wrong when I say that books belittle the environment. But life seen through books is reduced to a set of truths and facts; when learning about life is supposed to be flexible and confusing.

Many people think that to be educated is the only way to make a decent living, to have a job, to be able to make tough decisions, to be able to speak the English language, to have the financial capacity to look at budgets and other more complicated systems of control. Inuit see human life and how the body works differently from English. English reduces things to "a fact." " In Inuktitut it's not a "fact"—life doesn't lie to you—but it's a huge truth that takes your whole life to figure out: what love means, what truth means.

Inuktitut taught me the feelings towards hunting. The English language can be full of love and care, but love and care are only possibly effective and felt by your surroundings when you advocate fair and loose attitudes of respect for all living things, whether plants, animals, or us little human beings. And you can't separate the Inuktitut language from hunting and interacting with the environment; it would never work.[3] To keep and teach a language is a goal of mine and I will keep on doing what my language commands me to do. Inuktitut made sure that I care for the trees and grass and bees and insects of the south even though our language is not really made for the southern climate, but the respect the language teaches is inseparable from your own personal surroundings, so I felt I had no choice but to love the environment given me.

My language is so respectful that I learnt to respect every other race and being on this earth, no matter what they have done. But I'm only human and I might say a few things in English that might be taken wrong because my understanding of the environment was shaped in Inuktitut and sometimes the English words don't really mean what I think (but they come out that way in English).

I hope you have a great spring and summer and I'll write more this weekend.
—Tommy.

NOTES

1. Tommy: I found this paragraph was very important throughout the essay. What the elders were trying to say is the point I would like to have made. Might as well do it out on the land to get the best results, right? Derek: Hugh Brody's (2000) book *The Other Side of Eden* (especially the first chapter, "Inuktitut," pp. 9–64) makes this point really well. Also helpful for this is Jean Briggs' (2002) writing, for example her essay: "Language Dead or Alive: What's in a Dictionary?" In it the Inupiat elder Neakok says:

"a word is different when it is used by different people . . . When an Inupiaq reads a word, he'll be thinking that somebody else said something completely different" (p. 69).

2. Joanasie Akumalik is the former mayor of Arctic Bay and currently director of government relations for NTI; here is part of an e-mail he wrote us after reading our conversation: "First of all, qungapassi" [I smile at you all].

Smiling is part of the Inuit culture. It is a facial expression to express forgiveness, showing appreciation; welcoming, introducing, and just indicating happiness within. When Inuit are introduced or meet the first time with a person, usually just smiling is enough. The Canadian-European, on the other hand, will start expressing who they are and what they do and position themselves. For Inuit, it takes a while for us to come and say what we do. It's just that, we are not very expressive verbally, and would not want to "brag" about what we do at the first introductions. Inuit do not position themselves at the beginning. So I smile at all of you.

I read the excerpts by my *inuuqatiga* Tommy Akulukjuk and my ivory brother Derek Rasmussen and I totally agree with their concept of putting environment and language all together. It was interesting to see the different excerpts by a *qadlunnaq* and a young Inuk. Tommy seems to be very much in tune with his culture, by that I mean he knows how to express his way of being an Inuk.

I will try to attempt to explain my culture (I came from the "high arctic" region of Nunavut) and the way I see both worlds of Inuit and Canadian-European. I've done some schooling in a southern institute when I was young, in a Canadian city, Winnipeg, Manitoba, and where First Nation people are in large numbers. I have been involved in community development and did one term as a mayor in Arctic Bay. I have facilitated a number of conferences on economic issues, wildlife, climate change, and or just educational gatherings.

I was born in a sod house. A sod house in the high arctic is a structured house-like dwelling unit for a family, built with some sod, big rocks (boulders, if I may), canvass, some wood beams, if not traditional caribou antlers, narwhale tusks, whale bones, or some scrap of washed up old trees found along the shore. I was born in high arctic, dead winter in February. That is the coldest winter month up there. But I was adopted out to a family and I do associate a lot with my biological brothers and sisters to date. Both of my biological parents have passed away but I did stay and hunted with them a number of times. That is an Inuit way, to know and have full contact with your biological parents.

My father taught me to wake up early when I was about 11 or 12. I soon realize why I had to be up early, just like the farmers down south, so that you have the time to get to do what you have to do and hunt while there is still light. In the high arctic region, our sun disappears around the month of October and comes back up around the second week of February. To hunt in the twilight, and should the caribou be far (130 miles by snowmobile), you have to leave early enough to get to your destination and along the way, hunters can hunt seals and set up fishing nets. Once at the destination, you hunt the next day or two depending on how much you need. On the way back, hunters usually then check the fishing nets, if lucky, then hunters bring some caribou and fish home. This is done in the dead winter. It is different scenario in the other seasons.

Inuit are very much tied to the environment up in the arctic. We have to, otherwise life of an Inuk or entity would become false. Assimilation is the word I think I am looking for.

When Tommy indicated that his father was told go outside to "read" the weather as soon as he wakes up, that is so true. This is part of our exercise; to get the taste of the environment first thing before doing anything. I think it is like having your first coffee or shower in the morning before you do anything in Canadian-European way. The way I understand it is that when I wake, I want to see the light, feel the temperature and if not smell the environment, hear the environment, and just absorb the environment first thing. I have to disagree with Tommy with his attempt to explain "*Kajjaanaqtuq.*" This word encompasses so many meanings. I agree that it's to reflect positively but it goes beyond that. It touches your inner soul thereby providing serenity to one's self. Have you ever got up in the early morning by yourself and felt serene? The twilight, the slowness of things starting to move, the place you are in, hear the clock . . . I cannot translate it.

At home in Arctic Bay area, we have a traditional seal hunting season. That particular season we call "*qulaitiqtut*" meaning "the seal breathing holes 'covers' are opened" season. That is when we hunt all night long. The sun is up 24 hours a day. What is caught is all used up. For me, it's the season I love the most. While waiting for a seal, I can hear the snow melting. I can also hear the wind, feel the warmth of the sun, and the smell of the environment. I have always said: Gas for the skidoo: $40.00, Stainless steel traditional harpoon: $75.00, Carton of cigarettes $100.00, Seawater going up and down in the seal hole: priceless!"

3. David Joanasie, an environmental researcher with Inuit Tapariit Kanatami (ITK) also wrote to us (in Inuktitut, translated by Tommy into English): "You are right, this paper you've written with Derek is good news and fun to read and made me want to read it again even after I've read it. I agreed with you guys about our language and the connectedness with the environment. It is true the knowledge that Inuit hold is really connected to the land and the weather.... I have always heard our elders, like your father, how they were told to get out of the igloo each morning and feel the *sila* and take observance of it and feel it. It is like meditation as well.... Sometimes I think about the past and how they had expert knowledge of the land and were professionals at hunting and gathering animals and plants because they understood the land. They had so much knowledge that they could make clothes from sealskin and caribou skin and other tools from animals because they understood them. But today we do not understand/misunderstood our clothing and we live in houses now. We wear prefabricated clothing so much that we don't understand our environment anymore (as in how much we need to wear). Even right now I work in a huge building on the fifth floor with walls that have no connection to the outside world and the environment. I am physically far from the *nuna*. I have no idea what the state of the land is and what wildlife it holds or what plants are underneath the cement. Many lives are now disconnected from the *nuna* (land)."

REFERENCES

Amagoalik, J. (1977). Will the Inuit disappear from the face of this earth? *Inuit Today, 6*(4), 52.

Berger, T. R. (2006). *Conciliator's final report: Nunavut Land Claims Agreement implementation contract negotiations for the second planning period 2003–2013.* Vancouver: Bull, Housser & Tupper.

Bowers, C. A. (2005). Introduction; [and] how the ideas of Paulo Freire contribute to the cultural roots of the ecological crisis. In C. A Bowers & F. Apffel-Marglin (Eds.), *Rethinking Freire: Globalization and the environmental crisis* (pp. 1–12, 133–192). Mahwah, NJ: Erlbaum.

Briggs, J. (2002). Language dead or alive: What's in a dictionary? *Topics in Arctic Social Sciences 4,* 69–82.

Brody, H. (2000). *The other side of Eden: Hunters, farmers and the shaping of the world.* Vancouver: Douglas and McIntyre.

Cruikshank, J. (2002). Glaciers and climate change: Scientific research in sentient places. *Topics in Arctic Social Sciences, 4,* 7–16.

de Castell, S. (1990). Defining significant knowledge: Some limits to literacy. In S. P. Norris & L. M. Phillips (Eds.), *Foundation of literacy policy in Canada* (pp. 21–30). Calgary: Detselig Enterprises.

Harmon, D. (2002). *In light of our differences: How diversity in nature and culture makes us human.* Washington, DC: Smithsonian Institution Press.

Harmon, D. (2004). Fieldnotes: Diversity. *Audubon Magazine, 3,* 43.

Hillman, J., & Ventura, M. (1992). *We've had a hundred years of psychotherapy and the world's getting worse.* New York: HarperCollins.

Kane, S. (1998). *Wisdom of the mythtellers* (2nd ed.). Peterborough, ON: Broadview Press.

Maffi, L. (Ed.). (2001). *On biocultural diversity: Linking language, knowledge, and the environment.* Washington, DC: Smithsonian Institution Press.

Martin, C. L. (1992). *In the spirit of the earth: Rethinking history and time.* Baltimore: Johns Hopkins University Press.

Mitchell, T. (2002). *Rule of experts: Egypt, techno-politics, modernity.* Berkeley: University of California Press.

Muhlhausler, P. (1996). *Linguistic ecology.* London: Routledge.

Nadasdy, P. (2003). *Hunters and bureaucrats: Power, knowledge and aboriginal-state relations in the southwest Yukon.* Vancouver: UBC Press.

Philip, M. (2000, May 13). Aboriginal languages nearing extinction: Expert. *The Globe and Mail,* p. A1.

Rasmussen, D. (2000). Our life out of balance: The rise of literacy and the demise of pattern languages. *Encounter: Education for Meaning and Social Justice, 13*(2), 13–21.

Rasmussen, D. (2002). Qallunology: A pedagogy for the oppressor. In *Philosophy of Education Society Yearbook 2002* (pp. 85–94). Champaign: University of Illinois at Urbana-Champaign.

Ross, R. (1996). Watch your language. In R. Ross, *Returning to the teachings* (pp. 101–133). Toronto: Penguin.

Scott, J. C. (1998). *Seeing like a state: How certain schemes to improve the human condition have failed.* New Haven, CT: Yale University Press.

Skutnabb-Kangas, T. (2002, March). Mother tongues: An invisible, neglected and disappearing resource (Address delivered at U.N.E.S.C.O.'s "Mother Language Day"). *Langscape, 22,* 11–22. Washington: Terralingua.

Steele, B (1999). *Draw me a story: An illustrated exploration of drawing as pre- and post-literate language.* Winnipeg: Peguis.

Suckling, K. (2000, Sept.). Biodiversity, linguistic diversity and identity: Toward an ecology of language in an age of extinction. *Landscape, 17,* 15–20.

Wenzel, G. (1991). *Animal rights, human rights.* Toronto: University of Toronto Press.

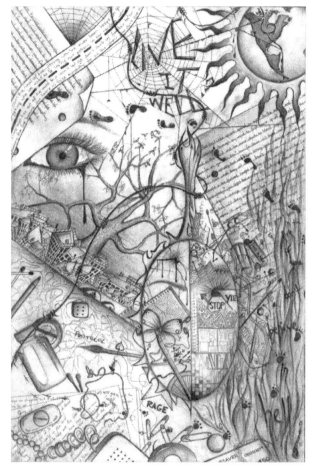

Serenne Romanycia (2005)

There are nine different words in Maya for the color blue in the comprehensive Porrúa Spanish-Maya Dictionary but just three Spanish translations, leaving six butterflies that can be seen only by the Maya, proving beyond a doubt that when a language dies six butterflies disappear from the consciousness of the earth. (Earl Shorris, The Last Word)

17

The Place of the City in
Environmental Education

Milton McClaren

Thirty-five years ago I was asked a question by a colleague that has affected my thinking about environmental education ever since. At the time we were in a group of faculty and associate teachers planning an in-service education program to help teachers make use of a newly developed environmental studies site in a forested area on the outskirts of a small interior city in British Columbia, Canada. My questioning colleague was a secondary school teacher with a background in social studies and geography, and an active outdoors person who had grown up in a rural area but now lived and worked in the large city of Vancouver.

He asked whether environmental education—a term only recently coming into general use at that time—was really only another name for outdoor education. More particularly, he asked whether we were planning to focus our efforts in teacher in-service education solely on wild, undeveloped places while neglecting the environments of cities where most of the teachers and their students lived. He challenged us to rethink our definition of *environment* and to ask whether environmental education was effectively the study of locales devoid of human constructions and significant or evident human influence.

The subtitle of this collection, *Restorying Culture, Environment, and Education* implies the telling of new stories or the renewal or revision of existing ones. It suggests the need to take a critical look at the discourses and narratives that constitute and frame contemporary education and, in particular, education that fosters thinking about human–environment relationships. My purpose here is to develop the premise that much of contemporary environmental education embodies underlying attitudes toward urban or constructed environments, revealing important assumptions about what is natural. I contend further that these attitudes and assumptions affect how and whether environmental education engages urban people and their knowledge of place. By becoming aware of this issue we may be able to widen the compass of environmental education, authenticate the lives of city-dwelling people, appreciate and recognize their stories, and perhaps in the process construct narratives of *Earth-Friendly Cities* (McClaren, Samples, & Hammond, 1993).

Given the importance of urban environments in our experience, it is strange how little attention we pay to these environments in school programs. In Canada, for example, the British Columbia Ministry of Education's official website lists the prescribed learning outcomes for social studies for grades from kindergarten to Grade 11. Only in the early years of kindergarten and Grade 1 is there mention of outcomes related directly to students' knowledge of their local neighborhoods and homes, whereas almost no space is given in the curriculum to the particular or general study of cities, except through abstract references to resource use and economic geography. This is notable given that one of the five major curricular themes in the B.C. social studies curriculum is "environment" (B.C. Ministry of Education, 1999). In an increasingly test-driven curriculum, what is prescribed and tested is often what gets taught, so the lack of clear and systematic attention to the environments in which students actually live is significant.

The idea that some students may not include cities in the ambit of "environment" was recently brought home to me with some force. In undertaking a content analysis of entries submitted online by students participating in the 2006 *Robert Bateman Wildlife Art and Writing* contest (McClaren, 2007), I looked at 148 entries from students between the ages of 7 and 19, living in five different Canadian provinces, with many in large urban centers such as Toronto and Vancouver. The students were asked to write on the theme, "Thinking about our future and the future of the Earth," and amazingly, the word *city* was absent among the entire set of online entries. One student mentioned the conservation of old houses and environmentally sound building design, and students made frequent references to environmental problems like smog, litter, and pollution, whereas some presented vivid descriptions of the future world they would like to inhabit (offering attributes more commonly associated with wild than urban places). The writers made 72 references to words that could be seen as referring to nonhuman or natural environments, including 26 occurrences of the word *nature* and 24 references to *trees*.

More generally, I find the omission of cities from the curriculum of environmental education fascinating. Is this because the reality of urban life is so apparent as to be taken for granted, so obvious that it requires no educational attention? Is the focus on getting students out—out and away from cities and back into environments presumed to be more "natural," healthier, less stressful, more beautiful? We need to examine these questions carefully. It is not my intention here to argue that it is not worthwhile for students to experience wilderness environments. Many writers (Louv, 2005; Miles & Priest, 1999; Suzuki, 2003) have offered effective arguments for wilderness experiences as components of environmental education, whereas others have described projects in which students have engaged in urban habitat restoration (Bell, 2001). However, the argument for developing urban awareness, although not absent (Hawkins & Vinton, 1973; Malone, 1999; Symonds, 1971), has not been strongly made.

Historical and cultural attitudes towards cites can be sorted along a continuum of descriptions, from opportunity and optimism to dreary toil and despair; from centers of learning and culture to centers of crowding, pollution, crime, and relentless competition. These are highly contrasting extremes; stereotypically, they lack detail, perpetuating misconceptions and grossly simplifying complexity, but examples of each can be found in any contemporary city. The point is whether one city story has more force in the discourse of environmental education than others. Consider for example the juxtaposition of words in the following passage from David Orr's (1994) *Earth in Mind*, in which he describes the current ecological crisis as "part of a larger pattern that includes shopping malls, glitzy suburbs and ozone holes, crowded freeways and climate change, overstocked supermarkets and soil erosion . . . technological wonders and insensate violence" (pp. 1–2). In this fairly dystopian view of at least some aspects of urban life and constructed environments, Orr links human constructions or technologies with significant, current environmental problems and with "insensate violence." In fairness, Orr notes that the environmental crisis is rooted not in technology as much as in the minds of those who create and use it. However, there is little here to suggest that cities might be considered as rich in human potential and possibility, rather than as sources of environmental problems.

In her classic *The Death and Life of Great American Cities*, Jane Jacobs (1961) notes that the view of cities as a sort of cultural and environmental blight is not new. She describes an early advocate of city planning, Ebenezer Howard, as follows: "He not only hated the wrongs and mistakes of the city, he hated the city and thought it an outright evil and an affront to nature. . . . His prescription was to do the city in" (p. 17). Howard proposed surrounding cities with planned Garden Cities where people could return to an imaginary bucolic rural village life and abandon urban squalor (of which there was plenty in Howard's time). Jacobs (1961) views this prescription as a sentimentalizing of nature and as a too-common trend among professional urban planners. Her critique is that nature, considered as the antithesis of cities, "is apparently assumed to consist of grass, fresh air, and little else" (p. 445). Furthermore, people who are to live in these "natural" landscapes apparently are expected to do little or nothing. She argues further that sentimentality about nature "degrades everything it touches" (p. 447), and denotes a "deep if unacknowledged disrespect" (p. 445).

The examples taken from Orr and Jacobs suggest several significant problems about the representation of urban places and city dwellers in the current discourses of environmental education, and expose deeper problems with environmental education, generally. Humans construct cities. If human constructions are not natural, then what does that make humans? Stated differently, how should humans behave naturally? Jacobs goes to the heart of these questions noting: "The cities of human beings are as natural, being a product of one form of nature, as are the colonies of prairie dogs or the beds of oysters" (p. 444). Richard Louv (2005) offers two definitions of nature attributed to the poet Gary Snyder (2004): *natura* from the Latin meaning "birth, constitution, character and the course of things" (p. 8), and *nasci* meaning to be born. Louv acknowledges that in its broadest sense, nature can be taken to mean all objects and phenomena in the material world. He notes that under this definition a machine and toxic waste are parts of nature. In this definition, a city like New York is natural; it complies with the laws of nature. Although Louv is clearly uncomfortable with such a broad definition, he is also unwilling to confine the term *natural* to virgin forests and habitats completely undisturbed by humans. Instead, he opts to apply the term *nature* to "natural wildness: biodiversity, abundance" (p. 8) and to see the process of wonderment (the capacity for wonder) as a profoundly important attribute of human nature: an interesting combination of process and attribute in a definition.

Additionally, there is a tension implicit in environmental education between a desire to integrate humankind in the fabric of life on earth (nature) on the one hand, and a tendency to place humans in a unique, separate position, somehow beyond or outside that fabric on the other. Phrases such as "man and nature" or "human and environment" reveal this tension. It is also found in some writings in the environmental management and stewardship genre. Orr (1994), for example, refers to a September 1989 special issue of *Scientific American* with the theme "Managing Planet Earth" as an example of the technological hubris in which humans view themselves as gaining control of the biosphere through technology and applied knowledge. David Suzuki (2003) also highlights this problem: "Inherent in the view is the assumption that human beings are special and different and that we exist outside nature" (p. 294). He adds, "If children grow up understanding that we are animals they will look at other species with a sense of fellowship and community" (p. 294).

Although environmental educators often argue for the importance of reconnecting humans with nature (Louv, 2005), the sort of natural places they describe appear to exclude that peculiarly human construction known as the city, even though growing numbers of the students of environmental education—not to mention environmental educators themselves—live most of their lives in urban settings. Many environmental educators feel a deep connection with other species and the places they inhabit, having life stories grounded in rich experiences in environments outside human influence (Durning, 1996; Hungerford & Volk, 1990; Louv, 2005). This love of so-called natural or wild places and of other species often motivates them to pursue careers in environmental education and related fields, and to find personal restoration and recreation in nonurban settings. Such experiences are part of a deeply situated knowledge—so deeply situated that, as Clifford Geertz (1996) writes, it is difficult to see what is always there. These naturistic stories can affect how we engage with urban people, especially young people who have spent their entire lives in densely populated, highly constructed city neighborhoods. If we do not appreciate the influence of our personal epistemologies, we may construct programs and projects of environmental education that deny or fail to acknowledge the realities and stories of urban dwellers, ignoring their senses of place. Those on the outside often make faulty, hasty judgments about how locals should view their situations. Jacobs (1961) describes many well-intentioned urban planning and renewal schemes which failed as a result of the inappropriate application of theory to actual situations. She comments:

> [T]hey have gone to great pains to learn what the saints and sages of modern orthodox planning have said about how cities ought to work and what ought to be good for people and businesses in them. . . . When contradictory reality intrudes, threatening to shatter their dearly won learning, they must shrug reality aside. (p. 8)

Ethnographers and cultural geographers are now more likely to defer or avoid making judgments about how people view their places. Sense of place, and the local, vernacular knowledge that is part of it, is understood as closely linked to identity. For example, Edward Casey (1996) writes, "To live is to live locally, and to know is first of all to know the places one is in" (p. 18), and further, "We are not only in places, but of them" (p. 19). For these reasons, we need to address the representation of both the nonhuman and human-constructed and modified elements of the environment in our treatment of environmental education. The failure of educational programs to represent and acknowledge the places and conditions of student life devalues students' experiences and fails to engage their prior knowledge, which many consider an essential element in all new learning (Bransford, Brown, & Cocking, 1999). Additionally, when educators present so-called natural environments as models of how reality should be arranged, we present implicit messages devaluing the urban environments in which students live. Finally, by assigning urban environments and the processes and structures of cities to the null curriculum (Eisner, 1985), we fail to allow students to consider alternative possibilities and develop appropriate, local action projects (McClaren & Hammond, 2005). As Casey (1996) writes, "To be cultural, to have a culture, is to inhabit a place sufficiently intensely to cultivate it—to be responsible for it, to respond to it, to attend to it caringly" (p. 34).

Critics of current urban and suburban life often point to the dreary repetition in many cities of the same shopping malls, fast food restaurants, house plans, and street layouts, regardless of climate, topography, local biology, culture, and history (Jacobs, 1961; Van der Ryn & Cowan, 1996). Sim Van der Ryn and Stuart Cowan refer to the power of standardized templates on the design and development of urban places, noting that these templates have insinuated themselves deeply into our perceptions and awareness of place. We expect and accept these patterns because they are so prevalent, and our knowledge of alternatives is so limited that the templates seem inevitable and inescapable (especially when supported and enforced by urban building codes, mortgage lenders, and zoning bylaws). If we were to bring the students' stories of their urban life experiences into the narratives of schooling, we might begin to make apparent the assumptions underlying the omnipresence of these design templates and escape the cycle of dumb design described by Van der Ryn and Cowan as "design that fails to consider the health of human communities or of ecosystems" (p. 14).

However, caution must be taken. It is important to begin from the students' perspectives of their places without assuming they share the value judgments that urban design is uninspired, monotonous, and anti-ecological. For example, rather than condemning shopping malls out of hand, we should let students offer their narratives of them in their own lives. Students have many important and insightful stories to tell about their towns, suburbs, and city neighborhoods. They can develop useful and creative suggestions, and designs for development. The urban planners' pencils can pass to those whose lives are most affected in the conventional planning process, thereby acknowledging a principle of ecological design, namely, that everyone is a designer (Van der Ryn & Cowan, 1996).

Our goal in bringing students' urban narratives into the school experience should also be to allow students to revisit their assumptions, their ideas about how cities work. In many ways cities are giant machines designed to obscure connections and attenuate feedback. For example, as Van der Ryn and Cowan suggest:

> Those of us who belong to industrial societies have come utterly to depend on far-flung sources for the basics of life. We have learned not to ask too many questions about how those basics are provided. . . . We need to ask questions, to intervene, to render visible what has so long been hidden from public discussion. (p. 14)

Survey research on public attitudes toward, and knowledge of, environmental issues (Coyle, 2005; Kempton, Boster, & Hartley, 1996; The National Environmental Education and Training Foundation, 2002) suggests that although many people are concerned about environmental issues and want to take appropriate personal actions, environmental problems seem too large scale or too abstract and complex for any local, personal actions to have effect (Durning, 1996). By bringing urban people's local knowledge and sense of place into the narrative of environmental education, we provide openings for people to develop action projects at the local level; experts, developers, and politicians can enter into the narratives not as authorities, but as informed participants willing to listen, learn, and contribute.

Any hope for a sustainable future lies in the personal choices and actions of millions of people all over the world, most of whom live in cities and towns, and their understandings and senses of place will play important roles in the choices they make or believe they can or should make. The world of the made is different from the world of the born, to use a phrase from the poet e.e. cummings,[1] but is no less natural for that. Environmental educators should create space in their discourses for stories of urban life in which both the problems and the richness of the urban experience can be expressed. We must also appreciate the power exercised on our thinking by our personal narratives about what is natural and what is not, lest our assumptions remain invisible and unexamined, affecting our practices in ways that may well disenfranchise and render voiceless those we seek to engage in education about the environment and our species' place in it.

NOTES

1. The phrase is taken from e.e. cummings poem, "pity this busy monster manunkind" which was included in the collection titled 1 × 1 [One Times One], XIV, (1944). The line is,

> "A world of made
> is not a world of born—pity poor flesh"

The entire poem is available online at http://www.geocities.com/soho/8454/554.htm

REFERENCES

Bell, A. C. (2001). Engaging spaces: On school-based habitat restoration. *Canadian Journal of Environmental Education, 6*, 209–224.

Bransford, J. D., Brown, A. L., & Cocking, R. R. (1999). *How people learn: Brain, mind, experience, and school.* Washington, DC: National Academy Press.

British Columbia Ministry of Education. (1999, January 28). *Social studies. Appendix A. Prescribed learning outcomes. Grades K–7.* [Online]. Retrieved August 22, 2006, from http://www.bced.gov.bc.ca/irp/ssk7/apatoc.htm.

Casey, E. S. (1996). How to get from space to place in a fairly short stretch of time. In S. Feld & K.H. Basso (Eds.), *Senses of place* (pp. 13–52). Santa Fe, NM: School of American Research Press.

Coyle, K. (2005). *Environmental literacy in America. What ten years of NTEEF/Roper research and related studies say about environmental literacy in the U.S.* Washington, DC: The National Environmental Education and Training Foundation.

Durning, A. T. (1996). *This place on Earth: Home and the practice of permanence.* Seattle, WA: Sasquatch Books.

Eisner, E. W. (1985). *The educational imagination. On the design and evaluation of school programs* (2nd ed.). New York: Macmillan.

Geertz, C. (1996). Afterword. In S. Feld & K. H. Basso (Eds.), *Senses of place* (pp. 259–262). Santa Fe, NM: School of American Research Press.

Hawkins, D. E., & Vinton, D. A. (1973). *The environmental classroom.* Englewood Cliffs, NJ: Prentice-Hall.

Hungerford H. H., & Volk, T. L. (1990). Changing learner behaviour through environmental education. *The Journal of Environmental Education, 22*(3), 8–21.

Jacobs, J. (1961). *The death and life of great American cities.* New York: Vintage Books.

Kempton, W., Boster, J. S., & Hartley, J. A. (1995). *Environmental values in American culture.* Cambridge, MA: MIT Press.

Louv, R. (2005). *Last child in the woods: Saving our children from nature-deficit disorder.* Chapel Hill, NC: Algonquin Books.

Malone, K. (1999). Reclaiming silenced voices through practices of education and environmental popular knowledge production. *Canadian Journal of Environmental Education, 4*, 231–242.

McClaren, M. (2007). *Content analysis of the online entries submitted to the 2006 Robert Bateman Wildlife Writing and Art Contest.* Unpublished manuscript.

McClaren, M., & Hammond, B. (2005). Integrating education and action in environmental education. In M. Mappin & E. Johnson (Eds.), *Environmental education and advocacy: Changing perspectives of ecology and education* (pp. 267–291). New York: Cambridge University Press.

McClaren, M., Samples, B., & Hammond, B. (1993). *Earth friendly cities.* Toronto, ON: Ginn.

Miles, J. C., & Priest, S. (1999). *Adventure programming.* State College, PA: Venture.

Orr, D. W. (1994). *Earth in mind. On education, environment and the human prospect.* Washington, DC: Island Press.

Snyder, G. (2004). *The practice of the wild.* Washington, DC: Shoemaker & Hoard.

Suzuki, D. (2003). *The David Suzuki reader. A lifetime of ideas from a leading activist and thinker.* Vancouver, BC: Greystone Books.

Symonds, H. (Ed.). (1971). *The teacher and the city. Urban studies project.* Toronto, ON: Methuen.

The National Environmental Education and Training Foundation/RoperASW. (2002, August). *Americans' low "Energy IQ": A risk to our energy future. The tenth annual national report card: Energy knowledge, attitudes and behaviour.* Washington, DC: Author.

Van der Ryn, S., & Cowan, S. (1996). *Ecological design.* Washington, DC: Island Press.

July 2, 1997

Woodhaven revisited...
Joan Burbridge has become
like an old friend & Woodhaven
a reservoir for the spirit.
The freshness of the sanctuary never
fails to fill my senses and lift my
spirit 'til it soars. An affirmation of
how important even a seemingl small natural
preserve can be to the human spir sense of
connectedness and good health... while an oasis for struggling

URBAN WILDLIFE

Bill Hammond

18

Postmodern *Oïkos*

Phillip Payne

This chapter focuses on the potential of the family household to act as a powerful teaching, learning, and sociopolitical site of environmental education and sustainable development. The ways in which families function in the intimacy of the home provide important pedagogical insights into the ethical and political renewal urged by critics of the current environmentally problematic human condition. To develop these ecologically framed pedagogical insights and their potential for a praxis of an intergenerational environmental ethics and ecopolitics, I focus on aspects of moral, social, and ecological "otherness" allegedly missing in modernity's and postmodernity's accounts of, and complicity in, the socioenvironmental predicament we now unavoidably confront in the "everyday."

The postmodern *Oïkos* anticipated here methodologically revisits aspects of the ancient Greek *Oïkos* (environmental home/economic household, as a dominant mode of material and social relationships) so as to add historical meaning to my recent studies of "green" households (Payne, 2005a, 2005b). Of particular intrigue in these empirical studies is how the home might act "ontologically" as a "primal" and "proximal" site of moral, social, and ecological *being, doing, belonging, dwelling, placing, and becoming*. The *Oïkos* of ancient Greece seems to provide an "ideal" reference point from which to "story" the future via these studies. The privacy and intimacy of (green) family households also seemed to provide for inquiry an exemplary "other" site of ethical and sociopolitical resistances to the consumerist, entertainment, and individualistic imperatives of postmodernity. This complex postmodern configuration is an ontological and epistemological condition in which so many young people are trapped (Kenway & Bullen, 2001), even as they are the next generation in whom we place our hopes for a more sustainable future. Hence, the storying of an *Oïkos* is a pragmatic type of philosophizing that is phenomenological, practical, ethical, and political. It reflexively weaves empirical findings with theoretical development and philosophical musings, and is (re)presented here as a "hybrid paper" (Reid & Scott, 2006, p. 584). Lessons learned from the *Oïkos* about various domestic forms of ecopedagogy and ecopraxis might inform inquiry into, and application in, a wide variety of settings—including in the classroom, work place, community; or in the theorizing of social ecology (Payne, 2005a, 2005b).

The historically based dialogue of the past, present, and future *Oïkos* and their ontological underpinnings ends up involving a less idealized and more critical return to a materialist and political conception of how some classical Greek households might have functioned "ecologically." Reference to the *primal* and *proximal* in restorying (environmental) education picks up on philosophical propositions about the *a priori* status in the family household and its social, moral, and ecological dimensions—offered respectively in the writings of Hannah Arendt, Zygmunt Bauman, and John Sanders, but "read through" the empirical zoom lens of the "best resistance" family ecopedagogies and praxis just mentioned.

POSITIONING THE POSTMODERN OIKOS:
SOME HISTORICAL, CRITICAL, ONTOLOGICAL, AND METHODOLOGICAL SIGNPOSTS

At the heart of this hybrid-like conversation[1] is my interest in identifying the enabling pedagogical and praxical conditions from which desirable ecological subjectivities and physical and psychosocial relations nurturing human agency and environmental praxis might flourish.

The term *postmodernity* is qualified by the notion of globalism in the section titled "Constitutive Abstraction." Postmodernity often refers to a globally dominant, technologically mediated, and economically driven condition where time and place are "collapsed" with a range of implications for who we are, what we know, and how we act and interact. Consumption, materialism, and markets are elevated in significance from their modernist origins, masquerading via hard and soft technologies as virtual templates for the environmentally problematic human condition. The individual, social, and environmental consequences of our current worldviews, ways of life, and knowing are increasingly clear on a wide range of fronts—locally, regionally, nationally, culturally, and globally. Indeed, The Stern Report (2006, p. 1) declares that climate change is "the greatest and widest-ranging market failure ever seen."

Less well appreciated is how postmodernity's various technologies and associated signs, markers, and templates also have a profound ability to make the everyday lifeworld and its dominant forms of socioecological relations and structures far more abstract. Such a nonpresenced lifeworld thus reconstitutes "by stealth" our personhood, the more-than-human world, and the relations between them. Indeed, the basic historical, material, and symbolic conditions of ontology are invisibly shaped, as are our subjectivities, and our social and environmental relationships.

The privacy of family life and the functioning and politic of the household have, ontologically and epistemologically, not escaped these often "invisible" social constructions and, therefore, social formations and arrangements. Most postmodern family members have mobile phones, credit cards, websites, and a range of hard and soft artifacts that, effectively, de/reconstruct "existing" moral and social relations and their invisible forms of interactions and exchange. The emotional costs of postmodernity's trajectories toward the abstraction of ordinary, everyday life, including the relations of family members, are high (Elliott & Lemert, 2006). Environmental education, even in its critical forms, is not immune from the juggernaut of technics, abstractions, extensions, and corrections of what it is to educatively experience the self and relationships with others and these relations to, with, or *for* the world (Payne, 2003).

Rampaging postmodernity presents extraordinarily difficult cultural, intellectual, and personal conditions that underpin the complexity, and perhaps the folly, of imagining a postmodern environmental ethics and storying it via educational policies and practices. Dealing globally and culturally with, for example, climate change (Flannery, 2005) urgently demands a pragmatic, ontologically aware imagining of how traditional, existing forms of social and environmental relationships are changing, as well as the demands placed on, for example, governments and individuals to reduce their greenhouse gas emissions. Consider one family example: The fortified, preservative-rich, perhaps genetically modified or chemicalized, and imported ingredients of one normal dinner eaten by one person in Australia will have collectively "travelled" up to 39,000 km by air, sea, and road to arrive on the dinner plate. Add to this family meal the distance, and environmental/economic costs/risks, then travelled by the disposal of the numerous wastes.

Dealing locally, personally, and more emphatically with the practical ethics of what we eat (Singer & Mason, 2006) also demands an urgent, pragmatic, and embodied reflection about our food and shopping preferences, as well as their social and environmental consequences (Payne, 1997).

The global and local challenges are (de)pressingly formidable. But there are real possibilities found in examining how the everyday household practices of green families can inform the ecopedagogies and ecocurricula that potentially translate to classrooms, school grounds, workplaces. Here, I bring into conversation the resistance work and best practices of green families with a more socially aware, material-driven, less idealized interpretation of the allegedly "noble" ancient Greek *Oïkos,* and the philosophical reinstatement of the moral, social and ecological by Zygmunt Bauman, Hannah Arendt, and John Sanders. One caution: Words, voices, language, texts, and discourses can only ever be mere approximations and, therefore, limited, reductive representations of human experience and agency, be they in empirical findings, theoretical development, or philosophical speculation (Abram, 1996; Lakoff & Johnson, 1999). The "conversation" of this hybrid text is then just that: the typeset and page the reader is currently experiencing, and the remainder of the text consists of the written epistemologies of more elaborate inquiries and understandings about the social ontologies we create and the agencies that flow from them. The conceptual purpose of these epistemologies is to sensitize the reader to the possibilities of further reconstructive work in environmental education.

CONSTITUTIVE ABSTRACTION AND ENVIRONMENTAL RELATIONS

Bearing in mind this textual purpose, but as a springboard for alternative definitions of postmodernity as cultural condition and postmodernism as entailing perspectives on knowledge and truth claims, my preferred entry point into storying a version of postmodern environmental ethics is the socio-ontological vantage point.

I propose here that the conceptions and practices of postmodernity and postmodernism are, inevitably, complicit in the chronic abstraction of the living and nonliving lifeworlds—that these "posts" disembody, disembed, dematerialise, and decontextualize the "world" by reembodying, reembedding, rematerializing, and recontextualizing the subject/object in increasingly more abstract, technologically mediated, "ordered/corrected" and global forms (Payne, 2003). *Globalism* (James, 2006) is a term that seems to capture the flux, exchange, and ambiguity of the terms *postmodernity* and *postmodernism.*

Abstraction of the self and world is the underlying ontological source and consequence of globalism, which serves further to rearrange and disconnect the "I" from the "we" and from a range of environments, including nature. The disconnections of inner, social, and outer natures are, it seems to me, the grist of the educational challenge and quest for revealing postmodern environmental moralities and agencies, along with their social ethics and ecopolitics. Clearly, the modern and postmodern abstractions and mediations of the self, the social, and the lifeworld have some advantages. Abstract theory can also sensitize us to the magnitude and global spread of the problems we now confront everyday. But I conclude that the ontologies of abstraction perpetuate a Cartesian-like severing and separation from the very environments with which we seek to have a more ethical relationship.

There is no advocacy here for "returning to nature" or "nature determinism." Indeed, my interest in a "critical, ecological ontology" focuses on the weak ecocentric notion of education *for being for the environment* as a form of *doing* and *becoming* (Payne, 1997, 2006), as that notion is approached philosophically and historically through the empirical studies of *ecological dwelling.*

The pragmatic quest in this study is to identify, explain, and imagine the sorts of morality, sociability, politic, and ecology that can be found *in situ*, lying dormant in the *Oïkos*.

The constitutive abstraction thesis—drawing upon four decades of theorizing by the Arena Group in Australia (James, 2006; Sharp, 1985)—focuses as much on the ontological formations through which social life is mediated as it does on the epistemological directions pursued in postmodernity that recursively reshape that ontology. This more theoretical thesis provides an alternative conceptual frame for clarifying the increasing messiness of the terms "postmodernity" and "postmodernism" and how they play off each other in obfuscating the environmentally problematic human ontological condition. My primary interests here in trying to (re)present a philosophical, historical, and phenomenological study of the home, as *Oïkos*, are the socio-ontological categories of temporality, spatiality and embodiment. But these categories are not only constituted by globalism's contemporary social conditions and views about knowledge but, indeed, are layered into the present and future by past social forms that live on in various ways—hence the "historicalism" in the storying methodology employed here. Paul James (2006) identifies these ontological formations as *tribalism, traditionalism, modernism*, and *postmodernism*. They layer over each other in ways that might be coherent, dissonant, or contradictory. For example, we continue to "live" time and, therefore, space and place "relations" via "body" time (e.g., circadian rthythms), cosmological time, seasonal time, day/night time, the arrow and linear mechanical/analogical time of modernity, and now the dot/spot/blip time of digitalized postmodernity. Indeed, their lived contradictions and subsequent social and environmental relations may be "unhealthy" and undermine individual, collective, and ecological "well-being." Thus, methodologically speaking, Arendt's account of the ancient Greek *Oïkos* is indicative only of how one ontological social formation around a certain form of temporality from the past partially lives on and informs this theorization of the *Oïkos*. Numerous other studies of families beckon, such as the "luddite" or "Amish" household.

Finally, to bluntly characterize the concept of abstraction and how it is socially framed and ecologically reconstituted, James (2006) views modernity's ontologies of time and space as "empty," whereas the postmodern is viewed as in transition to virtual and relativized "instantaneity" and "beyond space–time"; the ontologies of abstracting time, space, and embodiment can be understood primarily through the social forms in which we live. In "storying" or envisioning an *Oïkos*, we are now mindful that more abstract, empty, virtual, instantaneous modes of living and reimagining environmental relations are progressively layered over the more concrete modes of living and domestic dwelling: in this selective instance, families' "best resistance" practices. In this way, the *Oïkos* offered here should be seen as an attempt to socially and materially reconstitute rather than replace those prior, increasingly abstracting forms.

OÏKOS

Three vantage points are utilized in making additional sense of how the household potentially acts as a positive reconstitutive site for environmental education and sustainable living, and resistance to globalism's deepening objectification, commodification, textualization, and abstraction of self, lifeworld, and environmental relations. Each vantage demands that texts such as this incorporate a stronger sense of the materiality and social relations of the household conditions and resources in which sustainable living is already practiced.

First, "ecology," a key player in the often scientific, sometimes social, quest for a sustainable future, draws from the Greek term *Oïkos,* whose meaning in relation to the *polis* of classical Greece is far more morally, socially, and environmentally complex than what we in environmental education have textually been led to believe. Revisiting a passed human ecology, as I do here in reviewing the troubled private–public relations between the ancient Greek *Oïkos* (or household economy/environmental house) and *polis* (or politicized citizenship) furnishes a useful frame for restorying the postmodern possibility of an ecopedagogy.

Second, a critical foray into the Greek household is instructive. Vincent Pecora (1997) concludes that the *Oïkos* has been characterized as noble and, ironically, given the purposes of this volume of essays, is an "imaginary vision" whose discursive sources can be traced to the modern bourgeois longings for authenticity and social happiness. But here, the tension Pecora sees between the textually re-enchanted premodern *Oïkos* and the overwhelmingly disenchanted but nostalgic present is problematized further. Lisa Nevett (1999) asserts that our knowledge of how Greek families functioned is, indeed, poor. Nevett's "new" archaeology shifts methodologically from a reliance on textual sources only, to a heterogeneous study of the textual, iconographic, and material artifacts of Greek houses, and not only those in the cultural centre of Athens but also in its geographically decentered regional margins. Nevett wants to develop a clearer understanding of how relationships in the household were ordinarily enacted via a range of activities, interactions, artifacts, and material conditions, and how the household practices were routinely located in everyday relation to Greek society.[2]

Third, and in a similar materialist frame and praxical vein as Nevett's, my interpretive studies of a small number of inner-city and rural/regional "green" and "ordinary" families in Australia focus primarily on the environmental actions and inactions, or embodied relational experiences, "lived" use of resources and, hence, individual and collective ecopraxis of family members. These everyday "finding grounds" of individual and family practices inform the following philosophical storying.

GREEN HOUSEHOLDS: A MORAL, SOCIAL, AND ECOLOGICAL OVERVIEW

Of specific interest, therefore, to this empirically driven, historical–materialist, critical–realist, and philosophical work of restorying the idealized premodern *Oïkos* is how the green households studied act as highly intimate, proximal, and participatory sites for family members to embody, construct, frame, and craft versions of environmental ethics and ecopolitics.

These now 45- to 55-year-old "green" parents were exposed and immersed, often unavoidably, in the 1960s and 1970s to a life-changing mix of experiences that remain hugely influential in the way their lives are practiced and reimagined *for,* and *with,* their children, and each *other.* These significant experiences included the post-World War II baby boomers' eventual "escape" to university and free "higher learning" through which other social and political freedoms were expressed in opposition to the Vietnam war; the lifestyles and values attractions of feminist and local environmental politics and issues; the liberalizing lifeworld backdrop of hippies, communal living arrangements, and revolutions in popular music; being exposed to Rachel Carson's (1962) *Silent Spring*; and the nascent global environmental movement. Now "weary," these 50-ish parents struggle consistently and intensely—morally and socially—with the practical difficulties they confront culturally and globally in the abstracted "privacy" of their own households. The different values they commit to, and parenting practices they employ, often sit uncomfortably, even in competition, with those of their peers, their professional demands and roles, and, more generally, work against the dominant social and political templates by which they are abstractly expected to live.

Nonetheless, despite this cultural antagonism and obviously lived dissonance of many of the green parents, most of their "pale green" children were enthused by their parents and inspired to act as *other*, often confidently, in front of a peer and schooling culture that was overtly at odds with, or at best, ambivalent about, the children's and their parents' green interests and commitments. Most of the 10- to 16-year-old children and young adults who participated in these studies proudly accepted their own identity and lifestyle "differences" but also respected, even celebrated, their parents' green differences and family eco-functioning.

Despite these promising cross-generational practices, one speculative conclusion restrains the textual impulse here to imagine too freely a future *Oïkos* unsullied by any account of the prevailing cultural condition and its internally changing ontologies. Here, I remind the reader of the deepening encroachment into daily, "private" life of the symbolic and material sources of the constitutive abstraction thesis outlined earlier.

By and large, these once-activist, green parents were significantly "constrained" as children growing up in the 1950s and 1960s by a complex set of family arrangements, social expectations, and cultural "glue" that sustained depression-era and World War II "scarcity principles" in many households, and in related social arrangements. For example, an ascetic-like, modern "resourcefulness" rather than postmodern "buy-a-fix" consumerism underpinned their families' aspirations for better living conditions and enhanced intergenerational freedoms. Put simply, for the current green parents, their "living within one's means" in the formative years of the 1950s and 1960s were indebted to earlier "scarcity" ways of "grounded/concrete" life (provided by their parents and prevailing cultural context) that they, in turn, "re-traditionalized" or reimagined practically in the 1970s and 1980s due to the changing cultural climate of relative freedom, greater opportunity, and heightened sense of social and environmental angst and purpose. Despite the current postmodern affluence and "postscarcity" entitlement and consumerist framings of the "everyday" in which the current children live, the older scarcity resourcefulness cultural logic so "materially" and "socially" influential to the current green parents remains clearly embodied and framed in the parenting practices they now employ with their 10- to 16-year-olds. That is, in their retraditionalized parenting practices and green households there appears to be a strong dose of resistance to the abstracting trajectories of modernity and postmodernity and its ways of life.

If so, what horizons then exist for these "pale green" children's children, given the intense cultural, conservative, and domestic challenges the current 50-ish green parents experience and anguish about morally, socially, and practically? Such themes are addressed in the discussion of the primal nature of the responsibilities most of these green parents intuit, or have freely chosen, and whose intergenerational consequences for the future can really only be guessed at. How might we dare imagine a future horizon for the children of the current crop of "pale green" children different to the voracious present that the green parents studied here are so troubled by—one that is utterly precarious, risky, fluid, and abstracting in a wide range of familial, social, political, and environmental ways? Here, like the green parents studied, I am very cautious about the prospects for the next generation of pale green parents to live out their green inheritance or legacy. But, until the environmentally problematic human condition is acknowledged morally, socially, and politically, I see a glimmer of hope for environmental educators, researchers, and curriculum theorists/developers in the intergenerational ethic and ecopolitic currently practiced in these green households.

This is an empirical task that is partially revealed here in this philosophical restorying via Arendt, Bauman, and Sanders. Paul Ginsborg (2005) reminds us that families remain *the agents* and *preeminent site* of everyday politics, the emotions, affections, and the construction of opinion. David Herring (2003) invokes an array of evidence about how families, as agents of change, act as a subversive, primary form of association against the state's persistent corporate attempts to reconstruct "privatized" families along neo-liberal economic lines. For Bauman (1997), the "rocky road to justice" (in a world devastated and demoralized by local and global injustices) starts with the beginning of morality in the home, where the immediate proximity of the face-to-face encounter *before anything* is the primal site of morality from one for the other and, according to Bauman, provides the sensitization we need to reflexively think through in formulating a micro, then macro, ethics for more others.

OÏKOS: ARENDT AND THE PRIMACY OF THE SOCIAL

The household persists as one micro-ethical site of face-to-face encounters for family members, be it modern/nuclear, postmodern/blended/same, traditional/extended (Beck-Gernsheim, 2002; Berger, 2002) or arrested (Côté, 2000). There is also an abundant literature about the classical Greek *Oïkos*, which can serve as a reference point for interpreting how postmodern households function, irrespective of their contemporary differences and sheer diversity. In practical terms, the Greek household or "estate" of the fourth and fifth centuries most often discussed in the literature, was a large social arrangement made up of family members, slaves, animals, the house and property, and the various goods produced, consumed, and disbursed (Pomeroy, 1995). The central problematics for Nevett (1999) in understanding the underlying materiality of everyday family functioning of the Greek household are the somewhat misleading assumptions made about the nature of the intra- and interrelationships of the *Oïkos* and the civic body, or *polis*; or, as Arendt (1958) draws our attention to, the tensions between "the public and private realm" that are pursued here in restorying for an *Oïkos*.

Arendt's analysis of the values differentiation of Greek social and political life, and their blurring through to the present and, presumably, the future, is both intriguing and illuminating for those social and, inevitably, moral purposes emphasized here ecologically. A key idea in Arendt's interpretations of Greek life and culture was the *fundamental* status of the "social" in the human condition where active engagement and action, as distinct from individualized labour, was utterly dependent upon the co-presence of others. Arendt's (1958) analysis of social relations in the Greek household (noting the absence in Greek thought for the term *social*) sees these "private" relationships as naturally born of need in that there existed a "special relationship between action and being together" (p. 23). And, although a prescient Arendt does not dwell on the role of the human body in action, she links the demise of the embodied naturalness of the social within the privacy of the *Oïkos* to the (pejorative) rise of necessity, futility, and shame in the home. Effectively, Arendt claims that the body and its sociability, or perhaps, intercorporeality, were placed in the "hiding" of intimacy, subsistence, and the physical survival of the species.

Arendt traces how the rise in Greek political thought could only be achieved at the expense of that which was socially and morally embodied in those domestic realms and natural kinship relations. The "distinct, separate entities" (Arendt, 1958, p. 28) of private and public marginalized the household of material "necessity," while elevating participation in the civic sphere to the abstract realm of "freedom." Once the mundane, everyday *Oïkos* had been mastered by the male property owner, sometimes violently, the political realm was then accessed where that freedom gained and duly exercised inevitably became the "social" basis of "equality."

Axiomatic in Greek thought, according to Arendt, was that household necessity was the driving force of life, and the place for individual maintenance and species development. This "natural community" was essentially a pre-political phenomenon and material condition upon which freedom could be accessed and equally exercised by the (male) property owner, hence the "strict inequality," as Arendt argues, between the division of the private and the public spheres. This is a dualism that practically lingers on despite the "one-sided" ability of politics, markets and technologies to govern and penetrate the household.

Moreover, mindful of the abstraction of the postmodern lifeworld mentioned earlier, Arendt's (1958) account of the disconnection of the *polis* and its preoccupation with worldly human affairs from the *Oïkos* of gritty species survival extends to a discussion of how free speech in the public sphere is "separated off" from everyday action to become the esteemed domain of "words and persuasion." Aristotle's influential emphasis on the supremacy of the contemplative (and beyond speech) *nous*, according to Arendt, further confirms the political and discursive shift to the then public/civil abstraction of human action and free social interaction, and consequently, marginalization of the natural, social life of the *Oïkos*. Not coincidentally, politicians' "spin" and "weasel words" are now a target of (limited) criticism but most evident in the manner in which a number of world leaders have dismissed much of The Stern Report.

Arendt's analysis helps us see a little more clearly the early rise of the supremacy of the *polis* as "a way of life" where "only speech made sense" and the central concern of all (political, male) citizens "was to talk to each other" (p. 27). This division of private *Oïkos* (organic, social, material) and public *polis* (rhetoric, imagery, abstracting) remains a primary factor in the profound misunderstandings that continue to this day about the different natures of the moral-social interfaces of the private sphere and the ethico-political interfaces of the public spheres.

There is a need, as I attempt here, to critically clarify the continued blurring of the *Oïkos* (as a potential social realm of private resistance and moral/material necessity) with and against the de/reconstructive role played morally, socially, and ecologically by globalism's *polis* in "governing" the family according to postmodernity's economic, political, and cultural imperatives. All too often this anti-ecological governing of the household is "re-presented" in terms of a consumer-entertainment-lifestyle "choice" and "freedom" on one hand, and "fear" and "security" on the other.

This contradiction, I argue, provides fertile symbolic and abstracting "grounds" for the probable undermining of human agency and betrayal of action, and a moral "beginning" we hope, *for* the other. Or, in the simplest of terms, this may be why so many young people feel they cannot make a difference despite their increased environmental knowledge and concern (Fien, 2002). Resistance as (re)storying?

> Our approach to environmental parenting is to integrate it (the environment) into everything we do—in health, food, exercising, energy, composting, and so on—because we see the power of the social process we can create in the home and in the way our children grow. (Sarah, 53, partner to Jeff and mother of Rae)

BEING FOR: BAUMAN AND CHOOSING TO BE RESPONSIBLE FOR TAKING RESPONSIBILITY FOR THE OTHER

Arendt's interest in the difficult relationship of private necessity, survival, and sustainability in the *Oïkos* and the *polis* and its claims on freedom and equality invites further, deeper deliberation about a remoralized approach to (environmental) education. If Arendt is even partially correct about the *fundamental* status and household role of the social in the human condition, what primal or basic versions of morality in the intimacy of the household "place" might accompany a renewed sociability in the postmodern? This would be a postmodern morality that does not foreclose on the *other* and our intuitions, responsibilities and "choices" *for* it, including the otherness of the environment.

For Bauman (1993), the notion of "moral proximity" is key to understanding how postmodern ethics might be reimagined, because it is in the intimacy of the self and the other, "in the home," be it metaphorical or literal for Bauman, where morality is born and found.

"Distance" (and, inevitably, alienation and abstraction of social and environmental relations) is, according to Bauman, the "realm of estrangement and the Law."

Questions about the impoverished status of the moral in contemporary globalized cultures and societies have been posed and pursued relentlessly by Bauman (1993, 1995, 1997). More recently, Bauman (2006), in *Liquid Fear*, made his strongest statement yet on the links between postmodernity, morality, and the immediate prospect of the planet becoming unliveable. He sources what he refers to as the "horror of the unmanageable" in the combination of "anthropomorphic fallacy" and "moral lag" in modernity and its subsequent abyss in postmodernity. Bauman is highly critical of the ethics of modernity, its many failed ideals and illusions not grounded in morality, and the consequent emptiness of what now passes as ethics in postmodernity. Moral and ethical problems abound and, he argues, cannot escape the dilution of principle, fragmentation of known social contexts, including the family, and the increasingly episodic, mediated, and abstracted nature of multiple, often contradictory human experiences.

Bauman addresses this moral opportunity and ethical void by advancing the idea of "being for." This draws its inspiration and radical force from Emmanuel Lévinas' (1985) postulate of "before anything" *I* am framed for the service, self-sacrifice, and good of the *other*, where no senses of the we, as accumulations of the I, or reciprocity, are implied. For Lévinas, *being for* is pre-ontological. *Being for* is clearly at odds with the "me-ism" that authors other than Bauman align with modern possessive individualism and the rise of postmodern aesthetic individualism (e.g., McCarthy, 1991). But it is also at odds with directly related criticisms via the thesis of constitutive abstraction of the ideology of autonomy, the consumerist pursuit of "freedom," and their concomitant privileging of subjectivity(ies), all of which, unhesitatingly, are reconstitutive of the ecological problematic and its ontologizing of the risky, fearful, and precarious human condition.[3]

The notion of *being for* is still practically and anthropocentrically visible in, for example, that unconditional love many parents express for their children, day-in, day-out, in the home. Hence Arendt's philosophical scaffold here, alongside my interpretive studies of green parents and their children. That is, the primal and proximal "unconditionality" and intuiting of the moral (and, therefore, social) relationship we preconsciously and prediscursively embody, and existentially enact, of parental love *to* and responsibility *for* a child irrespective of any anticipation of moral and/or social reciprocity from that other signals the moral possibility *before anything* of *being for* the other. And, again, we sometimes do see that moral intuition or instinct of *being for* in the unambiguous biocentric (or organismic) caring often demonstrated by family members for the family pet.[4] This intuitive or organic type of "egalitarian" morality *for* the intrinsic worth of the other begins to elaborate the underpinnings of Arendt's *a priori* of the social in the necessity of the *Oikos*, and a renewed hope in our own postmodern *being* of a moral sensitisation or impulse *for* the ecological. But, to be sure, this proximal moral space is ambivalent and, according to Bauman (1993) is "torn apart by the impulse to stay and the impulse to escape" (p. 89).

Noteworthy, at this moral point of ambivalence, are findings from the study of green households on how many of the parents made choices about their (dis)engagement in public (social and environmental) politics. Most mothers, and some fathers, retreated to the privacy and intimacy of the domestic realm (Payne, 2005a, 2005b). This retreat to another version of Christopher Lasch's (1995) "haven in a heartless world," despite the encroaching abstraction constituting its membership, was primarily due to family circumstances in which hard moral, social, professional, and financial choices and priorities were made about the sustainability of a family way of life, particularly after the arrival of the first child.[5] Invariably, however, this initial retreat was followed by the parental reimagining and democratic development of the lived household ecopolitic/postmodern *Oikos* outlined earlier. Significantly, the majority of mothers participating in the studies relished the prospect of returning their temporarily withdrawn labours and commitments (eco/social) in the private, domestic realm of *Oïkos* politics to the public, activist *polis* realm in the not-too-distant future. But the family, in the first, proximal, face-to-face instance, had clearly taken moral and social priority.

Bauman (1993) is passionate about a "return" to the pre-ontological primal and proximal moral space. He raises the question of when "knowledge" from the other, or "third party," following Lévinas, intervenes that there are demands "I make it (the moral intuition) speak" (p. 90). Not only do we here encounter the problem of the "naming" of a pre-ontological intuiting of what might stand as a remoralized version of "inner nature," Bauman proceeds to the serious question raised by Arendt about "social nature" when he dwells inordinately on the "agony" *of choosing to be responsible for taking responsibility for the other*. And perhaps, we see some real evidence of a partial reconciliation between inner (moral) and social (ethical) natures in the "unconditional" manner "practised" in the retraditionalized postmodern everyday *Oïkos* outlined above. According to Bauman, choosing knowingly to be responsible for the other precedes any socially constructed modern ethical theories, many of which he claims are "blind alleys" (p. 2). Hence, the chronic agony and loneliness for the (potentially) postmodern moral agent (parent, teacher), whose "pain" for most of us has been made far easier with fewer moral choices due to modernity's legislating and substituting of ethical law for the pre-ontological but proximal moral spacing of *being for the other*.

> She's our only daughter and we had her late. We want her to have a strong sense of her self—a mix of values, ethics, equity, and spirituality—as a precondition to encountering the mixed difficulty we live in. (Jeff, 53)

Ecological Affordances; Sanders and "First Philosophy"

Sanders' account of the "ontological primitive" of an ecological approach to the observer's perception of affordances links indirectly with the pre-ontological form of moral intuition and choosing of responsibility for the *other* outlined earlier. Together, the social line of moral thinking I have drawn between Arendt, Lévinas, and Bauman now invites clarification of the term *other*, and responsibility for it, given the chronic rehearsal in the academy of that very open term whose openness potentially invokes anthropocentric assumptions, or becomes meaningless in its propensity to abstraction. At risk is the potential in the *other* and *otherness* for emptying, hollowing, and flattening of any ecocentric aspirations in retraditionalizing and restorying education and, reconciliation, even partial, of inner, social, and outer "natures."

Sanders draws heavily upon the influential works of Maurice Merleau-Ponty in phenomenological philosophy and J. J. Gibson in ecological psychology. Each play formidable roles in dismantling the subject–object and, in different ways, mind–body binaries and, therefore, I–world separation—that notorious Cartesian dualism (and associated values such as hierarchical thinking) that many suggest lay at the positivist heart of the human-over-nature sourcing of the ecological crisis and environmentally problematic human condition.

Following the deconstruction of the foundational truth of a hard subject-object distinction, we might well query, as does Sanders (1999), what version(s) of truth about "knowing" and "coming to know," or "epistemological primacy," are contained in, and conceived by, the mind–body and subject–object (re)connections. The "primitive" with which Sanders was concerned is the constellation and multiplicity of affordances, or attunements and opportunities for action available to the observer from within the environment. Affordances are "rich" in the *othered* perceptual possibilities offered to the actor *in "can do" relation* to that perceptual horizon. For an everyday example, the same river will be perceived as a social construction quite differently by the artist, the farmer, the engineer, the kayaker and the prime minister. This constellation and multiplicity of rich environmental possibilities and affordances of otherness, it seems to me, is conceptually (and practically) consistent with the choices, ambivalence, and agony of the moral agent that Bauman so passionately pursues in his persuasive account of reclaiming the primal moral place of *being for* and, consequently, the existential predicament of *choosing to take responsibility for being responsible*. The rich multiplicity of the *ecological otherness* of the *other* of the observed environment, it seems to me, *affords* the elusive ecological subjectivity and morality *from* which environmental educators might educate *for*.

And, it is at this juncture that I must gesture to literature that seriously addresses the *other* as including the *wild*, or vice-versa. For example, Gary Snyder's (1999) chapter on "the etiquette of freedom" is a poetic example in the English-speaking world of the much admired nature writing genre in North America that draws upon the inspirational insights of Ralph Waldo Emerson, Henry David Thoreau, John Muir, Aldo Leopold, Barry Lopez, and so on. Snyder, still confined by language and its severing from the depths of human experience, including the potentially pre-ontological and intuited morality and sense of sociability argued for above, invites a far more ecocentric play on the meanings of the terms like wild, nature, wildness, wilderness, as they are inner, social, and outer. Robert Briggs' (2001) philosophical deconstruction of environmental ethics highlights how "wild" thoughts are part of the missing otherness required in a reconstructed environmental ethics.

Sanders, like Merleau-Ponty and Gibson, is critical of that notion of affordances which implies a singular and often exploitative response by the *subject*, conditioned by culture (and embodied, invariably through instrumental reason), to the *object* of perception in the environment. Irrigators in dry, parched Australia do see rivers as unidimensional and profitable, notwithstanding the continent's well-known history and the "new" facts about climate change and its consequences. The barrage of possibilities available to the observer before that cultural conditioning not only opens up for the perceiver the wild otherness of the othered wild, as indicator of "nature," but effectively dismantles the mind–body and subject–object binaries conceived and predicted by the subject in behavioural responding to the environment's objectification and culture's denaturing of nature and taming of the wild. For example, the kayaker does not necessarily need to respond via particular performative skills such as pirouetting to prominent "storied" expectations of parts of a "river" in such a way that demonstrates his or her competence or expertise, or kudos. Here, a range of other environmental or perceptual affordances are "backgrounded" instrumentally to the "use and exploit" mentality, even if pirouetting is a relatively harmless action. Likewise in the postmodern *Oïkos* of the green household. Some families grew their own vegetables; one family chose to make its own bread because at least 200 plastic bags would be saved each year. Otherness and wildness were played out practically, ecocentrically, and socially in the domestic politic of the privacy of the home. Parents and families "chose" to resist the penetration of abstraction and consumerism.

The richness of river (including its othered "woundedness"[6]), its constitution and proximal and temporal surroundings can be experienced perceptually and in action in a multiplicity of ways by the *observer* using different media of embodied movement, less framed by, for example, the "ecological" footprints of culture and its technics (Payne, 2003). Likewise, for the reimagined *Oïkos* developed here, even as a socially constructed cultural artefact, its "green" materiality, creates the perceptual, relational, conceptual, and actional conditions of "otherness" of the socioecological type we are here keen to (re)present materially and socially, following Nevett's archaeological methodology.

Clearly, Sanders, and others want to ecologically reclaim embodied agency and its "primacy of practice" (Archer, 2000), for which "other" perceptions, sensibilities, affordances, and subjectivities are important. Sanders' first philosophy of an ecology of affordances stresses the fundamental character of what might best be termed an intercorporeal ecological agency about the way in which "worlds could be at all" (Sanders, 1999, p. 135). This is according to a much richer environmental *sensibility* in education about what, perceptually and conceptually, we *can do* (Payne, 2005d).

Ecology understood in this agential and perceptual manner—the constellation and multiplicity of affordances richly available in the environment to the reattuned wild observer—differs markedly from most conceptions of ecology and the environment by which we have become discursively and textually trapped, including what is represented in and by environmental education and its research. If my analysis is correct, Sanders' conception of an ecology of affordances is highly suggestive of the multiplicity or "wild otherness" of the other Bauman morally believes we might agonizingly choose in taking responsibility for that other. Strikingly prescient to the thought of Bauman and Sanders, Leopold (1966) observes that the promotion of perception is the only truly creative part of recreational engineering, that the outstanding characteristic of perception is that it entails no consumption and no dilution of any resource, and that it depends for its ecological qualities on the moral eye of the beholder.

> I love seeing wildlife like paddymelons and bandicoots but it is hard to describe nature because it was here before we came along. Humans are nature but it depends on different meanings— like the nature who you are, what you are like and nature as wildlife and animals, which I like. (Rae, 11, daughter of Sarah and Jeff)

THE MORAL, SOCIAL AND ECOLOGICAL PRIMACIES OF WILDLY IMAGINING ENVIRONMENTAL EDUCATION, AND ITS RESEARCH

Sanders, Merleau-Ponty, and Gibson textually sensitize us to the "otherness" of the others that Bauman morally believes in our responsibility *for,* beginning "in the home," and which Arendt sees socially in the *a priori* of the Greek household. That *other* has been opened up to its wildness or, for a more ecocentric (re)storying of education, we might well consider how the other is a dimension of wildness. The empirically qualified postmodern *Oïkos* outlined here aims not to be an othered, wild imaginary bequeathed by ideology, nor a textual exercise in seductive mythmaking. Rather, this pragmatic, hybrid, "grounded philosophy" of the *Oïkos* is offered as an intellectual resource[7] that serves to reawaken the social, moral, political, and ecological impulses that, possibly, are primal to the human condition but, probably, have been subjugated. The morally "humanist" choice and agony Bauman lays at our hearts and minds in *taking responsibility* for the other summons us all, be it as a parent, teacher, political leader, or plain old citizen. It summons because of the chronic problematics of the ethics of modernity and postmodernity that betray the moral and social story told here *for* educators, parents, and colleagues who agonize about their responsibilities and intuitions for the other, and all of which, when abstraction takes over, are anthropocentrically complicit in reconstituting the crisis-like environmentally problematic human condition.

Finding our morality, storying it, and making Bauman's choice an ecostory and pedagogical reality will not be an easy one, as the "green" parents and their "pale green" children demonstrate all too clearly in their intergenerational and agonizing efforts to resist dominant culture in being for each other and for the environment. Finding or retrieving, let alone consciously making, this choice about moral responsibilities, social, community, and environmental relations is, presumably, not for all who individually have, or confess to having, too much to lose. But, despite all of the cultural opposition these green parents and their children experience, ecopedagogically and ecopraxically in the home, but also at school and at work, we might well learn from their agential senses of purpose, engagement, resourcefulness, sheer mettle, and wild action. To story the home as a wild form of moral, social, and environmental relation will make it much easier to restory a postmodern *Oïkos* in education whose practical and theoretical gesture here is to an embodied, concrete, less individualized, and less abstract form of individual and collective eco-*being, doing, belonging, dwelling, placing and becoming* in a wider variety of places and spaces.

NOTES

1. Studies of the contemporary household practices of sustainable living and their preferred ecopedagogies have largely remained invisible in the social sciences, including environmental education inquiry, health promotion research, and family studies (Payne, 2005a, 2005b). Ray Ballantyne, John Fien, and Jan Packer (2001) examine how environmental lessons learned at school are translated into household understandings and practices.

2. Nevett concludes that her new archaeological methodology provides for a broader geographical perspective; that textual-only sources are often misleading and sometimes grossly oversimplify important complex matters that, in this instance, reify static models and accounts of the *Oïkos*.

3. The critique of individualism, individuation processes, subjectivity, and ideology of autonomy is well established. Less clear is its intensification in a globalized "economy," including "emotional" consequences that compound the chronic abstraction of the individual and his or her social conditions and environmental relations (James, 2006; Sharp, 1985).

4. Bauman (1993) sees deficiencies in notions like "being with" and "being aside" by drawing on Levinas' view that morality is before ontology, for precedes with, and both are before epistemology. Interestingly, the preposition *for* (the environment) in environmental education has generated considerable debate for reasons different to the empirically qualified restorying of a postmodern *Oïkos*. If imaginable, that debate might need revisiting and restorying along the moral, social, political, and ecological "lines" proposed here.

5. The highly educated parents consistently reported earning far less than their professional potential or that of their peers. One partner, mostly the mother, stayed at home, out of need/necessity for the child, following Arendt, but also as a consequence of democratic decision making in the home (contra the patriarchal *Oïkos*). Some mothers and fathers worked part time. One systematically "re"fathered himself to deconstruct his own father's negative legacy about parenting practices. Many families shunned material goods, in particular electronic forms of home entertainment creating considerable parental anguish that, surprisingly to me, was far less evident in the children studied.

6. I am indebted to my colleague, Dr. Brian Wattchow, for this term but moreso for the sustained practical and intellectual work he has undertaken in phenomenologically studying and poetically representing the ecopedagogies of river places.

7. For a "mapping" of an intercorporeal/ecocentric approach to methodology and inquiry, see Payne (2005c).

REFERENCES

Abram, D. (1996). *The spell of the sensuous: Perception and language in a more-than-human world.* New York: Vantage.

Archer, M. (2000). *Being human: The problem of agency.* Cambridge, UK: Cambridge University Press.

Arendt, H. (1958). *The human condition.* Chicago: The University of Chicago Press.

Ballantine, R., Fien, J., & Packer, J. (2001). School environmental education programme impacts upon student and family learning: A case study analysis. *Environmental Education Research, 7*(1), 23–38.

Bauman, Z. (1993). *Postmodern ethics.* Oxford, UK: Blackwell.

Bauman, Z. (1995). *Life in fragments: Essays in postmodern morality.* Oxford, UK: Blackwell.

Bauman, Z. (1997). *Postmodernity and its discontents.* Cambridge, UK: Polity Press.

Bauman, Z. (2006). *Liquid fear.* Cambridge, UK: Polity Press.

Beck-Gernsheim, E. (2002). *Reinventing the family: In search of new lifestyles.* Cambridge, UK: Polity Press.

Berger, B. (2002). *The family in the modern age: More than a lifestyle choice.* New Brunswick, NJ: Transaction Books.

Briggs, R. (2001). Wild thoughts: A deconstructive environmental ethics. *Environmental Ethics, 23*(2), 115–134.

Carson, R. (1962). *Silent spring.* Boston: Houghton Mifflin.

Côté, J. (2000). *Arrested adulthood: The changing nature of maturity and identity.* New York: New York University Press.

Elliott, A., & Lemert, C. (2006). *The new individualism: The emotional costs of globalization.* London: Routledge.

Fien, J. (2002). Australia. In J. Fien, D. Yencken, & H. Sykes (Eds.), *Young people and the environment: An Asia-Pacific perspective* (pp. 103–114). Dortrecht, Netherlands: Kluwer.

Flannery, T. (2005). *The weather makers: The history & future impact of climate change.* Melbourne: Text Publishing.

Ginsborg, P. (2005). *The politics of everyday life: Making choices changing lives.* New Haven, CT: Yale University Press.

Herring, D. (2003). *The public family: Exploring its role in democratic society.* Pittsburgh: University of Pittsburgh Press.

James, P. (2006). *Globalism, nationalism, tribalism: Bringing theory back in.* London: Sage.

Kenway, J., & Bullen, E. (2001). *Consuming children: Education-entertainment-advertising.* Buckingham, UK: Open University Press.

Lakoff, G., & Johnson, M. (1999). *Philosophy in the flesh: The embodied mind and its challenge to western thought.* New York: Basic Books.

Lasch, C. (1995). *Haven in a heartless world: The family besieged.* New York: Norton & Co.

Leopold, A. (1966). *A sand county almanac: With essays on conservation from round river.* New York: Ballantine Books.

Lévinas, E. (1985). *Ethics and infinity: Emmanuel Lévinas; conversations with Philippe Nemo* (Richard A. Cohen, Trans.). Pittsburgh: Duquesne University Press.

McCarthy, T. (1991). *Ideals and illusions: On reconstruction and deconstruction in contemporary critical theory.* Cambridge, MA: MIT Press.

Nevett, L. (1999). *House and society in the ancient Greek world.* Cambridge, UK: Cambridge University Press.

Payne, P. (1997). Embodiment and environmental education. *Environmental Education Research, 3*(2), 133–153.

Payne, P. (2003). Postphenomenological enquiry and living the environmental condition. *Canadian Journal of Environmental Education, 8,* 169–190.

Payne, P. (2005a). Families, homes and environmental education. *Australian Journal of Environmental Education, 21,* 81–95.

Payne, P. (2005b). Growing up green. *Journal of the Home Economics Institute of Australia, 12*(3), 2–12.

Payne, P. (2005c). Lifeworld and textualism: Reassembling the researcher/ed and "others." *Environmental Education Research, 11*(4), 413–431.

Payne, P. (2005d). "Ways of doing" learning, teaching and researching: Coherence, congruence and commensurability. *Canadian Journal of Environmental Education, 10,* 108–124.

Payne, P. (2006). Environmental education and curriculum theory. *Journal of Environmental Education, 37*(2), 25–35.

Pecora, V. (1997). *Households of the soul.* Baltimore: The Johns Hopkins University Press.

Pomeroy, S. (1995). *Xenophon: Oeconomicus—a social and historical commentary.* Oxford, UK: Clarendon Press.

Reid, A., & Scott, W. (2006). Researching education and the environment: Retrospect and prospect. *Environmental Education Research, 12*(3–4), 571–587.

Sanders, J. (1999). Affordances: An ecological approach to first philosophy. In G. Weiss & H. Fern Haber (Eds.), *Perspectives on embodiment: The intersections of nature and culture* (pp. 121–142). New York: Routledge.

Sharp, G. (1985). Constitutive abstraction and social practice. *Arena, 70,* 48–83.

Singer, P., & Mason, J. (2006). *The ethics of what we eat.* Melbourne: Text Publishing.

Snyder, G. (1999). *The Gary Snyder reader: Prose, poetry, and translations.* New York: Counterpoint.

Stern, N. (2006). *The economics of climate change.* Cambridge, UK: Cambridge University Press.

Morphing Geography
Nora Timmerman
Bill Timmerman

My father sees trees as flames. He sees cities as concentrations of energy with buildings rising and popping like bubbles as if the surface of the earth itself was boiling. Speeding up time so that every day equals 1 second, the rate at which trees and buildings rise and fall, flutter and grow, becomes such that forests and cities appear to be hot spots, burning and boiling. His philosophy, his thinking about the world, is intricately linked to the surface of the earth and a geological perspective on time. Sitting at home in the soft yellow light of his reading lamp, we would talk together for hours about these essentially unanswerable questions . . . What is this world that we live in? What is time? If we change our perspective on the world, how does that alter our understandings of what it means to be human, or what our individuality, actions, or values are?

Exploring different regions and places over time, I would return to the images of the flame and the boil, intrigued by the vast array of possibilities in which to view this planet. Sitting atop an exposed monocline, looking down at the valley below, I could see the rolling mountains as waves. Traveling down a cold, fast-moving river, I heard the grinding of rocks and could sense the rivers as knives and canyons as wounds on the surface of the earth.

Though they began years ago when I lived at home, these discussions with my father continue still now—he with his reading lamp, and I with my own. Lately, our questions explore the tensions and synergies that exist between a geologic perspective on time and so-called "real" issues such as poverty, desertification, extinction, and so on. I find myself asking, "while we sit here and muse on the relationships between time and the surface of the earth, who is suffering, dying, going extinct?"

Surely there are many. Yet, in the face of this suffering, I believe that this questioning does *do* something. Exactly how, why, or for whom I will never entirely understand. But, as time goes on, the discussions recur and the questions remain. We continue to ask, What *is* this world that we live in? I don't know, but how can we imagine it?

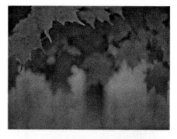

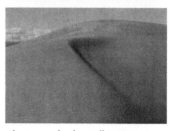

Photographs by Bill Timmerman
(from top: Sugar Maple,
Pennsylvania, 1978;
Monroe & La Salle,
Chicago, 2003;
Dune, Death Valley, 1998)

19

Being Here Together

Lucie Sauvé

Accomplishing such a basic but difficult and ever-renewed task as *Being humans on Earth*[1] fully and ethically, within our shared *Oïkos*, our place of belonging, caring, struggling, and becoming, would seem to be the ultimate goal of environmental education—or *environment-related education* (the generic expression adopted by Paul Hart, 2003).[2] We are embodied[3], localized, contextually grounded beings. Thus, "being" cannot be separated from "here." "Being" is constructed in and by the "here," at the same time as "being" transforms the places we inhabit. And being human is essentially a collective journey—dwelling in places together, weaving our cultures through dreaming, desiring, striving, constructing our environments, searching for meaning, and enacting values. Education is an ontological, cultural, and ethical process. It is about being here together, becoming fully human, consciously and meaningfully connected to our ecological world, expanding otherness to include the world beyond what is human. Education is environmental because "being" and "here" are intertwined realities. Environmental education is praxical because being human implies inhabiting (or acting in and on) a place, experiencing and transforming the milieu, interacting with other living beings, and reflecting on these interactions. Environmental education is political because it concerns togetherness in the *Oïkos*, our common "house of life," on a local community scale and in larger spaces of solidarity.

This vision of environmental education is grounded in an "ecology of time," where "being here" is situated "now" in a cyclical vision of past, present, and future. It is far different from instrumental and future-driven proposals. As is the case for all conceptions of environmental education, there is a need to define and discuss the foundations and implications. If we consider the rich spectrum of diverse theoretical and practical currents that researchers and educators—and researcher-educators—have developed in the last forty years in the field of environment-related education, bearing witness to the different and complementary ways of viewing and striving to enhance our relation to the environment (Sauvé, 2005), it is clearly very difficult to define environmental education without being limited to a specific and possibly reductionist vision. There are also so many perspectives and dimensions to take into consideration that any definition would remain necessarily incomplete. In the interests of stimulating pedagogical discussion and seeking relevance and coherence in the act of education, it is important for each educator to attempt to clarify how he or she views the juncture between education and the environment and coherently translate that into practice. I present here my own ever-evolving proposal, constructed through a dialogical trajectory with reflective and thought-provoking companions—colleagues, friends, and inspiring authors.

HUMAN-ENVIRONMENT RELATIONSHIP EDUCATION[4]

What is called the *environment* in this view of environmental education is not merely a topic to be studied, nor is it a theme among others, or an "organizer" for disciplinary didactics. Nor is it nothing more than a set of problems to be solved or resources to be managed. It certainly cannot be reduced to a simple condition for sustainable development. The woven fabric of the environment can be understood to be the network of life itself, at the juncture between nature and culture. The environment serves as the crucible where our identity is forged through our relations of otherness, via our relation to the world as beings within nature, living among the living. Encompassing education "about," "on," "in," "by," "through," "with," or "for" the environment, the specific object of environmental education is our relation to the environment.

Given the importance of this relationship, environmental education should be considered as an essential dimension of core education. It concerns our relation to the living milieu, or our shared "house of life." At the personal level, environmental education opens pathways to the development of an "ecological identity" (as defined by Thomashow, 1995), or a sense of our being in the world as part of the living milieu, thereby fostering a culture of belonging and commitment. At the community level and in expanded solidarity networks, it aims to mobilize and support social dynamics that adopt a collaborative and critical approach to socioecological realities, along with autonomous and creative problem solving and project development. Through holistic environmental education, the relationship to the environment becomes a reflexive, personal, and social project of self-construction, and of reconstructing our world through meaningful action.

Because the central object of learning is "being here together," environmental education implies a strong social dimension and a critical engagement. Such engagement refers to the deconstruction of accepted ideas, common places, dogmas, stereotypical language and power relations. This gives rise to "a fresh rethinking of the conventional" and is a condition to "foster thinking in new ways" (Burbules & Berke, 1999). A critical education thus invites us to reconstruct our own frames of reference, thereby reconstructing ourselves as individuals and as societies. Such an environmental education inspires the courage to recognize and take advantage of our "spaces" of freedom, and it would call for responsibility. Here, responsibility is not restricted to a legalistic, civic view of rights and duties, but rather a responsibility to be, know, relate, and act—requiring lucidity, authenticity, solicitude, and commitment.

Environmental education is an essentially political (but not politicized[5]) participatory process. To embrace the political dimension one takes part in the social and environmental realities that concern us all (Gutiérrez, 2002). Such education occurs *through* participation in a sociopolitical project—a creative and constructive project whose goal is to improve our living environment and contribute to individual and social transformation through involvement in shared action. We need to construct hope without naiveté.

As virtuous as that may appear at first glance, environmental education cannot be considered an instrument at the service of a universal and exogenous political-economic program responding to a predetermined vision of the world. A preferred approach is to deploy such education in a space of freedom and social criticism, with no ideological constraints. Our relationship to the environment is not *a priori* a matter of social compromise, historically negotiated by certain politically influential social actors. Neither can it be determined by a pseudo-planetary consensus. Environmental education primarily accompanies and supports the emergence and implementation of a project to improve our own relation to the world, whose contextually grounded meaning it helps to construct. From a global perspective, this contributes to the development of responsible societies. I am attempting here to clarify the deliberate vagueness that surrounds the word *development*, which generally refers to the growth of an exogenous economy where the environment is nothing more than a set of resources. The idea of "development of responsible societies" explicitly connects development with societies, each of them integrating an endogenous, culturally meaningful economy. Clearly, deeper than the equivocal and too often minimalist ethic of sustainable development ("provided that it lasts!") responding to the current "security crisis," an endogenous and integrated development promotes an ethic of responsibility.

Arising from an intense awareness that the breach between humans and nature is closely connected to the breach between humans—within and between societies—environmental education is an opportunity for educators to renew its basic pledge to contribute to the development of responsible societies. Such a pledge makes a deeper commitment to addressing ecological issues as they relate to poverty, social exclusion and inequities, health, abuse of power, overconsumption, and other social dysfunctions.

THREE COMPLEMENTARY PERSPECTIVES

The conception of environmental education articulated in this chapter comprises the confluence of three complementary perspectives that respond to three intertwined issues (Table 19.1): the degradation of life-support systems (the visible portion of the iceberg of socioecological disorders, which is rapidly increasing), the loss of meaning and sense of belonging, which induces an autistic regard toward the rest of our living world, and the lack of relevant education with which to face contemporary socioecological realities and effect transformation.

Table 19.1. Three Complementary Perspectives in Environmental Education

Perspective	Main Issue	Nature of Environmental Education	Focus
Socioecological	Degradation of life systems and and depletion of resources. Disparity of access to resources.	A strategy to promote environmental problem solving and management and eco-development.	The quality of the environment as a living milieu. The quality of life for human populations Empowerment in/for critical action.
Educational	A deep rupture between humans and nature, related to the many forms of rupture between humans and within and between societies.	An integrating and fundamental dimension of a holistic educational project. A life-long journey of personal and social development in relation to the environment.	The quality of being, at the individual and social levels. The achievement of an ecological self: belonging, resilience, care, and involvement.
Pedagogical	The inadequacy of the usual teaching–learning processes to construct environmental, transformative learning.	A contribution to a more relevant educational process to enhance our relation to the environment.	The quality of education through the ecologization of schools and curricula. The development of an eco-pedagogy.

A Socioecological Concern

The first issue is most frequently raised when addressing environmental issues. Socioecological concerns focus on the growing degradation of life systems as a result of our irresponsible ways of being here (acting here), our manner of occupying lands and overexploiting "natural resources," which become depleted and spoiled. The earth is not properly inhabited; it is abused for the benefit of a minority. For a growing number of human populations, this degradation is evidenced by problems with food security, access to drinking water, health, major risks, population displacement, uncertainty, and poverty. Here, environmental education is associated with problem-solving processes (a reactive approach) and eco-development projects (a proactive approach). This approach emphasizes the adoption of an ecosystemic vision of reality, and the rigorous construction of valid knowledge to induce relevant action. At the individual level, the notion of ecocivism is enriched when the objective of "behavioral change" (related to social desirability or reflex) is expanded to the "adoption of responsible conduct" (i.e., deliberate, grounded, coherent acting). At the collective level, we find the design and implementation of community projects and/or expanded solidarity initiatives.

This first perspective—of a socioecological order—is associated with action, with learning in and for a critical, environmental action that aims to transform, through an empowerment process, the problematic realities of our living environments, along with the people that live in them (as explained by Ian Robottom, 2003). This perspective has been adopted mainly by environmentalists and ecologists who are aware of the important contribution of education. Environmental education is considered a strategy of the highest order—a factor for social change that stimulates, upholds, and supports other types of intervention that respond to the need to survive and promote the quality of life (e.g., laws and regulations, economic incentives, technological innovations, land management, etc.). We must learn to conserve and construct healthy environments for ourselves and the other beings in our shared living milieu. We need to recognize the close links between the "development" modes of our societies and the quality of the environment, learning to cope with the silent stranglehold of large and small powers, globalization and the agents of world economization. The link between environment and consumption—the universe of "ownership," or owning as a way of being—appears to be at the heart of the current socioecological issues.

An Educational Project

The second and more basic issue is less frequently or explicitly considered in environmental education: the alienation of people and societies from their living environments and their ecological identities. There is a rupture with nature, with the living environment, with one's own human "nature," and between humans and societies. "Being" is isolated from "here," and there is no togetherness. We most often behave as individualistic users, consumers of the environment, "residents," says David Orr (1992), rather than "inhabitants." Here, environmental education is given an educational perspective adopted by educators concerned with our relation to the environment: It becomes an integrating and fundamentally holistic educational project. Through such education, we contribute to major cultural change and toward a culture of belonging and commitment. Here, environmental education is ontogenic: learning to be here together, fully and ethically.

A Pedagogical Process

Environmental education also responds to a pedagogical issue. The usual pedagogical conditions are characterized by disciplinary compartmentalization, learner heteronomy, and school isolation *vis-à-vis* the realities of the environment, among others. Such a context is not favorable to an education whose objectives are the construction of meanings for our human project of "being here together," the critical appropriation of relevant knowledge, and the development of a willingness and ability to act—which would empower youth and social groups to imagine and achieve socioecological changes within their own environments and effectively participate in larger social movements. From a pedagogical perspective, most often adopted by educators working in formal contexts, environmental education is perceived as a contribution to a more relevant global educational process. By means of a contextually and culturally adapted, holistic, meaningful, and coherent curriculum, we can stimulate the transformation of teaching and learning towards an "ecological epistemology" (i.e., integrating different modes and types of learning and adopting a dialogical process). Such a transformation calls for the participation of the different actors in the "educational community" and the larger "educational society" (Orellana, 2001). We can adopt cooperative, experiential, and reflexive processes that stimulate the development of dynamic qualities (the spirit of initiative, autonomy, commitment to a cause, and the ability to assume one's responsibility, according to Peter Posch, 1991; Michela Mayer, 2003), as well as action competencies (Jensen & Schnack, 1997), so that we might properly inhabit our shared world. From this perspective, "teaching" the environment is certainly not sufficient. There is a need to pursue the construction of an ecopedagogy (*Institut d'éco-pédagogie*, 1997), whereby the learners are accompanied in the global development of their cognitive, sensorial, sensual, affective, spiritual, and physical potentialities through (and for) holistic environmental encounters.

Finally, from a pedagogical perspective, the ecologization of schools and curricula is an essential condition in achieving a coherent and efficient environmental education: The context and processes themselves are learning vectors.[6] As Francisco Gutiérrez (2002) asks, for example, is it not true that we learn to cooperate better within cooperative processes? Similarly, the context (interior design and landscaping, daily practices, the human relationship atmosphere, etc.) carries implicit messages. Immersion in a specific context has a substantial and significant impact that must be recognized.

These three perspectives—socioecological (centered on the integrity of life systems, including human), educational (centered on personal and social "ecological" development), and pedagogical (centered on the relevant teaching and learning processes of an emergent ecopedagogy)—are essentially intertwined and complementary. These are inseparable for a comprehensive understanding of environmental education. However, it seems that the second perspective—the educational one— has been less explored or explicit. There is a need to shed light on the key role that relation to the environment plays in education—the *educere*—for the development of people and social groups. The following section attempts to clarify this role with a rationale for the integration of environmental education as an essential element of a core curriculum. The educational perspective justifies the key cross-curricular role of environmental education within educational projects in the school context, and imparts richer meaning to non-formal education processes.

ENVIRONMENTAL EDUCATION AS AN ONTOGENIC PROCESS

From a socioecological perspective, environmental education can enhance the quality of the environment, of our living conditions. But from an educational perspective, it is more fundamentally concerned with the "quality of being" manifested in people and social groups with respect to their relation to the environment. Educating means accompanying individuals as they actualize their own potential, and helping them become unique beings in the world, able to interact with other humans and the beyond-human world in a healthy and constructive way. In other words, it means helping them learn to "be here together." If we do not take the relationship to the environment into account, the educational process remains incomplete and we remain unfulfilled beings.

Here the environment is certainly not just a context, scenery or set of manageable "resources." It consists of all levels of being and manifestation. It corresponds to one of the three interactive spheres at the basis of personal and social development (concentric and interrelated spheres: Fig. 19.1). Closely related to the sphere of relation to oneself (construction of self-identity) and the sphere of human relationships (development of the relationship to human otherness) is the sphere of relationship to the environment, the beyond-human world. This third sphere is the one of interaction with *Oïkos* (from which "eco-" is derived), our matrix of life, both fragile and resilient. Environmental education focuses precisely on this third sphere of interaction, and is properly mindful that it cannot be separated from the other two.

The Psychosphere

The central sphere is the locus of the identity construction where the person develops through self-confrontation (confronting one's own characteristics, abilities, and limitations). This is where one learns to be, defines oneself, and enters into relationships (within the two other spheres), in a continuous, ever-changing process of individuation—"the profound and lifelong struggle" to become who we are, consciously or unconsciously integrating elements of the self into a whole (following Carl Jung, in Kovan & Dirkx, 2003). In this sphere we find the "differentiative desire"— knowing oneself and making personal sense of the world, as described by Chala Heller (1999). This is where integrity and integrality are sought (Kolb, 1984), and where self-esteem, autonomy, reflexivity, and the ability of critical distancing are developed. It is important, however, to consider that identity construction cannot be separated from the relation to otherness. Identity is built in relation to the other, within a culture of reference, where individual and social dimensions infiltrate

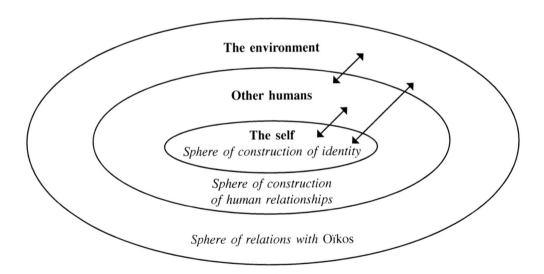

Figure 19.1. Three interrelated spheres of personal and social development.

one another. Moreover, identity cannot be separated from the relation to the *Oïkos*, as Thomas Berryman (2003) highlights in his concept of "eco-ontogenesis," whereby self-development occurs through interaction with places, living beings, and elements that, deliberately or not, consciously or not, become meaningful in our milieu. Similarly, in the words of Dominique Cottereau and Mitchell Tomashow:

> Between the being and its surroundings, there is no void, no impenetrable border, no impermeable juxtaposition. The air and the water course through our body and spirit, soul and heart. . . . Being in the world . . . is being aware of what happens between ourselves and the world in interactions that are vital for ourselves and for the world. (Cottereau, 1997, p. 21)

> The environment forms, deforms and transforms us, at least as much as we form, deform and transform it . . . In the space between us and the other (whether person, animal, object, or place . . .), each takes on the vital challenge of being in the world. This expression "being in the world" allows us to realize that the being is nothing without the world in which it lives, and that the world is clearly made up of all of the beings that populate it. Focusing on being in the world means entering into that which forms the relation of each human being to his surroundings . . . Biology is part of it since our organism survives with the help of elements outside of the body; but humans are also characterized by the drive to develop an essential and active symbolic relation to the world . . . the crux of human dynamics is in relationship, in ecodependence and in the question of the meaning that each one gives to his existence. (Cottereau, 1999, pp. 11–12)

> Ecological identity refers to how people perceive themselves in reference to nature, as living and breathing beings connected to the rhythms of the earth, the biochemical cycles, the grand and complex diversity of ecological systems. (Thomashow, 1995, p. xiii)

As "ecological subjects" (Carvalho, 2006), our ecological identity (Tomashow, 1995), ecological self (Naess, 1989), or environmental identity (Clayton, 2003; Weigert, 1997) is constructed at the juncture of the psychosphere and the ecosphere, and mediated by the sociosphere, through kinesic, cognitive, affective, spiritual, and esthetic experiences of the world. "How we understand ourselves in nature is infused with shared, culturally influenced understanding of what nature is—what is to be revered, reviled, or utilized" (Clayton & Opotow, 2003, p. 10).

Our identity is shaped by the places in which we have lived: where we became ourselves. Our innerscape is a synthesis of our life landscapes (Dansereau, 1973). Environmental education helps us clarify these dimensions of the self and gain an awareness of how they shape our relation to the *Oïkos* in turn.

The Sociosphere

Closely interrelated with the identity sphere is the sphere of human otherness or interaction with other humans, whether individuals or social groups. The "I" is forged and defines itself through the "you" (both singular and plural) and the "us" (Jacquart, 1999). Otherwise, there cannot be healthy otherness without a confirmed, assumed, and recognized identity. It is in this second sphere that we experience both the difficulties and advantages of living with others. It is where we develop a sense of belonging, and an awareness of our reference culture and its major influence on the way we relate to the world. We acquire a sense of responsibility toward others. Social identity is formed and the "associative desire" (to know other) is enacted (Heller, 1999). It is the locus of education for cooperation, peace, and human rights, where intercultural and international solidarity is learned. Political education finds its specific "niche" here:

> Political identity work is a series of reflective approaches that enable people to reconceptualize the role of power and controversy in their lives: how issues of authority, conflict and consensus are intrinsic to their sense of self and define their participation in a social system. (Tomashow, 1995, p. 105)

Citizenship education thus takes place in this sphere of human otherness. It implies learning a "dialogical democracy" wherein language is used with a view to mutual understanding and the other person is understood as on the same level as oneself, as an end in him or herself, and not as an instrument (Miguelez, 1997). In a continuous process of exchange, one learns to resolve conflicts in a positive manner, understand and accept differences, compromise if possible, and seek consensus where applicable. All this learning is essential to "being here together," "being humans on Earth." In fact, although the relation to the world—the *Oïkos*—implies personal and intimate dimensions linked to sensitivity and personal life histories, we should recognize that the relation to the environment is shaped through the sphere of interpersonal and social relationships and determined by the reference culture. Social identity plays a key role in constructing the values underpinning the human–environment relationship (Strang, 2005). Hence, it is at the interface between the sociosphere and the ecosphere that environmental education can contribute to developing an environmental citizenship—one that is sensitive to the social dimensions of environmental realities and works toward the establishment of environmental justice and the adoption of more integral forms of an "ethic of care" (Sullivan, 1977).

The Ecosphere

The third sphere is the specific domain of environmental education which invites us to reflect on and reconstruct our relations to the *Oïkos*, this house of life that is shared with each other and with other living beings. Our human environments are parts of the *Oïkos*; they are constructed and transformed at the juncture between nature and culture. They are made up of the biophysical components of the milieu, which closely interact with the sociocultural components of human populations. In the *Oïkos*, another form of otherness comes into play, a "beyond human" otherness. Environmental education invites us to renew our intrinsic connection to nature. We are part of an interconnected living system, where a single breath blows through plants, humans, and other living beings. It is a matter of becoming conscious of the transformative nature of our multidimensional interactions with the *Oïkos* (as in the concept of *écoformation* developed by Gaston Pineau, 1992) and of "expanding the margins of social responsibility in order to include all the components that weave the fabric of life" (Leff, 2000, p. 228).

In relation to the ecosphere, we find a threefold eco-education:

1. *Eco-logical education* can be defined as learning to know one's house of life in all its diversity, richness, and complexity; learning to locate oneself within it and identify and define one's human "niche" in the shared web of life; and learning to fulfill this niche joyfully, creatively and ethically, while learning to connect with, dialogue with, and achieve fundamental solidarity with the other, including the beyond-human world (being here together). Eco-logical education develops a sense of place, including a sense of belonging to one's place (whether temporary or migratory) as a basic condition for the practice of environmental responsibility. It invites us to repair the breaches and establish optimal conditions for humans and other beings to live together.

2. *Eco-nomic education* can be conceived as the process of learning to question the connection between being and owning, inhabiting shared space and using common resources; as well, this involves recognizing the political dimensions and socioeconomical impacts of production and consumption, and managing one's consumer choices and habits. In short, learning to become guardians of the *Oïkos*

(as a global environment), and responsible builders of our specific environments. In this perspective, "environmental management" does not mean to "manage" living systems for more efficient uses of natural resources and sustained development, but rather to reshape our own individual and collective relations to the environment in coherence with our ethical choices concerning production and consumption. In eco-nomic education, learning critical deconstruction occupies a broad terrain. We are invited to rethink and reconstruct the "eco-nomic" relation to the world towards a creative, endogenous economy based on solidarity (González-Gaudiano, 1999).

3. *Eco-sophic education* can be described as learning to define our cosmology or world vision so as to give meaning to our "being in the world." The tension between identity and otherness—a major contemporary social issue—may be resolved through the quest to impart ecological meaning to our "being here together" and the construction of an ecosophy. In such a process, ethics is a core concern. Environmental education highlights the close links between the intrinsic values in environmental and social relationships. Beyond simple respect, it is important to develop a deep sense of responsibility that encompasses care and solidarity. And beyond abstract principles, environmental education fosters the critical construction of an ethics that permeates everyday life (Jickling, 2004). It requires learning to live together and *with* the environment in the here and now and for the long term:

> The ecosophical outlook is developed through an identification so deep that one's own self is no longer adequately delineated by the personal ego or the organism. One experiences oneself to be a genuine part of all life. (Arne Naess, 1989, p. 174, cited in Tomashow, 1995, p. 21)

This model of three closely interrelated spheres, based on an ecological vision of human development, derives from a noninstrumental conception of education. The aim of education is to achieve a better quality of being—with integrality, integrity, and responsibility—in relation to oneself, other humans and the beyond-human world, in our shared *Oïkos*. In this perspective, environmental education is not first and foremost education for the environment, but rather education concerning our relation to the environment. Education is a quest for the meaning and connection underlying all responsible commitments to relevant action. Eco-education is not a prerequisite to action, but rather a continuous process that unfurls in the flow of life itself—a reflexive dimension that enriches the trajectory of action projects. Environmental education can contribute to "re-enchanting the world" and building hope.

Through the exploration of three complementary perspectives from which to approach environmental education and our focus on the educational perspective, we can better situate this essential dimension of global education at the heart of meaningful educational projects. Environmental education is not an accessory or just one theme among so many others. It is a major component of the core curriculum, and a dimension that cuts across all educational processes. This is an important clarification in the actual pragmatic era when the very notions of "education" and "environment" tend to be replaced by "learning" (a fragmented approach to the educational process, as observed by Gert Biesta, 2004, cited in Le Grange, 2004) and "resources" to achieve the worldwide politico-economic project of sustainable development.

NOTES

1. *Être humains sur la terre* is the title of a book by Augustin Berque (1996) that focuses on the ethical relationship to the earth, a relationship where the human is constructed in and by the world in which he or she lives, and a relationship of desire where the "is" merges with the "ought" for the co-construction

of this inhabited world. Because the human being is a point linked to the place where he or she lives, negation of place (a place perceived as neutral) corresponds to negation of being.

2. This expression is very close to the French *appellation éducation relative à l'environnement*.

3. Phillip Payne developed this theme in a very inspiring manner. Among other writings, see Payne (1997).

4. This expression is certainly not new. In his doctoral dissertation on environmental education, Gary Harvey (1976) identified "man–environment relationship education" as the core of the substantive structure of environmental education. Responding to a gender critic, he changed it to "person–environment relationship."

5. These ideas of criticality and the political dimension of environmental education were central to the discussions at the Environmental Education in the Light of Critical Education seminar organized by Regula Kyburtz-Graber and held at the University of Zurich in September 2005.

6. In this meaning, with reference to the "hidden curriculum" or "void curriculum," Orr (1992) observed that all education is environmental.

REFERENCES

Berque, A. (1996). *Être humains sur la terre* [Being humans on earth]. Paris: Gallimard.

Berryman, T. (2003). L'éco-ontogénèse: Les relations à l'environnement dans le développement humain—D'autres rapports au monde pour d'autres développements. *Éducation Relative à l'Environnement: Regards, Recherches, Réflexions, 4,* 207–230.

Burbules, N. C., & Berke, R. (1999). Critical thinking and critical pedagogy: Relations, differences, and limits. In T. S. Popkewitz & L. Fendler (Eds.), *Critical theories in education: Changing terrains of knowledge and politics* (pp. 45–65). New York: Routledge.

Carvalho de Moura, I. (2004). *Educação Ambiental: A formação do sujeito ecológico* [Environmental education: The genesis of the ecological self]. Sao Paulo: Cortez Ed.

Clayton, S. (2003). Environmental identity: A conceptual and operational definition. In S. Clayton & S. Opotow (Eds.), *Identity and the natural environment: The psychological significance of nature* (pp. 46–66). Cambridge, MA: MIT Press.

Clayton, S., & Opotow, S. (2003). *Identity and the natural environment: The psychological significance of nature.* Cambridge, MA: MIT Press.

Cottereau, D. (1999*). Chemins de l'imaginaire. Pédagogie de l'imaginaire et éducation à l'environnement.* La Caunette: Babio.

Cottereau, D. (1997). *Alterner pour apprendre.* Montpellier: Réseau École et Nature.

Dansereau, P. (1973). *La Terre des hommes et le paysage intérieur.* Montréal: Lemeac.

González-Gaudiano, E. (1999). Environmental education and sustainable consumption: The case of Mexico. *The Canadian Journal of Environmental Education, 4,* 176–187.

Gutiérrez, F. (2002). *Educación como praxis política.* México: Siglo Veintiuno.

Hart, P. (2003). *Teacher's thinking in environmental education.* New York: Peter Lang.

Harvey, G. (1976). *Environmental education: A delineation of substantive structure.* Unpublished doctoral dissertation, Southern Illinois University of Carbondale, Carbondale.

Heller, C. (1999). *Ecology of everyday life: Rethinking the desire for nature.* Montreal: Black Rose Books.

Institut d'Éco-pédagogie. (1997). *Recettes et non-recettes. Carnet de l'éco-pédagogue.* Liège: Institut d'Éco-pédagogie.

Jacquart, A. (1999). *L'homme est l'avenir de l'homme.* Liège: Alice Éditions.

Jensen, B., & Schnack, K. (1997). The action competence approach in environmental education. *Environmental Education Research, 3*(2), 163–178.

Jickling, B. (2004). Making ethics an everyday activity: How can we reduce the barriers. *Canadian Journal of Environmental Education, 9,* 11–26.

Kolb, D. A. (1984). *Experiential learning.* Englewoods Cliffs, NJ: Prentice-Hall.

Kovan, J. T., & Dirkx, J. M. (2003). "Being called awake": The role of transformative learning in the lives of environmental activists. *Adult Education Quarterly, 53*(2), 99–118.

Leff, E. (2000). *La complexidad aqmbiental.* Mexico: Siglo Veintuno Editores.

Le Grange, L. (2004). Against environmental learning: Why we need a language of environmental education. *Southern African Journal of Environmental Education, 21,* 134–140.

Mayer, M. (2003). Il progetto ENSI: Quindici anni di ricerca sull'educazione ambientale e la qualitá delle scuola. In M. Mayer (Ed.), *Qualitá delle scuola ed ecosostenabilità* (pp. 15–33). Milano: FrancoAngeli.

Miguelez, R. (1997). L'éducation au dialogue. Éducation pour la paix—Une approche philosophique. *Revue des Sciences de l'Éducation, 27*(1), 101–112.

Naess, A. (1989). *Ecology, community and lifestyle.* New York: Cambridge University Press.

Orellana, I. (2001) La comunidad de aprendizaje en educación ambiental. Una estrategia pedagógica que abre nuevas perspectivas en el marco de los cambios educacionales actuales. *Tópicos en Educación Ambiental, 3*(7), 43–51.

Orr, D. (1992). *Ecological literary education, and the transition to a postmodern world.* Albany: State University of New York Press.

Payne, P. (1997). Embodiment and environmental education. *Environmental Education Research, 3*(2), 133–153.

Pineau, G. (1992). *De l'air. Essai sur l'écoformation.* Paris/Montréal: Paideia.

Posch, P. (1991). Environment, and school initiatives: Background and basic premises of the project. In OCDE-CERI, *Environment, schools, and active learning* (pp. 13–18). Paris: OCDE.

Robottom, I. (2003). Communities, environmental issues and environmental education research. *Education Relative à l'Environnement: Regards, Recherches, Reflexion, 4,* 77–96.

Sauvé, L. (2005). Currents in environmental education: Mapping a complex and evolving pedagogical field. *The Canadian Journal of Environmental Education, 10,* 11–37.

Strang, V. (2005). Knowing me, knowing you: Aboriginal and European concepts of nature as self and other. *Worldviews, 9*(1), 25–56.

Sullivan, E. V. (1977). *Kohlberg's structuralism: A critical appraisal* (Monograph series, No. 15). Toronto: The Ontario Institute of Studies in Education,.

Thomashow, M. (1995). *Ecological identity: Becoming a reflective environmentalist.* Cambridge, MA: MIT Press.

Weigert, A. J. (1997). *Self, interaction and natural environment: Refocusing our eyesight.* Albany: State University of New York Press.

Love Is For Rejects Too: An Environmental Art Project
Hannah Jickling

During the winter and spring of 2002, I was an exchange student at the Glasgow School of Art. Throughout my time in the "Environmental Art Department," I carried-out a site-specific intervention, "relocating" chewing gum on the sidewalks by first removing it, then re-arranging it to form the shape of hearts on the concrete.

By manipulating the "randomness" with which people discard their gum on the streets, I wanted to create a similar experience as one might have when trying to identify shapes in clouds or inkblots. In contrast to most graffiti found on the surfaces of urban centres, I wanted to challenge the predictability of so-called "subversive" public intervention by using unexpected elements of the landscape as the material and site for art making. Gum "graffiti" direct from the mouths of unwitting Glaswegians, a re-arrangement of rejects into hearts, suggesting a gesture of love with no strings attached and no measurable outcome. As the early months of 2002 went by and I continued the project (seemingly rampant) speculation as to the origin and purpose of the hearts began to filter back to me, via friends, peers, and strangers on the street.

I am interested in the landscape, history, and myths that exist in all places. Local lore is developed over time by people, in communities and changes depending on whom you speak to. Conversely, the power of myth making also lies within governments, corporations, public relations firms, and mass media, and in specific cases is constructed to fuel tourism and/or the commercial desirability of a certain area.

Though the gum hearts are a distinct expression of their own, they were also, in part, a response to a recent urban regeneration project developed by the Glasgow City Council. The "Glasgow: City of Love" Festival was first launched in February 2002, to commemorate the relics of St. Valentine in possession of one of the city's churches. The festival advertised the modern, commercial aspects of Glasgow and featured "the biggest art show in the world," (cheesy heart-art in shop windows), reducing the role of art only to that of an economic tool. Although the original event literature claimed "this festival is about bringing benefits to the people of Glasgow,"

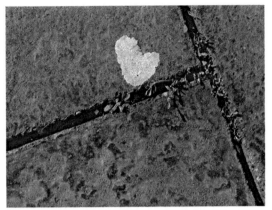

most scheduled events required £20 or more tickets, making such a "wonderful" event inaccessible to the majority of the population.

While City Council and friends were celebrating the relics of St. Valentine, I celebrated the wealth of relics on the streets. In total I made 57 gum hearts throughout Glasgow that could be "experienced"—or not—without a fee, at any time of the day or night.

For me, using an uncontrolled outdoor environment as an "exhibition space" presented issues of authorship, audience response, and effectiveness, as different challenges that are harder to qualify than they would be in most traditional art venues. These reject gum-wad arrangements held the most significance and meaning in the varied responses of individual viewers, there are a lot of anecdotes to recall. In "collaboration" with these stories and the interpretations of others, I like to believe that I have influenced a small part of Glasgow's urban landscape and local lore.

I have struggled with how to present this project after-the-fact. In February 2003, I lost nearly all of my documentation of this project in a house fire. A few months later, I returned to Glasgow to re-photograph the hearts in their various stages of deterioration. Many were in surprisingly good shape and could still be spotted around the city, two years after the project was initiated.

I feel it is important to share this context-specific work with a variety of audiences. In doing so, I hope to address the "grey areas" that site-specificity negotiates, the challenge of appropriate representation, and shifts between the worlds of "public art" and environmental education. This project points to ways in which we perceive our urban landscape and, most importantly, exemplifies the importance of participation and action in one's surrounding environment.

20

Gardom Lake to Tatamagouche

Climate Change, the WTO, and a Community Land Trust

Yuill Herbert

When I use the word *radical*, I have its deepest, original meaning in mind. The *Oxford English Dictionary* defines the word as "Going to the root or origin; touching or acting upon what is essential and fundamental; thorough." I've been lucky in my life so far to have belonged to some strong, radical communities, with rooted connections to people and place. These communities have given me the space and encouragement to be involved in unusual projects—like helping to found the Tatamagouche Community Land Trust in fall of 2003, a project inspired by my childhood connection to the land.

My first roots are in Salmon Arm, British Columbia, where I grew up in a rural area without a television. I missed out on the cartoons, and in high school I didn't follow the soaps. In many conversations at school I was left out and I felt "different." But not having a TV in my life gave me time, and I used that time to discover the forest.

The forest begins about 50 steps from the basement door at my parents' place near Gardom Lake, and it goes on for a long way. Towering over the forest is a cliff, a magical place. The forest around my house is a tangled mix of cedar, fir, spruce, white pine, and birch, but the top of the cliff is a meadow guarded only by widely spaced ponderosa pines that seem to gaze curiously out into the valley. I have often followed their example. From the cliff it is possible to see everything that happens below: farm tractors turtling around fields in endless circles, noisy little cars rushing to and fro, cattle meditating on the grass, and canoes lazing on Gardom Lake.

I came to know the other creatures that visited the cliff, like the ravens and red-tailed hawks that flew beneath the ponderosas and me. For two years in a row, a family of great horned owls lived in the pines. Every time I climbed up there, they would alight from their perch to my delight. I also found out that before I was born, cougars used to live in a cave on the face of the cliff. A farmer believed they threatened his winter bacon—the deer population—and shot them. After I learned about the cougars, I could feel their absence, a missing wildness.

When you get to know a place intimately and something threatens it, that something threatens you, too. I felt such a threat when a neighboring family decided to log their land. Logging seemed brutal and harsh, and I couldn't understand their motivation. My brother and I decided on a course of radical action. Inspired by the environmental writer Edward Abbey—whom I had discovered at the local library—and a hearty dose of teenage righteousness, we placed spikes in the path of the logging machinery. We got caught, and the resulting multiyear conflict with our neighbor gave us serious doubts about what we had done. But, as the forest became a slash pile, my regrets about my actions did not dampen my sense of loss.

Once your eyes are opened to injustice, it is hard to close them again. In my explorations of the forest I had found several veteran old-growth trees that dwarfed their neighbors. From my vantage point on the cliff I used to imagine how the now agricultural valley below used to look when it was filled with such majestic trees. Prompted by my discovery of these trees and the experience with my neighbors, I began to study the ecological impacts of clear-cutting. I joined a local environmental group that worked to preserve two pristine valleys north of Shuswap Lake and to prevent clearcutting in the region by organizing hiking trips and public debates and writing letters.

Then in summer of 1992 I followed the protests at Clayoquot Sound carefully because I was too young to make the journey there myself. Every day I cut out newspaper articles that covered the protests; I still have that file of yellowing clippings. More than 1,000 people were arrested in the nonviolent protests against the clear-cutting of ancient temperate rainforest—1,000 people who felt so deeply connected to Clayoquot Sound that they spent up to 4 months in jail.

As I grew up, my interest in ecological and social issues grew wider, at least in a geographical sense. I joined protests around North America against an alphabet soup of organizations: the World Trade Organization, the World Petroleum Congress, the Group of Eight, the Free Trade Agreement of the Americas, and the School of Americas. I was pepper-sprayed and tear-gassed, an activist's form of penance. It was thrilling and inspiring to flood the streets with thousands of people in the name of social justice. But going to protest after protest was not leading to systemic change—and the constant cycle of reacting to threat after threat made me feel empty and cynical. The supportive culture of committed activists tempered this feeling—it was exhilarating to see a diverse group coming together with a common purpose—but there is a nugget of truth when the likes of *The Economist* glibly dismisses activists as "protest junkies."

So I upped my level of commitment and decided to try to tackle one of the biggest, most intimidating challenges that we face: climate change. In summer of 2001, I cycled across Canada in the Climate Change Caravan, an initiative of a group of students at Mount Allison University. To me, the issue of climate change proved that social justice and ecological issues are inseparable: A small number of rich people, mostly in the rich countries, are guzzling fossil fuels at a grossly disproportionate rate and in so doing are causing hurricanes, floods, wildfires, and droughts that are literally killing poor people around the world. Those who are causing the least damage to the climate are suffering the most. For example, Andean farmers are losing their traditional crops due to drastically altered weather patterns, and they don't have the money to import food or seed. Our group wanted Canadians to understand that the ecological impacts of climate change have serious social implications.

The Climate Change Caravan included, at its peak, 40 cyclists and a bus that ran on used vegetable oil (we filtered out French fries with old pantyhose) and featured a serious speaker system powered by solar panels and a wind turbine. We challenged the Canadian government to a bet that individuals could do more to reduce greenhouse gas emissions than government initiatives, and we aimed to win that bet. We gave hundreds of presentations in schools, town halls, churches, living rooms, and university lecture theaters. Our presentations informed people about climate change and then asked them to commit to an eight-point plan to reduce their personal emissions. The plan included simple and practical steps such as biking to work 1 day a week, turning down the household hot water temperature and using a clothesline. In Toronto, we shut down an Exxon gas station to protest the company's denial of climate change. In every city and some small towns across Canada, we held Critical Mass bike rides that took over the streets from cars. We held a funeral for the future—complete with a coffin and a priest—at Parliament Hill in Ottawa. We illegally cycled across the Confederation Bridge to Prince Edward Island bridge to highlight the fact that it was the first major engineering project built for rising sea levels. Using a specially designed line-painting bike attachment, we outfitted Halifax with bike lanes.

Along our journey, we would move into and out of church halls, school gymnasiums, and campgrounds, and we experienced the exhilarations and struggles of a type of communal living that is seldom found in a society based on the nuclear family—imagine a summer camp with a serious purpose and equally serious responsibilities. The strength of the group persevered in times when an individual would certainly have faltered: in 4.5 months on the road we didn't miss a single day of our schedule despite extraordinary hurdles that ranged from a broken bus axle to flat tires, from rain storms to pure exhaustion. Our campaign went beyond simple reaction by promoting the benefits of what the Caravan itself embodied: long-lasting personal change supported by a strong community.

As our perhaps unrealistic hopes of mobilizing the entire Canadian population to tackle climate change evaporated—although people we encountered during our campaign had good intentions, we knew that breaking their dependency on cheap oil would require years of effort—the trip took on a new meaning. After almost 5 months on the bicycle seat and on the campaign trail, we came to an unexpected realization. On the Caravan, we made changes thanks to our collective effort that would have been difficult for an individual to achieve: Buying local organic food had become second nature for us, for example, and it was affordable when purchased in bulk. Our group's diverse interests and skills meant that each person found a niche, whether it was writing press releases or rebuilding bicycle hubs. And we built a culture around the bicycle as the primary means of transport. We came to believe that, as a collective, we would have more success implementing the radical personal lifestyle changes needed to help halt climate change.

When the Caravan ended in Halifax in October, we scratched our heads for a long time trying to map out a next step. Someone in the group suggested we create a community land trust (CLT). Robert Swann, the founder of E.F. Schumacher Society, invented CLTs in Massachusetts in 1980. Like a corporation or a cooperative, a CLT is a legal structure that can be incorporated. But they are radical in their premise that land, as much as air or water, is part of the common wealth and therefore should not be owned or sold for profit. At the same time, the CLT protects the individual need for a secure place to live by providing the long-term right for individuals to use the land, and it assigns a fair value to any improvements that individuals might make. It is a system that balances the needs of both the community and the individual.

In the fall of 2003, after 2 years of scraping together money and looking for land, a group of Caravaners purchased a farm in Nova Scotia with the eventual aim of donating the land to the Tatamagouche Community Land Trust. The 85 acres had previously been a dairy farm in the hands of one family for almost 200 years, and the father of the last owner, now in his 70s, still lives on a small piece of the land.

In the summer of 2005 we grew a hearty crop of vegetables and a weedy crop of heritage varieties of oat, barley, and wheat. We threshed the grain using a pre-1940s thresher, which resembles a Dr. Seuss machine, with belts and wheels everywhere. We built everything from a compost toilet to a greenhouse. We held amazing feasts and washed many dirty dishes. We raised chickens and ducks. We organized the annual Tatamagouche Summer Free School. At this school, anyone can teach anything, as long as he or she is passionate about the subject. In one day I learned about blacksmithing, the beauty of Euclid's proofs, and the history of residential schools.

I believe that in the Tatamagouche Community Land Trust we've found a community that includes both people and place. However, there are many questions we still need to address: How do we bridge the ideological and age gaps between the land trust and the wider community?

How can we carry the model of the land trust beyond Tatamagouche? How do we ensure that it's both relevant and realistic for people of different classes and different beliefs? And how do we make the farm economically self-sustaining?

The answer to at least some of these questions lies in the land. When we were harrowing a field, local farmers stopped by to offer advice, and when we threshed the grain, people stopped just to watch, commenting that they hadn't seen a machine like the thresher run since the days of their grandparents. The land offers the opportunity to grow food to sell. So it is rooted. So it is radical.

If you happen to be in the neighborhood, stop by. You will be welcome.

Conclusion

Repositioning Ourselves for the Tasks Ahead

Paul Hart, Marcia McKenzie,
Heesoon Bai, and Bob Jickling

One of the worst signs of our danger is that we can't imagine...
We must imagine the way.

—Herbert Marcuse

Fields of Green arose out of a reflexive interest in the future of environment in education and culture, in how their connection may be implicated in more ecologically sustainable practice. In a sense, this book is about how the intersection of knowledge, power, ethics, and desire crafts identities as cultural projects (Kelly, 1997). It is about how to productively employ that intersection to elicit participation in social life through education—by locating agency as the shape our dreams and identities can take in social activity. The collection points toward strategies for reimagining as well as resisting discourses of education embedded within textual densities of culture. It opens up particular concerns of environmental education reconceptualized by diverse and divergent interests of embodied, critical, postmodern, and radical pedagogies. Drawing on a variety of textual forms to frame and illustrate relationships of education, culture, and environment, it serves both to critique and to imagine positionings that environmental education may assume in transforming pedagogy. Seeking more complicated conversations, more embodied and sensuous subjectivities, more adventurous wandering and connective intelligence, more geophilosophical notions of place, the authors in this collected text provide ways to provoke and disrupt desires and dreams as specific social identities are constituted and negotiated.

Written from multiple and even contradictory positions, the chapters are haunted by creative dissonance and by intimate, emotional, and discursive workings of the imagination. The writers acknowledge, each in their own way, that they are working to reimagine fields of education with culture and environment in mind. Each creates conditions that raise critical and generative

343

questions about people–planet relationships, about ways of living well in the world. Each offers insight into complexities of the nature–culture relationships and calls into question how specific social/ecological identities are constituted and reconstituted continually. Recognizing that education needs (re)conceptual work, each offers sociocultural lenses and sites that foreshadow more conscious ecological educational practices. Each writer seems to know how "language produces us" and how to use its power strategically to disrupt established thought and practice. Recognizing that their attempts to disrupt old cultural patterns and invent new ones may provide insight into discursive mechanisms and regulatory frameworks that hold existing educational structures in place, they persist in imaginatively rewording the world. In the end, their reimaginings serve to foreshadow possible futures for environmental education. They engage us in more complex conversations (see Gough, chap. 1) about things exceedingly difficult to write about: tasks of representing and critiquing and connecting that can work to generate more hopeful educational interactions and action in the face of ecological and cultural loss.

TASKS OF REPRESENTING

This volume then, represents people who think critically and (re)constructively within and across various "fields of green," where the very nature of the terrain is uncertain and contested. What they have done, it seems, is to show how (post)modern representations of thought in education may be construed through a variety of poetic and political genres. They identify methods by which people represent, rationally as well as aesthetically, what is taken for granted within codified practices of making and seeing. Expressed creatively as working narratives, there is strength in their diverse images and trajectories: generative of "daydreams" and mind frames, of the "not yet thought possible," of new species of worldview. Although each chapter represents a somewhat distinct positioning, radical entanglements between the artistic, the ethical, and the political work to inform socioecological ways of knowing that impel us toward hopeful learning spaces that an uncomfortable profession cannot not act upon (see Price, chap. 4). In untangling mycelial interconnection relationships across diverse chapters as invitations to our own inquiries, we may gain insight into ways that discourses of education and environmental education have been imposed historically, institutionally, and discursively. Although we will never get it "right," both representational practices and the representations that are outcomes of such practices may help us understand how our socially and culturally embedded systems of education are implicated in both excavating and exploring change.

TASKS OF CRITIQUING

Well aware of the power of discursive formations in educational theory and practice, we see chapters in this volume pushing the limits of intelligibility, the boundary "where thought stops what it cannot bear to know, what it must shut off to think as it does" (Britzman, 1995, p. 155). To move beyond limits of ethical ideals such as ecological sustainability may challenge educators to interrogate the multiple and contextual meanings in their taken-for-granted policy rhetoric and slogan systems—not an easy task. Sean Blenkinsop and Kiera Egan (chap. 2) illustrate the difficulty in troubling rhetorical forms of thought that operate in educational systems as unexamined discourses and cultural practices. Where environmental, ecological, or sustainability education often operate in the same taken-for-granted manner within the dominant social discourse, Edgar González-Gaudiano and Rosa Buenfil-Burgos (chap. 3) invoke postfoundational-focused concern for ironies they see in disjunctures between theory and practice (see also González-Gaudiano, 2007). The fact remains that after more than 30 years of international conferencing on environment and education, we continue to tolerate metanarratives that, despite their "call to action," state that:

> We must reconsider our tools, methods and approaches, our politics and economics, our relationships and partnerships, and the very foundations and purposes of education and how it relates to the lives we lead. In making our choices we draw on, and are inspired by much work that has gone before us. . . . Environmental Education processes support and champion Education for Sustainable Development. Such education processes must be relevant, responsive and accountable. Research is encouraged to provide additional rigour and credibility and to identify increasingly effective methods of learning and sharing knowledge. (UNESCO, 2007, p. 1)

Is it not our task to question statements like this where words represent discourses we use in this field? As C. A. Bowers (2001) said, environmental education is subject to a limiting double bind by seeking to address environmental problems while reinforcing the use of language/thought patterns that are at the root of these very problems. If environment is not a neutral medium, then ideas of unified, rational, and universal systems whose moralities prop up unexamined discourses/practices have lost purchase here, as cultures network and education morphs itself into multiple identities.

Those in this book who encourage embodied or sensuous (rather than privileging intellect-based) resistance cannot comprehend change in environmental education without more profound educational reconfigurations than those contemplated in "official knowledge" discourses of UNESCO policy statements as just illustrated. These contributions interrogate our beliefs about what really counts as environmental education at deeper levels of consciousness. They suggest that what we remember is more likely to be found in mountain rivers than arcane analytic routines. If environmental education is reimagined to encourage pedagogies where plural interpretations of environmental issues are used to guide learners toward engaging issues and perspectives, could the focus in classrooms be directed more toward processes of inquiry rather than one particular solution (Price, chap. 4; Jickling, chap. 8; Bonnett, chap. 9)? In David Jardine's (chap. 7) terms, what constitutes the limits of our narrativity? Can more participatory forms of consciousness enable us to integrate the poetic and the rational (Bai, chap. 6)? To put it bluntly, these writers challenge us to stand "inside" ourselves, and to embed our actions with a more critical eye to the cultural worldviews and education systems that have failed the environment. They ask us to reinvent environmental education in ways that work to reposition ourselves "outside" these taken-for-granted or poorly constructed philosophical positionings or frames and within more grounded, dynamic and expanding notions of personal insearch and inquiry. They ask us to begin to take action knowing that the outcomes might not be "truths" or "solutions" to problems, but that they might be places that are "good enough" to take action (Price, chap. 4).

TASKS OF CONNECTING

As if in anticipation of questions from those who see humans as social/relational beings beyond the personal/sensual, another set of essays in this collection engage interactional concepts, social networking, and systems processes (as waves, hybrids, networks) in ways that implicate the social/interactional more centrally in learning and knowing. The idea that learning is always social complicates our questions about how we come to actually know and do anything. In our remembering, our (re)sources can be found in our relationships with things very basic. From the situated cartographies of Rebecca Martusewicz (chap. 5) and Leesa Fawcett (chap. 12), for example, our most basic ethic arises from our connection to the planet, whether through the collaborative intelligence of the metaphysical "city" or the feral sociality of embodied learning. How can we generate opportunities for embodied knowing and meaningful sensuous experiences through interaction? Where do we find and create the conditions for developing situated and nomadic ethics of community? How can people derive meaning from the sensuous experience? How do we begin to acknowledge the need for an a priori transformation of the roots of the contemporary mindset that has gotten us to this point? Through new metaphors, myths, and stories that imply some genealogical connection (Fawcett, chap. 12)? Through new forms of expanded, intersubjective, consciousness (Eppert, chap. 10)? Marcia McKenzie (chap. 11) attempts to sort through this complex, sticky web of desires and imaginaries by merging personal and social in considering education as transgression. Education, as a cultural and environmental phenomenon, these writers say, must begin now to support new stories, beyond those of cultivated subjects who can transcend nature, stories that invite critique and creative reimagining of culturally embedded habits of consciousness. Thus, for Michael Peters and Daniel Araya (chap. 13), these somewhat sticky cultural/relational or ecological questions remain for each of us: How do we do this *together* amidst particularized educational understandings and practices? What this set of essays seem to imagine are relational forms and hyperconnectivity, as learning systems that go straight to the heart of reimagined pedagogical process.

TASKS OF REGROUNDING

Part of the challenge and playful musement (Price, chap. 4) in this book comes in imagining, seeing, and dreaming how different philosophical framings can metaphorically and figuratively cut across forms of personal *and* social pedagogical praxis and inquiry. As educators we can reflect on specific, contextual possibilities and ethics of sociocultural change in terms of personally meaningful questions about, for example, the value of out-of-doors or first-hand experiences in natural settings or experiences in the virtual environment of modern technology. We can imagine how we can create conditions for our students to recognize, in our geographies of space and place (Greenwood, chap. 15), social cultural and relational as well as cognitive ways of learning (and knowing) (Sauvé, chap. 19). What more nuanced accounts of processes might we find in imaginative conversation about cultural and environmental loss (Rasmussen and Akulukjuk, chap. 16), reifications of nature in urban places (McClaren, chap. 7), personal (embodied) awareness of postmodern *Oïkos* (Payne, chap. 18), the role of place in exploring actively our sense of being *with* place (Herbert, chap. 20)?

TASKS OF IMAGINING

In the chapters in this volume, environmental education becomes part of a tangle of representative forms that anticipate productivities of difference, the possibilities of strangers in strange lands. But beyond mere narrative possibilities, Gough challenges us to "think and do" rather than just read and hope. So we use these physical and aesthetic metaphors and figurations of education, expanding these possibilities that may actually do something in future curriculum and education. This notion of doing is more than that it seems, for narratives that may activate our imagined poetics/aesthetics may also conjure up emotion in seeking and searching and engaging in interactivity.

But do these things come together right now? In her chapter on "Seeing" in *Pilgrim at Tinker Creek,* Annie Dillard (1974) writes about a different kind of "seeing" where sense impressions are not edited for the brain, where vision is less encumbered by meaning, where a sifting of values can set in. It is a nonessentialist expression of visioning like the person who watches a baseball game in an empty stadium. When I see this way, she says, I see the game purely; I am abstracted and dazed. But I cannot leave the stadium and go out and try to see this way. I will fail; I will go mad. All I can do is to try to gag the commentator, hush the noise of useless interior babble that keeps me from "seeing." The secret of seeing is complicated by conversation. It involves letting go of some sacred stories, and reimagining, reconceptualizing, re-programming, (re)placing learning and pedagogy. It involves gaining access to the continuities and discontinuities in the subjectivities of people. It involves exposing ourselves to new positionings and new discursive practices. It involves grasping the concepts of discourse, power, the good teacher, the good pupil, the good story. Perhaps, some of the time we may want to complicate our conversations and other times we may need to get away from conversation altogether.

The pedagogical process of education is so complex and so entrenched in mindsets that despite reimagining exercises, like stretching exercises, much of what happens remains unexamined, unintelligible, and unseeable. As educators, we have been so busy "doing" education that we can't see what is really going on in debates about the power of language to describe, let alone challenge, what we think is happening. Even where existing categories or frames no longer work, we have not learned how to think our way out of them. It is as if we have been taught how to think the world apart, and have not learned how to think it back together. It is here that these chapters offer help. Each of the contributors to this volume challenges us to think our way out of culturally determined assumptions and predispositions, to enlarge time-hardened categories to include alternative ways of knowing and being. Can we see how they have provided some opportunities for more complicated conversations, through personal reflexivity, social hyperconnectivity, or nomadic wandering? Can we see how these authors have expanded our metaphors and categories to include sensual, embodied, enfamilied dream data, as they write their ways into knowing/being, representing themselves in these ideas, generating relationality without getting lost in interstitial spaces?

If we believe that environmental education is itself a metaphor or a figuration for social-ecological-cultural learning and knowing grounded in a particular epistemology-ontology positioning, then having engaged these ideas as readers, we are called to think more deeply about educational possibilities with environment in mind. If we can do that and then begin to actually account for our thinking in terms of actions it may produce, we might just make a difference. Our mission, if our consciousness will permit us to see it, says Herman Hesse (1943) in *The Glass Bead Game,* is not so much to ask questions differently as to learn how, in relational ways, to ask different questions. The questions proliferate, once the structures/foundations of education are opened, and as these chapters suggest, the gates are open. And so we will continue to wonder which stories and daydreams to live by. Which make sense in which cultures and contexts, in places where values do exist, even if in resistance or in willful contradiction (McKenzie, 2004)? How do we enact and continue to reimagine these pedagogies of possibility, and when and where is it appropriate to consider education as the encouragement of disruptive daydreaming? Can revisioning projects, we wonder, be situated in educators' minds and hearts as meaningful and possible? Oh! we wonder . . . we exuberant ones!

You may say I'm a dreamer . . . but I'm not the only one!

—John Lennon

REFERENCES

Bowers, C. A. (2001). How language limits our understanding of environmental education. *Environmental Education Research, 7*(2), 141–151.

Britzman, D. (1995). Is there a queer pedagogy? Or, stop reading straight. *Educational Theory, 45*(2), 151–165.

Dillard, A. (1974). *Pilgrim at tinker creek.* Toronto: Bantam.

González-Gaudiano, E. (2007). Schooling and environment in Latin America in the third millennium. *Environmental Education Research, 13*(2), 139–154.

Hesse, H. (1943). *The glass bead game.* Harmsworth, Middlesex, England: Penguin.

Kelly, U. (1997). *Schooling desire: Literacy, cultural politics and pedagogy.* New York: Routledge.

McKenzie, M. (2004). The "willful contradiction" of poststructural socio-ecological education. *Canadian Journal of Environmental Education, 9,* 177–190.

UNESCO. (2007). Definition of education for sustainable development. Retrieved December 24, 2007, from http://portal.unesco.org/education/en/ev.php-URL_ID=27279&URL_DO=DO_TOPIC&URL_SECTION=201.html.

Out beyond ideas
of wrongdoing and rightdoing,
there is a field.

I'll meet you there.

When the soul lies down
in that grass,
the world is too full to talk about.

Ideas, language
—even the phrase "each other"
do not make any sense.
. . .

Rumi (1207–1273)

Chapter Contributors

Tommy Akulukjuk

Tommy Akulukjuk was born in Iqaluit, Nunavut, Canada and grew up in Pangnirtung, Nunavut. His youth included many seasons spent "out on the land" with his family. Tommy is a graduate of the 2-year Nunavut Sivuniksavut college program in Ottawa, and he has been published in the *Inuit Studies Journal*. He is interested in social issues and alternative education methods, and currently works with the environmental studies department of the Canadian national Inuit organization *Inuit Taparit Kanatami* (ITK). Tommy wishes to note that his contribution to this book is his interpretation of his father's understanding, not a quotation of his father's words.

Daniel Araya

Daniel Araya has a master's degree in sociology and education from the University of Toronto (OISE/UT) and is currently completing a doctorate in educational policy at the University of Illinois at Urbana-Champaign (UIUC). The focus of his research is the convergent impact of emerging technologies and cultural globalization on institutions of education. Daniel has published widely on subjects related to culture and technology including information networks, the knowledge economy, democratic innovation, cultural hybridity, peer-to-peer collaboration, technology design, and the cosmopolitanization of the university. He is currently working as a researcher with the Global Studies in Education program at UIUC and as a graduate assistant with Common Ground Publishing at the University of Illinois Research Park.

Heesoon Bai

Heesoon Bai is an associate professor in the Faculty of Education at Simon Fraser University in Vancouver, Canada. Her area of specialization is philosophy and education, and her current research interests include "psycho-ontology," perception and attention, pedagogy of mindfulness, ecological philosophy and education, moral and spiritual education, ethic of care, and democracy and education. As well, she researches Buddhist and Daoist philosophy, and applies their insights to education. Her research is currently funded by a Social Sciences and Humanities Research Council of Canada Standard Grant, and she has published a wide range of articles and book chapters. She is editor of *Paideusis: International Journal in Philosophy of Education*, which is affiliated with the Canadian Philosophy of Education Society.

Sean Blenkinsop

Sean Blenkinsop is an assistant professor in the Faculty of Education at Simon Fraser University in Vancouver, Canada. He has a Doctorate in philosophy of education from Harvard University and a Master's in experiential education from Minnesota State at Mankato. He has a long background in outdoor, environmental, and experiential education, and an ongoing interest in any debate that has to do with meaning-making. Current research interests include existentialism, imagination, and ecology as a way of being rather than an object of study.

Michael Bonnett

Michael Bonnett, formerly senior lecturer in the philosophy of education at the University of Cambridge, is currently reader in the philosophy of education at the University of Bath, and senior research fellow at the University of London Institute of Education in the United Kingdom. He has written numerous papers on education, published in academic journals and edited books, and he is the author of the books *Children's Thinking* (1994) and *Retrieving Nature: Education for a Post-Humanist Age* (2004). His current interests are in the philosophical exploration of issues arising from environmental concern, the philosophical implications of information technology for education, and the constitution of subjective identities and the nature and importance of self-knowledge in education.

Rosa N. Buenfil-Burgos

Rosa Buenfil-Burgos received her doctorate in government/discourse analysis from the University of Essex, United Kingdom, in 1990. She is now professor at the Departamento de Investigaciones Educativas, Centro de Investigación y Estudios Avanzados, in Mexico. Dr. Buenfil-Burgos is the author of three books about the educational discourse of the Mexican revolution. She has authored chapters, articles, and papers on philosophical debates on education, as well as recent educational policies in Mexico in the context of globalization and postmodernity.

Peter Cole

Peter Cole is a member of the Douglas First Nation of the Lower Stl'atl'imx in British Columbia, and is associate professor in Aboriginal and Northern Studies in the Faculty of Arts at the University College of the North. He is interested in orality, narrativity, and working with Aboriginal Peoples toward self-empowerment, sustainable communities and creating their own education. He is also interested in hiking and canoeing. His publications include poetry, literary and academic articles, book chapters and his book, *Coyote and Raven go Canoeing: Coming Home to the Village* (McGill-Queen's University Press, 2006). Peter is co-editor of *Speaking for Ourselves: Environmental Justice in Canada* (in press, UBC Press).

Rishma Dunlop

Rishma Dunlop is an associate professor of English and coordinator of the Creative Writing Program in English at York University, Toronto, Canada. She is cross-appointed to the Faculty of Education and School of Women's Studies. She is a poet, fiction writer, playwright, and essayist whose research interests extend across such disciplines as fine arts, aesthetics, literary theory, ecology, cultural studies, and human rights education. Among her publications are four books of poetry: *White Album* (2008), *Metropolis* (2005), *Reading Like a Girl* (2004), and *The Body of My Garden* (2000). Publications as editor include: *Art, Literature, and Place: An Ecopoetics Reader* (2008), *White Ink* (2007), and *Red Silk: An Anthology of South Asian Canadian Women Poets* (2004). She was the recipient of the Emily Dickinson Award for Poetry in 2003. She is founding editor of *Studio*, an international poetry journal (http://www.StudioPoetry.ca).

Kieran Egan

Kieran Egan completed his doctorate at Cornell University in 1972. His first job was at Simon Fraser University in Vancouver, Canada, where he has remained ever since. He is the author of about twenty books, and co-author, editor, or co-editor of a few more. In 1991 he received the Grawemeyer Award in Education. In 1993 he was elected to the Royal Society of Canada. Several of his books have been translated into about ten European and Asian languages. His most recent book is *The Future of Education: Reimagining our Schools from the Ground Up* (New Haven: Yale University Press).

Claudia Eppert

Claudia Eppert taught at Louisiana State University for eight years and is currently associate professor of English language arts education at the University of Alberta, in Edmonton, Canada. Her areas of research and teaching include: the history and philosophy of literacy and literature education; theories of reading and interpretation; literacies and curricula for social responsivity and responsibility; ethics of engagement with social and environmental suffering through literature, media, and the arts; and wisdom literature and contemplative pedagogical practices. In addition to publishing several book chapters and journal articles, she is co-editor with Roger I. Simon and Sharon Rosenberg of *Between Hope and Despair: Pedagogy and the Remembrance of Historical Trauma* (Rowman & Littlefield, 2000) and co-editor with Hongyu Wang of *Cross-cultural Studies in Curriculum: Eastern Thought, Educational Insights* (LEA/Routledge, Taylor & Francis, 2007).

Leesa Fawcett

Leesa Fawcett is an associate professor and coordinator of the graduate diploma in environmental and sustainability education in the Faculty of Environmental Studies at York University, Toronto, Canada. She is cross-appointed to the science and technology studies program and the children's studies program. She has worked in the environmental education field for more than 30 years, valuing educational praxis that is compassionate, inclusive, and wild. Her research interests include: critical (eco)feminist pedagogy, environmental philosophy and ethics, human/animal relationships, natural history and conservation, and organic agriculture. She lives with her family (including humans and other animals) on four acres beside the Nottawasaga River in the Hockley Valley, Ontario, where she is actively involved with community sustainability issues.

Edgar González-Gaudiano

Edgar González-Gaudiano is a researcher at the Institute of Social Research at the Autonomous University of Nuevo Leon. He has been a university lecturer and an academic consultant since 1972 at different institutes of higher education in Mexico and in five Latin American universities. He has provided support for the National Environment Commissions of Chile, Belize and Guatemala; the Ministries of Education in Brazil, Colombia and the Dominican Republic; and the Ministries of the Environment in Cuba and Argentina. This work has made him an important Latin-American liaison officer on environmental education issues. He has also taken part in seven collectively written books and he is sole author of three books and many articles in national and international journals.

Noel Gough

Noel Gough is professor of outdoor and environmental education and director of the Centre for Excellence in Outdoor Education and Environment at La Trobe University in Victoria, Australia.

His current research focuses on the diverse implications of globalization, internationalization, and multiculturalism for education, and on refining poststructuralist research methodologies in education, with particular reference to curriculum inquiry, environmental education, and science education. He is co-editor (with William Doll) of *Curriculum Visions* (Peter Lang, 2002), and is the founding editor of *Transnational Curriculum Inquiry*, the journal of the International Association for the Advancement of Curriculum Studies.

David Greenwood (formerly Gruenewald)

David A. Greenwood lives in the far eastern part of Washington State, just at the Idaho border where the Palouse Hills and dryland farming meet the Clearwater Mountains and forest logging. An associate professor at Washington State University, he has authored many papers on place-based and environmental education. He is co-editor with Greg Smith of *Place-Based Education in the Global Age: Local Diversity* (Taylor & Francis, 2007).

Paul Hart

Paul Hart is a professor of science and environmental education at the University of Regina, in Regina, Canada, where he teaches both undergraduate and graduate students. He has published widely in the areas of science and environmental education. He is an executive editor of the *Journal of Environmental Education* and consulting editor for *Environmental Education Research, the Canadian Journal of Environmental Education* and the *Southern African Journal of Environmental Education*. His research interests include the roots of teachers' implicit theories about their environmental education practices and children's ideas about the environment. He has received several research awards and national grants, served on the international board of the North American Association for Environmental Education, and has recently written a book on his research in teacher thinking.

Yuill Herbert

Yuill Herbert is originally from Salmon Arm, British Columbia, Canada. In the summers he grows grains at the Tatamagouche Community Land Trust in Nova Scotia. In the winters Yuill works with Sustainability Solutions Group (www.sustainabilitysolutions.ca), a worker's cooperative, on sustainability assessments of organizations and green-building consulting. Yuill is also the environment editor of the *Dominion* newspaper (www.dominionpaper.ca).

David Jardine

David Jardine is a professor of education at the University of Calgary in Calgary, Canada. In addition to numerous articles on educational theory and practice, he is the co-author, with Sharon Friesen and Patricia Clifford, of *Back to the Basics of Teaching and Learning: "Thinking the World Together"* and *Curriculum in Abundance.* He is also the author of *Piaget and Education: A Primer.* His research interests include the intersections between ecology, pedagogy, and hermeneutics; reconceptualization of the idea of "the basics" in educational theory and practice; and the implications of these areas for curriculum theory and teacher education.

Bob Jickling

Bob Jickling is an assistant professor in the Faculty of Education at Lakehead University, in Thunder Bay, Canada. He is the founding editor of the *Canadian Journal of Environmental Education*, and has published widely in international circles of environmental education. His research interests include relationships between environmental philosophy, ethics, education, and teaching. A long-time outdoor pursuits instructor and wilderness traveler, much of his passion is derived from journeying through the Yukon's magnificent northern landscape by foot, ski, and canoe.

Rebecca Martusewicz

Rebecca Martusewicz is a professor of education at Eastern Michigan University, where she teaches undergraduate and graduate courses in the social and theoretical foundations of education. She is the creator of a new Master's of Arts in EcoJustice Education, and is editor of two journals: *Educational Studies* and *The EcoJustice Review: Educating for the Commons*, an internationally juried online publication. She is author of three books, including: *Seeking Passage: Post-Structuralism, Ethics, Education*. Her current research interests include the cultural foundations of the ecological crisis, as well as the theoretical foundations of ecojustice pedagogy and community education. She has an EdD from the University of Rochester.

Milton McClaren

Milton McClaren is an emeritus professor of education in the Faculty of Education at Simon Fraser University (SFU), and an adjunct professor in the School of Environment and Sustainability at Royal Roads University, both in British Columbia, Canada. At SFU, he initiated the environmental education program in the Faculty of Education and developed the Summer Institute in Environmental Education, a program currently in its 36th year of operation, as well as the undergraduate Minor in Environmental Education, and MA (Education), MSc (Education) and MEd cohorts focusing on environmental education. Milt is a recipient of the B.C. Minister's Environment Award, the Canadian EECOM Award, the Canadian Wildlife Federation's Certificate of Merit, and the Taft Campus Award from the University of Northern Illinois for his work in the field of environmental education.

Marcia McKenzie

Marcia McKenzie is an assistant professor in Social Justice and Education in the Department of Educational Foundations as well as jointly appointed to the School of Environment and Sustainability at the University of Saskatchewan in Saskatoon, Canada. Her research interests center on education and socio-cultural practice, youth agency and activism, and the politics of social science research. Her current SSHRC-funded research centers on a collaborative web-based project entitled, *Discursive Approaches to Teaching and Learning about Social and Ecological Issues*. She has published in a range of journals and edited volumes, and has been involved with a number of community-based nonprofit organizations.

Pat O'Riley

Pat O'Riley is of Irish, French, and Mohawk heritage, married into the Lower Stl'atl'imx community of British Columbia, and is assistant professor in the School of Social Sciences at York University. Her interests include canoeing, ethics and protocols relating to research with Aboriginal peoples; intersections between traditional and contemporary technologies; poststructuralisms (Deleuze & Guattari in particular); and housing design. Her publications include a book entitled *Technology, Culture and Socioeconomics: A Rhizoanalysis of Educational Discourses* (Peter Lang, 2003), and a co-edited book, *Speaking for Ourselves: Environmental Justice in Canada* (in press, UBC Press).

Joe Paczuski

Joe Paczuski is a photographer and a Toronto high school teacher. His photography and the works of his students have been exhibited at a variety of venues and appeared in numerous publications. His work has been featured on the covers of books and journals, as well as in articles and chapters, including: *Poeisis: Journal of Arts and Communication*; *ARM Journal*; *English Teaching: Practice and Critique*; and *Canadian Journal of Environmental Education*. Exhibitions at public and private venues include: Queen West Art Crawl; Great Art Glad Heart: Benefit for Nellie's Women's Shelters; Gladstone Hotel; Praxis Gallery, and the Samuel J. Zacks Gallery. His current research for a Masters Degree at York University focuses on documentary photography as an agent of social change for disadvantaged youth.

Phillip Payne

Phillip Payne is an associate professor in the Faculty of Education at Monash University in Australia. He leads the Research Group "Movement, Environment and Community" that is engaged in the development of socioecological theory and its interface with experiential education pedagogies through the promotion of active lifestyles and communities, their well-*being,* and sustainable *becoming.* Prior to joining Monash University in 2006, in the early 1980s Phillip founded, led, and headed the first undergraduate degree program in Australia (at La Trobe University) specializing in outdoor/environmental education. His major interests in environmental education lie in evidence-based formulations of curriculum theory; ontological, epistemological and methodological tensions in framing and conducting socioecological inquiry; the place/site of the mediated human body(ies) in their phenomenological relations with various social constructions of "nature"; and, consequently, the "nature of experience" in education.

Michael A. Peters

Michael A. Peters is professor of education at the University of Illinois at Urbana-Champaign and adjunct professor in the School of Art at the Royal Melbourne Institute of Technology. He was research professor of education at the University of Glasgow (2000–2005) and in the School of Education at the University of Auckland, NZ (2000–2003). His research interests are in the areas of philosophy, education and policy studies. He has written some 30 books, including, most recently: *Education, Globalization and the State in An Age of Terrorism* (2005), *Derrida, Deconstruction and Education* (2004), *Poststructuralism and Educational Research* (2004), *Critical Theory and the Human Condition: Founders and Praxis* (2004), and *Futures of Critical Theory: Dreams of Difference* (2004). He is currently executive editor of the journal *Educational Philosophy and Theory* (Blackwell), the international e-journals, *Policy Futures in Education* (Symposium) and *E-Learning* (Symposium), and co-editor of the on-line *Encyclopedia of Philosophy of Education*.

Leigh Price

Leigh Price is a Zimbabwean, living in Harare. Originally an ecologist, she teaches a part-time course on environmental ethics at Arrupe College of Philosophy and Humanities. She spends the rest of her time working as an environmental education consultant. Leigh recently completed her PhD with the Education Department at Rhodes University, South Africa. Her thesis was entitled: *A Transdisciplinary Explanatory Critique of Environmental Education*. It included two volumes, the first entitled *Business and Industry* and the second entitled *Ironic Musings*. Leigh has published a variety of papers on environmental education, covering topics such as business and industry, discourse analysis, Indigenous knowledge, participation, and social epistemology.

Derek Rasmussen

Derek Rasmussen is resident teacher at the Morin Heights Dharma House in Quebec. Derek lived in Iqaluit, Nunavut, from 1991 to 2001, serving as a social policy advisor to Nunavut Tunngavik Incorporated (NTI), the representative body for the Inuit of the Nunavut Territory in Canada. He is a graduate of the Kinmount Seminary and Academy, a Buddhist seminary school in Ontario, Canada, and received an MA in Education from Simon Fraser University in British Columbia, Canada. Derek has also been active in peace and anti-intervention movements, and was a cofounder of the Canadian East Timor Program in the early 1980s. Derek's writing has been published in the *Annual Journal of the Philosophy of Education Society* (Chicago), as well as in *InterCulture* (Montreal), *Holistic Education Review* (NY), *Cultural Survival Quarterly* (Boston), *l'Ecologiste* (France), *Forests-Trees-People* (Sweden), the *Canadian Journal of Native Studies* (Edmonton), and the *Globe and Mail* (Toronto).

Lucie Sauvé

Lucie Sauvé is Professor at the Faculty of Education of the Université du Québec à Montréal (UQAM) in Montreal, Canada, and holds a Canada Research Chair in environmental education. She is director of the UQAM post-graduate program in environmental education and co-director of the international research journal *Éducation relative à l'environnement—Regards, Recherches, Réflexions*.

Vignette Contributors

Daniela Bouneva Elza

Daniela Bouneva Elza is a doctoral student in Philosophy of Education at Simon Fraser University. She dwells in chaordic spaces, where imagination takes us and invents us. Her work is forthcoming in *Van Gogh's Ear, Vancouver Review, Journal of Environmental Philosophy, Rocksalt, A Verse Maps of Vancouver,* and *Poetic Inquiry: Vibrant Voices in the Social Sciences.*

Lorri Neilsen Glenn

Lorri Neilsen Glenn's poetry collections include *All the Perfect Disguises, Saved String,* and *Combustion* (2007, Brick Books) and *Lost Gospel* (Brick Books, 2010) from which this poem is taken. Her work has appeared in *Arc, Prairie Fire, CV2, The Malahat Review, The Antigonish Review, Event, Grain,* and anthologies such as *White Ink, Nth Position, Dropped Threads 3, Common Magic,* among others. As an ethnographer, she has written several books in the field of literacy as well as works of creative nonfiction. She is Poet Laureate of Halifax for 2005–2009 and currently Professor in literacy at Mount Saint Vincent University in Halifax, Canada.

Hannah Jickling

Hannah Jickling recently completed her BFA at the Nova Scotia College of Art and Design where she majored in Media Arts. Her work takes form through various disciplines such as video, printed matter, site-specific intervention in public spaces, installation, performance, textiles, and photography. She has developed and shown her work in the Yukon, various locations in Canada and the United States, the United Kingdom, and Germany. She works individually and collaboratively, often using everyday materials as art supplies.

Artin Lahiji

Artin Lahiji is a multi-media artist currently living in Saskatoon, Canada, where he studies, produces, and teaches multi-media. He studied art, design, and media at the Ontario College of Art and Design and interdisciplinary research at the University of Saskatchewan. He is currently engaged in media education research exploring creativity and media of expression at the University of Saskatchewan.

J. B. MacKinnon

J. B. MacKinnon is the author of the bestseller *The 100-Mile Diet: A Year of Local Eating.* His other works include *I Live Here,* a collaborative book on displaced people; and *Dead Man in*

Paradise, which won the 2006 Charles Taylor Prize for Literary Nonfiction. As a journalist he has earned three National Magazine Awards. A past editor of *Adbusters* magazine, MacKinnon has written on topics ranging from civil war in Sudan to anarchism in America to prehistoric tortoises in the Chihuahuan Desert.

Serenne Romanycia

Serenne Romanycia is a Vancouver-based freelance artist. Her work focuses on mirroring the shared consciousness of the world. Her artist credo: "Keeping your mind open to change and letting your observational skills teach and change you is very important. You create what you are, and it creates you. My style reflects a lot of motion and movement, because that's how the world is to me; I've always felt that it's important to never let yourself become static. As an artist, I'd like to be able to not capture motion, but keep it flowing." She currently works in acrylic and canvas, but her earlier work was mostly in pencil and ink. More on her website: www.serenne.net.

Bill Timmerman

Bill Timmerman is an architectural photographer in the Sonoran desert city of Phoenix, Arizona. His personal photographs can be viewed at the Joseph Bellows Gallery: www.josephbellows.com.

Nora Timmerman

Nora Timmerman is a PhD student in the Department of Educational Studies at the University of British Columbia in Vancouver. She studies ecological justice and higher education.

Author Index

Subject Index

LaVergne, TN USA
18 August 2010
193660LV00003B/3/P